# THE NIRVANA EXPRESS

MICK BROWN

# The Nirvana Express

*How the Search for
Enlightenment Went West*

HURST & COMPANY, LONDON

First published in the United Kingdom in 2023 by
C. Hurst & Co. (Publishers) Ltd.,
New Wing, Somerset House, Strand, London, WC2R 1LA
Copyright © Mick Brown, 2023
All rights reserved.

The right of Mick Brown to be identified as the author of
this publication is asserted by him in accordance with the
Copyright, Designs and Patents Act, 1988.

Distributed in the United States, Canada and Latin America by
Oxford University Press, 198 Madison Avenue, New York, NY 10016,
United States of America.

A Cataloguing-in-Publication data record for this book
is available from the British Library.

ISBN: 9781805260196

www.hurstpublishers.com

Epigraph to part one reproduced with the kind permission of City Lights Books.
Fernando Pessoa (as Álvaro de Campos), excerpt from 'Ode (an excerpt)', translated
by Edwin Honig and Susan M. Brown, from *Poems of Fernando Pessoa*. English
translation copyright © 1986 by Edwin Honig and Susan M. Brown. Reprinted with
the permission of The Permissions Company, LLC on behalf of City Lights Books
citylights.com. Quotations from the letters of Aleister Crowley © Ordo Templi
Orientis; used by kind permission.

Printed and bound in Great Britain by Bell and Bain Ltd, Glasgow

# CONTENTS

*List of Illustrations*                                     vii

*Acknowledgements*                                           ix

*Preface*                                                    xi

### FIRST WAVE
### THE BOOK

1   The Light of Asia                                         3

2   The Swami Comes West                                     31

3   Lady Emily's Dilemma                                     57

4   The Bhikku and the Beast                                 73

5   Hyman, the Bootmaker's Son                               99

6   Meher Baba Comes to the West                            123

7   Ramana Maharshi                                         153

8   Mercedes and Somerset                                   173

9   The Life and Death of Paul Brunton                      195

### SECOND WAVE
### THE SACRAMENT

10  'We are all Hindus in our essence'                      213

11  Allen Ginsberg's Vision                                 229

12  Love Is All You Need: The Maharishi and the Beatles     253

13  Rajneesh: The Last Guru                                 285

14  Down on the Ranch                                       319

*Notes*                                                     339

*Select Bibliography*                                       375

*Index*                                                     381

# LIST OF ILLUSTRATIONS

1. Sir Edwin Arnold. Stereoscopic Co., Public domain, via Wikimedia Commons.

2. Swami Vivekananda. Ramakrishna Mission Delhi, Public domain, via Wikimedia Commons.

3. Allan Bennett with members of the Buddhasansan Samagam. Photo courtesy of Frater Orpheus, Astrum Argenteum.

4. Aleister Crowley in ceremonial regalia. Public domain, via Wikimedia Commons.

5. Jiddu Krishnamurti. Public domain, via Wikimedia Commons.

6. William McGovern. © National Portrait Gallery, London.

7. Meher Baba. © Meher Nazar Publications.

8. Meher Baba with Margaret Craske, Margaret Starr, Kim Tolhurst and Meredith Starr. © Meher Nazar Publications.

9. Mercedes de Acosta. Arnold Genthe, Public domain, via Wikimedia Commons.

10. Ramana Maharshi, Paul Brunton, disciples and calf. Photo courtesy of Sri Ramanasramam.

11. Somerset Maugham. Library of Congress, Prints & Photographs Division, LC-DIG-ggbain-36664.

12. Timothy Leary. Everett Collection Historical / Alamy Stock Photo.

13. The Beatles meet the Maharishi. Keystone Press / Alamy Stock Photo.

14. Maharishi Mahesh Yogi at the Royal Festival Hall, London, on his world tour to usher in the Age of Enlightenment. Trinity Mirror / Mirrorpix / Alamy Stock Photo.

# LIST OF ILLUSTRATIONS

15. Shrine to 'the Mother', Mirra Alfassa. Author's photo.

16. John McLaughlin, Carlos Santana and Sri Chinmoy. Apic, Getty.

17. Rajneesh and his personal secretary Ma Anand Sheela, leaving Immigration and Naturalization Services. Rob Crandall / Alamy Stock Photo.

# ACKNOWLEDGEMENTS

I am immensely grateful for their help and advice to Odin Biddulph, John Brauns, William Breeze, Andrew Brown, Jeff Cox, Hamish Dewar, Allan Downend, Don Eales, Anth Ginn, Dot Ginn, David Godman, Andrew Harrison, Christopher Howse, Bruce Johnston, Mike Jones, Naomi Levine, Carole Mansur, Louise Marchant, Jeffrey Moussaieff Masson, John May, John McLaughlin, Philip Norman, David Robson, Christine Ryder, Deryck Solomon, Michael Stoeger, Adam Stout and Dennis Wills.

I am particularly indebted to Robert Ward for his generosity in sharing his extensive research into the life of Paul Brunton, and to Evangeline Glass and Melody Talcott for their great kindness in sharing their personal memories of Brunton. I am also immensely grateful to John Crow for sharing the benefit of his boundless knowledge of Allan Bennett.

This book would not have been written without the backing and encouragement of Mike Jones. And I am indebted as ever to my brilliant agent Elizabeth Sheinkman.

Thanks too to my editor Alice Clarke for her patience and perfectionism, and to the book's copy editor Rose Bell, for her meticulous attention to detail.

Above all, words are not sufficient to express my gratitude to my wife Patricia, for everything.

# PREFACE

In 1897, an Indian yogi named Bava Lachman Dass exhibited himself at the Westminster Aquarium in London, demonstrating for the benefit of a packed and curious audience forty-eight yoga positions, drawn from what *The Strand*, a popular periodical of the day, described as the 'repulsive Indian religion'. Four years earlier, another emissary of that 'repulsive' religion had spoken at the first World's Parliament of Religions in Chicago, where more than 150,000 people gathered to listen to representatives of different faiths from all over the world. Narendra Nath Datta, who would become better known as Swami Vivekananda, had travelled 8,000 miles from his native Calcutta to address the Parliament. His speech on the need for universal brotherhood was greeted with rapturous applause, and Vivekananda hailed as a hero. 'Purposeful, virile, strong, he stood out, a man among men,' wrote the social campaigner and Theosophist Annie Besant, 'his inborn sense of worth and power subdued to the exquisite beauty of the spiritual message which he had brought to the sublimity of that matchless truth of the East which is the heart and the life of India.'

The Victorians had a particularly conflicted view of the religious beliefs and practices of the Indian subcontinent, compounded of fascination, admiration, bemusement and suspicion. For almost 300 years the British had maintained a presence in India, firstly through the East India Company, before in 1858 India came under the rule of the British Crown. India was the jewel in the crown of the British empire, yet to most it remained a faraway place, little known and even less understood—and nothing in Indian life was understood less than its rich spiritual traditions. That was about to change. The social and cultural revolutions afoot in late Victorian England, the challenge to traditional Christian belief posed by scientific progress, the quiet revolt against what the social reformer Edward Carpenter would describe as the 'smug commercialism and materialism of the mid-Victorian epoch'—all contributed to an awakening interest in Besant's 'matchless truth of the East'. Within the span of three generations, tens of thousands of young Westerners would be following the 'hippie trail' halfway across the world in search of spiritual enlightenment, and the world's most famous pop group, the Beatles, would be meditating at the feet of the bearded, giggling Maharishi Mahesh, converts to his 'simple technique of living in peace and happiness'.

The truth seekers and dreamers, scholars and idealists, the poets, occultists, hippies and earnest enquirers into the nature of self and soul that populate the pages of this book, were people ahead of their time. Adventurers of the spirit, for them the East was a place not simply of fascination, romance—or exploitation—but also of deliverance, a spiritual Eldorado. For there, it seemed, lay the answer to mankind's eternal problems—unhappiness, separation from the self and from God. For some this pursuit would end in disappointment and disillusionment, for others in madness, and for a very few, perhaps, in the attainment of that most elusive holy grail of enlightenment—although who other than the truly enlightened can tell what enlightenment truly is?

This book traces a path from the publication in the Victorian era of Edwin Arnold's poetic life of the Buddha, *The Light of Asia*, which became a best-selling sensation; through Vivekananda and Annie Besant; Allan Bennett, the first Englishman to become a Buddhist monk; the spiritual tourist and self-styled sage Paul Brunton; Mercedes de Acosta and Somerset Maugham; from the Beats to the Beatles and beyond, it explores how Eastern teachings, and teachers, first came to the West, to be received firstly with bewilderment and curiosity, and later to become familiar figures on the Western cultural stage, in the persons of such gurus as the Maharishi Mahesh, the 'boy god' Maharaj Ji and—the most controversial figure of the modern era—the Bhagwan Rajneesh.

To the spiritual seeker, the figure of the guru held out the promise of a personal path to God which conventional religion had patently failed to provide, in an age when science seemed to be pushing God and mystery further to the margins. Eastern mysticism appeared to offer a deeper, richer explanation for human existence—a promise of realising the divinity within that the materialistic view of the world, which argued that man was simply a collection of 'selfish genes', did not provide.

Many of the ideas expressed in this book, which were once regarded as eccentric, exotic, foreign or cranky, are now part of everyday life. Where once Christian ministers and clerics railed against the heresies of Hinduism, yoga classes are now held in church halls. Meditation has been stripped of its spiritual connotations and rebranded as 'mindfulness'.

# PREFACE

Statues of the Buddha have become a ubiquitous accoutrement in design magazines. The term 'guru' has floated free of its Eastern connotations—and its original meaning of 'teacher'—and is now applied to almost any expert or authority in any field, and to many who aren't.

It is ironic that at the same time the distrust in Eastern gurus should have grown. The guru system demanded an altogether different kind of relationship from that of congregant and priest or pastor. The guru was seen as a path to—or in some cases an embodiment of—the divine. In philosophical systems that emphasise the disintegration of the ego, unconditional devotion to the guru has all too often fostered a child-like dependence in the follower, leaving them open to emotional, financial or sexual abuse.

Emissaries of enlightenment, or holy con men? For some, the guru's teachings would help to lead them to a spiritually fulfilled life. For others, the result was bitter disappointment, when the guru proved to be all too human—all too fallible—or the promise of enlightenment faded. From the 1970s up to the present day, scandal has enveloped some of the most famous gurus who came to the West. Sai Baba, certainly the most extraordinary and enigmatic guru of the late twentieth century, who commanded a huge following in India and the West, became enveloped in allegations about sexual misconduct with young male followers. Sai Baba never commented on the allegations, leaving it to his apologists to explain the behaviour as being part of a 'spiritual development' which those crying abuse had failed to understand.

Buddhism too has had its share of scandals. In 1983, allegations surfaced that Swami Muktananda, who had urged his students at his ashram in Fallsburg, New York, to observe celibacy, had conspicuously failed to follow his own advice, having regular sexual encounters with female followers, some of them in their early to middle-teens. (Muktananda responded to the allegations by quoting the fifteenth-century poet-saint Kabir, 'The elephant strides at his own gait, but the dogs do trail behind and bark.') In 2018, two of the leading lamas in the West, Mipham Rinpoche and Sogyal Rinpoche, were engulfed in allegations of sexually—and in the case of Sogyal, physically—abusing followers, allegations that resulted in both stepping down from the organisations they led. All these incidents and more have served if not to bring Eastern religious teachings into total disrepute, then at least to suggest that claims of enlightenment, and expectations of a guru's perfection, are no defence against the pitfalls of ordinary human fallibility.

This book begins with a long ago world, when the editor of an English newspaper wrote the first poetic telling in English of the life of the Buddha, and when congregants at that first World's Parliament of Religions in 1893 rose to their feet as one to applaud a man lecturing them on the principles of Vedantic thought; it moves on to a time when Meher Baba took Hollywood by storm, and when Somerset Maugham fainted in the presence of perhaps India's greatest saint; when the LSD messiah Timothy Leary pronounced that 'we are all Hindus' now, and the Beatles sat at the feet of the Maharishi, writing songs that, inadvertently, would inspire the murder spree of the man who embodied the dark side of 1960s freedoms, Charles Manson.

It ends with Rajneesh, whose ninety Rolls-Royces (or was it ninety-three? Nobody could be sure) made him the most instantly recognisable and controversial guru of the late twentieth century, and whose utopian vision to create a 'New Man' ended in murder plots and midnight flights from the grasp of the American authorities. It could be said that the golden age of gurus in the West ended with Rajneesh. This book describes how it began, how it flowered and how it withered—if not died.

# FIRST WAVE

# THE BOOK

*The East where everything comes from, daylight and faith,*
*The fanatical East with its high pomp and its heat,*
*The teeming East I shall never see,*
*The East of Buddha, Brahma and Shinto,*
*The East having everything we have not,*
*The East being all that we are not*

Fernando Pessoa

# 1

## THE LIGHT OF ASIA

Standing in the corner of an airy, high-ceilinged room in a tall Victorian house on a leafy square in central London is a handsome armchair, fashioned from mahogany and upholstered in red velvet. The house is the headquarters of the English Buddhist Society, and the armchair once belonged to the Victorian educator, poet and journalist Sir Edwin Arnold—a man who, as much as anybody, was single-handedly responsible for introducing the religious and philosophical teachings of India to the West.

It is a ritual to invite important visitors to the Society to sit in 'Sir Edwin's chair'. The Dalai Lama, the 16th Karmapa and the King of Thailand have all settled themselves on the red velvet upholstery, and run their fingers along the carved mahogany arms, while considering, perhaps, the relationship between comfort and inspiration.

A portrait of Arnold hangs on the wall in the Society's library. It shows a distinguished looking man in late middle age, formally dressed in a frock coat, wing collar and cravat, with a cavalier's beard and swept-back wings of greying hair. There are two medals attached to his lapel: one the Order of the Star of India, the other signifying Arnold as KCIE—a Knight Commander of the Indian Empire. In a long and distinguished life, he would also be honoured with decorations by the rulers of Turkey, Persia, Japan and Siam. He wears an expression of enquiring intelligence, his gaze fixed on the middle distance. He holds a notebook in his left hand, a pen in his right, as if captured in a moment of contemplation before putting pen to page. He looks every inch the eminent Victorian that he was.

Arnold was a linguist who spoke nineteen languages including Hindi, Urdu, Sanskrit, Persian and Turkish; a journalist who wrote authoritatively on everything from blush roses to the Prusso-Danish war; a poet who was at one time considered for the post of Poet Laureate following Alfred, Lord

Tennyson. Alfred Austin got the job, despite Queen Victoria's preference for Arnold.

A man of formidable erudition and intellect, he was also possessed of a surprisingly playful spirit—a man, according to his son Emerson, who was as 'simple as a little child and would turn readily from his high thoughts and philosophies to enjoy any harmless and witty joke'.[1] His most eccentric whim was to carry a bag of semi-precious gemstones, which he had acquired in the bazaars of Ceylon. Using his carpenter's tools he would bore holes in a staircase, a sideboard or a chair, in which he would secrete a topaz, garnet or sapphire—simply for the fun of it. Running your fingers along the mahogany frame of his chair in the Buddhist Society you may detect certain crevices and indentations that do not seem to be part of the natural grain of the wood, and find yourself wondering—but topaz, garnet or sapphire is there none. Attached to its back is a plaque explaining that it was while sitting in this chair that Arnold wrote The Light of Asia, his epic prose poem about the life of the Buddha, which was published in 1879, and that was to enthral Victorian society.

There had been scholarly works, translations and academic treatises on Buddhism published in the West before The Light of Asia, but Arnold's poem was something very different. The first original poem written in the English language on the life of the Buddha, it would go on to sell more than a million copies in Britain and America and be translated across the world. It would also prove a formative influence on many of those we shall meet in this book.

For Arnold himself it brought praise and unique recognition. The King of Siam initiated him as an Officer of that country's Order of the White Elephant. And in what was then Ceylon, he was honoured as a champion of the Buddhist faith, and presented with the yellow robe and begging bowl of a Buddhist monk—the first, and so far as one can determine, only, editor of The Daily Telegraph, or indeed any Fleet Street newspaper, ever to be accorded this honour. The apparently conventional Victorian proved to be very unconventional indeed.

The second son of a Sussex magistrate, Robert Coles Arnold, Edwin Arnold was born on 10 June 1832 at Gravesend in Kent. He was educated at King's School, Rochester, where he displayed an early facility for poetry and the classics, winning a scholarship to King's College, London, before going on to University College, Oxford. Here, living in rooms that had previously been occupied by the poet Shelley, Arnold threw himself into college life, founding an organisation called the Fez Club, whose members adopted the Egyptian headdress, smoked Oriental tobacco and vowed to practise misogyny, celibacy and a programme of 'keeping women in their place'.[2] In many respects, Edwin Arnold was very much a man of his time. In 1852 he won the Newdigate prize for poetry with 'The Feast of Belshazzar', and his first book of verse, *Poems Narrative and Lyrical*, was published a year later. After graduating from Oxford, he became a schoolmaster at King Edward VI School, Birmingham. He married Catherine Biddulph, who gave birth to a son, and in 1857, at the age of just twenty-five, travelled with his new family to India to take up the post of Principal of Deccan College at Poona.

Arnold's arrival coincided with the outbreak of the so-called Sepoy Rebellion (now often referred to as the First Indian War of Independence) which was brutally put down by the British, and which, a year after Arnold's arrival, led to the charter of the East India Company, which had determined British interests in India for more than a hundred years, being cancelled by Parliament and India coming under the direct rule of the Crown.

The Rebellion did not extend to what was then the Bombay Presidency, where Poona lies, but feeling against the British nonetheless ran high. Arnold took the precaution of keeping a loaded revolver beside his plate at mealtimes. On one occasion, a notice was discovered on the gate of the school offering a reward of several thousand rupees for the head of the Principal. Arnold coolly addressed the students, expressing his hope that they would find him more useful alive than dead, and the threat passed.

Arnold loved India, and the three years he spent as a teacher at Poona would leave him with a profound admiration for the country's culture and its religion. He studied Persian and Marathi and, with the help of local pandits, Sanskrit, enabling him to read the great epic tales of Indian literature, the Ramayana and the Mahabharata. At the same time, he availed himself of less taxing pleasures, riding, hunting, shooting and, he would recall, 'watching the endless movements of the Nautchnees [dancing girls] and listening to their songs'.

He particularly deplored the prevailing colonial attitudes of racial and cultural superiority, 'the precipitate ignorance', as he put it, 'which would set aside as "heathenish" the high civilization of this great race'. Nonetheless, throughout his life he would remain an unapologetic imperialist, never deviating from his belief in Britain's divine right to rule, and that 'The hope of Hindostan lies in the intelligent interest of England.'[3] The idea of Indian self-government would have been anathema to him.

In 1860, Arnold was forced by Catherine's ill health to return to England. (She died in 1864, and four years later Arnold got married for the second time to Jennie Fanny Channing, the daughter of William Ellery Channing, a Unitarian minister and Christian socialist.) He took a job as a leader writer on *The Daily Telegraph*, eventually rising to the position of editor-in-chief. His son Emerson (whom Arnold named after his friend Ralph Waldo Emerson) would put it more poetically in his memoirs, explaining how India was his father's first love, but that he was 'obliged by circumstances to remain under grey Western skies and labour for more than 40 years in London on the staff of *The Daily Telegraph*'.[4]

In fact, this grim sentence of servitude seemed to suit Arnold rather well. *The Daily Telegraph* had been founded in 1855 as a four-page sheet selling for tuppence. By the time Arnold joined the paper its circulation was climbing rapidly, on the way to making it the biggest-selling newspaper in Britain. (Karl Marx, living in London at the time, was an avid reader, but evidently not a fan. 'By means of an artificially hidden sewer system all the lavatories of London spew their physical filth into the Thames,' Marx wrote. 'By means of the systematic pushing of the goose quill the world capital spews out all its social filth into the great papered central sewer called the *Daily Telegraph*.'[5])

Arnold's position as a leader writer afforded him the opportunity to roam freely over a wide diversity of subjects—over the years he would write more than 10,000 'leaders' on matters ranging from the perfidy of Russia to the cultivation of blush roses, frequently embroidering his thoughts and opinions with what his colleague George Augustus Sala, the most famous journalist of the Victorian age, described as 'an Oriental exuberance of epithets'.[6]

Lord Burnham, the proprietor of the *Telegraph*, would remember Arnold in later years as 'a rugged, rather ugly old man in a black velvet skull cap', but with 'the soft serene dignity of an Oriental mystic'. This, and the rosette of the Order of Medjidie (a knightly order of the Ottoman Empire, another of Sir Edwin's awards) that he wore in his button-hole, made him a distinctly exotic figure in a Fleet Street office.[7]

By his son Emerson's account, Arnold was an exceedingly gentle, almost saintly man. 'It is not too much to say of him that his own life was indeed "like soft airs passing by"', he wrote:

> He had 'goodwill to all that lives,' and the sweetness of his soul radiated
> a constant benediction on those of us who were privileged to be in daily

and intimate association with him ... 'Let your minds be like sundials,' he would say, 'and only record the sunny hours of life.' I never heard him utter a malicious, cruel or unkind word.[8]

A man of indefatigable energy, he wrote books on Indian education, a two-volume history of Lord Dalhousie, the Viceroy of India, memoirs of his travels in America, India and Japan, and several volumes of poetry. He abhorred time-wasting and would exhort his children always to 'use the ten minutes of life' to do something useful.

In India, he had learned the Sanskrit alphabet by writing it out and hanging it over his dressing table to peruse as he dressed in the mornings. And according to Emerson, his pockets were always bulging with some volume of Greek, Latin or Oriental classics to dip into at an idle moment. He had an astonishingly retentive memory and could recite screeds of classical poetry verbatim.

Arnold composed much of *The Light of Asia* at his weekend retreat, Hamlet House, a cottage overlooking the Thames estuary near Southend in Essex, but he would also scribble on his knee as he travelled on the District Line between his home in South Kensington and the *Daily Telegraph* office in Fleet Street. He had formidable powers of concentration, and was able to write anywhere and on whatever was to hand—a menu, the margin of a newspaper, his shirt-cuff. He would assemble these scraps into bundles that he called 'brick piles', and from them copy the lines into a blank book.

*The Light of Asia* comprises some 5,300 lines of verse, divided into eight books. Told in the voice of a narrator described as 'an imaginary Buddhist votary', the poem recounts the story of Gautama Buddha from his birth into a royal family, through his gradual awakening to the sufferings of the world, his attainment of Buddhahood, meditation in the shade of the Bodhi tree, his first teachings and the establishment of the first *sangha*, or order of monks. It ends with a summary of Buddhist doctrine: the law of karma and dharma, the Four Noble Truths, the Eightfold Path and an exposition on Nirvana—the 'nameless quiet, nameless joy,/ Blessed NIRVANA— sinless, stirless rest,/ That change which never changes', as Arnold had it.[9]

*The Light of Asia* would prove hugely influential in introducing Buddhist teachings for the very first time to the public at large, bringing to an enormous popular audience a subject that had hitherto been largely the domain of Orientalists, scholars and (usually disapproving) theologians. It was an astonishing commercial success in both Britain and America. In

Britain the book appeared in some forty editions, in America in around eighty editions, and many more in pirated form (at that time British works were not protected by copyright). It was translated into German, Dutch, French, Italian, Czech, Japanese and even Esperanto, making Arnold both internationally renowned and rich. It was turned into a play, an opera and later a film—made in India—for which the Maharajah of Jaipur provided the locations, costumes, camels and elephants (despite there being no mention of camels or elephants in *The Light of Asia*).[10]

Christmas Humphreys, the barrister and founder of the British Buddhist Society, noted that it was 'little exaggeration to say of this great work that it obtained for the *Dhamma* [the Buddhist teachings] a hearing which half a century of scholarship could never have attained'.[11] That 'half a century' seems to err on the low side. Long before Zen Buddhism was taken up by the Beats in the 1950s, long before such popularisers as Humphreys himself, or the Zen pioneer Alan Watts, and long before the rising eminence of the Dalai Lama in the West, Sir Edwin Arnold made Buddhism fashionable.

\* \* \*

The extraordinary success of *The Light of Asia* was a milestone in the long and frequently tortuous history of Western understanding—and misunderstanding—of India's great religions.

To the Greeks who first encountered Indian sadhus, or 'gymnosophists', as they called them, more than 2,000 years ago, there was much that seemed admirable in their teachings that 'the best doctrine was that which removed pleasure and grief from the mind'—as bizarre as the range of austerities and self-mortifications that were apparently necessary to achieve them must have appeared. Later travellers were bewildered and horrified to encounter Hinduism's pantheon of deities: blue-faced gods and goddesses, riding on tigers or seated in lotus flowers, snakes coiled around their necks; a god that is half-elephant, half-man; another riding on a rat; an eight-armed goddess, wearing human skulls as a necklace and severed heads at her waist—a taxonomy that must have seemed to the outsider as chaotic and disordered as the rest of Indian life. 'You should scarce believe me, shou'd I name the vile and infamous creatures to which they pay divine honours', wrote the eighteenth-century Jesuit Pierre Martin, ''Tis my opinion, that no idolatry among the antients was ever more gross, or more horrid, than that of these Indians.'[12] The religious practices of the vast majority of Indians did not even have a name—

at least not one commonly agreed upon by Europeans—until 1877, when the British anthropologist Monier Monier-Williams published his book *Hinduism*.

Early travellers in India were considerably hampered in their understanding by being unable to read Sanskrit, the so-called language of the Gods in which the sacred Vedic texts, believed to date from between 1700 and 1100 BCE, were written, and the knowledge and understanding of which was jealously guarded by the priestly Brahmin caste. It was not until the eighteenth century that a group of European and predominantly British scholars, most of them enthusiastic amateurs, began the translation of Sanskrit texts in earnest, unlocking for the first time for the West an extraordinary trove of knowledge about Asian religion and culture.

The catalyst was the British East India Company, which in 1617 was granted permission by the Mughal emperor Jahangir to trade without payment of duties in the Indian province of Bengal, and which in 1757 established de facto rule over the territory, after troops under the command of Major-General Robert Clive defeated the Nawab of Bengal at the Battle of Plassey, thereby establishing Britain's first colonial foothold on the subcontinent. The Company brought with it merchants, administrators, lawyers, soldiers and craftsmen, many of whom took an interest in India's cultural and religious life that went far beyond the pragmatic necessities of trade and governance, and who would ultimately make an incalculable contribution to the Western world's understanding of Indian history, culture and religious traditions.

John Zephaniah Holwell arrived in India in 1732 as a surgeon for the East India Company, before becoming the *zamindar*, or chief revenue collector, for Calcutta. Holwell was also in charge of the Company garrison of Fort William, and was among those who in 1756 were incarcerated in the so-called Black Hole, the small dungeon in Fort William where the Nawab of Bengal imprisoned British prisoners and their families. By Holwell's account, of the 146 prisoners held there, 123 died.

After serving briefly as Governor of Bengal in 1760, Holwell returned to Britain and set to work on his monumental study of Indian customs, beliefs and practices, which was published in three volumes between 1765 and 1771, arrestingly entitled *Interesting Historical Events, Relative to the Provinces of Bengal, and the Empire of Indostan With a seasonable hint and perswasive to the honourable the court of directors of the East India Company. As also the mythology and cosmogony, fasts and festivals of the Gentoo's, followers of the*

*Shastah. And a dissertation on the metempsychosis, commonly, though erroneously, called the Pythagorean doctrine.*

Holwell claimed to have based his writings on sacred Brahmin texts that had come into his possession but then been lost at the time of his hellish incarceration in the Black Hole (scholars have never been able to identify exactly what these texts might have been). He argued that all the world's religions rested on the same 'primitive truths revealed by a gracious God to man', and that 'to attentive inquirers into the human mind, it will appear, that common sense, upon the affairs of religion, is pretty equally divided among all nations'. Rather than following the conventional prejudice of seeing the abundance of different deities in the Hindu pantheon as evidence of a berserk paganism, he recognised that belief in 'one God, eternal, omnific, omnipotent and omniscient' was fundamental to Hinduism, and that the multiplicity of deities were 'to be taken only in a figurative sense'.[13]

Indeed, to Holwell, the Vedic teachings constituted 'the most ancient, and consequently most pure' of religions. Indians might well have been as 'degenerate, crafty, superstitious, litigious and wicked a people as any race of beings in the known world', but the Vedic teachings on good and evil were 'rational and sublime' and those Brahmins who lived by the code were 'the purest models of genuine piety that now exist or can be found on the face of the earth'.[14] He looked particularly kindly on the Hindu teachings on the transmigration of souls—or reincarnation. The Brahmins, he wrote, hold that

> [the] metempsychosis of the delinquent spirits extends through every organised body, even to the smallest insect and reptile; they highly venerate the bee, and some species of ant, and conceive the spirits animating those forms are favoured of God, and that its intellectual faculties, are more enlarged under them, than in most others.[15]

(Holwell himself was an ardent vegetarian.)

It was passages such as this, perhaps, that led *The Critical Review* to the opinion that the religious practices described by Holwell constituted 'such a continued series of nonsense, rhapsody, and absurdity, that the quoting it must insult the common understanding'.[16]

It would be a further twenty years after the publication of Holwell's book before the appearance of the first translation in English of the single most important text in Hinduism. The Bhagavad Gita—or Song of God— is part of the epic historical and philosophical poem the Mahabharata, which is believed to date from between the fifth and fourth centuries BCE. Written in a sublime poetic form, barely 20,000 words in length, the Gita, as it is known, recounts the conversation on the eve of battle between the warrior prince Arjuna and his charioteer, the god Krishna come to earth in human form, which extemporises the essential Vedic teachings on duty, karma, right and wrong action, reincarnation and the requirement to surrender to the Divine.

As Krishna describes it, life is an impermanent, dreamlike state in which the soul is beset by dreams and illusions. The wise man learns to recognise these illusions for what they are and, freed from desires and attachments, goes through life with complete serenity, at the end of it merging into eternal unity with Brahman, the omnipresent spirit of all created things. Those who fail to achieve this blessed state are bound to be reborn over a countless succession of lives until liberation is finally achieved.

The man responsible for the first English translation of the Gita was a printer and 'writer'—or clerk—for the East India Company named Charles Wilkins. Born in Frome, Somerset, in 1749, Wilkins travelled to India at the age of just twenty-one to take up work with the Company. He learned Persian and Bengali, and with the help of local craftsmen cast the first complete fount of Bengali characters for a *Grammar of the Bengali Language* that had been compiled by another Company writer, Nathaniel Halhed.

At Halhed's urging, Wilkins began to learn Sanskrit. When his health started to decline due to overwork and the sweltering heat and malarial climate of Calcutta, on the advice of Warren Hastings, the Governor General of Bengal, he decamped to the city of Benares—'a place which is considered as the first seminary of Hindoo learning', as Hastings described it. There, with the help of a Brahmin pandit named Kalinatha, Wilkins embarked on a translation of the Mahabharata from Sanskrit into English. He would never complete the full translation, but at Hastings' instigation Wilkins' translation of the Gita was published in London in 1785, under the title *The Bhagavat-Geeta, or Dialogues of Kreeshna and Arjoon*. It was the first Sanskrit text to be translated into a European language.

In his introduction, Wilkins wrote that 'The Brahmans esteem this work to contain all the grand mysteries of their religion.' Writing to Nathaniel Smith, the chairman of the East India Company, to introduce Wilkins' translation, Warren Hastings described the Gita as 'one of the greatest curiosities ever presented to the literary world', declaring it to be 'of a sublimity of conception, reasoning and diction almost unequalled'. But he cautioned Smith that he was likely to find some passages in it 'cloathed with ornaments of fancy unsuited to our taste, and some elevated to a track of sublimity into which our habits of judgement will find it difficult to pursue them'.[17] And it was as a curiosity that the work was generally received—'a curious specimen of mythology and ... an authentic standard of the faith and religious opinions of the Hindoos', as one reviewer put it.[18]

Wilkins' translation of the Gita was itself translated into French, Greek, Russian and German, becoming an important influence on the European understanding of Hindu philosophy. Ralph Waldo Emerson extolled it as 'the first of books; it was as if an empire spake to us, nothing small or unworthy, but large, serene, consistent, the voice of an old intelligence which in another age and climate had pondered and thus disposed of the same questions which exercise us';[19] while William Jones, the co-founder with Wilkins of the Asiatic Society, and the most distinguished of all the Orientalists, considered Wilkins' translation to be the summit of scholarship, advising anyone who wished to form 'a correct idea of Indian religion and literature' to disregard 'all that has been written on the subject, by ancients or moderns, before the publication of the Gita'.

A painting of William Jones by Sir Joshua Reynolds hangs in the headquarters of the Asiatic Society in what is now known as Kolkata. It depicts him at the age of about thirteen, an angelic-looking child, dressed in a crimson velvet jacket, his head buried in a book—as it invariably seemed to have been—apparently lost to the world. Born in London in 1746, Jones was a child prodigy who was reciting Shakespeare at the age of four, and by the time he was 13 years old was able to write down the whole of *The Tempest* from memory. He mastered Greek, Latin, Persian, Arabic and Hebrew at an early age. By the end of his life he was proficient in twenty-eight languages. After graduating from Oxford and studying law at London's Middle Temple, he went on to serve as a circuit judge in Wales and was then appointed to the Supreme Court of Judicature at Fort William in Calcutta, the highest court in British India.

Jones arrived in Calcutta in 1783, and the following year, with Charles Wilkins, he co-founded the Asiatic Society (or 'The Asiatick Society'), with the ambitious objective of furthering the study of 'whatever is performed by man or produced by nature' in Asia. From 1808, the Society occupied a handsome neoclassical building on Park Street in the centre of Calcutta, which today is a museum. The Society's headquarters are in an adjoining building, a scruffy, nondescript block next door to a store selling sewing machines.

An antiquated cage-lift carried me to the third floor. Along a dingy corridor, the walls were lined with a series of fading photographs—Sri Aurobindo Ghose, the freedom fighter turned mystic, and the Indian nationalist Subhash Chandra Bose. A row of worn leather chairs were pushed against the wall, under a notice: 'For the use of guests only'.

Mr Roy, the Society's secretary, greeted me in his office. He talked of Jones having 'two missions' when he came to India: 'One was to study, and the other was espionage.' Espionage? Mr Roy smiled: 'To spy. If you want to rule the country, you must understand the minds of the country—who were these Indians? But Jones was special, I think. He had a love of India.'[20]

Mr Roy was right. Jones did love India and made it his aim to 'know India better than any other European ever knew it'. He adopted local customs, at home dressing in kurta pyjamas for comfort, and took daily language lessons from scholars and pandits. A man of extraordinarily far-ranging interests and abilities and, too, of phenomenal energy, over the next ten years he would produce an abundance of works on botany, geography, literature, language, local laws and customs and religious philosophy and practice.

Jones made the first English translations of several important works of Indian literature from the Sanskrit, a language that he considered 'more perfect than the Greek, more copious than the Latin, and more exquisitely refined than either'.[21] He was one of the first European scholars to note the correspondences between Sanskrit, Greek and Latin, and to suggest a common origin for these languages. He took an unusually sympathetic and nuanced view of Hinduism, and his essays 'On the Hindus', which were published in *Asiatick Researches*, the journal of the Asiatic Society, in 1789 and 1780, were, for many years, regarded as the definitive account, for a European readership, of Hindu beliefs and practices.

While the civilisation of Europe was 'transcendently majestick', Asia, Jones acknowledged, had 'many beauties, and some advantages peculiar to herself', not least the Hindu classics, including the Mahabharata, which he described as 'magnificent and sublime in the highest degree'. Jones gave a favourable account of what Christians found most difficult to countenance in Hinduism, the doctrine of monism—or non-dualism—the unity of the individual soul, or Atman, and the supreme Brahman, as expounded in the Upanishads and the writings of the Vedanta school. Brahman, in this sense, is not God exactly, but the Absolute—the fundamental unchanging Reality of existence itself, which is held to be the Godhead. Atman is the Brahman within—the spark of the divine that is the Self. This is not to be confused with our individual ego. Atman is beyond individuality, and not to be identified with any of our functions, such as thought or emotion.

This idea of the divine within was a teaching that most Christians regarded as rank heresy on the grounds that it seemed to give licence to man to believe he was God. But Jones wrote that while human reason could neither 'fully demonstrate, nor fully disprove' the teachings of the Vedantists, 'nothing can be farther removed from impiety'.[22] Like Holwell, Jones was also much taken by the Hindu doctrine of transmigration, regarding it as 'incomparably more rational, more pious and more likely to deter men from vice' than the Christian view of eternal damnation for sinners. But although Jones found much to admire in Hindu philosophy, there was nothing sufficient in the end to shake the 'adamantine pillars of our Christian faith'.

Jones died in 1794 at the age of forty-seven. He was buried in the South Park Street cemetery in Calcutta, the final resting place of numerous British soldiers, adventurers, administrators and merchants, among them George Bogle, the first British envoy to Tibet, and the singular Major General Charles 'Hindoo' Stuart, who each morning bathed in the Ganges, worshipped Hindu gods and (unsuccessfully) urged the British ladies of Calcutta to cast off their whalebone corsets and dress in saris, the better to display 'those charms that the bounty of nature hath bestowed'.

It is a fitting tribute to Jones' contribution to the understanding of Indian culture and history that, among the weathered and lichen-encrusted tombs and broken statuary of the cemetery, his mausoleum, surmounted by a soaring pinnacle, should be the most striking of all. His epitaph reads: 'Here was deposited the mortal part of a man who feared God, but not death. And maintained independence but sought not riches. Who thought none below him but the base and unjust, none above him but the wise and virtuous.'

The tolerant, open-minded and enquiring view of Hinduism embodied in men like Jones, Wilkins and Holwell would begin to subside in the mid-nineteenth century, as theologians and Christian evangelists renewed their attack on the 'paganism' and 'idolatry' of Hinduism. From the moment it gained its foothold in India in the early part of the eighteenth century, the priorities of the East India Company had been trade and power, not religious conversion. Missionaries were prohibited on the simple grounds that Christian proselytising would interfere with business. But by the end of the century, demands were mounting from evangelical Christians in

Britain that the territories of the East India Company should be opened up to missionary work.

The most zealous champion of this cause was Charles Grant, a Scotsman who had arrived in India in 1768 to take up a military position with the Company and gone on to make a small fortune as a silk merchant, becoming a member of the Company's board of trade. Grant led a particularly dissolute life, but after losing two children to smallpox he became a devout Christian. In 1787, with a handful of fellow evangelicals, Grant drafted a proposal for launching missions in India, in which he described Hindus as 'universally and wholly corrupt ... as depraved as they are blind, and as wretched as they are depraved'—and therefore pressingly in need of conversion.

His initial attempts were unsuccessful, but following his return to Britain in 1790, he took up the Christian cudgel with renewed fervour. In 1792 he wrote the tract, *Observations on the State of Society among the Asiatic Subjects of Great Britain, Particularly with Respect to Morals and on the Means of improving It*, attacking the liberal attitudes of men like Hastings, Wilkins and Jones who had contrived to 'exalt the natives of the East, and other pagan religions, into models of goodness and innocence', and arguing that India would be advanced socially and morally by compelling the East India Company to permit Christian missionaries into India. By 'communicating light, knowledge and improvement', Grant argued, 'we shall attach the Hindu people to ourselves'.

In 1804 Grant joined the East India Company's board of directors, and the following year became its chairman. He also acquired a powerful ally in William Wilberforce, one of the founders of the Church Missionary Society (and the man who would later lead the campaign for the abolition of slavery). In 1813 Grant's broadside was presented to Parliament as part of the debate on the renewal of the Company's charter, and in 1815 the first missionaries of the Church Missionary Society arrived in India.

The merchants, soldiers and writers who set out to make their fortunes with the East India Company were for the most part young, single men. They embarked from Britain on the long and hazardous voyage to India—a journey that could take up to six months—with little expectation of returning soon, if at all. Few took their wives and children with them (William Jones was an exception, bringing his wife Anna). Some adopted local customs and habits and took Indian wives or mistresses. It has been estimated that as many as a third of the 'Company men' had Indian wives and Eurasian children, on whom they settled money or property, creating an 'Anglo-Indian' class that would in time suffer discrimination from both the British rulers and the Indian population.

Grant strongly disapproved of such assimilation. But he believed that Indians should be encouraged to adopt the customs and habits of the English, the objective being, in the words of the Whig politician Thomas Babington Macaulay, to form among the Indians an elite class that was 'Indian in blood and colour, but English in taste, in opinions, in morals and in intellect'.[23]

While the earlier generation of Orientalists had argued for the importance of educating Indians in their own texts, traditions and language, Macaulay's 'Minute on Indian Education' (1835) claimed the innate supremacy of European culture, and argued that proficiency in English would be of greater value to Indians than their own languages. It was a proposal intended to lay the foundation for a class of English-speaking Indians that would reinforce colonial dominance, and at the same time diminish the value placed on the study of Indian culture, history and language.[24]

It would require the coming of a new generation of Orientalists to once more restore respectability to Indian studies—and to open the door to a greater understanding of India's other great legacy to religious thought: Buddhism.

\* \* \*

When Edwin Arnold wrote *The Light of Asia* towards the end of the nineteenth century, knowledge and understanding in the West about the life of the Buddha and his teachings was still very much in its infancy. Writing in his introduction, Arnold noted that as recently as 'a generation ago little or nothing' was known in Europe of 'this great faith of Asia', which, according to Arnold, surpassed 'in the number of its followers and the area of its prevalence' any other creed or religion—470 million people, as Arnold had it, 'from Nepal and Ceylon, over the whole of the Eastern Peninsula, to China, Japan, Tibet, Central Asia, Siberia and even Swedish Lapland'. More than a third of mankind, he wrote, 'owe their moral and religious ideas to this illustrious prince, whose personality, though imperfectly revealed in the existing sources of information, cannot but appear the highest, gentlest, holiest and beneficent, with one exception, in the history of Thought.' The exception, for Arnold and most of his readers, was, of course, Christ.

Arnold's 'illustrious prince', the historical Buddha, Gautama or Shakyamuni—the sage of the Sakya clan—was born in Lumbini, in what is now southern Nepal, sometime in the fifth century BCE (Arnold dated his life from about 620 to 543 BCE). According to Buddhist teachings, he attained enlightenment at what is now called Bodh Gaya, in the state of Bihar, going on to preach the gospel of the Four Noble Truths at Deer Park, near the town of Benares, now Varanasi.

From there, his teachings spread throughout northern and central India. But Buddhism had all but disappeared from the land of its birth by the thirteenth century, persecuted by Hindu kings, disparaged by Brahmin priests, its relics largely destroyed by the Moghul invaders who would rule most of India for the next four centuries.

While traces of India's Buddhist past still existed in the form of temples and shrines, it was not until the nineteenth century that British surveyors and archaeologists would begin to put together the various pieces of evidence that would finally establish India as the cradle of Buddhism. So it was that the earliest accounts of Buddhism to reach the West came from other lands where the teachings had spread.

Early travellers in China, Japan, Tibet, Ceylon (Sri Lanka), Siam (Thailand) and other parts of Asia, encountered the stories and worship of a great saint variously called Sakmomia, Sakyamuni, Fo, Xaca, Shaka, Buddu and other names, but had no idea that it was the same teacher and the same philosophy that was being followed, albeit with doctrinal and regional differences, throughout Asia.

As early as the thirteenth century, the Venetian trader Marco Polo had observed Tibetan monks at the court of the Mongol emperor Kublai Khan and determined that they revered a prophet whom they called Sakyamuni. But Polo made no attempt to understand the monks' philosophy, describing them simply as idolaters and being more impressed by their powers as healers and sorcerers, 'knowing so many enchantments'. The Jesuit writer Daniello Bartoli, in his history of Francis Xavier and the Jesuit missions in India, Japan and Asia called *L'Asia*, which was published in 1653, wrote of 'Xaca' as being 'one of the most famous gymnosophists of India', the son of a king in the Gangetic basin who had lived 'about a thousand years before Christ' and whose surname was 'Budda', meaning 'a wise or lettered person'.

But most travellers agreed that what they encountered was heathenism and idolatry of the highest order, and that the Buddha, by whatever name, was variously 'a Devil', 'a monster' and, as Francis Xavier had it, 'the pure invention of demons'. Reading an account of the Buddha, or 'Schiaca', originating in Japan, the sixteenth-century French priest Guillaume Postel concluded that the Buddha's story was actually a garbled account of the life of Christ, a theory elaborated on by the Jesuit missionary Matteo Ricci, who died in Beijing in 1610. Ricci wrote that Emperor Ming of the Han dynasty, hearing of the teachings of Christ, had despatched emissaries on a mission to the West to bring back the Christian writings. But the emissaries had been waylaid in India and mistakenly brought back Buddhist texts instead. The Buddha, according to Ricci, had 'borrowed' the doctrines of heaven and hell from Christianity 'in order to promote his private views and heterodox teachings'—adding: 'We transmit the correct Way.'

However, by the eighteenth century, after piecing together historical accounts from missionaries, traders and diplomats, scholars were finally able to determine that the religion practised under different names in Ceylon, Burma, China, Japan and throughout the Indies all had at their root the same historical Buddha; that Buddhism had originated in India some 600 years before the birth of Christ; and that while Buddhism and Hinduism had much in common, they were two quite separate religions. As the French scholar Joseph Eudelin de Jonville observed in 1801, 'From the similarity of the two religions, there can be no doubt that the one is the child of the other; but it is hard to know which is the mother.'

Most of the early accounts of Buddhist practice were based on anecdote, local conversation and the observation of rituals—and quite often misunderstanding them—at first hand. Just as a fuller knowledge of Vedic thought depended on an understanding of Sanskrit texts, so unlocking the mysteries of Buddhism depended on a knowledge of the languages in which the canonical texts were written—Sanskrit and Pali, the derivation of Sanskrit in which the Buddhist texts of Sri Lanka were written. The breakthrough was to come primarily through two men: the English grammar school boy Brian Houghton Hodgson and the Transylvanian Alexander Csoma de Koros.

A graduate of the East India Company training college at Haileybury, Hodgson arrived in Calcutta in 1818. In 1820 he was posted to Kathmandu as political assistant and secretary to the British Resident to the Court of Nepal. He would remain in Nepal for the next twenty-six years, thirteen of them as British Resident. Hodgson's principal enthusiasms were for botany and ornithology. Buddhism, by his own admission, was 'foreign to my pursuits', but in the interests of research he began to gather material on the subject, helped by 'an old Bauddha' of his acquaintance, named Amrita Nanda Pandya. Hodgson acquired Buddhist texts in both Sanskrit and Tibetan, including two complete sets of the Kanjur—the body of the Buddha's teachings—but was left distinctly unmoved by them. Hodgson wrote that he had 'no purpose to meddle with the interminable sheer absurdities of the Baudhha religion or philosophy'. The aim of his studies was 'to seize and render intelligible the leading and least absurd of the practices of these religionists'.[25]

While continuing his research, Hodgson had been corresponding with the scholar and traveller Alexander Csoma de Koros, who had set off for Asia on a quixotic search for the origins of the Hungarian language, taking him to Constantinople, Egypt, Syria and Afghanistan, and culminating in him spending nine years studying Tibetan at monasteries in Ladakh and Zanskar. In the course of his travels, de Koros compiled a Tibetan grammar and Tibetan–English dictionary, as well as accumulating a collection of Buddhist texts written in the Tibetan language. In 1830 he travelled to Calcutta, where he worked in the library of the Asiatic Society, publishing numerous articles on Tibetan Buddhist teachings, among them a detailed study of the life of the Buddha drawn from Sanskrit texts.

In the meantime, a collection of Hodgson's texts, along with a copy of de Koros' *Tibetan Grammar* and *Tibetan–English Dictionary*, found their way to Paris, and to an obsessive scholar and philologist named Eugène Burnouf, who had recently been appointed to the first Chair of Sanskrit at the Collège de France. In 1844, having wrestled with what he described as 'an immense metaphysical apparatus, an endless mythology; everywhere disorder and a dispiriting vagueness on questions of place and time', Burnouf produced *L'Introduction a l'histoire du buddhisme indien*—a 600-page, densely detailed volume that would provide the most comprehensive study of Buddhist history and doctrine yet to be published in the West. In America it would be read by Emerson and Henry David Thoreau, and in Germany by Arthur Schopenhauer and Friedrich Nietzsche, becoming a vital piece in the growing understanding of Buddhism among scholars, intellectuals and the general public, and determining the shape of Buddhist scholarship for the next fifty years.

\* \* \*

The growing field of Eastern religious studies—and what came to be known as 'comparative religion'—presented a fundamental challenge to conventional Christian teachings, which were already coming under assault during the first skirmishes in what would prove to be a protracted war between religion and science.

In 1859 Charles Darwin published *On the Origin of Species*, offering a non-theistic explanation of evolution that confounded a literal interpretation of biblical teachings, hastening what the poet and educator Matthew Arnold called the 'melancholy, long, withdrawing roar' of the sea of faith, 'Retreating, to the breath/ Of the night-wind, down the vast edges drear/ And naked shingles of the world.'

By the mid-nineteenth century, there were some thirty secular societies active in London alone, recruiting members under the banners of atheism, materialism and 'free thought'.[26] As the German chemist Heinrich Caro, writing at the end of the nineteenth century, would put it, 'Science has conducted God to its frontiers, thanking him for his provisional services.'[27] And then, Caro might have added, ushered Him on His way, closing the door behind Him as He left.

To the Victorians, Buddhism provided a different and more subtle challenge to Christianity than Hinduism. The fact that Buddhism—like Christianity—had spread from its land of origin throughout Asia and China lent it the authority as 'a world religion' that Hinduism lacked. To many commentators, Buddhism seemed more rational, the solitary, austere figure of the Buddha more clearly understood than the proliferation of gaudy deities in Hinduism. Buddhism, as the Scottish scholar William Erskine wrote, seemed 'not only a simpler but a more intellectual religion'.[28]

If the Buddha was a historical figure and not, as had long been believed, just one of the confusing pantheon of Indian gods—and, furthermore, a figure who had essayed a series of philosophical and ethical teachings that bore comparison with the teachings of Christ—then this gave Buddhism a new legitimacy. But it also made it a more significant threat—'the only moral adversary that Western civilisation will find in the Orient', as the nineteenth-century Belgian Sanskrit scholar Felix Neve described it.[29]

Not everybody felt threatened. Commenting on the doctrinal similarities between Buddhism and Christianity, Max Müller, the most distinguished Oriental scholar of the day, wrote that 'far from being frightened, I feel delighted, for surely truth is not the less true because it is believed by the majority of the human race'.[30] Born in Germany, Müller had studied Sanskrit under Eugène Burnouf in Paris, and at Burnouf's encouragement embarked on a translation of the complete Rig Veda, the Vedic Sanskrit hymns believed to date from between 1500 and 1200 BCE.

In 1846, he moved to England to study Sanskrit texts held in the collection of the East India Company, going on to take up a position as professor of modern European languages at Oxford.

Müller was a practising Christian, who believed that Christianity would benefit from a wider study of other religions, and that the religion of the future—what he called 'the true religion'—would be a fulfilment of all the religions of the past. After publishing a six-volume collection of the Rig Veda in 1879—the same year as the publication of *The Light of Asia*—Müller published the first of his monumental series of 'The Sacred Books of the East'—English translations of the texts of Hinduism, Buddhism, Islam, Taoism, Confucianism, Zoroastrianism and Jainism, of which a total of fifty titles were published in the years up to 1910. (The *Bhagavad Gita* was published as the eighth book in the series in 1882—a year before the more clandestine publication of the first Western translation of another Indian literary masterpiece, *The Kama Sutra*.)

The humorous periodical *Funny Folks* greeted Müller's series, noting that:

> One of the volumes contains the Satapatha-Brahmana according to the text of the school of Madhyandin; another comprises the 'Pattimokkha' (who was he bye-the-bye and why did he mock Patti?); while in volume eight is found 'The Bhagavadgita with the Sanatsugatiya, and the Anugita' translated by Kashinath Trimbak Telang, M.A. Fancy sending your servant to a bookseller's to ask for such works! Why, she would be sure to drop half a dozen syllables on the road.[31]

That Müller's series should have been the subject of gentle mockery in a popular magazine was a measure of the growing public awareness and interest in Eastern philosophy. The time was right for a popular telling of the Buddha's story. And Edwin Arnold provided it.

Orientalists and scholars might have complained that *The Light of Asia* gave a fancifully embroidered and not altogether accurate account of Buddhist doctrine, but to most readers that was hardly the point. Arnold cast the Buddha's life in a deeply romantic light. The story of the Indian prince renouncing the world and finding Nirvana would have seemed both a fascinating novelty, yet at the same time profoundly universal in its themes of nobility, virtue, struggle and self-sacrifice. Arnold's lapidary language, his luxuriant descriptions of the Indian landscape and his depiction of the Buddha as a figure of unimpeachable virtue, all sounded a resonant chord for an audience enamoured of the high romantic poetry of Tennyson. One could almost imagine his descriptions of the Buddha's enlightenment under the Bodhi tree rendered as a series of paintings by those Pre-Raphaelite arch romantics John Everett Millais or William Holman Hunt.

Readers of *The Light of Asia* might also have been struck by the strong correspondences in the story of the Buddha to that of Christ, from the miraculous circumstances of his conception and birth to the temptation of the Buddha by Mara—'he who is the Prince of Darkness'—so reminiscent of Christ's temptation by the Devil. And Arnold seemed deliberately to nudge them towards a judgement of equivalence between Christ and the Buddha—'greater than the King of Kings', as the poem has it.

To some, the analogy with the life and teachings of Christ sounded a resonant chord—the American writer Oliver Wendell Holmes, Sr., considered *The Light of Asia* worthy enough to be compared to the New Testament; but Christian writers considered it close to heresy. In a booklet entitled 'Edwin Arnold as Poetizer and Paganizer' (1884), the Baptist preacher, theologian and poet William Cleaver Wilkinson described Arnold as an apostle of the Antichrist, articulating a common worry that the 'transient whim' of popular interest in Buddhism provided an insidious challenge to Christian belief, which threatened a 'letting up in the sense of obligation, on the part of Christians, to Christianise the world'. Samuel Kellog, the American Presbyterian missionary who spent many years in India and played a major role in the translation of the Hindi Bible, was sufficiently alarmed by *The Light of Asia* to write his own book combating what he called 'the Buddhist menace', and the danger of Arnold's book in particular. 'Many who would have been repelled by any *formal*, drily philosophical treatise upon Buddhism, have been attracted to it by the undoubted charm of Mr Arnold's verse', he warned.[32]

To its critics, whatever virtues were to be found in Buddhism as a laudable set of ethics could in no way compensate for its absence of a Supreme Being who could act as an instrument of deliverance and eternal life. The first of the Four Noble Truths, that all is *dukkha*, or suffering, was misinterpreted by critics as 'nihilism' and 'pessimism'—a 'religion of total perishableness', in the words of the nineteenth-century Welsh theologian Rowland Williams.

Christian writers particularly struggled to understand what was meant by Nirvana. That the ultimate objective of the struggle of life should be the absorption of the Self into the Infinite, rather than its eternal existence with God and one's loved ones in Heaven—seemed mystifying and unconscionable. What Arnold in *The Light of Asia* rhapsodised as 'Blessed NIRVANA—sinless, stirless rest —/ That change which never changes', to others seemed rather to be some sort of horrific total extinction, despite Arnold's argument that 'a third of mankind would never have been brought to believe in blank abstractions, or in Nothingness, as the issue and crown of Being'.[33]

For more sympathetic readers, part of the appeal of Arnold's poem would doubtless have been the way in which it seemed to reinforce the growing body of opinion about the compatibility of Buddhism and science, a belief based not on divine revelation but on personal practice; a path that denied the binary philosophy of salvation or damnation, and which put man's fate firmly in his own hands. The Buddha's exhortation to be 'lamps unto yourselves', not to blindly believe but to test against one's experience, 'like an analyst buying gold, who cuts, burns, and critically examines his product for authenticity', appeared to chime with the scientific method of experimentation and verification.

Arnold numbered among his friends many of the most eminent scientific thinkers of the day, Darwin among them, and argued that 'a close intellectual bond' existed between Buddhism and modern science, and that Buddhism was compatible with Darwin's theory of evolution:

> When Darwin shows us life passing onward and upward through a series of constantly improving forms towards the Better and the Best, each individual starting in a new existence with the records of bygone good and evil stamped deep and ineffaceably from the old ones, what is this again but the Buddhist doctrine of Dharma and of Karma.[34]

As he noted in his preface to *The Light of Asia*, the doctrine of reincarnation would doubtless be 'startling to modern minds'. But his exposition in the poem seemed to chime serendipitously with Darwin's theories:

> Life runs its rounds of living, climbing up
> From mote and gnat, and worm, reptile and fish,
> Bird and shagged beast, man, demon, deva, God,
> To clod and mote again, so are we kin
> To all that is.

All part of 'the fixed arithmetic of the universe,' as Arnold put it, 'Which meteth good for good and ill for ill'.

The success of *The Light of Asia* encouraged Arnold to turn his attention to other Oriental works. He produced a translation of the Gita Govinda,

*The Indian Song of Songs* (1875), the twelfth-century poem describing the relationship between Krishna and Rada, and episodes from the Mahabharata, which Arnold described as 'The Iliad of India', culminating in his translation of the Bhagavad Gita, published in 1885 under the title *The Song Celestial*.

Arnold's translation of the Gita was the first introduction to the classic work for a young Indian named Mohandas Gandhi, who had arrived in London in 1888 to study at Inner Temple with the intention of becoming a barrister. Gandhi, who heretofore had expressed scant interest in religion, would later describe Arnold's 'magnificent rendering' of the Gita as the first step in his understanding of the teachings of *ahimsa*, or non-violence, which would become the abiding philosophy in his struggle to free India from the yoke of colonial rule. 'I devoured the contents from cover to cover and was entranced by it', Gandhi wrote in an article for the nationalist weekly newspaper, *Young India*, published in 1925, 'I have since read many translations and many commentaries, have argued and reasoned to my heart's content but the impression that first reading gave me has never been effaced.'[35]

Gandhi would carry Arnold's translation with him thereafter, maintaining that it was unimprovable. He also read Arnold's *The Light of Asia*, 'with even greater interest than I did the Bhagavad Gita. Once I had begun it I could not leave it off.' Reading *The Light of Asia*, the Bhagavad Gita and Christ's Sermon on the Mount, Gandhi wrote, would form the basis of his belief in renunciation as 'the highest form of living'. Arnold and Gandhi, despite an age difference of thirty-seven years, became good friends, and both were committee members of the London Vegetarian Society.

*The Song Celestial* consolidated Arnold's standing as the foremost interpreter of Oriental wisdom—'a revealer to his generation', as one newspaper described him.[36] His friend Oscar Wilde wrote of Arnold that 'He knows India better than any living Englishman knows it and Hindoostanee better than any English writer should know it.'[37]

Arnold's son Emerson, who described himself as a student of 'Theosophy and Oriental Occultism' and was a firm believer in reincarnation, wrote that such was his father's knowledge and understanding of Eastern philosophy that he, Emerson, was convinced that Arnold must have lived in India in previous lives:

> My father, although very patriotic and intensely British in many ways, was always semi-oriental: in outlook, tastes, manners and thoughts and

even in appearance. I believe that his brief visit to India resuscitated the subconscious memories of former lives spent there and that these gave him his wonderful knowledge and insight and his love for and attraction to Eastern life and philosophy.[38]

In the autumn of 1885, Arnold returned for the first time to the country he had left almost twenty-five years earlier. At Poona, he found that the college where he had once been Principal had been destroyed in a fire and rebuilt. He moved on to Benares—the 'Oxford and the Canterbury of India in one'—and then travelled the 13 miles to Deer Park at Sarnath, the spot where following his enlightenment the Buddha gave his first teaching on the Four Noble Truths, and where the Buddhist sangha was first formed. Sitting beside the stupa marking the spot, it seemed to Arnold that 'more consecrated ground could hardly anywhere be found'.

From Deer Park he moved on to Bodh Gaya, the holiest site in the Buddhist world. In 250 BCE the emperor Asoka had constructed the first shrine to mark the place where, nearly 300 years earlier, the Buddha had attained enlightenment; at some point between the fifth and sixth centuries, a magnificent temple had been erected on the same spot. But in the centuries since, Buddhism had been driven from India, the temple had fallen into disrepair and the holy site purged of all memory of its origins. Following the arrival of the British in India, the site had been visited sporadically by travellers, including the artist James Crockett, who on a tour of the region in 1799 paused to paint a view of what was described as 'the Hindoo Temple', towering out of dense undergrowth and entwined with vegetation.

In 1811, a party under the command of Dr Francis Buchanan, a surgeon, geographer and botanist of the East India Company, came upon the site during an extensive survey of the region. Buchanan had some knowledge of Buddhism; he had lived for some years in Burma and published an article in *Asiatick Researches*, the Asiatic Society journal, called 'On the Religion and Literature of the Burmas' (1799). He found the site to be in the possession of a group of Hindu ascetics under the direction of a head priest, the Mahant.

Its Buddhist origins had been long forgotten. Masonry and statuary from the temple had been scattered far and wide or plundered for local use; some of the statues of the Buddha had been appropriated for worship and given the names of Hindu deities. It was only in recent years, Buchanan was told, that the Mahant had learned of the site's original religious significance, when two separate delegations despatched by the

Burmese King of Ava and arriving just a few years apart had informed him that it was here that their god Gautama had lived. At the great pipal, or Bodhi tree, under which the Buddha had sat and gained enlightenment, Buchanan was informed by his guide that it was revered by Hindus as a tree planted by the great god Brahma, 'but the worshippers of Gautama on the contrary assert that it is placed exactly in the centre of the earth, and call it *Bodhidruma*'.[39]

Further visitors to the site had served only to contribute to its decline. Some fifty years after Buchanan's visit, Alexander Cunningham, a British soldier and the first archaeological surveyor to the Government of India, carried out excavations at the site, which had the unfortunate effect of exposing the Mahabodhi temple to the elements, and leaving parts of it on the point of collapse.

In 1877, a delegation of Burmese monks, officials and artisans were given permission by the Government of India to construct a small monastery on the outskirts of the site and undertake some restoration work on the temple and its surroundings. (The Mahant raised no objections, stipulating only that several Hindu idols near the temple should not be interfered with.) The results were disastrous. Rajendrala Mitra, an archaeologist sent by the government to inspect the work, reported back with horror that the Burmese were 'perfectly innocent of archaeology and history, and the mischief they have done by their misdirected zeal has been serious'. It required a further party under the direction of Cunningham's deputy, J. D. M. Beglar, to rectify the damage done by the Burmese.

This was the situation that greeted Arnold when he arrived in Bodh Gaya in January 1886, eager at the prospect of at last casting his eyes on the holy site that he had conjured so vividly from his imagination in verse in *The Light of Asia*:

> The Bodhi-tree (thenceforward in all years
> Never to fade, and ever to be kept
> In homage of the world), beneath whose leaves
> It was ordained the Truth should come to Buddh.

But his excitement quickly turned to dismay. In a subsequent report for *The Daily Telegraph*, he described how stones bearing images of the Buddha were being used as weights to the levers for drawing water; statues were buried under rubbish; local villagers had appropriated elaborately carved blocks of stone as doorsteps; and the Asoka pillars—which had once graced the temple pavement and that Arnold described as 'the most antique memorials of all India'——were being used as posts in the Mahant's kitchen.

Arnold wandered around the site in growing despair. When he asked his Hindu guide if he might take a leaf from the Bodhi tree, he was told 'Pluck as many as ever you like, sahib; it is nought to us.' 'Ashamed of his indifference', Arnold wrote, he took 'the three or four dark shining leaves' which the priest pulled from the branches of the trees and 'having written upon each the holy Sanskrit formula', carried them with him on the next stage of his journey to Ceylon. 'There I found them prized by the Sinhalese Buddhists with eager and passionate emotion', he wrote.[40]

At the temple at Kandy, a leaf that Arnold presented to the temple custodians was placed in a casket of precious metal, to be made the centrepiece of the temple rituals. In a ceremony in the town of Panadura, he was lionised as a scholar who had 'eclipsed the fame of other learned men as a mountain of diamonds would the luster of mountains of other precious stones'.[41] In yet another ceremony in Kandy to mark his departure from the island, he was presented with the yellow robe and begging bowl of a Buddhist monk.

For Arnold, it was not simply the state of disrepair that Bodh Gaya had fallen into that was the cause of anguish; it was the fact that the most important site in the Buddhist world should remain in Hindu hands. At a dinner with the Governor of Ceylon, Sir Arthur Hamilton Gordon, Arnold proposed a campaign to restore the temple and return the site to Buddhist possession, and with Gordon's support began lobbying British politicians and Buddhist leaders in Burma, Tibet, Siam and Japan. As a token of goodwill, he despatched a copy of The Song Celestial to the Mahant in Bodh Gaya—who not surprisingly gave Arnold's proposal short shrift.

Arnold's plan got nowhere until, in 1891, a young Sinhalese Buddhist named Angarika Dharmapala, inspired by Arnold's account, visited Bodh Gaya himself, going on to found the Maha-Bodhi Society with the intention of reviving Buddhism in India and restoring Bodh Gaya and other Buddhist sites. Arnold became an enthusiastic proselytiser for the cause. In March 1893, in an article for The Daily Telegraph called 'East and West: A Splendid Opportunity', he appealed for public support for the campaign:

> I would today, in these columns, respectfully invite the vast and intelligent British public to forget, for a little while, home weather and home politics, and to accompany me, in fancy, to a sunny corner of their empire, where there centres a far more important question, for the future of religion and civilisation, than any relating to parish councils or parish pumps.

Outlining his hopes for the campaign, Arnold went on: 'I am quite certain that my own policy of appealing to Reason and Right, and of relying upon friendly negotiations with the present Hindoo tenants of the shrine, will and must eventually prevail.'

And so—eventually—it did. In 1953 the Hindu owners finally relinquished ownership, and after 700 years Bodh Gaya was returned to Buddhist custody.

\* \* \*

In 1888, Arnold was knighted. The following year his second wife, Jennie, to whom he had been married for twenty years, died of pleurisy. Arnold sought consolation in travel. He embarked on a lecture tour of America and then journeyed to Japan, where *The Light of Asia* had been rapturously received.

Arnold fell in love with the country, lauding the Japanese for 'that ceaseless grace in the popular manners, that simple joy of life ... that almost divine sweetness of disposition which, I frankly believe, places Japan in these respects higher than any other nation'.[42] He would spend almost two years living in Japan, adopting Japanese dress and immersing himself so deeply in the culture that an obituarist would later note that English residents 'refused to receive or countenance him'.[43]

It was there that he met the woman who would become his third wife, Tama Kurokawa. Arnold was sixty-five; Tama was twenty. It was doubtless Tama that Arnold was thinking of when he wrote:

> I am still inclined to believe that the average or abstract Japanese female comes, all things considered, nearest among her sex, as regards natural gifts, to what we understand by an angelic disposition ... She is, in point of fact, the most self-denying, the most dutiful and the most patient woman in the world, as well as the most considerate and pleasing.[44]

With his new wife, Arnold returned to Britain and his London home at 31 Bolton Gardens, South Kensington. The Japanese marriage ceremony was not recognised under English law, but as a point of principle—and to the consternation of his friends and family—Arnold refused to undergo a second, English, ceremony, that might be seen to cast doubt on the sanctity or legitimacy of the first. He eventually surrendered to propriety and agreed to an English ceremony in 1897, making his wife Lady Tama. The union was reported even in the United States, with *The Milwaukee Journal* noting, in a tone of barely disguised bemusement, that the author of *The Light of Asia* had married a Japanese woman, 'and seems to be very happy with her'.

Was Arnold a Buddhist? He never described himself as such, and never took Buddhist vows, but clearly he took the Buddhist teachings greatly to heart. He gave up the sport of shooting animals and birds, and his son Lester would later recount a charming story about his father's adherence to the teaching of *ahimsa*—non-violence to all living things—which Arnold defined as 'the desire to help, the readiness to love'. According to this, in 1897, when Arnold was cruising in the Mediterranean, the boat he was on was three hours out from Sicily when a member of the crew brought on deck a box of lizards he had captured on the island. When Arnold enquired how he intended to feed the creatures, the sailor replied that he had no idea, and they would have to starve. Arnold insisted the boat turn back to the island, where the lizards were released, and the cruise duly resumed.

The most compelling evidence of Arnold's convictions comes in the exultant closing stanzas of *The Light of Asia*:

> Ah Blessed Lord! Oh, High Deliverer!
> Forgive this feeble script, which doth thee wrong,
> Measuring with little wit thy lofty love.
> Ah! Lover! Brother! Guide! Lamp of the Law!
> I take my refuge in thy Law of Good!
> I take my refuge in thy Order! OM!
> The dew is on the Lotus! Rise great sun!
> And lift my leaf and mix me with the wave.
> Om Mani Padme Hum, the sunrise comes!
> The dewdrop slips into the shining sea!

But Arnold, of course, was writing in the voice of a 'Buddhist votary', not himself. It would have been almost unthinkable for an Englishman of Arnold's generation and position publicly to have declared himself a Buddhist, far less to have adopted the ascetic rigours and demands of a monastic life.

In 1891—possibly as a response to the criticism from Christian writers over *The Light of Asia*—Arnold published a second lengthy narrative poem on the life of Christ, *The Light of the World*. The poem lacked the novelty of *The Light of Asia*. Reviews were lukewarm, and sales poor. The general public, it seemed, preferred Arnold the champion of the Buddha, to Arnold the disciple of Christ.

But the truth, surely, was that for Sir Edwin, it was not so much a question of 'either/or' as 'both'. He was a liberal Christian, able to reconcile his Christian beliefs with a deep respect for Buddhism. But if ever he wore the bhikku's robes he had been gifted in Ceylon, he did so in private.

'It seems strange to say,' Margaret Scott, the wife of *The Daily Telegraph*'s drama critic Clement Scott, once remembered, 'but when speaking to me of death, as he did on many occasions, Edwin Arnold appeared to await it with almost eager curiosity.' Sir Edwin Arnold died on 24 March 1904. Two years earlier, a man named Allan Bennett had become the first Englishman ever to be ordained as a Buddhist monk. The starting point for his journey to taking robes was his reading of *The Light of Asia*.

2

# THE SWAMI COMES WEST

The first World's Parliament of Religions, held in Chicago in September 1893, was a historic attempt to bring together for the first time in a public forum the spiritual traditions of East and West.

Held over the course of seventeen days, as part of the World Columbian Exposition, the Parliament of Religions drew more than 150,000 people to listen to representatives of different faiths from all over the world, heralding, in the words of the opening address by the Parliament's chairman, a Chicago attorney named Charles Bonney, 'a new era of religious peace and progress ... dispelling the dark clouds of sectarian strife'.

Not everybody thought this a commendable idea. The Archbishop of Canterbury had declined an invitation on the grounds that 'the Christian religion is the one religion', and he had no wish to affirm 'the equality of the other intended members and the parity of their position and claims'. The Sultan of Turkey lodged a similar objection on behalf of Islam, leaving the Parliament with just one Muslim representative, an American convert named Alexander Russell Webb, a writer and publisher who was also the United States Consul to the Philippines.

But while the overwhelming majority of delegates were from Christian denominations, there were also representatives of Shintoism, Zoroastrianism, Jainism and Confucianism, as well as the 'new religions' of Spiritualism and Christian Science. Anagarika Dharmapala, the young Sinhalese Buddhist who inspired by Edwin Arnold's account of Bodh Gaya had founded the Maha-Bodhi Society, attended as the representative of 'Southern Buddhism'—the term then used for Theravada Buddhism. Also present was the Japanese teacher D. T. Suzuki, representing Mahayana Buddhism. But the greatest stir would be caused by a 30-year-old Hindu swami, the first ever to speak publicly in America, named

Narendra Nath Datta—or as he would become universally known, Swami Vivekananda.

On the first day of the Parliament, 7,000 people packed the hall, the majority of them women—as one newspaper reported, 'ladies, ladies packing every place—filling every corner'. Vivekananda's turn came in the late afternoon—he was the thirty-first delegate to speak. Called to the stage he was suddenly seized with stage fright and, unsure what to say, asked for more time to prepare himself.

At length, clad in a belted robe and a saffron turban, looking every inch the exotic spiritual figure, the Swami stepped up to the podium to begin his address: 'Sisters and Brothers of America ...'. No sooner had he begun than he was interrupted by a fervent round of applause, which, according to newspaper accounts of the day, lasted between two and four minutes.

His speech, when he was finally able to deliver it, was not much longer. He talked of Hinduism as 'the mother of all religions' that had taught the world tolerance and universal acceptance, and which accepted 'all religions to be true'. He continued:

> I will quote to you brethren a few lines from a hymn which I remember to have repeated from my earliest childhood, which is every day repeated by millions of human beings: 'As the different streams having their sources in different places all mingle their water in the sea, so, O Lord, the different paths which men take through different tendencies, various though they appear, crooked or straight, all lead to Thee'.

The Parliament, 'which is one of the most august assemblies ever held', he went on, was 'in itself a vindication, a declaration to the world of the wonderful doctrine preached in the Gita: "Whosoever comes to me, though whatsoever form, I reach him; all men are struggling through paths which in the end lead to me."'[1] 'He is an orator by divine right,' *The New York Critique* enthused, 'and his strong, intelligent face in its picturesque setting of yellow and orange was hardly less interesting than those earnest words, and the rich, rhythmical utterance he gave them.'

Among those enraptured by the spectacle of Vivekananda was Annie Besant, the English-born writer and social campaigner, who had come to Chicago as the representative of the Theosophical Society. Vivekananda was short—barely 5 feet 6 inches tall—and given to a certain pudginess, but his noble bearing had a liquefying effect on Besant, who wrote:

A striking figure, clad in yellow and orange, shining like the sun of India in the midst of the heavy atmosphere of Chicago, a lion head, piercing eyes, mobile lips, movements swift and abrupt—such was my first impression of Swami Vivekananda, as I met him in one of the rooms set apart for the use of the delegates to the Parliament of Religions. Off the platform, his figure was instinct with pride of country, pride of race—the representative of the oldest of living religions, surrounded by curious gazers of nearly the youngest religion. India was not to be shamed before the hurrying arrogant West by this her envoy and her son ... Purposeful, virile, strong, he stood out, a man among men, able to hold his own.

She continues:

On the platform, another side came out. The dignity and the inborn sense of worth and power still were there, but all was subdued to the exquisite beauty of the spiritual message which he had brought, to the sublimity of that matchless truth of the East which is the heart and the life of India, the wondrous teaching of the Self. Enraptured, the huge multitude hung upon his words; not a syllable must be lost, not a cadence missed! 'That man, a heathen!' said one, as he came out of the great hall, 'and we send missionaries to his people! It would be more fitting that they should send missionaries to us!'[2]

Annie Besant was not the only woman to go weak at the knees at the sight of Vivekananda. A Mrs S. K. 'Roxie' Blodgett, the wife of a wealthy Chicago businessman, who would later become an ardent devotee, would recall how

When that young man got up and said, 'Sisters and Brothers of America', seven thousand people rose to their feet as a tribute to something they knew not what. And when it was over and I saw scores of women walking over to the benches to get near him ... I said to myself, 'Well, my lad, if you can resist that onslaught you are indeed a God.'[3]

Vivekananda would address the conference some dozen times over the next seventeen days. By its end, he had been acknowledged not only as 'undoubtedly the greatest figure in the Parliament of Religions', as *The New York Herald* described him: he had become the most famous Indian in America.

\* \* \*

Before the arrival of Vivekananda in the West, the popular idea of the Indian holy man had largely been derived from colonial accounts of sadhus, fakirs and *soi-disant* miracle workers—many of whom, as one observer noted, appeared to follow 'a life of easy, irresponsible indolence and mendicancy'.

In March 1829, for example, *The Asiatic Monthly Journal* offered an account of a Madras yogi who gave exhibitions of 'sitting in the air', and reported on yogis being buried for up to forty days with no harmful effects. In a diverting study of sadhus and mystics, John Campbell Oman, the Professor of Natural Science at the Government College in Lahore, wrote of tales of one sadhu who was able to conjure up *bhuts* (or goblins) in a jungle clearing, and offered vivid descriptions of others engaged in the traditional practices of self-mortification, including lying on their backs in the open air, exposed to the elements, for weeks on end. Another man, Oman wrote, would stand for hours on one leg while holding a beam of wood 'three cubits long', and yet another would fix his gaze on the rising sun and continue to stare at it while following its progress across the sky throughout the day.

In 1895 a correspondent for *The Civil and Military Gazette* in Lahore offered an extraordinary account of a yogi in Shimla who was said to have burnt himself on a funeral pyre, and then ascended to heaven for ten days before reappearing in front of the whole village. Villagers, it was reported, were inclined to believe the story as the man was able to give them a detailed account of heaven. 'This, of course, settles the matter,' the correspondent noted, possibly sarcastically. 'It is manifestly impossible for any man to describe heaven unless he has been there to see.'[4] The *Gazette* seemed to have a particular fascination with miracle workers. A month earlier it had reported on a yogi in Trivandrum who had lived for three years 'in divine contemplation, without partaking a morsel of food', adding the melancholic news, 'A few days ago he died.'[5]

Such was the typical British view of the Indian holy man.

'A wonder faquir was in view in the main street, who all the time he says his prayers goes through acrobatic performances that would earn him a fortune in England,' another traveller reported. 'As we approached he was standing on one leg with the other curled round his waist; in another second he was on his hands, head downwards, and his legs round his neck: when we left him he was tied up in something resembling a reef-knot and clove hitch combined.'[6]

One of these so-called religious posturists, named Bava Lachman Dass, would indeed subsequently exhibit himself at the Westminster Aquarium in 1897, demonstrating forty-eight yoga positions drawn from what *The Strand* magazine described as the 'repulsive' Indian religion. Whether this earned him a fortune or not, history does not record.

\* \* \*

The man who had inspired Vivekananda in his religious mission was neither a 'posturist', fakir nor miracle worker. But he was certainly one of the most extraordinary and revered religious figures in India. Ramakrishna, or Gadadhar Chatterji, to give him his proper name, was born to a poor Brahmin family in rural Bengal on 18 February 1836, and claimed to have had his first experience of spiritual rapture at the age of six: walking through some paddy fields, he looked up at the sky and saw a flock of white cranes passing across a thundercloud, and was so intoxicated by the sight he 'completely lost consciousness in ecstasy'.

Scorning conventional education, he made his way to Calcutta where he took up the duties of a priest, tending to a temple at Dakshineswar devoted to Kali, the divine mother. Lost in a devotional trance, he would converse with the goddess, bring her food and behave for all the world as if she was a living reality for him. In any other society Ramakrishna might have been considered mad—indeed he was widely feared to be so by many among his neighbours; but others recognised him as 'god intoxicated'—a saint who had attained the state of *nirvikalpa samadhi*—the merging of the Self with Brahman, or God.

His most devoted disciple was his wife Sarada Devi, whom Ramakrishna considered to be the Divine Mother in human form. They had married when Sarada was just five—a purely religious union. The marriage was never sexually consummated, and she continued to live with her family until she was nineteen, when she joined Ramakrishna at the Kali temple. Following his death she would be recognised as the Holy Mother of the Ramakrishna Order. Ramakrishna claimed to have realised God through the paths of all the great religions. He was initiated as a Sufi, he claimed to have visions of Christ and pronounced the Buddha and the Sikh gurus as saints, declaring that 'it is the same God towards whom all are directing their steps'.

The young Vivekananda, who would later articulate much the same sentiments to a standing ovation at the World's Parliament of Religions, was, on the face of it, an unlikely disciple for a 'God intoxicated' saint like Ramakrishna. Born in Calcutta on 12 January 1863, Narendra Nath Datta was the son of an affluent attorney-at-law at the High Court in

Calcutta. According to his biography, Narendra was a high-spirited, often troublesome, but sweet-natured child, a pleasure seeker, a sweet singer and 'the leader in all innocent fun'. He was also of exceptional intelligence. Both his Indian and British teachers at the General Assembly's Institution, a school run by the Scottish General Missionary Board, were said to be 'astounded by his brilliant intellect'. The college principal, a Church of Scotland clergyman named William Hastie, remarked that despite his habit of chain-smoking, 'Narendra Nath Datta is really a genius. I have travelled far and wide, but have never yet come across a lad of his talent and possibilities, even in the German universities amongst philosophy students.'[7]

As a student, Narendra developed an interest in politics and became a member of Sadharan Brahmo Samaj, a reformist Hindu movement that advocated the abolition of the caste system, and the education and emancipation of women. But it was Hastie—evidently a most unusual Scottish clergyman—who would inadvertently steer Narendra's destiny towards a spiritual life.[8]

One day, while teaching a class on the themes of transcendence and ecstasy in the poems of William Wordsworth, Hastie suggested that to understand the true meaning of 'trance' his students should visit Ramakrishna, whom Hastie had personally witnessed in that ecstatic state. Narendra duly made his way to the Kali temple at Dakshineswar, where Ramakrishna greeted the boy and asked him to sing him two songs, which moved him so deeply that he entered a state of *samadhi*. Crying tears of joy, he told Narenda that he had been waiting for him, and that the boy had a great spiritual mission to fulfil. Not surprisingly, perhaps, Narendra's first thought was that Ramakrishna was a madman, but over the course of several visits he came to believe that Ramakrishna was a saint, and in time became his most devoted disciple.

In 1886, following Ramakrishna's death, and in accordance with his final instructions, Narendra organised Ramakrishna's disciples into a monastic order, eventually establishing a *math*, or monastery, at Baranagar, a few miles upriver from Calcutta—where it still stands today. Narendra took to the life of the wandering mendicant. He spent two years travelling through India and the Himalayas, visiting sacred sites and witnessing at first hand the demoralising effects of British colonisation on the Indian people. He became fired with the belief that India's renaissance depended on a revival of her great religious tradition of Vedic thought, and with a mission to 'raise' the masses. 'The Hindu, the Mohammedan, the

Christian, all have trampled them underfoot,' he wrote. 'Again, the force to raise them must come from inside, that is from the orthodox Hindus. In every country the evils exist not with, but against religion. Religion therefore is not to blame, but men.'

Narendra resolved to travel to the West and speak on behalf of India and his religion. Learning that religious leaders would be gathering in Chicago, and with funds provided by a disciple, the Maharajah of Khetri, in May 1893 he sailed from Bombay for America, vowing not to return 'until I can burst on society like a bomb and make it follow me like a dog'. His journey took him from India to Ceylon, on to Singapore, Hong Kong, Nagasaki and Yokohama, across the Pacific to Vancouver, and from there by train to Chicago, where he arrived towards the end of July. 'With a bleeding heart I have crossed half the world to this strange land seeking help', he wrote.

Presenting himself at the offices of the Exposition, he was shocked to learn not only that he had arrived six weeks early, but also that no one would be admitted as a delegate without proper references. On the long train journey from Vancouver, he had fallen into conversation with a wealthy lady from Massachusetts, who, impressed by his mission and good character, had invited him to stay at her home. Vivekananda now made his way to Boston, where his new friend introduced him to a professor at Harvard University who furnished the Swami with an introduction to the Chairman of the Committee of the World's Parliament of Religions and the train fare back to Chicago.

Arriving back in the city, Vivekananda discovered to his dismay that he had mislaid the Chairman's address. Unable to find lodgings, he passed the night in an empty boxcar in the railway freight yard. The following day, he wandered the streets until sitting down, exhausted, at the roadside. At that moment a woman stepped out of a house opposite, and spying Vivekananda enquired whether he was a delegate for the Parliament of Religions. Learning of his difficulties, she provided him with breakfast and walked him to the hall on Michigan Avenue where the Parliament was being convened, and where, at last, he was accepted as a delegate.

Addressing the Parliament in his final speech, Vivekananda spoke powerfully about the need for amity between all religions:

> The Christian is not to become a Hindu or a Buddhist, nor is a Hindu or a Buddhist to become a Christian. But each must assimilate the spirit of the others and yet preserve his individuality and grow according to his own law of growth. If the Parliament of Religions has shown anything

to the world, it is this: It has proved to the world that holiness, purity and charity are not the exclusive possessions of any church in the world, and that every system has produced men and women of the most exalted character. In the face of this evidence, if anybody dreams of the exclusive survival of his own religion and the destruction of others, I pity him from the bottom of my heart.[9]

Vivekananda's speeches, his personal magnetism and his powerful sense of conviction made him an instant celebrity. He was signed up by an agency in Chicago to give lectures, and he became the star attraction at Green Acre, a spiritual retreat founded in 1890 by Sarah Farmer in the town of Eliot, Maine, where invited speakers lectured on a variety of topics to do with moral and physical improvement.

The philosopher William James was among those who attended Vivekananda's lectures on Vedanta and his demonstrations of Raja yoga. A Harvard colleague of James remarked that the Indian Swami 'had swept Professor James off his feet', and James would borrow from Vivekananda's teachings on Raja yoga at some length in his highly influential work, *The Varieties of Religious Experience* (1902).

Vivekananda proposed Vedanta as a practical way of realising the divine within, compared to the Christian belief of praying for an infusion of Grace from God. But he was greatly influenced by the Christian ideas of charity and service. It was not enough, he argued, simply to meditate in pursuit of one's own enlightenment. And the Ramakrishna Missions, set up by Vivekananda and his disciples, emphasised social engagement and service to humanity.

A recurring criticism levelled at Eastern religions in Victorian times—and ever since—was that they were passive, introverted and inimical to Western ideas of industry and progress; it was the contradiction, as one observer put it, between 'the busy practical West and the tranquil, dreamy East', between the Western ideal of 'the man of action' and the Eastern veneration of the man of contemplation, dedicating his life to the pursuit of God. It was religion, according to this argument, which had held India back. Vivekananda taught that India's spirituality—what he called 'the silent mesmerism' of Indian thought—was the country's great gift to the world:

The one characteristic of Indian thought is its silence, its calmness. At the same time the tremendous power that is behind it is never expressed by violence ... Like the gentle dew that falls unseen and unheard, and yet brings into blossom the fairest of roses, has been the contribution of India to the thought of the world. Silent, unperceived, yet omnipotent in its effect, it has revolutionised the thought of the world, yet nobody knows when it did so.

But while India had given the gift of spiritual truth to the world, he did concede that 'unfortunately sometimes we think so deeply that there is no power left for expression'. Thus had India come to be considered, as he put it frankly, 'a dead nation'.

Vivekananda saw the future lying in the revival of Vedantic thought— the 'spiritual greatness that made India the greatest nation of the then existing races of the world'—allied to the purposefulness and drive of the West:

> The most stupendous powers of civilisation, and progress towards humanity and social progress, have been effected by that wonderful race—I mean the Anglo-Saxon. We should learn from the West her arts and her sciences. From the West we have to learn the sciences of physical nature, while on the other hand the West has to come to us to learn and assimilate religion and spiritual knowledge. We Hindus must believe that we are the teachers of the world.[10]

Vivekananda espoused a vigorous sense of altruism, service and selflessness. And his biographies and hagiographies overflow with elevating parables about his emphasis on action above contemplation. 'Sir,' a young man once addressed him, 'even now I sit in a closed room, and meditate as long as I can. Yet, peace is far, far away from me. How am I to gain peace?' Vivekananda replied:

> My boy, if you have any respect for my words, the first thing I will advise you to do is to throw open all the doors and windows of your room! In your quarter there are lots of poor people sunk in degradation and misery. You will have to go to them and serve them with all your zeal and enthusiasm. Arrange to distribute medicines to those who are sick, and nurse them with all care, supply food to him who is starving, teach with as much as lies in you the ignorant; and if you begin to serve your brethren in this wise, I tell you, my child, you will surely get peace and consolation.

Following his appearances at the World's Parliament of Religions, Vivekananda would make several visits to Britain and America. In 1899, he returned to the United States to establish Vedanta centres and instruct his growing number of devotees. Among these were three sisters in Pasadena, California, where Vivekananda spent six weeks in 1900. When he returned to India, one of the sisters, a widow named Carrie Mead Wyckoff, made contact with two Indian disciples of Vivekananda who had followed him to America, and was given permission to establish a centre in San Francisco. She was given the Sanskrit name Sister Lalita.

She later moved to Los Angeles, where in 1928 she met another of Vivekananda's disciples, Swami Prabhavananda. The following year she put her home in Los Angeles at his disposal, and it became the centre for the newly inaugurated Vedanta Society of Southern California. It was here that the English novelist Christopher Isherwood would arrive in 1936, becoming an ardent disciple of Prabhavananda.

Vivekananda's message of ecumenicalism and universal love seemed to have a particularly powerful purchase on the female imagination—an early precursor of the appeal of the Indian mystic to Western women of a certain age and class. Photographs of the Swami at Green Acre, the retreat in Maine, show him seated amidst a circle of admiring women, dressed in their finest Sunday flummery; an image that would be repeated over the decades to come with different gurus, different followers.

It is tempting to see these religious savants not simply as emissaries of a powerful spiritual vision, but as the embodiments of an enticing glimpse of the romantic other—an exotic antidote to the stuffy, rigid English Victorian idea of manhood.

Not atypical of his followers was Josephine MacLeod, who described her first meeting with Vivekananda, on 29 January 1895, in the sitting room of an apartment where he was staying in New York, in almost supernatural terms: 'He said something, the particular words of which I do not remember, but instantly to me that was the truth, and the second sentence he spoke was truth, and the third sentence was truth.'[11] MacLeod described the meeting as the most important event in her life, and became a lifelong devotee.

For his part, Vivekananda was undisguised in his admiration for American womankind. 'Well, I am almost at my wit's end to see the women of this country!' he wrote to his disciples in Bengal a year after the World's Parliament of Religions, continuing:

> They take me to the shops and everywhere, as if I was a child! They do all sorts of work—I cannot do a sixteenth part of what they do. They are like Lakshmi [the goddess of Fortune] in beauty, and like Sarasvati [the goddess of Learning] in virtues—they are the Divine

Mother incarnate, and worshipping them, one verily attains perfection in everything. Great God! Are we to be accounted among men? If I can raise a thousand such Madonnas, incarnations of the Divine Mother, in our country before I die, I shall die in peace ... Most wonderful women these. They are about to corner the men, who are nearly worsted in the competition.[12]

Perhaps his most celebrated Western disciple was Margaret Noble, the daughter of a Congregationalist minister, who first heard Vivekananda speak on a visit to London in 1895. In 1898, Margaret followed Vivekananda to Calcutta, where she took the name Sister Nivedita, dedicating her life to missionary and social work, and founding a girls' school in one of the poorest quarters of the city. She also became active in the Indian nationalist movement. Vivekananda described Nivedita as 'the fairest flower of my work in England'. She died in India in 1911 at the age of forty-three.

The redoubtable Mrs Blodgett put her finger on it—or on part of it— when she remarked that she knew Vivekananda personally but for a short time, 'yet in that time I could but see in a hundred ways the child side of Swamiji's character, which was a constant appeal to the Mother quality in all good women'. It was an appeal that Vivekananda well recognised. In 1902 Mrs Blodgett wrote to her friend Josephine MacLeod, reminiscing about her time with Vivekananda:

Were you present at a lecture when one of those ladies who love to make themselves conspicuous by some ill-timed remark asked: 'Swami, who is it who support the monks in your country? There are so many of them, you know.' Like a flash Swami replied; 'The same who support the clergy in your country, madam. The women!' The audience laughed. Madam was for the time effaced and Swamiji proceeded with his lecture.[13]

* * *

It was a long and tortuous journey that had brought Annie Besant to the exotic shores of Indian mysticism, involving an unhappy marriage, the threat of imprisonment, estrangement from her children and, through it all, a fierce and unwavering commitment to a multitude of good causes.

Born Annie Wood on 1 October 1847, she was the daughter of an impoverished London doctor, who died when Annie was five. Unable to support her, her mother sent the child away to be brought up by a wealthy spinster, Ellen Marryat, who instilled in the young Annie a sense of deep religious calling. At the age of 20 she married a 26-year-old Anglican curate, Frank Besant, settling in the Lincolnshire village of Sibsey.

From the very beginning the marriage was unhappy, the couple hopelessly mismatched. Frank was a Low Church evangelical, conservative in his views and narrow-minded in his character. Annie was intellectually his superior and radical by disposition. In 1869 she gave birth to a son, Digby, and the following year to a daughter, Mabel, who almost died in infancy from whooping cough. Annie wrote short stories and books for children, but as a married woman she had no financial independence; whatever she earned went to her husband.

Her growing domestic unhappiness contributed to a crisis of faith, bringing her to question all the received tenets of eternal punishment, the divinity of Christ and the revealed truth of the Bible. In 1873 she separated from Frank—a move that effectively rendered her an outcast from polite society. She now threw herself into the free thought movement and joined the National Secular Society, presided over by the radical politician and atheist Charles Bradlaugh, quickly rising to the position of Vice-President, and becoming Bradlaugh's deputy on the *National Reformer*, a secularist newspaper.

Among the causes taken up by the National Secular Society was a 'preventive check' to population—birth control—that Bradlaugh saw as one solution to the problem of poverty. In 1877, Besant and Bradlaugh were prosecuted for obscenity after republishing an 1832 pamphlet by the American physician Charles Knowlton on marriage guidance and birth control under the title *Fruits of Philosophy, A Treatise on the Population Question*.[14] The book had already been published in Britain by a Bristol bookseller, who, for his pains, had been successfully prosecuted for obscenity.

Besant defended herself in court, arguing passionately for the right of working-class women to be educated in sexual matters and have control over their own bodies. But both she and Bradlaugh were found guilty and sentenced to six months' imprisonment and ordered to pay heavy fines. The Court of Appeal subsequently overturned their conviction on a legal technicality. But the case was to have a calamitous effect on Besant, who, following manoeuvring from her husband, was prevented from having any access to her own children.

Inflamed by this injustice she threw herself even more eagerly into the cause of women's rights, travelling the country, drawing large crowds and earning standing ovations wherever she went. As well as becoming one of the first women to embark on a science degree at University College, London, she took up the cause of Home Rule for Ireland and embraced Fabianism.

George Bernard Shaw described Besant as the greatest orator in England, and the pair enjoyed what Shaw described as an intimacy of 'a very close and personal sort, without, however, going further than friendship'. According to Shaw, Besant had 'absolutely no sex appeal', and absolutely no sense of humour either. 'Comedy was not her clue to life', he wrote, 'No truth came to her first as a joke. Injustice, waste, and the defeat of noble aspirations did not revolt her by way of irony or paradox; they stirred her to direct and powerful indignation and to active resistance.'[15] This active resistance reached its apotheosis in July 1888, when Besant took a leading role in the strike by 1,400 women matchstick makers at the Bryant & May factory in London's East End—one of the most significant actions in the drive towards establishing trade unions in Britain.

The following year her life took an even more momentous turn when she was invited by *The Pall Mall Gazette* to review a book by the Russian émigrée, self-styled clairvoyant and co-founder of the Theosophical Society, Madame Helena Blavatsky. *The Secret Doctrine* was a ponderous, rambling dissertation on the relationship between science and what Blavatsky called 'the Accumulated Wisdom of Ages'—the universal truths embodied in the ancient religions of Egypt and the East.

Published in two volumes in 1888, the book elaborated on Blavatsky's theories on the origins of mankind and its evolution over the course of several million years through a series of what she described as 'root races'. The first of these, according to Blavatsky, was 'ethereal'; the second, semi-corporeal root race had inhabited a realm called Hyperborea. The third root race, and the first to be truly human, had existed on a lost continent called Lemuria, while the fourth had inhabited Atlantis. The fifth was the Aryan race, which had inhabited earth for around one million years. Through reincarnation, each root race, Blavatsky theorised, had become more spiritually and intellectually evolved than the last. Traces of the less-evolved pre-Aryan race were still to be found on earth, Blavatsky wrote, notably the 'narrow-brained' South Sea Islander, the Australian aborigine and the African native. (This pernicious theory would find an obvious legacy in the theories of Aryan supremacy that surfaced with venomous force in twentieth-century Europe.)

These musings were not exclusively the author's own. According to Blavatsky, the philosophies of *The Secret Doctrine* had been transmitted to her by a hierarchy of realised beings, or as she had it, 'ascended Masters', whom Blavatsky claimed resided in a Himalayan redoubt, patiently watching over mankind and guiding it towards knowledge and salvation. In the book's preface she paraphrased Montaigne, writing, 'I have here made only a nosegay of culled flowers, and have brought nothing of my own but the string that ties them.'

That Annie Besant, the rationalist and Fabian, should have been persuaded by this dense and fanciful occult stew seems incredible—but persuaded she was. Besant's review appeared in *The Pall Mall Gazette* on 25 April 1889, under the title 'Among the Adepts: Madame Blavatsky on the "Secret Doctrine"'. 'Let it be said at once,' Besant began, 'that the great majority of average easy-going folk will do well not to begin "The Secret Doctrine" at all. A certain mental position must be acquired ere any reading thereof can be aught save weariness and futility.' But her conclusion was one of fulsome praise:

> The book deserves to be read; it deserves to be thought over; and none who believes in the progress of humanity has the right to turn away over-hastily from any contribution to knowledge, however new in its form, from any theory, however strange in its aspect.

So impressed was Besant that she sought out a meeting with Blavatsky, who was at that moment domiciled in London. Besant was confronted with a plump woman with doleful eyes, clad all in black, chain-smoking cheroots and speaking in a thick Russian accent. They passed an afternoon together in intense conversation. By the end of the meeting, Annie Besant—lapsed Christian, socialist campaigner, fierce atheist—had found a new faith. In the membership list of the Fabian Society, its founder Edward Pease crossed out Besant's name, adding the note 'Gone to Theosophy'.

\* \* \*

The daughter of a Russian aristocrat and army officer, Helena Petrovna von Hahn was born in the town of Ekaterinoslav (Dnipro) in what is now Ukraine, but was then part of the Russian Empire, on 12 August 1831. Her mother, also Helena, a writer of romantic novels, died when Helena was nine, and she was raised by her maternal grandparents. She was taught French, music and art and became an accomplished horsewoman; but by her own account much of her spare time was spent poring over the esoteric books in the extensive library of her great-grandfather, Prince Pavel Vasilevich Dolgorukov, an initiate in Rosicrucian Freemasonry.

In 1848, at the age of seventeen, Helena was married off to Nikifor Blavatsky, the vice-governor of Yerevan province in Armenia. Her husband was thirty-nine. It was evidently an unhappy marriage, for within a matter of weeks, having refused her husband conjugal rights, Helena had fled the marital home, en route to Constantinople. It was the beginning of an extraordinary odyssey, which over the next few years, by Blavatsky's account, would see her travelling through Asia and Europe, working in a circus, fighting with Garibaldi's army in Italy and communing with Buddhist lamas in Tibet. It was in the course of these peripatetic wanderings that Blavatsky claimed to have first encountered what she called the 'Hierarchy of Masters'. According to Blavatsky, these Masters, or Mahatmas, were members of what she called the Great White Brotherhood, whose spiritual advancement had invested them with supernatural powers, including an ability to communicate telepathically or materialise themselves in their etheric form for those enlightened enough to see them—i.e. Blavatsky. Her association with the Masters had supposedly begun with an encounter with one of their number, whom Blavatsky named as Morya, in July 1851, at the site of the Great Exhibition in London's Hyde Park. Evidently recognising Blavatsky's special gifts, Morya explained that she had important work to do for the benefit of mankind, thereby initiating the relationship on which the edifice of Theosophy would come to be built.

Blavatsky had found her vocation. In 1871 she found herself stranded in Cairo following a shipwreck. Here she set herself up as a clairvoyant, founding a 'Société Spirite' 'for the investigation of mediums and phenomena'. The organisation didn't last long, and Blavatsky made her way to New York, supporting herself as a seamstress. America was convulsed by an enthusiasm for spiritualism, table-tapping and poltergeists, which had begun in 1848 when the sisters Margaretta and Kate Fox claimed to have experienced strange rappings in their house caused by visitors from the spirit world.

In November 1874, Blavatsky travelled to a farmhouse in Vermont to investigate the case of a medium named William Eddy, who was supposedly materialising a variety of ethereal beings ranging from a Russian peasant girl to a serving boy from the Caucasus. Blavatsky concluded that these materialisations were not in fact spirits of the dead, but the 'etheric double' of the medium Eddy, 'escaping from his body and clothing itself with other appearances'.

But of more significance to Blavatsky was her meeting in Vermont with Colonel Henry Steel Olcott. Born in 1832, Olcott had been a journalist, served as a signals officer for the Union Army during the American Civil War, and then become a lawyer specialising in revenue and fraud. Divorced and the father of four children, Olcott was in search of some meaning in his life, which had led to an interest in mesmerism and spiritualism, and thus to Vermont to investigate the Eddy case on behalf of the *New York Sun* newspaper. Forceful, charismatic and with what seemed to be a direct line to disembodied entities, Blavatsky quickly had the disillusioned Olcott under her spell. The American colonel and the Russian mystic were soon fast friends, or in their term, 'chums', with their own pet names for each other. She called him 'Maloney'. He called her 'Jack'.

In 1875 they founded the Theosophical Society, listing as its objects:

(1) To form a nucleus of the Universal Brotherhood of Humanity, without distinction of race, creed, sex, caste or colour.

(2) To encourage the study of Comparative Religion, Philosophy, and Science.

(3) To investigate unexplained laws of Nature and the powers latent in man.[16]

Olcott was named the Society's first President, but the philosophy was mostly Blavatsky's—a dense stew of Egyptology, occultism and Buddhism. At its heart—and the font of her authority in these matters—was Blavatsky's relationship with the Masters.

At the head of the hierarchy, according to Blavatsky, was the Lord of the World, who had originally come from Venus, and now resided in Shamballah—a magical kingdom said to be located somewhere in the region of the Gobi Desert. The hierarchy had included all the great religious teachers and philosophers of the past, among them Confucius, Solomon, Moses and Plato. But the greatest of them was yet to come. This was the Lord Maitreya, whom Blavatsky maintained would return to earth as the next 'world teacher'. According to Blavatsky's teachings, the Lord Maitreya had twice before appeared in a human body at a critical juncture in mankind's history—firstly as Sri Krishna in the fourth century BCE, and then as Jesus.

Blavatsky had borrowed the prophecy from Mahayana Buddhism, which holds that Maitreya will be the Buddha of the next aeon (Shakyamuni, or Gautama, being the Buddha of the present aeon). Buddhist texts are unspecific about when the next aeon might be. But preparing the way for Maitreya's arrival would become a central part of the Theosophical Society's purpose.

Blavatsky's first book, *Isis Unveiled: A Master-Key to the Mysteries of Ancient and Modern Science and Theology*, published in 1877, argued the validity of the 'occult sciences', and that Hinduism, Christianity, Buddhism and Zoroastrianism all shared their roots in an ancient 'Wisdom Religion'. For refugees from organised religion, in search of a creed of universal brotherhood that purported to reconcile science with the ancient spiritual verities, Theosophy proved a surprisingly alluring proposition, and attracted a remarkably diverse following. The painter Wassily Kandinsky, the biologist and naturalist—and friend of Charles Darwin—Alfred Russel Wallace and the poet W. B. Yeats were all Theosophists.

The British army officer and Orientalist Francis Younghusband dismissed Theosophy as a philosophy for 'neurotic and partially educated ladies'; while the French historian and Indologist Alain Daniélou would later disparage Theosophists as 'dropouts from society, people vaguely interested in spiritism, "the Orient", vegetarianism, ghosts and other such nonsense'.[17] But amidst the convulsions in religious, intellectual and cultural thought that were sweeping through late Victorian England, 'other such nonsense' was gaining widespread popularity.

The Theosophical Society was just one thread in a broad tapestry of enthusiasms—from Eastern religious thought to social hygiene, from 'natural' living and food reform to anti-vivisection—that 'marked the coming of a great reaction from the smug commercialism and materialism of the mid-Victorian epoch, and a preparation for the new universe of the twentieth century', as the writer and social reformer Edward Carpenter wrote.[18]

The young barrister Mohandas Gandhi wrote that Madame Blavatsky's book *The Key to Theosophy*, which was published in 1889, had been the first book to stimulate in him a desire to read books on Hinduism, and 'disabused me of the notion fostered by the missionaries that Hinduism was rife with superstition'. Gandhi was taken to meet Blavatsky and Annie Besant, and urged to join the Theosophical Society himself, but politely declined, explaining, 'With my meagre knowledge of my own religion I do not want to belong to any religious body.'[19]

Theosophy might have purported to find the common ground between all the world's great religions, but Blavatsky was largely hostile to Christianity and showed next to no interest in Islam. Her principal enthusiasm was Buddhism, in which, she maintained, the apparent opposites of science and religion were best reconciled. Blavatsky professed to have sat at the feet of Buddhist masters in the Himalayas, but her claim that she was revealing an 'esoteric Buddhism known only to Gautama's closest followers' was mocked by serious scholars, including Max Müller—'Though I must say,' Müller added, 'what she does divulge seems very harmless.'[20]

Müller disparaged *Isis Unveiled* as 'an immense amount of drudgery and misdirected ingenuity', but he did not question Blavatsky's sincerity. He described her as a 'clever, wild and excitable girl' in search of a new religion that she could honestly embrace. (The irony is unmistakable: nobody would have thought to describe Blavatsky—a heavy, ponderous woman noticeably lacking in any feminine graces—as an 'excitable girl'; even Olcott expressed the opinion that Blavatsky was actually 'a very old man, and a most learned and wonderful man ... a Hindu man'.[21])

In 1879, ostensibly on the direction of her masters, Blavatsky and Olcott travelled to India, where they established a new headquarters of the Theosophical Society on an estate called Huddleston Gardens, which Olcott purchased for £600, at the mouth of the Adyar river, south of Madras. The following year the pair travelled to Ceylon, where on 19 May they took *pansil*, a form of Buddhist confirmation. They are believed to be the first Westerners ever to do so.

Blavatsky was too stubborn—and egotistical—a figure to fully subordinate herself to any particular creed; but Olcott had found his vocation in what he called 'pure, primitive Buddhism'. He was to remain in Ceylon, establishing a Buddhist Defence Committee, helping to organise monks to fight for the preservation of Buddhist rights in the face of pressure from Christian missionaries. And in 1881 he produced an English *Buddhist Catechism*, sowing the seeds for the establishment of schools run by the Buddhist Theosophical Society. When Edwin Arnold arrived in Colombo in 1886, following his visit to Bodh Gaya, his first port of call was the new premises of the Theosophical Society to present Olcott with some pages of the original manuscript of *The Light of Asia*.

Olcott would also prove to be a particularly energetic educationalist. There were just four Buddhist schools in Ceylon when he first arrived in the country. By 1898 there were 99, and by 1914 there were 230. While Theosophy would largely fade into obscurity throughout the rest of the world after the 1930s—for reasons that we shall shortly discover—its legacy in what is now Sri Lanka was to prove remarkably enduring. In 2013 there were 420 Buddhist schools that owed their existence to Colonel Olcott. And the Colombo Buddhist Theosophical Society continues to occupy handsome premises on the street that bears Olcott's name.

With Olcott living in Ceylon, a new figure now entered Blavatsky's life—an erstwhile Anglican curate who would go on to become a critical, and highly controversial, figure in the Theosophical Society. Charles Webster Leadbeater was a tall, determined man with leonine features, who had arrived at the Theosophical Society with an extraordinary story to tell. By his own account, Leadbeater could trace his family back to Old Norman stock, arriving in Britain at the time of William the Conqueror.

At the age of twelve, he travelled with his parents and his younger brother Gerald to Brazil, where his father worked as the director of a railway company. Travelling in the interior, Leadbeater survived attacks by Indians and was forced to watch his brother die at the hands of the leader of a rebel army. Leadbeater avenged his brother's death by bettering the rebel in a swordfight, and then watched as the rebel was shot dead in front of him.

Returning to England, apparently none the worse for his adventures, Leadbeater entered Queen's College, Oxford. But his studies were cut short by the tragic loss of his family fortune. He then worked as a shipbroker and in banking until, having been called by God, he was ordained into the Church of England.

Fantasy! All of it! Leadbeater's father was not the director of a railway company—he was a humble book-keeper—and there was no family fortune. Leadbeater's father died at the age of thirty-six, leaving his widow and son impoverished. Leadbeater had never been to Brazil. He did not have a brother. Nor had he ever studied at Oxford. Born in Stockport, on leaving school he had worked in a series of lowly clerical jobs before entering the church through family connections, taking up the position of curate in the village of Bramshott in Hampshire.

Leadbeater applied himself diligently to his duties. He took a particular interest in the moral improvement and physical fitness of the young boys in the parish, taking responsibility for church-affiliated groups such as the Union Jack Field Club and the Church Society, in which members had to promise not to lie and to be 'pure and good'. But the daily round of a curate's life proved uninspiring. Before long, Leadbeater was dabbling in spiritualism and the occult, keenly trying to make contact with the spirits of the departed.

At length his enthusiasms led him to the Theosophical Society and a meeting with Madame Blavatsky. For Blavatsky, a clergyman leaving the Christian flock—even an insignificant country curate and an incorrigible fantasist—was a good catch, and she quickly took Leadbeater under her wing.[22]

In November 1884 Leadbeater travelled to India with Blavatsky. En route they stopped in Ceylon, where, following her and Olcott's example, and after being assured by Blavatsky that it would not involve the renunciation of what she described as 'the true Christian faith', Leadbeater took refuge as a Buddhist. Leadbeater's belief that he was not compromising his Christian beliefs was somewhat misplaced, as an account of his initiation ceremony, published in *The New Zealand Craftsman and Masonic Review* in March 1885, suggests:

> It was a sight heretofore seldom seen—a Christian minister seated at the feet of the yellow-robed priests of the followers of Buddha, and solemnly repeating after them, 'I take my refuge in Buddha! I take my refuge in the law; take my refuge in order.'
>
> On being requested by the high priest to state his reasons why he desired to become a follower of Lord Buddha, Mr Leadbeater stated that it was his desire to arrive at the truth, and that he had found the truth expressed in a purer form in Buddhism than in any other system with which he was acquainted. He further stated that, while the Christian doctrines were all based upon hearsay evidence and upon doubtful authority, and required him to believe many unreasonable things, the teachings of Gautama Buddha, which stands forth most prominently, is that we should believe nothing which our reason cannot accept as true, because faith, to be lasting, must be based upon sound reason and common sense.[23]

Having thus driven the final nail into the faith of his upbringing, Leadbeater and Blavatsky travelled on to India.

\* \* \*

For Charles Leadbeater, arriving at Adyar was the fulfilment of his fantasy of the East as a repository of esoteric wisdom, where the holy writ of the 'Masters' ruled:

> What it was for me to find myself at last upon the sacred soil of India, among dark-skinned brothers of whom I had heard so much—any one of whom, for all I knew, might be a pupil of one of our holy Masters—all of whom, I thought, must at any rate have been from childhood students of the sacred lore, knowing far more about it all than we Westerners could know.[24]

Leadbeater would remain at Adyar for two years, steeping himself in Blavatsky's teachings, and cultivating his own psychic connections with her 'Master' Kuthumi, who according to Leadbeater taught him to be clairvoyant in just forty-two days.

Leadbeater embraced the occult aspects of Theosophy with an evangelical zeal. He would take a particular interest in the subject of past lives and the practice of travelling on the astral plane and consulting the Akashic records—a sort of cosmic encyclopaedia in which the history of all previous lives is supposedly stored, which could be accessed by those with the right clairvoyant gifts, and which offered the humble country curate abundant potential to conjure himself an exotic pedigree.[25] 'My first touch with anything that could definitely be called Theosophy', he later wrote, 'was in the year 504 BC, when I had the wonderful honour and pleasure of visiting the great philosopher Pythagoras.'[26]

But all was not well in the Theosophical Society. In India, Blavatsky's heretical ideas had made her a target for Christian missionaries; and her association with the Arya Samaj, a movement calling for national regeneration through a revival of the ancient Vedic teachings, aroused the suspicion of the British authorities. At the same time, the Society for Psychical Research in London launched an investigation in 1884 into Blavatsky's supposed clairvoyant and paranormal activities, after a disgruntled housekeeper accused her of forging the letters that had supposedly been materialised from the Masters. The Society's 200-page report concluded that Blavatsky should be regarded as 'neither the mouthpiece of hidden seers, nor as a mere vulgar adventuress: we think that she has achieved a title to a permanent remembrance as one of the most accomplished, ingenious and interesting imposters in history'. Blavatsky beat a retreat from India and settled in London. It was then that Annie Besant came calling.

To her friend, the playwright George Bernard Shaw, Besant was an actress whose progress through life could be read as a series of starring roles. 'She was successively a Puseyite Evangelical and Atheist Bible smasher, a Darwinian secularist, a Fabian socialist, a strike leader and finally a Theosophist exactly as Mrs Siddon was a Lady Macbeth, Lady Randolph, Beatrice, Rosamund and Volumnia', he wrote.[27] But it was Theosophy that would provide her greatest and most enduring performance.

In 1890, fired with new-found zeal, Besant was formally initiated into Theosophy. Her first act was to invite Blavatsky to move into her large London house at 19 Avenue Road, St John's Wood. But within a year Blavatsky would be dead, victim of an influenza epidemic that was sweeping through London. She was just sixty. With Blavatsky's passing,

Annie Besant assumed the role of head of the Society's 'Esoteric Section'. This was dedicated to the innermost workings of the Society, in particular to communications with the Masters. And nobody was more assiduous in those communications than Charles Leadbeater.

Besant was headstrong, dogmatic and 'the most tactless person I ever knew', according to Charles Bradlaugh's daughter, Hypatia. Leadbeater had a pathological aversion to women—he refused to shake hands with a woman on the grounds of purity, or even to stay alone in a room with one—but he was prepared to make an exception for Besant. And his years of communicating with the Masters and travels on the astral plane would make a powerful impression on her (Annie would have her own encounters with the Masters, but they never seemed to possess quite the vivid clarity of Leadbeater's).

In 1895, Besant invited Leadbeater to move into the house at Avenue Road, which had now become the Theosophical Society headquarters. Leadbeater had published his first book, *The Astral Plane: Its Scenery, Inhabitants and Phenomena*, the year before ('a landmark for the intellectual history of humanity', according to the master Kuthumi, known as K.H.), and now with the help of the Masters, he was busy with the monumental task of scouring the Akashic records with a view to determining the past lives of the most important members of the Theosophical Society. These researches, the results of which would appear over the next twenty years, revealed, extraordinarily, that all of the prominent members of the Society had been intimately connected with one another over the course of millennia, and, furthermore, that they had played significant roles on the stage of world history.

Elaborating on Madame Blavatsky's theories about root races, Leadbeater revealed that a small group of leading Theosophists had actually lived on the moon, where they inhabited monkey-like bodies and were servants of those who were now the Masters. In 40,000 BCE, Leadbeater himself had been Annie Besant's wife. Many thousands of years later, Besant had apparently married Leadbeater's daughter. In Peru, around 12,000 BCE, Leadbeater had been married to another prominent Theosophist, Francesca Arundale, producing three more eminent Theosophists—Basil Hodgson-Smith, Bertram Keightley and A. P. Sinnett—as their sons, and adopting George Arundale—Francesca Arundale's nephew.

Over the years, 'the lives' would be extended to include many prominent Theosophists; indeed, to have one's past lives divined and recorded by Leadbeater became the ultimate act of one-upmanship within the Society. Those who were not included consoled themselves with a popular, mocking poem:

> In the Lives, in the Lives,
> I've had all sorts of husbands and wives,
> I've been killed and reborn,
> Many bodies I've worn,
> But my higher anatomy thrives.
> In the Lives, in the Lives,
> We've been busy as bees in their hives —
> Whether Arab or Turk,
> We were pining to work,
> In the Lives, in the Lives.[28]

\* \* \*

Charles Leadbeater's keen enthusiasm for the education of young boys was always likely to cause trouble. In 1906 he found himself embroiled in scandal when two boys he had been teaching, the sons of Theosophists, claimed that he had been encouraging them in the habit of masturbation. The damning evidence was a coded letter that Leadbeater had written to one of them: 'Glad sensation is so pleasant. Thousand kisses darling.'

Leadbeater protested that the letter was a forgery, although he admitted to advocating masturbation as a release from frustrations that might otherwise lead a boy to the services of a prostitute or an unhealthy obsession with erotic thoughts. Despite the support of Annie Besant, Leadbeater was pressured into resigning from the Theosophical Society, and would spend the next two years in purdah, firstly in England and then the Channel Island of Jersey.

In February 1907, Colonel Olcott died at Adyar. He had supposedly been visited several times on his deathbed by one or another of the hierarchy of Masters pressing him to appoint Annie Besant as his successor, and in June 1907 she was duly elected as President of the Theosophical Society. With Besant's support, Leadbeater was now able to come in from the wilderness, and to press ahead with the great crusade of Theosophy, to fulfil Blavatsky's prophecy of bringing forward the next world teacher, or the Lord Maitreya.

'We look for Him to come in the Western world this time—not in the East as Christ did two thousand years ago', Annie Besant announced at a public lecture in Chicago in 1909. In fact, the 'vehicle' for the

Lord Maitreya had already been selected by Leadbeater, in the person of a young American named Hubert Van Hook, who conveniently enough just happened to be the son of Dr Weller Van Hook, the General Secretary of the Theosophical Society in the United States. Hubert was duly put on a boat to India to receive special training for his august role. But by the time the young boy arrived at Adyar, Leadbeater had changed his mind, and Hubert found his place usurped by a new putative Messiah.

The candidate could not have been more unlikely. One afternoon in the spring of 1909, walking on the beach at Adyar with some friends, Leadbeater spotted a group of Indian boys paddling in the shallows. Among them was a 13-year-old boy named Jiddu Krishnamurti. The son of a clerk working at the Theosophical Society, Krishnamurti, who had lost his mother at the age of ten, lived with his father and three brothers in a small cottage on the outskirts of the Adyar estate.

Outwardly, there seemed to be nothing about the young boy to arouse Leadbeater's interest: he was slack-jawed and vacant-eyed, and evinced a vagueness that, as he himself would later admit, bordered on the moronic. Yet Leadbeater told his companions that he felt a particular sense of wellbeing in the presence of the boy; he was a being 'devoid', as Leadbeater would put it, 'of any particle of selfishness'.

Leadbeater was vain, delusional, conceited and manipulative, but as time would prove, he was undoubtedly correct in intuiting something extraordinary about Jiddu Krishnamurti. The young boy, Leadbeater revealed, would one day become the vehicle for the Lord Maitreya, 'unless something went wrong', and it was to be Leadbeater's task to train him for that purpose.

In order better to establish Krishnamurti's credentials, Leadbeater set about 'reading' his young protégé's past lives, publishing his findings in a series of articles which were published together as *Lives of Alcyone* in 1924. This serendipitously confirmed that the young boy had been linked with Leadbeater and Annie Besant in a series of previous incarnations stretching back to 40,000 BCE, when Leadbeater and Besant were man and wife and Krishnamurti and his younger brother Nityananda were among their numerous children.

When Besant arrived in Adyar in November 1909 and met Krishnamurti for the first time she was similarly impressed. For the next four weeks Krishna and Nitya spent every day with Besant. It was the beginning of a deep attachment between Besant, who had been deprived of her own children, and the fragile young Krishnamurti, who had been deprived of his mother, and now saw Besant as fulfilling that role. 'My Dear Mother,' he wrote in a letter to her in December 1909, after she had left Adyar, 'Will you let me call you mother when I write to you? I have no other mother now to love, and I feel as if you were our mother because you have been so kind to us ...' He signed it, 'Your loving son, Krishna'.[29]

Before long, supposedly under instructions received by Leadbeater from the Master Kuthumi, Krishnamurti and Nitya were moved out of their father's home and took up residence in the main house on the estate, where they were placed under the care and tutelage of Leadbeater and another member of the Society, A. E. Wodehouse (the A stood for Armine), the elder brother of the novelist P. G. Wodehouse.[30]

The process of turning the slack-jawed, sleepy-eyed Indian boy into a facsimile of a young English gentleman now began in earnest. Indian customs and habits were abandoned. The Masters had stipulated a regime of tooth and nail brushes, knives and forks, and never sleeping in pyjamas—a garment, according to one instruction, apparently 'responsible for so much evil in your civilisation'. Underclothes, the instructions went on, 'must always be of silk, linen or cloth and no wool or flannel must touch the skin'.[31] Plans were laid to take the vehicle for the Lord Maitreya to England to continue his education. European clothes were bought for Krishna and Nitya, and a doctor performed the task of sewing up the holes in their ears, which had been pierced when they were small children in accordance with Hindu custom.

On 22 April 1911, Krishna and Nitya set sail from Bombay for England on the S.S. *Mantua*. On 5 May, the would-be Messiah arrived at Charing Cross station. He was just fifteen. Waiting to greet him as he stepped off the train was a woman named Emily Lutyens.

# 3

## LADY EMILY'S DILEMMA

As a boy, Jiddu Krishnamurti had the liquid eyes and trembling sensitivity of a young deer, and there was not a woman who met him who did not want to protect him. As a young man, taking on a poise and an air of authority, there was hardly a woman he met who did not want him as their son, their teacher or, more covertly, their lover—a role that he could never play.

And therein lay the problem for Lady Emily Lutyens.

When Krishnamurti arrived at Charing Cross station in May 1911 in the company of his brother Nitya and Annie Besant, on his first visit to Britain—after a journey that had taken him from Bombay to Brindisi in Italy, to Turin, to Calais, and thence to London—a welcoming party of excited Theosophists was gathered to greet him. As the slender Krishna, buttoned uncomfortably in a tweed Norfolk jacket, walked towards them, with Besant clutching his arm protectively, one woman almost fainted, overwhelmed by his spiritual aura.[1] For another, it was as if she had been struck by lightning. 'I had eyes for none but Krishna, an odd figure, with long black hair falling almost to his shoulders and enormous dark eyes which had a vacant look in them', wrote Emily Lutyens.[2] It was to be the beginning of a relationship that would span more than fifty years and change her forever.

When Emily first met Krishna, she was thirty-six, the wife of Britain's most distinguished architect, Edwin Lutyens, the mother of five children, unhappy in her marriage and in search of meaning in her life—a life that, thus far, had been utterly conventional. She was born in 1874 in Paris, the daughter of Robert Bulwer-Lytton, 1st Earl of Lytton, a career diplomat who was then the secretary to the British Embassy in Paris. She was one of two children to be born in the British Embassy that year. The other was the novelist Somerset Maugham, whose father was the embassy lawyer.

Her grandfather was Edward Bulwer-Lytton, 1st Baron Lytton. An eccentric figure who smoked opium in a hookah, and who attempted to rid himself of his troublesome Irish wife, Rosina, by twice having her committed to an asylum, Bulwer-Lytton was a politician and a poet, but was better known as the author of a string of phenomenally successful novels, written in vividly purple prose, and featuring occult and fantastical themes. The most popular of these was *Zanoni*, published in 1842, which tells the story of a Rosicrucian who sacrifices his chance for immortality for the love of a beautiful opera singer. Bulwer-Lytton died in 1873, the year before his granddaughter Emily's birth, but she would grow up steeped in his books and in stories about her eccentric grandfather's taste for fern seeds, and his reputed abilities to render himself invisible.[3]

When Emily was 2 years old, her father Robert was appointed Viceroy to India. His tenure was not a success. During his first year in the post, India was struck by a great famine that took the lives of more than 6 million people, and possibly as many as 10 million. Lytton's implementation of British trading policy was held partly to blame. Two years later, he ordered an invasion of Afghanistan, sparking the Second Anglo-Afghan War—resulting in a pyrrhic victory which brought to an end 'the Great Game' between Britain and Russia, but which also led to the downfall of Disraeli's Conservative government in 1880. Lytton resigned as Viceroy and returned to England. He died in Paris in 1891, and was buried in the family mausoleum at the family estate of Knebworth in Hertfordshire.

Emily was sixteen at the time of his death, an awkward, unhappy girl who by her own description was 'shy by nature and bored by Society'.[4] A photograph from the period shows a plain, somewhat mournful looking young woman with a large, aquiline nose and prominent jaw, her hair gathered in two buns in the Victorian manner, a string of pearls around her neck.

At the age of eighteen, Emily fell in love with a 53-year-old married philanderer named Wilfred Blunt. The relationship was never consummated, but her obsession with Blunt overwhelmed her, and the discovery that he was seeing another woman left her broken. It was at this point that she met Edwin Lutyens, a brilliant, ambitious, but impoverished young architect. Their natures could not have been more different.

Edwin was a gregarious and jovial man with a puckish sense of humour ('Doctors', he joked, 'are luckier than architects; they can bury their failures')—a workaholic, who was desperate for social approval. Emily was shy, introverted, with an indifference to matters of class and position that only someone born into the aristocracy could possess.

In 1897 they married in a ceremony at Knebworth House. From the outset the marriage was difficult; the honeymoon a disaster. Emily being 'seedy', as she called menstruation, delayed consummation. When the moment finally arrived, Edwin's inexperience made him a clumsy and unsatisfying lover—a state of affairs that their years of marriage would never properly remedy. Emily seemed to find no joy in sex.

Added to this was a further, abiding problem. As much as Edwin loved Emily, he would always remain married, first and foremost, to his work. 'I did not find in my marriage the companionship I had hoped for, nor a release for my energies,' Emily wrote.[5]

Religious conviction—and in particular Edwin's lack of it—was a further cause of friction. Growing up, Emily had been a devout Christian, earnestly believing—hoping and fearing—that the Second Coming of Christ would occur in her lifetime. As an adult she continued to read the Bible daily. Edwin had the traditional Englishman's view of religion—that it was all good and proper, but should not be allowed to dominate or interfere with one's life. And, in his case, certainly not with one's work. 'The deep things of life—God, religion in any form—mean so much to me,' Emily wrote to Edwin:

> you only scoff, till I have shut all these thoughts away from you … All I know of your work is its worries … I want more of you, not your body, but your soul and intellect, something big to take hold of and share, and when I am in a mood of longing for sympathy and all you give me is criticism and jokes, then I feel as if I bleed inwardly.[6]

In an attempt to improve the marriage, Emily persuaded Edwin that they should both read Edward Carpenter's 'beautiful book' (as she described it) Love's Coming of Age, a collection of essays on relations between the sexes, which was first published in 1896 and went on to sell over 100,000 copies. 'What Woman most needs today, and is mostly seeking for,' Carpenter wrote, 'is a basis of independence for her life.' He describes the ideal marriage as

> so free, so spontaneous, that it would allow of wide excursions of the pair from each other, in common or even in separate objects of work and interest, and yet would hold them all the time in the bond of absolute sympathy, like the relation of two suns which, revolving in fluent and rebounding curves, only recede from each other in order to return again

with renewed swiftness into close proximity—and which together blend their rays into the glory of one double star.

Emily's was certainly a marriage of 'wide excursions'—mostly Edwin's—but the blending of rays into the glory 'of one double star' was sadly absent.

With Edwin's reputation as an architect in the ascendant, Emily—in the familiar manner of privileged women of the Edwardian era—took to 'good works'. She became a supporter of the cause of women's suffrage—her younger sister, Constance, was an ardent suffragette, and had spent a short spell in prison for throwing a stone at a car carrying Lloyd George, the Chancellor of the Exchequer. She joined the Fabian Society, played an active role in the Moral Education League and took a keen interest in women's sexual health and hygiene, particularly the effects of venereal disease on prostitutes.

In search of something to further satisfy her keen intelligence, sense of idealism and religious leanings, it was entirely logical that she should have found her way to Annie Besant after a friend sent her a copy of Besant's 1907 London lectures on Theosophy. One line on the universality of the theosophical teachings struck Emily most forcefully: 'To us, truth is so supreme a thing that we do not desire to bind any man with conditions as to how, or where, or why, he shall seek it.'[7]

Emily attended a meeting of the Theosophical Society, where readings from the Bhagavad Gita and Edwin Arnold's *The Light of Asia* were followed by a lecture by Besant herself. Listening to Besant speak about Krishnamurti and the coming of the next World Teacher, 'I was completely carried away,' Emily wrote, 'and felt myself face to face with something immeasurably greater than anything I had ever known.'[8]

All her life she had been filled with a devotion to Christ and given of an 'inborn conviction that he would come again to earth'. Seeing a photograph of Krishnamurti, she believed that he had: 'As soon as I looked at his face I knew in a flash the answer to my question, and that he, and no other, was the coming Teacher.'[9]

\* \* \*

Krishna's arrival in London in 1911 was the beginning of a spiritual *folie d'amour* in which the middle-aged Emily would find herself increasingly drawn into the world of the Theosophical Society and estranged from her family.

Three days after his arrival, Annie Besant called a meeting at the Society's headquarters in Bond Street to announce the founding of a new group, the Order of the Star in the East, 'to proclaim the coming of a World-Teacher and to prepare the world for that event'. Emily was named as the National Representative for England and rewarded with a five-pointed gold star. 'I seem to have embarked on a shoreless sea of wonder and beauty and gladness,' she wrote, 'Only it does make most things seem a little empty and wearisome by comparison.'[10] Emily was caught between her maternal feelings for Krishna, her spiritual feelings and a deeper, more demanding urge that she could hardly acknowledge even to herself.

It was a confusion of emotions, complicated even further by the rigid conventions of the day, which under normal circumstances would have made any sort of relationship between a middle-aged aristocratic British woman and a 16-year-old Indian boy unthinkable. But from the moment of Krishna's arrival in England, Emily found it almost unbearable to be separated from him, and seldom left his side.

In London, Krishna was introduced to a new and providential circle—the wealthy, middle-aged and elderly women who were the bedrock of the Theosophical Society. Foremost among them was Mary Dodge, the daughter of William E. Dodge, a controlling partner in the Phelps Dodge Corporation, one of the largest copper mining corporations in the United States. 'The most nobly generous woman I have ever met', as Emily observed, Mary would become a stalwart source of support—and money—in the mission to promote Krishnamurti as the world teacher, settling an annual allowance of £500 on Krishna and £300 a year on Nitya while he was a student at Oxford. She also gave Lady Emily £100 annually so that she could travel with Krishna.

The two brothers were taken to Savile Row and measured for suits, and to Lobb of St James's for bespoke shoes, which Krishna would find excruciatingly uncomfortable. (Charles Leadbeater would report that even his Master grew concerned at Krishna's discomfort, instructing Leadbeater to take 'special care of the feet'.[11]) It was a sartorial exactitude lacking among most Theosophical Society members, whom Emily noted tended to look 'rather arty-crafty', but that would remain with Krishna all his life. Wherever he travelled, on whatever occasion, he never looked anything less than impeccable.

Under Emily's watch the two brothers were treated to all the cultural and tourist delights that London had to offer: theatrical productions of *Macbeth*, *The Scarlet Pimpernel* and *Julius Caesar*; the Oxford and Cambridge and Eton and Harrow cricket matches at Lords; Madame Tussauds and the Royal Tournament. On 22 June 1911, the day of the Coronation of

King George V, they watched from a privileged position at Admiralty Arch as the royal procession made its way up The Mall.

The arrival in London of the new Messiah had not escaped the attention of the newspapers. Krishna had been derided as 'a chocolate-coloured Jesus', and he was recognised as they walked through the crowds towards Covent Garden. 'God bless his beautiful face', exclaimed one woman as he passed, while others jeered and there were shouts of 'Get yer 'air cut.'

A stranger in a strange land, separated from his father and with his 'mother replacement' Annie Besant frequently travelling, Krishna found himself turning increasingly to Emily for comfort. It was a role she was only too happy to play. 'He drew out all my maternal tenderness,' she wrote, 'He seemed so lonely and unhappy.'[12]

And so the bonds deepened. 'I really love Lady Emily,' Krishna wrote to Leadbeater, 'She is very devoted to me and thinks that I am her Master.' By the time she met Krishnamurti, as the mother of five children, Emily had, as she saw it, performed her 'duty' to husband and country. Edwin was busy with his work. There were servants and nannies to look after domestic affairs. She was free to indulge her enthusiasm for her new Messiah, promoting him at meetings and in articles for periodicals, and dutifully following him wherever he travelled, preparing for his mission as the World Teacher. 'I was never really happy away from Krishna,' she wrote, 'My husband, my home, my children faded into the background. Krishna became my entire life and for the next ten years I suffered all the difficulties of trying to sublimate a human love.'[13]

Edwin was initially tolerant of his wife's obsession and her mission of spreading the good news of the coming world order, or 'popjawing', as he called it. But he soon grew tired of it, complaining of the Theosophical Society's 'priestcraft, popery and hypocrisy' and its promulgation of Oriental religions. He wrote to Emily, 'I am frightened of the Buddha that sits on his haunches and star-gazes and lives a world away from the surface of this.' He worried about the influence of Emily's beliefs on his children and their growing closeness to Krishna, particularly that of his son Robert, whom Edwin believed should be spending his time with English boys and not be influenced 'by the darkie ones'.[14] But whatever his fears, Emily observed, Edwin was always polite and charming to Krishna. Any jealousy he may have felt was directed 'rather unfairly', Emily thought, against Annie Besant.

When Annie approached Edwin Lutyens to plan a new headquarters for the Theosophical Society, Emily insisted he waive his fee. Edwin reluctantly agreed, and Besant rewarded him for his pains by christening him Vishvakarman ('architect to the gods') and giving him honorary membership of the Society (nothing could have pleased him less). For her part, Emily was rewarded by being admitted to Besant's 'special group' entitling her to wear a yellow silk Indian shawl. She wrote to Edwin:

> I know I am odd and perhaps growing odder, but so much happier and so loving of my darling husband. I feel just like a flower that has been living in a cold clay soil and is suddenly transplanted into sunshine and congenial soil and now I feel daily as if I was opening out and growing and stretching glad petals to the sun.[15]

Annie's time was increasingly being taken up by unpleasant developments back in India. Krishna's father, Narianiah, had never taken kindly to his sons being taken from him, and becoming suspicious of Leadbeater and the attention he lavished on Krishna he initiated a lawsuit to have his sons returned. Narianiah was supported in his efforts by orthodox Hindus, who resented Besant and wished to see her expelled from the Central Hindu College at Benares, which she had founded. It took all of Besant's powers of diplomacy and persuasion to see off the threat.

Even the loyal Theosophist Emily Lutyens harboured doubts about Leadbeater, and his 'rather funny mincing walk' and 'rather drawly parsonic voice'. 'He has a very courteous manner and has been most cordial to me,' she wrote to Edwin, 'But under all one feels a mild contempt for all women and I feel I am only tolerated as the mother of Robert. He has a quite polite way of making you feel small and ridiculous which is not pleasant.'[16]

In 1912 Edwin was commissioned to design the principal buildings for New Delhi, which had been designated as the site of the new capital of British India, replacing Calcutta. It was the confirmation he had yearned for that he was now at the pinnacle of his profession, the most distinguished and famous architect in Britain. It was also to be another nail in the coffin of his marriage. Over the next twenty years he would travel back and forth frequently between England and India, leaving Emily abundant time and opportunity to indulge her passion for Theosophy in general, and Krishna in particular.

Edwin, like many British visitors to the subcontinent, was appalled by the poverty, the squalor, the climate and the unfamiliar food, and fulsome in his prejudices, lamenting 'the sly slime of the Eastern mind'. 'The low intellects of the natives spoil much and I do not think it is possible for the Indians and whites to mix freely', he wrote.[17] As Lutyens' biographer Jane Ridley notes, for Edwin, India was 'a metaphor for everything that threatened his own family'—Theosophy, Annie Besant, Charles Leadbeater and his wife's obsession with Krishna—'the embodiment of fear and the dangers of the unknown'.[18]

With Edwin away in India, in January 1914, exhausted by family life and displaying all the characteristics of a love-struck teenager, Emily fled the family home, leaving the children with Nannie, to join Krishna and Nitya relaxing in Taormina, Sicily. (Mary, Emily's youngest child, who would become Krishna's biographer, would remember being brought up almost entirely by Nannie.)

A tutor, George Arundale, had now joined Krishna's party. Arundale had been orphaned at an early age and brought up by his Theosophist aunt, Francesca. As a child he had been privately tutored by Charles Leadbeater, then moved to India with Aunt Francesca where he taught history at the Central Hindu College in Varanasi, before taking up his role as tutor to Krishna and Nitya. Arundale was as fiercely possessive of Krishna as Emily was, and their relationship became one of jostling for the boy's attention and affection—a familiar scenario of jockeying for position and favour among the followers of gurus. When Emily turned up at Taormina Arundale reported her to Annie Besant, who wrote Emily a stiff letter reprimanding her for deserting her own children to be with Krishna.

Emily's infatuation, and what Besant described as the 'very curious relationship' between her and Krishna, was a cause of growing concern to Besant and Leadbeater. Annie warned Emily to keep her feelings under control, and not do anything that would throw Krishna's spiritually refined nature 'out of tune'. In an effort to keep any improper feelings firmly in check, Annie agreed to Emily's request that she be allowed to assume what had hitherto been Besant's role as Krishna's adoptive mother. Besant conducted an awkward little ceremony giving Emily and Krishna her blessing, and, Emily recounted, 'we were very happy'.

But matters were less harmonious in her marriage. In 1914 she wrote to the unfortunate Edwin telling him that their marriage could only continue with a severance of their physical relationship. 'I have suffered *intensely physically* during all my married life,' she wrote:

> There were compensations when I wanted the children and had them. But now we are both entering upon middle age. I have done my duty to you

and my country as regards children and I could never face another. With that incentive gone your coming to me has been increasingly difficult for me to bear.[19]

Edwin had no choice but to accept it. They seldom saw each other, and when they did the mood was invariably strained. Their rare meals together passed in awkward silence, with Edwin doing *The Times* crossword while Emily read throughout the meal, usually a Wild West novel.[20] Emily was already a vegetarian, but now became a strict vegan, forcing her children to follow her example. Edwin refused to bow to this demand, and two separate meals would be served at the family table.

Annie Besant now spent much of her time in India, her attention largely focused on the question of Indian Home Rule, for which she had become an ardent campaigner. In 1917 she was arrested by the authorities and interned at a hill station for three months. On her release she was greeted by cheering crowds, and she was elected President of the Indian National Congress. Emily dutifully supported Besant's campaign—much to the annoyance and embarrassment of Edwin, who not only depended on the Government of India for his livelihood but was also busy cosying up to sympathetic Maharajahs in search of new commissions.

Emily was becoming progressively unhinged, her obsession with Krishna dominating her life completely. 'I looked upon Krishna as both my son and my teacher', she wrote.[21] But more than that, she was consumed by 'an overwhelming personal love' for him: 'Religion for me could never be separated from love, and my love for Krishna was now blended with my early love for Christ.'

In the summer of 1914, the simmering feud between Emily and George Arundale came to a head. Krishna and Nitya were now installed at the home of Arundale's Aunt Francesca at Bude in Cornwall. Emily took a house nearby with her five children, but spent most of her time with Krishna. The highly strung Arundale now went on the attack, writing to accuse her of 'self-centredness' and of leading the putative World Teacher astray. 'You have used Krishna more for your own convenience and satisfaction than for any other purpose,' he wrote, 'You have hindered the Master's work by emphasizing Krishna's lower nature at the expense of the higher.' He rebuked her for stirring 'big whirlpools of emotion for yourself, and you have awakened them in him', interfering with his spiritual progress. 'Therefore, no more occult progress could be possible until these are entirely gone.'[22]

Krishna, already struggling unhappily with the expectations being placed on him as the vehicle for the new Messiah—'Why', he would often lament, 'did they ever pick on me?'—was now faced with the difficulty of negotiating the feelings of a woman he had come to love as a mother, Arundale's jealousy and the growing disapproval of Besant and Leadbeater about the relationship. He wrote to Leadbeater:

> I love in the *whole* world four people and they are, you, Mrs Besant, George and Lady Emily and that will never change whatever happens ... [Arundale and Lady Emily] both are very fine people in their way and I love them very much. George was a bit jealous of her but now, thank goodness, it is all over. I love her *very*, *very* purely and I am glad that I am not like usual people in that respect. I am *not* that way and *never* shall be.[23]

\* \* \*

The promotion of Krishnamurti as the new world teacher had a galvanising effect on membership of the Theosophical Society. The horrors of the First World War and its millions of needless deaths had left a bitter disillusionment with established political orthodoxies and the onward march of scientific materialism. In this mood of millennial expectation, news of a coming Messiah who would usher mankind into a new age of peace, tranquillity and salvation would prove to have a powerful appeal—at least to some. Membership of the Theosophical Society grew from 13,000 in 1907 to 36,000 by 1920. By 1928 it would reach its peak of 45,000.

In 1921, Krishnamurti was introduced to the young Dutch aristocrat and Theosophist Baron Philip van Pallandt, who offered his home, Castle Eerde in Ommen, in the eastern Netherlands, as the headquarters of the Order of the Star in the East. Starting in the summer of 1924, Krishna would speak at the annual summer Star camps in the castle grounds, attended by thousands of mostly young people.[24]

The author Rom Landau visited Ommen, but was frustrated by his inability to discern any deep meaning in Krishnamurti's teaching, or among his followers:

> I had been hoping to find those answers among the people who stayed at the castle and who must have known exactly what was to be understood. They were only too willing to help me; but it seemed to me that they had all sacrificed their personalities in order to become members of the Order of the Star in the East. I talked to many of them in the course of the day, but they left too little impression to enable me to distinguish them in

my mind later on … They would talk of reincarnation and karma with an understanding smile on their lips and as though they were speaking of the next train from Ommen to the Hook of Holland.

Landau thought 'their new spiritual experience' would have given the devotees a greater understanding of the world at large, but concluded that, on the contrary, it had only made them more insulated from it:

> There were political and economical congresses, religious disputes, naval conferences going on all over the world; new movements in art, in literature, music, the theatre, the cinema were being experimented with; the world talked of unemployment and reparations; there were thousands of things that had to be discussed, improved upon but none of them seemed to have penetrated the woods of Eerde.[25]

\* \* \*

The figure of the Indian guru was now sufficiently embedded in the British consciousness to be taken for a figure of fun. In 1920, the English novelist E. F. Benson published *Queen Lucia*, the first in what would become a highly popular series of 'Mapp and Lucia' novels. This series of gently biting satires on life in the quintessentially English village of Riseholme concern its self-styled 'Queen' Emmeline Lucas, known to all as 'Lucia', who holds dominion over the village's other inhabitants by a combination of browbeating, vaulting snobbery and sheer force of will. Foremost among Lucia's subjects is Daisy Quantock, who is fatally subject to every passing fad and enthusiasm of the day, be it Christian Science, spiritualism, Ouija boards, vegetarianism or the latest nostrums from her favourite periodical 'The Uric Acid Monthly'. Daisy's gullibility reaches new heights with the sudden appearance in the village of an Indian guru preaching a 'Great Message, a Word of Might, full of Love and Peace'.

The guru is a pantomime figure, dressed in a saffron robe, '*violently green*' girdle, chocolate-coloured stockings, short pink socks and red slippers, salaaming and unctuous, purporting to see into 'the clear white soul' of everyone he encounters. Falling for his nonsensical pronouncements, the credulous Daisy—'I don't even know his name, and his religion'—is soon contorting herself in yoga positions and practising chanting 'Om'.

Loathe to let Daisy take the lead in anything, Lucia claims the guru as her own, running him as her 'August stunt' and establishing herself as 'dispenser of Eastern mysteries and Mistress of Omism to Riseholme'. Inevitably, enlightenment eventually comes with the revelation that the

'Brahmin of Benares' is not, after all, a bona fide guru, but a thief who works as a cook at an Indian restaurant in London.[26]

* * *

Krishna's association with Castle Eerde was to create further inadvertent heartache for Lady Emily. On his first visit to the castle, he was introduced to a 17-year-old American girl of Dutch extraction named Helen Knothe. Elated to be in the company of a sweet, highly intelligent and attractive girl of his own generation, within a week Krishna had confessed his love for her. He wrote to Lady Emily to share his news: 'I *am* awfully in love & it is a great sacrifice on my part but *nothing* can be done. I feel as if I had an awful wound inside me; don't think I'm exaggerating ... I hope you are not jealous, dear old Mum?'[27]

How that 'dear old Mum' must have hurt.

It was left to Annie Besant to manage the situation with characteristic adroitness, offering no discouragement to Krishna, and writing kindly to Helen:

> About Krishna, dear, I know something of the tie between you. He will help you immensely, I know but the affection may have a good deal of pain in it, from the ordinary standpoint. He has a great deal of work to do and it may keep him much from you physically. For the world needs him and he cannot, as it were, belong to any one of us. Are you big enough and strong enough, I wonder, to help him and not to hinder him.[28]

So it was that before it had ever truly caught fire, the relationship was quietly and effectively extinguished.

In 1922, on a visit to America, Krishna was taken for the first time to Ojai in California, a small community set in the rolling hills 80 miles northwest of Los Angeles. He was suffering from exhaustion, and the debilitating effects of what he called 'the process', in which he would experience bouts of excruciating pain combined with a sense of mystical breakthrough, which was taken to be evidence that his body was being made ready for the spirit of Maitreya to descend. He was put up in a rented house called Pine Cottage. The clement surroundings, the orchards of orange trees, the clean air—all proved soothing to his spirits. He told Annie he could happily stay there forever, and the ever-obliging Mary Dodge provided the money with which to purchase Pine Cottage and a larger house nearby, which was renamed Arya Vihara, meaning noble monastery.

Expectation that the spirit of Maitreya would soon descend into Krishnamurti reached fever-pitch in December 1925 at the Theosophical Society's Jubilee Convention at the Society's headquarters at Adyar. Addressing a large gathering under the giant banyan tree in the grounds on the subject of the World Teacher, Krishnamurti slipped from saying 'he' to 'I'. 'He [the World Teacher] comes only to those who want, who desire, who long,' he said, then paused before resuming, 'And I come for those who want sympathy, who want happiness, who are longing to be released, who are longing to find happiness in all things.'[29] An enthralled Annie Besant declared afterwards that 'the voice not heard on earth for two thousand years had once again been heard'.

But at the same time, it was becoming worryingly obvious to some that Krishnamurti's talks were beginning to deviate from the party line espoused by Besant and Leadbeater. His lectures increasingly emphasised self-knowledge and the requirement for each individual to find their own way to the truth—a teaching directly at odds with Leadbeater and Besant's ideas of there being just one 'path of discipleship' regulated by a self-styled elite of initiates. Leadbeater began to quietly express the view that 'The Coming has gone wrong.'

In 1926, when Krishna returned to Ojai, Lady Emily dutifully trailed after him. Finally, she had time with him to herself, but that only made her feelings of physical and emotional attraction for him harder to control. 'My personal feelings for Krishna occasionally got the better of me,' she wrote, 'He was much less the teacher and more his human self while we were there, and in consequence I found it more difficult to keep my feelings at a sublime level. He gave me many lectures about being personal and I was often reduced to tears.'[30] Aware of the unhappiness that her feelings were causing her, Krishna warned Emily against possessiveness, telling her, 'If I become necessary to you, you will not be free and it will spoil it all. We love each other. That is sufficient'; and 'Everybody is the same—they all think they have some special claim, some special road to me.'[31]

Krishna was moving slowly but ineluctably further away from all the ties that bound him to the Theosophical Society, and to the calling it had imposed on him. In 1927, addressing a gathering at Ommen, he returned to his argument that people should seek the truth within themselves rather than relying on any external authority—namely Besant and Leadbeater. 'Until now,' he said, 'you have been depending on the two Protectors of the Order for authority, for someone else to tell you the Truth, whereas the Truth lies within you.' In what amounted to a fundamental heresy of Theosophical thought he declared that the descriptions of the Masters proposed by the Theosophical hierarchy were delusional mental images conjured by the imagination, and largely irrelevant. Instead, he talked of the ultimate reality, which he called 'The Beloved':

> To me it is all—it is Sri Krishna, it is the Master K.H., it is Lord Maitreya, it is the Buddha, and yet it is beyond all these forms. What does it matter what names you give? ... What you are troubling about is whether there is such a person as the World Teacher who has manifested Himself in the body of a certain person, Krishnamurti; but in the world nobody will trouble about this question.[32]

In 1929, at another gathering at Ommen in front of Annie Besant and 3,000 members of the Order of the Star of the East, Krishna finally made his fateful break with the Society, rejecting the study of the occult, religious ceremony, initiations and rituals—basically, everything that had been assembled in his name since the moment he had been discovered, slack-jawed and vacant-eyed on the beach at Adyar—and dissolving the Order, declaring that 'Truth is a pathless land, and you cannot approach it by any path whatsoever, by any religion, by any sect.' From that moment on, he vowed, he would not be concerned with 'creating new cages, new decorations for those cages. My only concern is to set men absolutely, unconditionally free.'

For the next fifty-seven years until his death in 1986, Krishnamurti travelled the world delivering this message, living out the paradox of being an anti-guru with a devoted following hanging on his every word. His abdication from his role as the chosen one, his renunciation of the organisation that had grown up in his name, was an act of great honesty, moral integrity and considerable courage. And it sent shock waves through the Society, devastating Annie Besant and causing deep anger to Leadbeater and his cronies. 'They are out for my scalp', he wrote to Emily.

She would soon follow in resigning from the Society. From the moment she set eyes on him, Emily's loyalty was always to Krishnamurti rather than to Theosophy. She wrote:

> One is driven to the conclusion that those who were the most eager to proclaim him have been the last to welcome him; that those who urged upon their followers the necessity for an open mind have closed their own minds against the new presentation of truth which has swept away, as they prophesised it might, the old conceptions and theories. I for one will no

longer be a party to a policy which plays upon the credibility, the vanity and ignorance of men and women.[33]

While she lost faith in Theosophy, her faith in Krishna remained constant. But for the next few years, she wrote, she felt that she had 'hopelessly lost my own way. My life had suddenly become empty':

> I was still ready to be Krishna's disciple, and had he called me to give up everything and follow him into the wilderness I would have done so unhesitatingly—it was, I think, what I was really longing for—but he did not want disciples, he did not want followers. He wanted to make people think for themselves, find truth in their own hearts and stand on their own feet. He had cut the ground from under mine and I felt I was dropping into nothingness.[34]

As time passed, so Emily's sense of loss and confusion grew. She found Krishna's message of austere self-reliance daunting and 'inadequate'. What she craved was comfort and direction. Krishna, who had written and spoken so beautifully of 'the Beloved', who declared that he and the Beloved were one, now seemed to Emily to be rejecting all beliefs, denying the Beloved's existence: 'For me, a "Beloved", someone to worship, was a necessity.'[35] Her own 'Beloved', who had once depended on her for personal affection, now seemed to reject affection in all its forms. When, in 1931, she wrote telling Krishna of problems that she was having with her children, he wrote back urging her to detach herself from her family, and to 'free myself from all human ties'. She wrote that

> Krishna had managed to transcend personal love but I could not ... It was not that he did not love, but no one person was necessary to him any longer. He had attained to universal love. As he said himself: 'Pure love is like the perfume of the rose, given to all ... The quality of true love, of pure love, knows no such distinctions as wife and husband, son, father, mother.'[36]

But the 'universal love' that Krishna advocated was beyond her:

> I realized that I did not want to lose personal love in the love for all. There was a cold aridity, a dullness about the idea which repelled me. I could strive to make my love for the few purer, greater, nobler, less possessive, but I did not want to lose it altogether.[37]

Finally, it dawned on her that her years of devotion to Krishna and to Theosophy 'had largely separated me from a very wonderful human

71

love'—for her husband Edwin. Krishna would go on as a teacher, but Emily could no longer follow: 'I felt as if I had been left behind like driftwood on the shore.'

Annie Besant died peacefully in Adyar on 20 September 1933. She had been suffering from Alzheimer's disease, but when Krishna visited her a few months before her death, shortly after he had suffered a debilitating bout of chickenpox, she was able to recognise him, complimenting him on the beard he had grown, and telling him he must drink grape juice to build up his strength. 'Dear Amma,' he wrote to Lady Emily, 'it is so tragic to see her like this. It's all so sad for them all.'[38]

In search of spiritual sustenance, Emily had tried to reignite her Christian faith, but found she could not. Krishna had replaced Christ long ago, and even in Krishna's absence there was no place for Christ to return to. But, however estranged she now felt from Krishna's teachings, 'for me,' she wrote, 'he will always remain unique, the purest and most beautiful being I have ever come across, the perfect flower of humanity'.[39]

Edwin Lutyens died on New Year's Day, 1944. His marriage to Emily had lasted forty-seven years. Emily would live for another twenty years. Krishna would continue to write to her and to visit whenever he came to Britain, even when Emily could no longer recognise him, sitting with her, holding her hand and chanting, which seemed to give her some comfort.

Lady Emily died at the age of eighty-eight on 3 January 1964 of an aneurism. Her daughter sent a cable to Krishna, who was in Madras, to tell him the news. He replied on 16 January:

> Life's a strange business. One could not have wished for Mum to go on living, but all the same, London won't be the same. It has been a long friendship, more than that, for nearly fifty-two years, almost one's whole life. What we have all been through! It will be very strange, all the same, not to see her. I loved her.[40]

4

# THE BHIKKU AND THE BEAST

By the reckoning of all who knew him, Allan Bennett was a man of unimpeachable purity and integrity. And there is some irony that one of his closest friends, the man who esteemed Bennett above all others and who would be the most eloquent witness to his life, should have been vilified by the popular press of the day as the 'Wickedest Man in the World'.

Aleister Crowley, the poet, mountaineer and occultist, was not usually generous in his praise of others, but he would describe Allan Bennett as 'the noblest and gentlest soul I have ever known', a man possessed of 'a mind pure, piercing and profound beyond any other in my experience'.

Allan Bennett was not, in fact, his real name at all. He was born in Holland Park, London, on 8 December 1872, the illegitimate son of a woman named Mary Corbyn and a man who was said to have been a scientist prominent in society. In order to protect the reputations of her children—Mary also had a daughter, Charlotte Louisa—their father and herself, Mary invented the story that she was the widow of an electrical engineer named Charles Bennett. Thus her son was Charles Henry Allan Bennett.

Mary Corbyn died of ulcerated tuberculosis of the throat when her son was aged ten. Allan was a sickly child; he suffered badly from asthma, and throughout his life he would be haunted by two things: ruinous health and a perennially empty bank balance. On leaving school he went to work for a chemist named Bernard Dyer, described on his letterhead as 'Public analyst and official analyst to the London Corn Trade Association', of Great Tower Street in the City of London.

The author Paul Brunton, who knew Bennett towards the end of his life, would claim—somewhat fancifully perhaps—that by the age of seventeen, Bennett had 'a profounder and wider scientific knowledge than that possessed by any youth in England'.[1] What is clear is that he was possessed of a highly original and inventive mind. While working as a chemist, Bennett also studied extensively in the field of electromagnetism, and throughout his life he would work on a series of inventions including an early refrigerator, a gramophone that played records of unlimited length, and a machine to read people's thoughts—none of which, alas, ever came into production.

Bennett's mother had raised him as a devout Catholic, but in later life he would explain that it was scientific knowledge that had destroyed his faith 'in the religious lessons of my childhood'. Aleister Crowley provided a more colourful explanation, claiming that Bennett developed a fatal aversion to Christianity at the age of sixteen, following a conversation among his fellow workers at the laboratory about human reproduction. Bennett drew jeers of derision from his workmates when he protested that the facts of life were 'bestial blasphemy' and that children were actually brought down to earth by angels. When one of the boys turned up next day with a manual of obstetrics, Bennett was appalled; if the omnipotent God whom he had been taught to worship could devise 'so revolting and degrading a method of perpetuating the species' then God 'must be a Devil, delighting in loathsomeness'. To Bennett, Crowley wrote, 'the existence of God was disproved from that moment'.[2] Overly dramatic as this response may appear—even if the story is true—it does seem to have put Bennett not only off Christianity but also off sex; he was seemingly to remain a celibate for the rest of his life.

Two things in particular seem to have aroused Bennett's interest in Eastern teachings. The first, according to Crowley, was an incident at the age of eighteen, when Bennett had 'an accidental' experience of the mystical state of Shivadarshana—an annihilation of the ego, and a sense of being totally at one with the Universe.[3] So profound was this experience, Crowley wrote, that it was a marvel that Bennett survived it and kept his sanity. And it was this glimpse of transcendence, according to Crowley, that would determine the whole course of Bennett's life: 'His one object was to get back into that state.'

The second factor in Bennett's transformation, according to Bennett himself, was reading Edwin Arnold's *The Light of Asia* at the age of eighteen. Perhaps it was the anguish of his mother's early death and his own physical frailty that would impress on Bennett the first Noble Truth of Buddhist teaching, that all life is *dukkha*, or suffering. Bennett would later say that he was a Buddhist from the moment he read *The Light of Asia*; if that was indeed the case, it would be some years before he actually realised it himself. But when Arnold died in 1904, three years after Bennett had become the first Englishman to become a Buddhist monk, Bennett would pay tribute to *The Light of Asia*, noting that even though Arnold had written it in the turmoil of a busy life, it still breathed 'the calm sweet atmosphere of Buddhism; even as the lotus springs uncontaminated from the mire and water into the fresh, pure air'.[4]

It was Bennett's early interest in Buddhism that led him in 1893, at the age twenty-one, to join the Theosophical Society. He took an active role in Society activities; the minutes for the Society's Bow Lodge record him delivering lectures on alchemy, astrology and the Egyptian Book of the Dead.[5] He became a member of the Society's 'Esoteric Section', an elite group of Theosophists that occasionally met with Madame Blavatsky in private. It was probably through the Theosophical Society that Bennett met Samuel Liddell 'MacGregor' Mathers, the co-founder of an occult group called the Hermetic Order of the Golden Dawn, which brought together a rich brew of Rosicrucianism, Freemasonry, Enochian magic and Egyptian lore. In February 1894 Allan Bennett joined the Order and embarked on his journey into the occult.

\* \* \*

Samuel Mathers was born on 8 January 1854 in Hackney, London, the son of William Mathers, a merchant's clerk. Following the death of his father, Mathers moved with his widowed mother to Bournemouth where he worked as an estate agent's clerk. At the age of twenty-three, Mathers was initiated into a Freemason lodge in Bournemouth, the Lodge of Hengist. There he became acquainted with two high-ranking Masons, William Woodman and William Wynn Westcott, who in turn introduced Mathers to the Societas Rosicruciana in Anglia, a Rosicrucian group open only to the highest initiates in Masonry.

In 1887, Westcott, who would later become the coroner for North East London, and whose eccentricities included using a human hand as a paperweight, came into possession of a collection of sixty folios which became known as the cipher manuscripts, outlining a series of initiation rituals and practices in Kabbalah and hermetic magic. Westcott had supposedly been given the manuscripts by a senior Mason and church rector named Adolphus Woodford. Using these manuscripts as a basis, Westcott, Mathers and Woodman established the Order of the Golden Dawn. The first published reference to the founding of the Order appeared in a small article in Madame Blavatsky's *Lucifer* magazine, on 9 February 1889.[6]

Mathers threw himself into his occult enthusiasms, more or less abandoning gainful employment. He married Moina Bergson, an artist and the sister of the philosopher Henri Bergson, who became the first woman to be initiated into the Golden Dawn. Their marriage is said to have been purely 'magical', and never to have been sexually consummated. The Mathers lived on a small allowance from another recruit to the Order, Annie Horniman, the daughter of the wealthy tea merchant John Horniman. Annie obtained for Mathers a post at her father's private museum in Forest Hill, South London, and continued to support the couple after they settled in Paris in 1892. Mathers would later reward her for her kindness by expelling her from the Order for 'mischief-making'.[7]

By 1897, Westcott had withdrawn from the Golden Dawn leaving Mathers as the organisation's leader. The Golden Dawn attracted a mixed bag of Theosophists and occultists, among them W. B. Yeats and his lover Maud Gonne; the actress Florence Farr Emery; the artist Pamela 'Pixie' Smith (who together with Arthur Edward Waite co-created the Rider-Waite Tarot pack); the writer Arthur Machen; and Constance Wilde, the wife of Oscar Wilde—who would reputedly be inspired to write *The Picture of Dorian Gray* (1891) by Constance's stories about the Order. According to the writer Gerald Yorke's account, at its height the Order numbered some two hundred members, in five separate lodges, or temples, with at least thirty of those members actively practising ritual magic. Aleister Crowley—who would become the Order's most famous (or infamous) member, would later describe the membership as 'an abject assemblage of nonentities ... as vulgar and commonplace as any other set of average people'.[8] But it was seemingly not so abject, vulgar and commonplace as to discourage Crowley from joining himself.

Mathers, who liked to be known as 'Brother God', had a fondness for titles, adopting the 'MacGregor' in his name from the Scottish clan motto, 'S Rioghail Mo Dhream (Royal Is My Race), and styling himself variously as the Chevalier MacGregor and the Comte MacGregor de Gleestrae. He loved nothing better than dressing up, whether in military uniform, full Highland fig, or in the costume of an Egyptian high priest. Photographs show him in a robe and skull cap, with a leopard-skin thrown over his shoulder, clutching a stave wreathed in flowers. W. B. Yeats would describe him as 'half-lunatic, half-knave'.[9] Mathers is sometimes said to have been Allan Bennett's 'foster father', and Paul Brunton maintained that Bennett was 'adopted' by Mathers as an 'orphaned boy'.[10] But this seems unlikely in the literal sense of the term—Bennett was most likely in his early twenties when he met Mathers for the first time—although he did later adopt the name 'MacGregor' out of admiration for his magical mentor, whom he once described as someone 'whom I revere more than any man', and he continued to use it intermittently throughout his life.[11]

Allan Bennett took the Neophyte initiation into the Order, and a year later was initiated into 'the Second Order', taking the name Frater Iehi Aour (Hebrew for 'Let there be Light').[12] He was evidently a quick study. Crowley wrote that Bennett was esteemed second only to Mathers in his abilities in ritual and ceremonial magic, and 'was, perhaps, even more feared'—the one magician 'who could really do big-time stuff'.[13] Crowley described how Bennett would carry a glass lustre—a long glass prism with a neck and a pointed knob, such as might be seen on a chandelier—which he used as a wand, and which he once turned on a Theosophist who was sceptical about the power of Bennett's 'blasting rod', with the result that 'It took fourteen hours to restore the incredulous individual to the use of his mind and muscles.'[14] This demonstration of power, if true, would have doubtless amused Crowley, but it seems strangely out of character for the gentle and thoughtful Bennett.[15]

Photographs of Bennett show a tall, stooping, cadaverous man with a shock of dark hair and deep-set eyes, dressed in a funereal, ill-fitting suit and looking like a character from a story by Edgar Allan Poe. 'The face', Crowley noted, 'would have been handsome had it not been for the haggardness and pallor due to his almost continuous suffering.'[16] Illness was to haunt Bennett throughout his life. He would attempt to self-medicate his acute asthma by a regime of drugs: he took opium for a month, then, when the effect wore off, injected morphine; he then moved on to cocaine, which he took until he began to 'see things', when he would be reduced to chloroform—often taking to his bed for up to a week at a time, 'only recovering consciousness sufficiently to reach for the bottle and the sponge'. He would then gradually convalesce, only for the vicious cycle of spasms and cure to repeat itself.[17]

It was possibly Bennett who first introduced Crowley to the drugs that Crowley used throughout his life and would become addicted to. Kenneth Grant writes that the two men conducted several experiments together with hemlock, 'and obtained glimpses of the world behind the veil; but these glimpses were fleeting and sporadic'.[18]

Occult practice seemed to provide some relief from Bennett's illnesses, if not for his bank balance: 'At this time of year I feel my occultism returning, and when I am occult I am really quite indifferent to my physical state.' Bennett led an impoverished existence, moving from one set of shabby furnished rooms to another. In 1895, when Bennett was twenty-three, his sister Charlotte married Godfrey Johnson, described on the marriage certificate as 'a professional agent'.[19] Godfrey's father Robert was a devout Christian, a philanthropist and an educationalist, who in 1887 founded Hollesley Bay Colonial College in Suffolk for the purpose of training young men for life in the Colonies, teaching a range of subjects from agriculture to geology, veterinary science to soil chemistry. In many ways the college resembled a public school—and it was often referred to as the Public Schools Colonial Training College.

It is likely that Bennett had spent some time at Hollesley as a teenager. The 1891 English census lists him as a lodger in St Margaret, Suffolk, with a profession of 'student of electricity and chemistry'. Bennett would have been sixteen at the time. What is clear from a number of his letters is that he spent some time at Hollesley Bay between 1895 and 1897 (Bennett, unfortunately, did not date his letters). In one letter, written to his friend Frank Gardner from Hollesley Bay, he talks of his need to try and find science-teaching work, admitting that 'I can't be spongeing [sic] on here much more.'[20] Another letter from Bennett's sister Charlotte, written on his behalf, possibly to Gardner, from Hollesley Bay, dated 28 December 1895, talks of Bennett feeling unwell—'He has been rather seedy lately.'[21]

Hollesley Bay would later become a borstal. It is now a prison for young offenders. Like many of its graduates, Bennett too would find his way to the Colonies, but not quite in the fashion anyone might have anticipated.

\* \* \*

Aleister Crowley was just twenty-three when he joined the Order of the Golden Dawn in November 1898. He was born in Leamington Spa in Warwickshire, the son of a wealthy brewer, Edward Crowley, who retired to dedicate his life to preaching the doctrines of the Plymouth Brethren.

The Plymouth Brethren is a rigidly fundamentalist Christian sect that believes in the literal word of the Bible, and his parents' extreme religiosity had the predictable effect of cultivating in Crowley an early contempt for what he called the 'fiendish superstition' of Christianity. In his Bible classes he acquired a particular fondness for the Beast in the Book of Revelation, whose number is 666. A wilful child, his mother came to refer to him as 'the Beast'.

Crowley's father died when he was eleven—the same year that Crowley, by way of a scientific experiment, killed his first cat. His mother's strict puritanism had the adverse effect on Crowley of inculcating an interest in sex that would, in time, become a dominant motif of his life. At the age of fourteen he lost his virginity to a servant-girl—in his mother's bed.

As a student at Cambridge, Crowley developed an interest in both Eastern philosophy and the occult, and an introduction to an 'alchemist' named George Cecil Jones led to him being inducted into the Golden Dawn, taking the name 'Perdurabo'—'I will endure to the end.' But it was not until the spring of the following year, at a magical ceremony, that he had his first encounter with Allan Bennett. 'I was aware of the presence of a tremendous spiritual and magical force,' Crowley wrote of that meeting. 'It seemed to me to proceed from a man sitting in the east, a man I had not seen before, but whom I knew must be Very Honoured Frater Iehi Aour, called among men Allan Bennett.' He continued:

> After the ceremony we went into the outer room to unrobe. I was secretly anxious to be introduced to this formidable Chief. To my amazement he came straight to me, looked into my eyes, and said in penetrating and, as it seemed, almost menacing tones: 'Little Brother, you have been meddling with the Goetia!' I told him, rather timidly, that I had not been doing anything of the sort. 'In that case,' he returned, 'the Goetia has been meddling with you.'[22]

Chastened, Crowley returned home, resolving to visit Bennett the next day. He found him living in 'mean, grim horror' in a tiny tenement in Southwark, in the company of a fellow member of the Golden Dawn called Charles Rosher—'a widely travelled Jack-of-all-trades', according to Crowley, whose myriad accomplishments included inventing a patent water closet and being court painter to the Sultan of Morocco, as well as writing 'some of the worst poetry I have ever read'.

Deeply impressed by Bennett's accomplishments, and 'instantly aware that this man could teach me more in a month than anyone else in five years', Crowley, who lived comfortably on a private allowance, invited Bennett to stay with him in his rooms at 67/69 Chancery Lane, where he was living under one of his several pseudonyms, Count Vladimir Svareff. (Others employed over the years included Sir Alaster de Kerval and Guru Sri Paramahansa Shivaji.)

A detailed impression of Crowley's accommodation might be gained from his short story, 'At the Fork of the Roads':

The poet's rooms were austere in their elegance. A plain gold-black paper of Japan covered the walls; in the midst hung an ancient silver lamp within which glowed the deep ruby of an electric lamp. The floor was covered with black and gold of leopards' skins; on the walls hung a great crucifix in ivory and ebony.[23]

Here, Bennett gave his friend private tuition in the full range of the magical arts, including astrology, divination, scrying and the Kabbalah. The two men became close friends. 'He showed me where to get knowledge; how to criticise it; how to apply it,' Crowley would later write. 'We also worked together at ceremonial Magick; evoking spirits, consecrating talismans and so on.'[24]

An unpublished manuscript by Crowley, cited by Kenneth Grant, adds more:

We called him the White Knight, from Alice in the Looking Glass. So lovable, so harmless, so unpractical! But he was a Knight, too! And White! There never walked a whiter man on earth. He never did walk on earth, either! A genius, a flawless genius. But a most terribly frustrated genius.[25]

But as Crowley's friend and biographer, C. R. Cammell, noted, the two men differed greatly in their attitudes to the application of these techniques: 'Unfortunately, Crowley's methods of applying Bennett's teaching, and the objects to which he devoted the knowledge he acquired, were far from what Bennett could have approved or indeed visualised.'[26]

To Bennett, magic was a deeper exploration of the natural sciences, a practical method of investigating the physical, and metaphysical, properties of the world. But it is clear that he became frustrated with its limitations in his spiritual development. Bennett wanted power over his desires, not the power to fulfil them. The more of his magical knowledge he passed on to Crowley, it seemed, the less interested he became in it himself, and the more his enthusiasm turned to yoga and to Buddhism, which increasingly he came to see as a philosophy that provided the perfect reconciliation between the scientific and the spiritual, an ethical system without the encumbrance of a revealed religion.

By 1899, at the age of twenty-eight, Bennett's asthma was becoming progressively worse. With George Cecil Jones, Crowley practised a ritual to conjure up the spirit Buer of the Goetia, whose function is to heal the sick. It was only partially successful—'a helmeted head and the left leg being distinctly solid, though the rest of the figure was cloudy and vague'.[27] With his doctors warning that Bennett would not survive another English winter, it was agreed that he should make a new life in the warmer climes of Ceylon, where he could also pursue his interest in Eastern philosophy and learn the techniques of yoga and meditation from an established master.

But there was another familiar problem. Bennett had no money. Crowley had an abundance of it, but rather than paying for Bennett's ticket himself, he instead turned to his mistress. Lilian Horniblow was the wife of Lieutenant Colonel Frank Horniblow of the Royal Engineers, who at the time was conveniently stationed in India. Lilian called herself 'Laura Grahame' for the purpose of her assignations with Crowley. At Crowley's request, the 'seductive siren', as he referred to her, duly stumped up £100, and early in 1900 Bennett set sail for Ceylon, leaving his magical manuscripts and impedimenta in Crowley's care. Tapping up 'Laura', Crowley explained, was 'for the good of her karma'. Thus, he observed, she 'saved to humanity one of the most valuable lives of our generation'.[28] Its effect on Crowley's karma was almost immediate. When his interest in the 'seductive siren' dwindled, she began to wonder when her £100 might be returned. Soon the police were involved. But anxious not to embarrass her husband or herself, 'Laura' declined to press charges.

With Bennett on his way to Ceylon, Crowley applied himself with renewed zeal to his magical practices. He had constructed two temples in his flat, one white and lined with six huge mirrors; the other black, with an altar supported by the figure of an African man standing on his hands, and with a human skeleton which Crowley would feed from time to time with blood, small birds and the like—'the idea,' he explained 'was to give it life, but I never got further than causing the bones to become covered with a viscous slime'.[29] The experiments were abandoned shortly afterwards when Crowley gave up the apartments to take occupancy of his new residence, Boleskine House on the shores of Loch Ness. However, his baleful presence continued to haunt the Chancery Lane apartments; visiting workmen were 'put out of action for several hours', while callers at the flat fainted or were attacked with cramps and dizziness.[30]

The environs of Loch Ness were to provide their own problems. Shortly after moving into Boleskine House, Crowley found it necessary to write a letter complaining to the local Vigilance Society that 'prostitution is most unpleasantly conspicuous' in the area. An officer of the society was sent to investigate and, deeply puzzled, reported that they could find no evidence whatsoever of prostitution. Crowley wrote back: 'Conspicuous by its absence, you fools!'

Ceylon had become a British Crown colony in 1815 following the collapse of Dutch rule, and after overcoming bitter resistance from the small Kingdom of Kandy in the mountainous centre of the island. Initially, the Kandyans had finally accepted the role of the protectorate when the British promised that they would not try to impose Christianity on the kingdom and that they would respect the local Buddhist beliefs. Within two years, however, the Kandyans were in rebellion over the failure of the British authorities to honour their assurances that Buddhist traditions would be upheld. A massacre of the rebel forces in 1817 eventually ensured British dominion over the entire island.

The population of Ceylon was largely divided between the Sinhalese, who were Buddhists, and the Hindu Tamils, with a smaller proportion of Tamil Muslims. This delicate balance would be disturbed from early in the twentieth century, when the British began importing hundreds of thousands of Tamils from southern India to work firstly in the coffee and then the tea plantations.

One of Bennett's first ports of call on arriving in Colombo was the headquarters of the Theosophical Society, where he met Colonel Henry Olcott for the first time. Bennett's most pressing need was for money, and through Olcott he found work as a tutor to the children of the Hon. Ponnambalam Ramanathan, Solicitor-General of Ceylon. Ramanathan was a remarkable man and an accomplished yogi, who under the name of Sri Parananda had written commentaries on the gospels of Matthew and John, interpreting the sayings of Jesus as instructions in yoga. He was a close friend of Olcott, and was active in promoting Buddhist education in schools. In order properly to study the Buddhist texts, Bennett learned Pali, at the same time taking instruction from Ramanathan in yoga, quickly mastering the physical postures and breathing techniques.

In the summer of 1901, Crowley arrived in Ceylon en route to the Himalayas, where he planned an attempt on the mountain known as K2, the second highest in the world after Everest. Crowley was astonished at the improvement in Bennett's health. He wrote to his friend (and future brother-in-law) the painter Gerald Festus Kelly, describing Bennett as 'cured, clean, shaved and very good-looking, but weak and weary'.[31]

From Colombo the two friends travelled north into the hill country to Kandy, where Bennett rented a furnished bungalow with the quintessentially English name, Marlborough. Nearby was a waterfall and pool. As part of his Buddhist practice, each morning Bennett would allow the leeches in the pool to feed off his arms, releasing them by means of certain breathing techniques which made the limbs rigid, causing the leeches to fall off.

Crowley was deeply impressed by Bennett's new attainments as a yogi, recording that his friend was now able to meditate in the full lotus position for days at a time. On one occasion, Bennett was on a meditation retreat in a little bungalow a short distance away from the main house. It was Crowley's duty to leave food and water in an adjoining room, for Bennett to take at his discretion. But when Bennett missed two successive meals, Crowley became alarmed and entered his friend's room. He was astonished to find Bennett seated not on his meditation mat, but in a corner of the room, in a deep meditative state, resting on his head and right shoulder 'like an upturned statue', his legs still knotted in the full lotus position.

Crowley concluded that Bennett must have levitated, lost his balance and become wedged against the wall. Crowley set Bennett the right way up and he slowly came out of his trance, apparently quite oblivious to the fact that anything unusual had happened. (Crowley's friend and disciple Edward Bryant offered a more fanciful account of the story. Entering the bungalow, he wrote, 'to his amazement and horror' Crowley found Bennett 'suspended in the air at eye level' in the draught from the open door, being 'blown about like a dry leaf'.[32])

Possibly hoping to master the same trick, Crowley took lessons in yoga from Bennett, applying himself, as he wrote to Kelly, to 'cleansing myself physically and morally' with breathing exercises, or *asanas*, 'breathing up one nostril and down the other 80 times after every six hours. This is not funny.'[33]

After two months' practice under Bennett's direction, Crowley claimed to have attained *dhyana*, one of the highest stages of realisation. However, he then appeared to lose interest in continuing with his yoga practice. The careful itemisation of terms and techniques in his notebook petered out into a long sequence of blank pages—culminating in a final entry on ways of maintaining his briar and Meerschaum pipes. Bennett, Crowley noted with some irritation, was 'already at heart a Buddhist'—Buddhism being a philosophy that 'got on my nerves'. What Crowley called 'the egocentric psychology' of Hinduism at least 'seemed to lead somewhere'. Buddhism, on the other hand, repelled him in what he construed as its inaction and its idea that sorrow was inherent in all things—a philosophy, he said, which perfectly suited Bennett, 'whose only idea of pleasure was relief from the perpetual pain which pursued him'.[34]

Crowley left Ceylon for India. On his arrival, waiting to take a train, a white man with a beard approached him offering help, explaining that he was a Theosophist. 'It was the first act of kind thoughtfulness that I had ever known a Theosophist perform,' Crowley noted, '– and the last.'[35]

In 1904, while staying in Egypt, Crowley claimed to have been contacted by his Holy 'Guardian Angel', a messenger from the god Horus, known as Aiwass, who directed him to compose the *Liber AL vel Legis*, or *The Book of the Law*, the crux of which is the command that became Crowley's motto: 'Do what thou wilt shall be the whole of the law.' Crowley claimed *The Book of the Law* was the 'answer [to] all possible religious problems', enshrined in its exhortation to 'Be goodly therefore: dress ye all in fine apparel; eat rich foods and drink sweet wines and wines that foam! Also, take your fill and will of love as ye will, when, where and with whom ye will! But always unto me.' 'We are forced to conclude,' he wrote, 'that the author of *The Book of the Law* is an intelligence both alien and superior to myself, yet acquainted with my inmost secrets; and, most important point of all, that this intelligence is discarnate.'[36]

*The Book of the Law* would become the bible for Crowley's invented creed of Thelema (the Greek word for 'will'), which he described as encompassing 'the method of science—the aim of religion'—the motto of the magical order, 'the A.A.' (Argenteum Astrum, or Silver Star), that Crowley founded in 1906. Crowley predicted that Thelema would supplant Christianity as the major world religion, with himself as its prophet. At the age of twenty-eight, 'the Beast' had discovered his messianic calling. He took to signing his letters 'Saint E. A. Crowley'.

The author Clifford Bax, who would later become a close friend of Bennett, met Crowley in 1905 while staying at a hotel in Switzerland. Bax was just nineteen at the time, but was already developing a keen interest in metaphysical subjects. Over games of chess, Crowley exhorted the young man to become his disciple. When Bax hesitated, nervously protesting that perhaps he needed to 'read a little more first', Crowley snapped back at him: 'Reading is for infants. Men must experiment. Seize what the gods have offered. Reject me, and you will be indistinguishable from all these idiots around us.' Crowley then asked abruptly, what is the date? 'January the 25th', Bax answered. And what is the year? Crowley asked. Bax replied: '1905'. 'Exactly,' Crowley said, 'And a thousand years from this moment, the world will be sitting in the sunset of Crowleyanity.'[37]

Crowley was finished with goodness. He wrote to his friend Gerald Kelly:

After five years of folly and weakness, miscalled politeness, tact, discretion, care for the feeling of others, I am weary of it. I say today: the hell with Christianity, Rationalism, Buddhism, all the lumber of the centuries. I bring you a positive and primaeval fact, Magick by name; and with this I will build me a new Heaven and a new Earth. I want none of your faint approval or faint dispraise; *I want blasphemy, murder, rape, revolution, anything, bad or good, but strong.*[38]

Bennett wanted nothing to do with it. He had done with 'Magick'—or at least Crowley's version of it. 'No Buddhist would consider it worthwhile to pass from the crystalline clearness of his own religion to this involved obscurity', he wrote. In Buddhism he had found a far higher and finer alchemy than anything that could be achieved through Magick—the transformation of the self:

> It is a part of Buddhist teaching that a person can gain control over the hidden forces of his own mind as they develop, and the power to affect the minds of others in various ways. Certain of these would distinctly come under the heading of the so-called miraculous. But although these powers over the minds of others, and even over what we should term objective phenomena, are said naturally to come to most in the natural course of their interior development towards *Arahanship*, it must not be supposed that, according to Buddhist teaching, the possession of these powers, or their exercise, proves a man to be of high and spiritual development. Rather, indeed, in some ways it is the opposite.[39]

To the aspirant himself, he wrote, the development of these powers is regarded as a possible snare, 'because he may become so interested in them, and in the new worlds which their possession opens to his investigation, as to forget the higher teaching, and to neglect his training for the Path itself'.[40] Bennett cited the Buddhist parable of the Wrong Marvel and the Right, where the Buddha takes up the challenge by a group of fire-worshipping ascetics to test his powers against theirs. Attempting to kindle a fire by their magical mastery of the fire element, the ascetics are thwarted by the Buddha, and immediately declare themselves to be his followers. But such marvels, the Buddha tells them, prove nothing for or against any body of teachings. They were mere worldly powers that anybody could take the time or trouble to acquire. The 'greatest miracle', as Bennett described it, was the miracle of the power of Truth to conquer falsehood; 'even when the Truth is hard to bear, when the falsehood appeals to every hope and passion in our hearts'.[41]

Unlike his old friend, Bennett had no interest in forging his own world religion—although he would become a tireless proselytiser on behalf of his adopted one, Buddhism. Rather, he yearned for the quiet, modest bliss of nirvana—'the apotheosis of sanity', as he put it:

> no vain longing after future states of bliss, but the attainment even in this life of that Goal of Happiness after which humanity has craved, since first speech became articulate—the bliss that comes to him who has put aside the causes of woes—who lives freed from the passions, hatreds and illusions that enchain us—his mind filled with inutterable Peace, his heart filled with love and helpfulness to all living things.[42]

Bennett was now fixed on the idea of formally taking the vows of a Buddhist monk, deciding that a purer form of practice was to be found in Burma than in Ceylon where, according to Crowley, the Sinhalese monks were 'ignorant, idle, immoral and dishonest'.[43]

Bennett had been offered the post of treasurer at a monastery near Colombo—'for the avowed reason,' Crowley observed, 'that they could not trust anyone of themselves'. But he turned down the offer, and at the end of 1901 he travelled to Akyab (now Sittwe), on Burma's west coast, some 600 miles northwest of the capital Rangoon, where he entered a Buddhist monastery.

On 12 December 1901, Allan Bennett was ordained as a novice monk, or bhikku, taking the name Ananda Maitriya Sasanajotika. Ananda means joy; Maitriya is the name of the Buddha to come, and also means loving kindness; Sasana is the word for dispensation of the teachings; and jotika means light or radiance.[44] He would subsequently change his name from the Sanskrit 'Maitriya' to the Pali 'Metteyya', dropping Sasanajotika altogether for the sake of brevity. Six months later, on 21 May 1902, he took the *upasampada* (higher) ordination and became a full bhikku. Seventy-five priests took part in the ceremony, and the town was reported to have been 'golden with the robes of the priests'.

Bennett was not content only to follow the simple monastic life of a bhikku. He was, at heart, an evangelist. Buddhism was a creed, as he put it, that 'asks from its followers not faith but understanding', and which to Bennett's mind perfectly reconciled the search for higher truth with the application of reason and provided the only answer to the problems of modern mankind. The great teachings of science and 'the outgrowth of the spirit of humanity' that would be unleashed through Buddhism, would, he optimistically believed, liberate mankind from ignorance, and dispel 'the old barbarous race-hatreds ... till the whole folly and fanfaronade of militarism and its evil fruits of warfare are swept away forever'.[45] At his ordination he delivered a stirring address, declaring that 'the work that is before me' was to carry 'to the lands of the West the Law of Love and Truth declared by our Master, to establish in those countries the Sangha of his Priests'.

Within a few months of his ordination, he founded the International Buddhist Society, or Buddhasasana Samagama, with the objective of translating and publishing Buddhist scriptures and works, and promoting Buddhist education in the face of a colonial education system that prioritised the teaching of Christianity in schools. Bennett did not find his new calling easy. He was living with Burmese monks in conditions that he described as 'disgusting',[46] and he was facing his familiar problem of a chronic shortage of funds. The Burmese, he complained, were 'not in the least imbued with the ancient missionary spirit of Buddhism'.[47]

Help would arrive in the form of a wealthy benefactor, Mrs M. M. Hla Oung, the widow of the Comptroller of the Indian Treasury. Mrs Hla Oung was a steadfast supporter of Buddhist causes; she had founded two Buddhist schools in Burma, one for boys and one for girls, which had been praised by Annie Besant in the pages of *The Theosophist*. Now she undertook to support Bennett, building a small monastery on her land in Kyang—in effect a compound of small huts, where he lived with a German who had also taken monastic vows.[48]

In Britain, the ground for Bennett's mission to the West was already being prepared by a handful of like-minded spirits, among them Colonel J. R. Pain, an army officer who had been introduced to Buddhist teachings while stationed in Burma, and Ernest Rost, a doctor who had served in the Indian Medical Service. Learning of Bennett's work, they resolved to found an organisation to promote his mission in Britain, and on the evening of 3 November 1907, the first meeting of the Buddhist Society of Great Britain and Ireland convened in a house in Harley Street, presided over by the society's first president, T. W. Rhys Davids, with the objective of preparing the ground for the bhikku's arrival.

On 23 April 1908, a small deputation gathered at the Royal Albert Dock in London to greet the ship carrying Allan Bennett from Burma. The curiosity of an Englishman becoming a Buddhist monk had excited the attention of the English newspapers, and a number of journalists were awaiting his arrival and went on board to interview him.

The bhikku, one newspaper reported, shivered in his cabin, warm and comfortable though it was, smoking what were described as 'asthma cigarettes, to drive away the cold and damp of London's unoriental weather'.[49] He sat in one corner, clad in the yellow robe of his Order, 'With his head clean-shaven and his feet bare, he looked deathly pale, as he nervously fitted a cigarette into an amber holder', it was reported. 'Averting his eyes, he said in a low voice, in which the Scottish accent was noticeable, "Ask me what you desire to know, and I will answer".'[50]

It was noted that as a monk, Bennett had renounced all personal property except his robe, a razor, a begging bowl and a water-filter: 'He must drink only filtered water, not because the living organisms might do him harm, but because he might harm the living organisms', one paper reported. Although he could not look upon the face of a woman, the article added, 'he may speak to her; but his eyes must be downcast or his face turned aside'; 'There was one pathetic incident amid the quiet and distant greetings which the Bhikshu permitted. A lady, who had known him in the old days, approached. "Allan—welcome!" she said. The monk's eyes fell on his rosary. He bowed, and turned quickly away.'[51]

Bennett had been accompanied on the voyage by Mrs Hla Oung, who had defrayed the entire cost of the mission, along with her son and his wife. Because of the precept forbidding a bhikku from sleeping in the same house as a woman, the Society had been obliged to rent two separate residences in the leafy London suburb of Barnes for the duration of Bennett's stay. The house at 101 Elm Grove Road, where Bennett stayed, was designated as the temporary headquarters of the International Buddhist Society. A shrine was installed in the living room. To avoid breaking the precept against 'high and soft' beds, Bennett slept on the floor, and ate his food at specified hours, taking nothing after noon. 'Apparently he takes but one meal a day,' noted one newspaper report, 'and less than seven of the twenty-four hours are spent in bed, so that his life is not one of worldly pleasure.'[52]

Because he was not allowed to handle money, he was unable to travel far on his own. The Vinaya rules also forbade riding behind a horse—which was seen as a sign of vanity—an inconvenience in a city where much public transport was still horse-drawn. The spectacle of a shaven-headed Englishman, dressed in bright saffron robes, drew curious stares and sometimes ribald comment on the streets. Despite these difficulties, Bennett was still able to maintain a busy schedule of talks. He spoke at the Theosophical Society, the Highgate Unitarian Church and the City Temple Debating Society, as well as at numerous meetings in private homes.

He also met his old friend Aleister Crowley, although according to Crowley's friend and disciple Edward Bryant there was a widening gulf between the two men, with Crowley confining his interests to 'Magick' and Bennett devoted completely to Buddhism, 'and also because Allan tended to acquire a circle of woolly sisters whom Aleister loathed'.[53] A new journal was established to support his mission called *The Buddhist Review*, and in its first issue Bennett addressed his readership as those who regarded Buddhism 'not merely with the interest of the philosopher, the linguist, or the antiquary, but as a Religion, as the Religion they are proud—and yet humble—to call their own'.[54]

Wherever he went, Bennett seems to have impressed everyone he met with his integrity, devotion and the simple nobility of his demeanour. But while he was a gifted writer, able to convey the essence of Buddhist teachings with a tremendous clarity and conviction, he was considerably less effective as a public speaker. One member of the Buddhist Society, Edward Greenly, lamented that having apparently never learned the first rule of public speaking, Bennett would read with his eyes glued to his notes, and was completely unable to gauge the mood of an audience, writing that 'Nature, when enriching him with so many gifts, man of science, thinker, writer, not to mention the originality, daring and leadership which could conceive such an enterprise, had fatally omitted the essential gift of eloquence.'[55]

Bennett's presence in London had been noted by another journal, *The Nature Cure*, which opened its edition of June 1908 with a full-page portrait of the English bhikku. *The Nature Cure* was the creation of another eccentric adornment to Edwardian English life—George Watson MacGregor Reid: socialist, union organiser, founder of the British Nature Cure Association and the father of modern Druidism.[56] The journal aimed at a broad constituency—'all Food Reformers, Vegetarians, Temperance Enthusiasts, Anti-Vivisectionists, Anti-Vaccinists and believers in Simple Life ideals', reflecting the eclectic enthusiasms of its editor, who described himself as 'a peculiar mixture of clergyman, philosophic teacher, health advisor and dietic guide'.[57]

It is possible that Bennett and MacGregor Reid were acquainted from their days in the Theosophical Society. But MacGregor Reid was clearly impressed by the figure that Bennett now cut as a Buddhist monk. In *The Nature Cure* he extolled Bennett as 'certainly the most remarkable man who has ever appeared in our midst'.

In September 1908, shortly before Bennett's departure for Burma, MacGregor Reid chaired a valedictory lecture by Bennett on the topic of

'Self Renunciation, the Basis of Buddhist Practice', at Battersea Town Hall, that was attended by almost 1,000 people. But despite the warm welcome that had been extended to him, and the numbers that had attended his lectures, Bennett returned to Burma a disappointed man. To Bennett, Buddhism was a religion that should be lived and practised, not an interest to be followed in an academic way. The problem as he saw it was that the Buddhist Society in England contained members who were curious about Buddhism, but not committed to it.[58]

Bennett expressed his feelings in an article published in *The Buddhist Review* in 1910, writing that 'We must strive to be [the Buddha's] Followers not in name alone, but must so rule our hearts and lives that men may understand the meaning of that noblest holiest life that ever human being lived.' Before leaving England, a despondent Bennett wrote to MacGregor Reid, lamenting the difficulties in generating enthusiasm—and more particularly funds—for the Buddhist sangha. Beginning his letter with warm salutations and a warning that MacGregor Reid should be more careful when cycling (the stout and bearded advocate of healthy living was apparently prone to falling off his bike), Bennett went on to complain that 'The work here has, with the exception that it has brought me a few earnest and devoted colleagues, like yourself, been a failure: financially— just as with your own movement, none of the wealthy members will do anything—nothing can be got even to keep the movement barely floated.'[59]

Arriving back in Burma, Bennett kept his disappointment to himself, saying he had been 'highly gratified' by his visit to Britain in an interview given to a Rangoon newspaper. He returned to his monastery at Kyang resolving to devote his energies to developing new inventions that he hoped would subsidise the Buddhasasana Samagama and—his ultimate dream—the building of a monastery in Britain (a dream that would never be realised). Foremost among these was his plan for a 'consciousness-reaction apparatus', which would, he believed, 'if successful be of considerable commercial value as patented'. He wrote to MacGregor Reid again, pleading for money for 'Ananda M's Engine Fund' to buy the necessary tools and materials for his work. It was a pity, he lamented, that while 'millions of money' should go to Christian missionaries, 'many of themselves not really believing the doctrine they teach', no funds could be found for a teaching 'so perfectly adapted to the modern Western mind' as Buddhism.[60]

Bennett continued to write for *The Buddhist Review*, to produce his own magazine, *Buddhism*, and to make the occasional contribution on Buddhism to *The Equinox*, the journal edited by his old friend Aleister Crowley. In 1911 he published *An Outline of Buddhism; or, The Religion of Burma*. But the vicissitudes of life as a bhikku had begun to take their toll. His health was now in serious decline. As well as chronic asthma he had also developed gallstones, necessitating being operated on twice.

In 1913 he was visited at Kyang by Ethel Powell-Brown, an Englishwoman who had travelled to Rangoon to join her husband, a ship's officer, who was billeted in the city. Having been told about the English bhikku and being curious to meet him, Powell-Brown made her way to Bennett's monastery. She would later give a vivid description of his circumstances in a letter to Gerald Yorke, later adapted and printed in *The Westminster Gazette*. She noted that Bennett's habitation was on two floors. The ground floor was 'fitted up as a laboratory', with test tubes and a spirit lamp. Upstairs, 'all was confusion, a very welter of dust and disorder'. Tall bookcases lined the walls, crammed with 'the latest works of scientists, philosophers, mathematicians, together with those of astrologers, numerologists, vegetarians, spiritualists and other extraordinary people whom the world generally labels as "cranks"'. Magazines littered the floor and the chairs, and an antiquated typewriter and piles of proofs sat on the table.

Bennett, Powell-Brown recorded, was in poor health. His asthma was now so bad that he could barely cross a room without bringing on an attack, and he was also suffering from liver problems, with his skin 'yellow as a Burman's with jaundice'. Yet his intellectual capabilities remained undiminished. Powell-Brown described him as 'the most interesting man I have ever met in my life. He was ill, but a most brilliant and stimulating talker.' They talked of Buddhism, and 'later the talk ranged on to lighter subjects: levitation, palmistry, the relation between sound and colour, the photographing of auras; all came up for consideration and each question touched upon he illuminated with a new light'. Bennett also talked of his inventions and claimed that he had developed a method of sterilising food to prevent it rotting by means of the rays from a 'special lamp', as well as a method for making ice much more cheaply and simply than the manufacturers of refrigerators, but that they would kill the idea rather than scrap their machines.

He also described an experience in meditation which he said had been 'an exaltation and a liberation', and which he likened to

> travelling upwards in an elevator. And at each stage of the journey, the four walls fell outwards and he found himself in an immensely large space

91

which itself began to move upwards until the walls of that fell out, and the roof rolled back, and he was again in immensities, but moving higher.

The recollection so exhausted him, Powell-Brown recorded, that 'he dropped suddenly into a chair fighting for breath'. The Burmese servants told her that they had seen Bennett levitate while in meditation, and that on another day he had raised a thunderstorm, 'but as it was near the beginning of the monsoon which always commences with a heavy storm I was rather inclined to doubt'. Despite his failing health, Bennett still strictly observed his precept against eating after noon:

> The arm that the monkish robe left bare was incredibly thin, and from the bony shoulders the robe itself hung in gaunt and angular lines like the folded wings of an adjutant bird. But the black eyes under the up-tilted eyebrows were as burningly alive as ever, and the welcoming words just as cordial.[61]

Fourteen years earlier, Bennett had been told that his life depended on him leaving Britain to travel East; now, it appeared to depend on him leaving the East to go home, and he pleaded to Mrs Powell-Brown for her help. At her insistence, her husband approached a friend, the editor of *The Rangoon Times*, who agreed to raise an appeal on Bennett's behalf. In a curious case of serendipity, the editor happened to be Channing Arnold—the son of Sir Edwin Arnold, whose book *The Light of Asia* had first put Bennett on the path of Buddhism that would eventually lead him to Burma. Now it was Arnold's son who would be responsible for bringing Bennett home.

With his fare provided for, Bennett set sail for Britain on the same ship as the Powell-Browns. In a rambling and feverish letter to Captain Powell-Brown, written before their departure, Bennett thanked him for all that he and his wife had done, and implying that he, Bennett, had effectively been held prisoner by Mrs Hla Oung, who did not wish him—and the accumulation of merit his presence as a monk carried with it—to leave Burma. Powell-Brown, he wrote, had saved him from 'some vile black hole, on point as it were, of actual suffocation … I regard my life itself as having been saved by your kindest action.' When the boat carrying Bennett docked at Plymouth, he bid farewell to his saviours. 'We saw the last of the bhikku in town,' Mrs Powell-Brown would recall. They never heard from him again.

The marriage of Bennett's sister Charlotte to Godfrey Johnson had ended in divorce in 1911, and she had invited her brother to come and live with her in California, believing that the climate would be more congenial to his health. Together with Charlotte, he travelled to Liverpool to make passage to America. But when Bennett attempted to board the ship, he was turned back by the ship's doctor on the grounds that because of his ill-health, he would inevitably be refused entry to America by the immigration authorities. Charlotte set sail without him.

A distraught Bennett was taken in by a local member of the Buddhist Society. The 'fanfaronade of militarism and its evil fruits of warfare' had now engulfed Europe. Bennett saw out the first two years of the Great War meditating in a room in Liverpool, supported by a fund raised by the Buddhist Society to pay for his food and lodging. (Aleister Crowley was in America, writing propaganda for the German cause. 'A great deal of damage was done at the suburb of Croydon,' he wrote of one Zeppelin raid over London, 'especially at its suburb Addiscombe, where my aunt lives. Unfortunately her house was not hit.'[62])

\* \* \*

In 1916 Allan Bennett returned to London. He had now given up his robes and was living as a layman. He lived for a while in a hostel for the poor, and then, with the support of friends, took lodgings in a house in Eccles Road, Battersea, a working-class district of shabby but respectable terraces, railway viaducts and small factories south of the river Thames. Bennett lived in a small room furnished with a camp bed, two wicker chairs and a washbasin. Books rose in stacks from the floor. A Burmese Buddha stood on the mantelpiece.

He had become friends with Clifford Bax, the playwright, poet, critic and editor whose eclectic accomplishments included translating haikus from the original Japanese and writing a biography of the cricketer W. G. Grace. Bax had first encountered Bennett in 1908 during his 'mission' to England, when he attended one of Bennett's lectures at the Theosophical Society. But now the acquaintance was rekindled through a mutual friend, the Egyptologist and erstwhile Theosophist Battiscombe Gunn.

Gunn described how Bennett was living in a 'small dingy room of a jaundice-coloured villa in a Battersea side street', with two elderly ladies living downstairs who, it seemed, did not much like the look of Bennett's gilded Buddha, but put up with him because 'he composes the quarrels of the household'. Like almost everyone who met Bennett, Gunn described him as 'the most remarkable man I've known'. He told Bax a story about how Bennett, out on the streets of Battersea one night 'to buy a packet of fags' (an unusual purchase for an asthmatic bhikku, surely), had come across a soldier lying huddled on the pavement. Seeing that he was ill, Bennett took him back to his lodgings and put him to bed and sat all night at his bedside. 'He put himself onto one of the higher levels of consciousness—jhanas, they call them,' Gunn went on, 'And towards morning the soldier woke up and said "Where am I? I've been in paradise."'[63]

A few days later, Bax was introduced to Bennett at Gunn's home in Chiswick. The man that ten years earlier he had seen speaking, shaven-headed and dressed in a saffron robe, was now dressed in a shabby suit and moth-eaten overcoat, but his impoverished appearance did nothing to diminish his impact on Bax. Bennett's thick hair, he wrote, was 'so fine in texture and so intensely black that anyone must have recognised its beauty'; while his face was 'the most significant that I have ever seen':

> Twenty years of physical suffering had twisted and scored it: a lifetime of meditation upon universal love had imparted to it an expression that was unmistakable. His colour was almost dusky, his mouth firm but in-sunken like that of an old man, and his eyes had the soft glow of amber. At first glance I realised that he never could have played at being a man of mystery. Indeed, he thought nothing of himself. He had passed, I believe, through experiences of more importance than those of any man in England, but he regarded them as early milestones on a road which all men, in the end, must travel. Above all, at the moment of meeting and always thereafter, I was conscious of a tender and far-shining emanation, an unvarying psychic sunlight that environed his personality.[64]

Like supplicants at the feet of the master, Bax and Gunn listened as Bennett expounded on the doctrine of Anatta, or 'no-self' (or as Bax put it, 'no soul')—the central tenet of Buddhist teaching. Man, Bennett explained, 'is like an onion. Peel off layer and layer, attribute after attribute, and you will come to no centre in the onion and to no immortal essence in man. His mind, like his body—in fact like everything—is in a state of flux.' The self, Bennett went on, is an illusion, and to cling to it leads only to suffering: 'Until we have dissolved our egoism we cannot cease to oscillate between pleasure and pain.' And, Bax asked him, is it possible to escape? 'Yes,' Bennett replied, 'That is the meaning of Nirvana.' The great dissolvent of selfhood, he went on, is love: 'True love is a union of the perceiver with the perceived; and I think you will not deny that the more nearly you come to union with another human being, the less emphatically are you yourself.' When our selves are 'blown out,' he continued, 'something immeasurable and indescribable is released' to take its place. And that is Nirvana.

As a Buddhist, Bennett was an alert and powerful personality; 'but as a poor man dwelling unknown in London,' Bax observed, 'he was a sick creature prematurely old'. As Bennett was leaving, Gunn's wife Meena remarked on his moth-eaten coat and insisted that she would buy him a new one—'This coat is too full of holes.' 'But, you see,' Bennett joked, 'I'm supposed to be a holy man.'[65]

In his room in Battersea, Bennett continued to work on his inventions. He told Bax that he had developed a gramophone that would play records of unlimited length, but when applying to take out a patent on his new invention he discovered that a similar instrument had been patented twenty years earlier. He also had plans to devise an instrument that could read thoughts, and then project them onto other minds (presumably the same 'consciousness-reaction apparatus' that he had been trying to raise funds to develop more than ten years earlier). 'It would revolutionize education', he told Bax.[66]

Bennett had resumed editorship of *The Buddhist Review*, publishing it as a quarterly, but unable to cope with the workload it entailed he sought the help of a young acquaintance named Raphael Hurst, who became his part-time assistant. Hurst, who would later become a well-known author under the name Paul Brunton, would describe the distressing spectacle that Bennett presented—the 'tragic look' he constantly wore, 'illuminated by fitful smiles'; the skin 'turned quite yellow through tropical liver trouble':

> Shocking spasms of asthmatic cough racked his lungs every day. Yet his serene face would immediately break into a smile the next moment and he would utter some light humorous phrase or profoundly spiritual remark, as his mood went. Here one saw how his meditation, training and Buddhistic detachment had proved their worth, for although his body was stricken his mind proved invulnerable.[67]

Few of the Indian yogis that Hurst would later go on to meet, he wrote, could 'hold a candle' to Bennett: 'He had realized the phenomenal character of all things in this parade of flickering shadows which we call life, as most of them have never done.'

To Hurst, who kept a photograph of Bennett on his living-room wall, Bennett was 'a bodhisattva ... come from a higher plane to penetrate those Western minds which could appreciate, and benefit by, Buddhism as meeting their intellectual and spiritual needs. He gave the hidden impetus, but others came later to do the outer work.' Bennett, he continued, 'lived the doctrine of love for all beings to its fullest extent;

none was exempt from the sweep of his compassion'.[68] Love, Bennett once told Clifford Bax 'is the great unraveller—love that expects nothing in return; and the immemorial heresy of the human mind is egoism ... All egoism is in some measure insane, and what we admit to be insanity is but egoism overdriven.'[69]

He might have been talking of his old friend Aleister Crowley. There is no record of Bennett and Crowley having communicated at all following Bennett's return to Burma in 1908, after which Crowley had fallen ever deeper into the pit of disrepute.

Kenneth Grant believed that one of the great ironies of Crowley and Bennett's friendship lay in Crowley's belief that by prolonging Bennett's life by magical means (which Crowley thought he had done) and enabling him to travel to the East for the good of his health, Crowley hoped that his friend would 'plant the banner of Thelema in foreign lands'. Instead, Bennett brought Buddhism to the West.

In 1920, Crowley, along with a handful of acolytes, moved to Sicily, establishing his Abbey of Thelema in a ramshackle farmhouse in the town of Cefalù. There he practised sexual magic, earning the fervid attentions of the British yellow press, who recounted lurid stories of sexual orgies and animal sacrifice. (In his defence, his friend Gerald Yorke would point out that in a long life, Crowley 'only sacrificed a few sparrows, two pigeons, a cat, a goat and a toad, and of these the cat and goat were killed at ceremonies extemporized by request.'[70]) The death in 1922 of an Oxford student who was staying at the farmhouse was the final straw. Crowley was denounced by the press as 'the wickedest man in the world' and kicked out of Sicily on the orders of Mussolini.

According to his friend Edward Bryant, 'the Beast' always maintained the deepest respect for Bennett the 'Bhikku'. 'It often struck me that in one corner of his mind at least he thought of himself as the Disciple to Allan's Master', he recalled.[71] Bryant claimed that Crowley told him that he had always wanted to write a biography of Bennett, but the particulars of Bennett's life were so confusing and unclear the task would have been impossible.

In January 1923, Bennett published his last book, *The Wisdom of the Aryas*—a collection of lectures he had given for a small audience in Clifford Bax's studio. The book contained a ringing summary of his abiding hope and belief for Buddhism—'surely the Western world, amidst this present darkness ... may well find in this ancient Truth some answers to its deepest problems; some solace for the sorrows and nescience of life'. He died on

9 March 1923, two months after its publication, at the age of fifty-one, a member of the Buddhist Society at his bedside. It was recorded that his dying wish was to give his last few pence to a beggar he heard passing beneath his window.

The death certificate listed the cause of Bennett's death as asthma and intestinal blockage. He was buried in Morden cemetery, South London, where a large gathering assembled for a Buddhist funeral service, arranged by his friend Francis Payne. 'We took the lovely passage describing the Buddha's last days,' Payne wrote, 'the very last words that the Master uttered, and then we added his beautiful passage on the nature of Nibbana, and those present by the graveside were deeply impressed.'[72] 'This white Buddhist,' as Raphael Hurst put it, in characteristically purple prose, 'whose ship has sailed for the infinite waters of Nirvana.'

There was no memorial stone placed at his grave.

Crowley's friend Bryant would record that on one occasion, exhausted by a lifetime of illness, Bennett had sighed to Crowley, 'I don't understand why I should have to suffer this way', to which Crowley replied: 'There's a fine thing for a Buddhist to say.'[73] 'Allan never knew joy', Crowley wrote:

> He disdained and distrusted pleasure from the womb. Is it strange that he should have been unable to conceive life as aught but ineluctable and fatuous evil? For myself, I saw pleasure as puerile, sorrow as senile; I was ready, when mine hour should arrive, to accept either amicably or dismiss both disdainfully.[74]

Crowley would survive Bennett by twenty-four years. Having spent much of his life travelling the world and failing in his attempts to persuade, variously, Stalin, Hitler and the British government to accept Thelema as the state religion, in 1945 Crowley came to his last resting place—a boarding-house called Netherwood House, perched on the cliffs above the East Sussex seaside town of Hastings. He arrived there looking like a spectre from another age, a balding, crow-like man, dressed in knickerbockers, stockings and silver-buckled shoes. Given the choice of which room he wanted as his own, he chose room number 13. An addict to his last breath, his heroin would be dispatched by Heppells the chemists in London. He was said to be taking 11 grains of heroin a day—approximately 666 milligrams.

On 1 December 1947, Crowley died of asthma and chronic bronchitis. The nurse at his bedside reported that his last words were, 'Sometimes I hate myself ...'

# 5

## HYMAN, THE BOOTMAKER'S SON

Raphael Hurst was a small, bearded man, little more than 5 feet tall, fastidious about his appearance, who spoke in a pronounced Cockney accent, and in moments of levity would claim to have come from the planet Sirius.

Raphael Hurst was not, in fact, his real name. As a journalist and author, he wrote under a variety of pseudonyms, including Raphael Meriden and Raphael Delmonte. But it was under the name Paul Brunton that he would become famous as one of the first interlocutors between Eastern spiritual teachings and the mass Western audience, most notably with his best-selling book *A Search in Secret India*, published in 1934.

A chronicle of the author's encounters with yogis, swamis and miracle workers in his quest for a guru, *A Search in Secret India* was a key work in the creation of two interlinking mythologies. The first was of India as a repository of lost or hidden spiritual teachings and miracle-working yogis, that could provide an answer to the West's headlong rush into materialism and spiritual crisis. The second was the picture of 'Paul Brunton' as the archetype of the solitary, questing traveller on the spiritual path, which would eventually lead to his own elevation to the status of sage and guru—a role that Brunton himself always professed to despise.

Paul Brunton liked secrets. *A Search in Secret India* would be followed by another book, *A Search in Secret Egypt* (1935), and much of his life was devoted to the revelation of hermetic wisdom. But there was one subject about which he always remained determinedly secretive—himself.

Before there was Paul Brunton, even before there was Raphael Hurst, there was Hyman Abraham Isaacs. The son of Jewish migrants from Lithuania, who had settled in the melting pot of London's East End, Brunton—as we shall call him, since that is the name by which he became best known—was born in Whitechapel on 21 October 1898.

Brunton seems to have been something of a stranger even to his own son Kenneth, who in his biography of his father wrote that he knew next to nothing of his father's family background; as a parent, too, Brunton appears as a curiously remote and elusive figure, cultivating a relationship with Kenneth that was more along the lines of guru and disciple than father and son.

Hyman's father, Rubin, was a bootmaker who became successful enough to open two small factories in Commercial Road, the busiest business street in the East End. The young Hyman attended the local Central Foundation School, which had originally been established for the sons of skilled workmen and tradesmen who were able to pay only a limited amount towards their children's education, and which would prepare them for entry to business and the professions.

When he was thirteen, his mother Fanny died of tuberculosis; Rubin remarried, and Hyman was brought up largely by his stepmother, whom he called 'Auntie'. It was around this time, it seems, that Rubin Isaac made the decision to rename his son Raphael Hurst, apparently in order to improve his prospects by disguising his Jewish identity.

Brunton would later write of how his boyhood years had been 'shadowed by a terrible and tremendous yearning to penetrate the mystery of life's inner meaning'.[1] At an age when most boys were reading adventure stories or comics, he was reading the Letters of St Paul and Edward Bulwer-Lytton's feverishly overblown occult romance *Zanoni* (1842)—a book, Brunton would later write, that 'opened a new and eerie world for me, a stripling yet at school! It gave me dark brooding ambitions. I, too, would take the path of the Rosicrucian neophyte and strive to fling aside the heavy curtain which hides the occult spheres from mortal gaze.'[2] But it was another book, *The Awakening of the Soul*, by the twelfth-century Sufi philosopher Ibn Tufail, which Brunton would credit as the first book to introduce him to mystical ideas and encourage his first attempts at meditation.

After six months of 'unwavering daily practice', he would later recount, 'and eighteen months of burning aspiration for the Spiritual Self', he experienced a series of ecstatic mystical states, 'a happiness beyond which it is impossible to go', which he attributed to being at one with what he called 'the Overself'. 'The glamour and freshness of mystical ecstasies subsided within three or four weeks and vanished,' he wrote, 'But the awareness kindled by them remained for three years.'[3]

Brunton's son Kenneth—his hagiographer and his disciple—would write that these experiences were so at odds with 'the harsh materialistic big-city vibrations' surrounding his father that he was driven to the brink of suicide. It was only reading books on spiritualism in the British Museum Reading Room, Kenneth maintains, that dissuaded him from this course.[4]

On leaving school, Brunton worked as a civil servant in the Government Patent Office. In 1917, at the age of nineteen, he went to war, enlisting in the Tank Reserve Corps. His military record names 'H. A. Isaacs' at the rank of Private. The first tanks had been introduced into the British Army a year earlier during the Battle of the Somme. Each tank had a crew of eight men confined in a cramped and claustrophobic space; Brunton's small stature would have made him perfect for such a role. Being confined in a tank in the heat of battle was hell. Temperatures inside the vehicle could reach 50°C (122°F), and the atmosphere was thick with poisonous carbon monoxide, fuel and oil vapours, and the pungent smell of cordite from the tank's four cannons. To protect from concussion and flying metal, crews had to wear a thick leather helmet and chainmail masks. It was not unusual for whole crews to pass out inside the vehicle.

At the end of the war, Brunton took work with Foyles, the famous London booksellers. He also returned with some enthusiasm to his esoteric studies. He joined the Theosophical Society and the Spiritualist Society. The development of occult powers seems to have greatly interested Brunton. He told his son Kenneth that he possessed such powers himself, relating an incident concerning a well-known public speaker whom Brunton claimed to have discovered was using black magic for immoral purposes. Brunton decided to attend his next lecture: 'As soon as the "magician" began to speak, my father concentrated his own force and thereby extinguished every light in the hall. When the lights were switched on again, [he] this time concentrated with such force as to explode every light bulb!'[5]

According to Kenneth, Brunton began revelling in his new-found powers until an 'inner message' warned him that he had to make a choice between occult powers or spiritual development. Once he had chosen the latter, 'his occult powers left him and he was no longer able to indulge them'.[6]

\* \* \*

One of Brunton's closest friends was Michael Hurwitz—who went under the name Michael Houghton—a Theosophist (he would introduce Brunton to the Theosophical Society) and an associate of Aleister Crowley, who would go on to become the editor of *The Occult Observer*, a monthly publication that covered a range of topics from Buddhism and yoga to clairvoyance and astral travel, and which numbered among its contributors Crowley, Dion Fortune and, later, a young Alan Watts.

In his book *The White Brother: An Occult Autobiography* (1927), written under the pen name Michael Juste, Houghton paints a vivid picture of the occult and bohemian fraternity in London in the years immediately before and after the First World War, with a myriad of societies, groups and cults promulgating Theosophy, spiritualism, yoga, Rosicrucianism, Buddhism, Gnosticism and a dozen other creeds and beliefs. Houghton himself had made the journey from a conventional Christian background to atheism, socialism—'a realm where Suspicion and Misrule were the true sovereigns'—and thence to 'the dark valleys' of 'Anarchism', before arriving at the sunny uplands of the Theosophical Society and a broad interest in occult matters.

Brunton appears in *The White Brother* under the pseudonym of 'David', of whom 'Juste' writes:

> David was of short and somewhat slight stature, pale and intensely sensitive (he originally disliked me because I was too crude, and argued with him), serious, and, I used to think, much too casual about the incidents of the world, and much too deeply engrossed in the world within. He always appeared to move in a perpetual haze. He had had some interesting experiences of an occult nature when young, which helped me to prove the existence of unknown states of consciousness, and when I first met him his air of other-worldliness puzzled me greatly. I remember particularly one day, when I was waiting for him in the shadow of a staircase, he touched me to see if I was real or a ghost. Life to him was then very insubstantial, although since that period he has had experiences which have taught him the wisdom of planting his feet firmly on earth.

'Juste' continues:

> David strove to live the mystical life, and gave to every beggar he met his last few pence. Unfortunately the people to whom he gave were sometimes the least deserving. In fact, his mystical life did not develop the power of discrimination; a characteristic I have noticed among many who live in too mystical an atmosphere.[7]

Brunton and Houghton led a life of self-consciously penurious bohemianism, sharing rooms in Tavistock Square, Bloomsbury (the same rooms that two or three years later Leonard and Virginia Woolf would occupy as the first offices of the Hogarth Press), from where they would venture out to the cafes of Fitzrovia and Soho—'David because he hoped to become acquainted with those who had mystical beliefs.' 'Juste' continues:

> Here our little group would sit and watch the fantastic pageant, drinking from thick glass tumblers weak and highly priced Russian tea, and listening to the loud, shaggy voices of women and low-pitched, giggling, sexual laughter of young students and frowzily clad men.[8]

Brunton worked as a journalist, contributing articles and book reviews for a range of small publications including *The Occult Observer*. He also became acquainted with Allan Bennett and helped him in editing *The Buddhist Review*. In 1922 he married Karen Tottrup, whom he had met at a meeting of the Theosophical Society, and in the same year he and Houghton opened a bookshop on Lamb's Conduit Street in Bloomsbury, selling occult and esoteric material. But it closed after just six months. Houghton would have more success setting up as a bookseller on his own. In the same year he opened another bookshop on Museum Street, the Atlantis, which is still trading today.

Brunton's marriage was short-lived. In 1929 he and Tottrup divorced. The following year Brunton founded his own magazine called *Success*—an unlikely project for an esotericist—promulgating the principles of positive thinking in business through such articles as 'Promotion and How to Get It!' and 'Effective Speech for Salesmen'. The object of the publication, he wrote in one editorial, was

> [not] to glorify the money spinner ... The gilded ruffian who tramples on others is not a success in our view. Because we seek to portray in some of these pages such careers as have inspirational value for others, it will never be our purpose to bend the knee and worship Mammon. Character is to a man's career what the steel reinforcement is to concrete: without it all his works will one day perish into the dust.

As, indeed, did *Success*. In 1929 Wall Street crashed, and after just six issues, *Success* crashed with it.

It was shortly after this in 1931 that Brunton co-wrote his first book, *Are You Upward Bound*, under the name Raphael Delmonte, with William G. Fern, a prolific author of books on salesmanship and self-improvement including *The Master Salesman* and *How to Make Money More Easily: Being the Philosophy of the Master Money Maker*. Raphael Delmonte would never write another book. But for Paul Brunton, the title would prove curiously prophetic.

\* \* \*

It was through the Theosophical Society that Brunton met an engineer and veteran of the Great War named Frederick Fletcher. Much like Brunton, Fletcher is a frustratingly elusive character. In his biography of Brunton, Kenneth Hurst refers to Fletcher simply as 'Bud', and describes him as the scion of 'an aristocratic family', who was regarded as a black sheep and was paid a retainer to keep away from the family home. Fletcher himself left few clues about his background.

The application form that he submitted in 1912 to become a member of the Institution of Mechanical Engineers in London, states that Frederick Charles Fletcher was born on 7 November 1880 in Birmingham, and that he was educated at Parmiter's public school and at Mansfield College, Oxford. But Mansfield College has no record of a Frederick Fletcher having ever studied there. In his application, Fletcher states that he had worked as an apprentice for an iron works, as a draughtsman, and for a short while as an engineer for the London Underground railway. In 1909 he travelled to Ceylon to take up a job with the Colombo Engineering Company, remaining in the country for two years before returning to Britain to work as a design engineer for the British American Tobacco Company. Fletcher had apparently developed an interest in Buddhism as a student after reading Edwin Arnold's *The Light of Asia* and the works of Madame Blavatsky, and his time in Ceylon would have afforded him ample opportunity to witness Buddhist practice at first hand.

At the outset of the First World War, Fletcher enlisted in the Royal Engineers. He was 33 years old. He would later maintain that he rose to the rank of major; other evidence suggests he was the lower rank of sergeant major. He fought in the battles of Ypres and Mons and was awarded the Victory Medal and Star, and the Mons Ribbon. For Fletcher, witnessing the industrialised slaughter of trench warfare sowed an abiding disenchantment with the modern world, and strengthened his conviction that Buddhism was the one true path to sanity.

In 1922, he joined an expedition to Tibet, called the British Buddhist Mission, which had been organised under the aegis of the British Buddhist Association. While the occasional Western explorer and adventurer had penetrated Tibet, and in 1904 the military expedition of Sir Francis Younghusband had reached as far as Lhasa, the country retained its mythical allure as the font of mystery and wisdom, only exacerbated by its remoteness and its traditional antipathy to outsiders.

Despite its name, the British Buddhist Mission to Tibet did not appear to have been conceived out of any particularly strong religious enthusiasm. Its leader, George Knight, was not even a Buddhist. He was a journalist and a member of the Royal Botanic Society, whose interest in Tibet was primarily botanical—and commercial. Travelling on a London bus, Knight had picked up a trade journal left by another passenger and lighted on a paragraph about the 'splendid opportunity' that awaited anybody who could secure the first motion pictures of Lhasa, 'the Forbidden City of Tibet'. 'From that moment,' he wrote later, 'the idea haunted us, and we set about thinking very hard, a thing we are quite unaccustomed to do.'[9]

Knight conceived an expedition that would penetrate to the very heart of Tibet and make a record of its people, its customs and religious traditions, and, in particular, that would meet and, if possible, film the fabled Dalai Lama himself. Knight began to assemble a team to carry out his plan. Captain John Ellam was an author and journalist, one of the founding members of the British Buddhist Society in 1907 and its honorary secretary; the following year he had accompanied Allan Bennett—Ananda Metteyya—on his public engagements during his 'mission' to Britain. During the Great War, Ellam had served with distinction in France and Flanders with the Manchester Regiment; he would assume responsibility for the study of the political and religious institutions of Tibet encountered on the expedition.

The third member of the party, William McGovern, was an American anthropologist and adventurer who had studied Buddhism in Japan, where he had graduated as a Doctor of Divinity at the Buddhist monastery of Nishi Honganji in Kyoto, before going on to study at the Sorbonne and Oxford. He has been cited as the inspiration for the fictional adventurer Indiana Jones. McGovern's granddaughter Elizabeth would achieve her own renown as an actress, playing the role of Lady Cora in the popular television series *Downton Abbey*.

McGovern had only been recruited to the expedition at the last minute in the belief that his knowledge of the Tibetan language and customs would prove useful. The party was completed by William Harcourt, its youngest member and the expedition's cinematographer, and Frederick Fletcher, who was listed as 'Geologist and transport officer'.

It was planned that the expedition should begin in Darjeeling, and enter Tibet through the small semi-independent state of Sikkim.

As a result of the Younghusband expedition in 1903–4, the British government had secured permission from the Tibetan government to establish trading stations in Tibet at Yatung, just across the border from Sikkim, and at Gyantse, 150 miles into the Tibetan interior, to which specially approved persons might travel along a designated route. But travellers wishing to penetrate further into the country and to reach Lhasa required special permission from the Tibetan government. In London, the Buddhist Mission secured the permission of the India Office to proceed as far as Gyantse, on the understanding that they would not proceed any further without the consent of the Indian and Tibetan governments.

A photograph taken on 14 July 1922 shows Fletcher, McGovern, Harcourt and Knight at Liverpool Street railway station preparing to embark on their epic adventure. They are dressed in the customary formality of the age, in overcoats, suits and ties and sturdy brogues, as if on an excursion to nowhere more inclement than Bournemouth. (Two years later the British mountaineer George Mallory would make his ill-fated ascent of Everest dressed in gaberdine and hobnail boots, sustained by cake from Fortnum & Mason.) Fletcher stands awkwardly facing the camera, a trilby hat pulled down low over his brow, with deep-set eyes and a facial expression that looks almost quizzical.

In his steamer trunk, Captain Ellam carried a silver urn containing an elaborate scroll, bearing fraternal greetings to the Dalai Lama: 'We come to your wonderful country of Tibet as Messengers of Peace, strong in the belief that Your Holiness, Your Ministers and Your People would receive us, reciprocating the sentiments of warm friendship and esteem from the Country which we represent.' Ellam would never be given the opportunity to present the scroll personally.

After landing in Calcutta, the expedition made its way to Darjeeling—a town, Knight noted, that thronged with a polyglot variety of Tibetans, Nepalese, Bhutanese and Mechis, 'happy-go-lucky' types who 'make excellent servants on the whole'. McGovern, impatient to make progress, pressed on ahead with his own team of bearers, crossing the border into Yatung. The remainder of the party followed at a slower pace. Their journey was not without incident. The cine-camera was damaged after one of their bearers dropped it on the head of another bearer during a drunken argument. Crossing a particularly treacherous mountain pass, a mule carrying a considerable quantity of foodstuffs and clothing disappeared over a precipice, and Fletcher almost followed suit, only just reining in his mule in time, addressing it, as Knight observed, 'in terms that only Sergeant-Majors know how'.[10]

Eventually arriving at Yatung, they met Major F. M. Bailey, the British Political Officer, who was responsible for maintaining Britain's diplomatic interests in the region, not least the fragile relations with the government of Tibet. Bailey, who was based in Gangtok, had made several journeys into Tibet, including reaching Lhasa with the Younghusband expedition.

Knight noted that Bailey was 'a most charming host'—but privately the Political Officer formed a dim view of the expedition and its members. On learning that they hoped to make money by selling the film taken in Tibet, Bailey filed a disobliging report to the Foreign and Political Department in Simla, claiming that the group, and George Knight in particular, 'show very clearly the cloven hoof of commercialism'.

McGovern and Ellam, he wrote, were 'genuine'. Harcourt was not a Buddhist: 'He is really nothing but a cinema operator.' Knight was also a Buddhist, but 'is, I am convinced only out to make money from the cinema films'.[11] Frederick Fletcher was dismissed almost as an afterthought: 'He seems to be of little importance to the Mission', Bailey wrote.

Bailey left Yatung shortly afterwards, but not before laying down firm conditions for the expedition. He insisted they should not depart from the main route to Gyantse and extracted a solemn promise from each of them that in the event of the Tibetans refusing them permission to go further, they would return directly to India. He further insisted that even if the expedition received permission to proceed to Lhasa the 'cinematograph camera' would be left behind in Gyantse. Each member solemnly signed the guarantee.

Sticking obediently to the route designated by the government of India, the group pressed on. In the town of Phari they were greeted by the Jong-pon, or governor of the district, who demanded tribute from the party. He was given cartons of cigarettes (smoking being strictly forbidden in Tibet), tea, sugar, a hatchet and a medicine chest. Still not satisfied, he pressed his guests for more. Delving deeper into their provisions, the group produced a gramophone and records, a Kodak camera, a pair of opera glasses and a pair of silk stockings as a gift for one of the Jong-pon's wives, and a silk jumper for another. Knight would describe him as 'one of the greediest men it has been our great misfortune to meet'.[12]

In Phari, Knight noted, 'the filth of ages' had been allowed to accumulate on the pathways to a degree that the roofs of the houses were almost on a level with the street: 'Pharians have to enter their dwellings by a passage cut through the layer of garbage to their doors.'[13] Tibetans were not in the habit of washing. A minor diplomatic incident threatened when the party made a gift of a powder-puff to a local lady, with the suggestion that it would be more efficacious if she washed the thickly engrained grime from her face before applying it. 'Were we not aware that when one loses one's dirt in Tibet, self-respect and virtue go with it?' he observed. Tibet, Knight concluded, was a land of dubious hygiene ('Hundreds of Tibetans pass through this "vale of tears" without indulging in cutaneous ablution'), appalling poverty and rampant disease, where peasants believed that the world terminated at the edge of the mountains and that the sun was made of yak dung. Yet the people were resolute, industrious and immensely hospitable (the Jong-pon notwithstanding).

On the plain above Phari the party encountered a yogi, dressed in a simple loincloth. Knight was told that the man had lived in the hollow of a mountain for over twenty years, a vantage point from where 'he could look down upon the world, and commiserate with long-suffering humanity, for whom he had feelings of the deepest pity'. 'Favoured by gods and spirits', the yogi could reputedly manifest supernormal powers at will. He could turn lightning from its path, float in the air, walk on water and shoot flames of fire from his body, and had no need of food and water. The party was invited to observe him closely. 'With a few peculiar movements of the body, the yogi disappeared in a very mysterious manner', Knight observed:

> We could not vouch for any feat in levitation, but he certainly did disappear on a piece of level ground with no obstacles within fifty feet of the observer. No trace of the yogin could be found. Then suddenly, out of the ground as it were, he re-appeared. We asked how it was done, and received the reply that we should have to re-incarnate ten thousand times before we could make such an approach to excellence in things spiritual![14]

Notwithstanding this seemingly miraculous display, Knight was singularly unimpressed by Tibetan religious practices and what he described as the 'rather depressing system of Lamaism', although one suspects he was not a particularly vigilant observer: he could, quite correctly, find no common dogma with Christianity, but nevertheless managed to note some resemblances of 'ritualistic details, such as the cross, the mitre, choir singing, benedictions, celibacy, [and] spiritual retreats'. Quite how the cross had arrived in Tibetan religious ritual, Knight failed to explain. The 'great tragedy of Tibet', he concluded, was its isolation from the rest of the world. 'This isolation bred in the people and their rulers a conservatism that is almost incapable of uprooting. All the evils of a mediaeval priest craft are everywhere obvious in Tibet.'[15]

In October the Mission finally reached Gyantse. There they were held for more than a month, awaiting permission from the Tibetan authorities to proceed further into the interior. Eventually, word came back. Permission was denied, on the grounds that 'other foreigners may ask for permission to come to Lhasa'.

Major Bailey would later file a report to the Foreign and Political Department of the Indian government stating that 'the Tibetans were very unfavourably impressed by the Mission. They quarreled among themselves at Gyantse and the Tibetans were surprised at their ignorance of Buddhism.'[16] Ellam, however, would attribute the rejection to political infighting in the Tibetan government. While the Dalai Lama was minded to welcome the Mission, he wrote, 'reactionaries' within the Tibetan government who wished to keep the country closed to the outside world had prevailed against him. Ellam took it as an insult: 'The action of the Tibetan Government in refusing to receive the Mission which ... carried with it undeniable credentials, would seem to indicate that Tibet has treated the whole Buddhist World outside her borders with contempt.'[17]

Thwarted, the members of the Mission were now obliged to return to Darjeeling. According to McGovern's account, Knight, Fletcher and Harcourt 'immediately returned to India by the same way by which we had come'.[18] McGovern and Ellam remained in Gyantse pleading to be allowed to proceed. When their appeals fell on deaf ears, they too returned to Darjeeling.

Reasoning that he was now freed from his promise to Bailey, McGovern determined to enter Tibet in secret. Hiring a group of porters, he disguised himself as a coolie, dying his hair and staining his skin with iodine and walnut juice. Then, posing as the servant of his Sikkimese headman, he set off for Lhasa. After an arduous journey in freezing temperatures, living on a diet of raw dried meat and barley flour, and during which he contracted dysentery, McGovern finally reached Lhasa, weak and emaciated, on 15 February 1923, where he sought refuge in the house of the Sikkimese postmaster named Sonam.

He would later write a vivid account of his journey in the book *To Lhasa in Disguise: A Secret Expedition through Mysterious Tibet* (1924). In this, he described the harrowing ordeal of his trek to Lhasa, and how on arrival he had narrowly escaped death when a mob, angry at the presence of a foreign intruder, had besieged the house of the postmaster. Donning a disguise, McGovern had actually slipped out of the house and joined the mob. 'Not to be outdone by the others,' he wrote, 'I occasionally let out a yell myself, and to make things very realistic picked up a small stone and threw it at my own window.'[19]

By his own account, McGovern befriended Tsarong Shape, the commander of the Tibetan Army and the Dalai Lama's 'favourite minister', and through him was introduced to the Prime Minister and then accorded the extraordinary privilege of a secret meeting with the Dalai Lama himself, before eventually leaving Lhasa.

McGovern's book was serialised in eleven parts in *The Daily Telegraph* between September and November 1923, before its book publication the following year. It would become one of the classic stories of an adventurer in the 'Forbidden Land' and add immeasurably to the popular idea of exotic Tibet. But was it the full and unexpurgated truth?

In July 1924, Major Bailey paid his own visit to Lhasa. Apparently still smarting at McGovern having gone behind his back, he made enquiries about the American's sojourn in the city. In a subsequent letter to the India Office, he wrote that both Tsarong Shape and the Tibetan Prime Minister had denied ever meeting McGovern, and had 'ridiculed the idea' that the American had met the Dalai Lama, stating that it would be 'impossible for anybody to approach the Dalai Lama without the knowledge of at least fifty court officials and servants and that such a thing could not be done secretly'. Bailey had also spoken with 'the Telegraph Master' Sonam, whose house McGovern had stayed in. Sonam told Bailey that his house had not in fact come under siege, as McGovern had claimed, and reiterated that to his knowledge McGovern had not met the Dalai Lama nor anyone else of importance. Bailey concluded:

> From the above enquiries I am forced to the conclusion that Dr McGovern was ignored by the Tibetans and that his account of his stay in Lhasa bears little relation to the truth and that his object in writing as he did was to obtain money by a sensational story.

Bailey drove a final nail into McGovern's story, stating that the Dalai Lama himself had denied ever meeting the American adventurer: 'He said that Dr McGovern did not even ask for an audience.'[20] Bailey's report was never made public, and McGovern's tale of his hair-raising adventures was allowed to burnish his legend thereafter.

But what of Frederick Fletcher? According to Bailey's reports, Fletcher dutifully returned from Gyantse to Darjeeling with the rest of the Mission. However, an account that Fletcher gave to an Australian newspaper some twenty years later tells a different story. By this account, Fletcher—having either remained in Tibet, or returned there under his own steam—made his way to the town of Shigatse. There, he claimed, he entered Tashilhunpo monastery—the seat of the Panchen Lama—where he lived for a year, becoming the first Westerner ever to be ordained as a Gelugpa monk. According to Fletcher, when rioting broke out in the city, he was urged by his fellow monks to flee. Dressed only in his robes, and carrying nothing but a begging bowl, he trekked for 400 miles across high mountain passes to finally arrive in Darjeeling.

It is an incredible story—and not an altogether plausible one. William McGovern was the only member of the Buddhist Mission to speak any Tibetan, and it is hard to imagine how Fletcher could have made his way singlehandedly to Tashilhunpo and then persuaded the monastic authorities to accept him as a monk, let alone acquiring the position of a lama. While the account of trekking across the cold and dangerous mountains, dressed only in robes and with nothing but a begging bowl, beggars nothing so much as belief.

By Fletcher's account, having returned from Tibet he remained in India, travelling through the country, living for some months with the digambar sadhus, until finally arriving in Ceylon. Here he took ordination as a Theravadin monk, taking the name Bhikku Prajnananda. In 1925, he travelled to Burma, where he established a small ashram in Rangoon that he called the English monastery.

At some point in these travels, the austerities and deprivations of the renunciate's life apparently began to take their toll. When a relative made an offer of an office job in London, Fletcher accepted—entering, as he would later put it, 'once again the sordid commercial world'. 'For a month,' he later wrote, 'I struggled with ledgers and invoices, lived the drab suburban existence, and saw the hollowness, cruelty and madness of modern civilization. At the end of that time I said: "I'm going back to the Homeless Life again."'[21]

He returned to Ceylon, and then travelled through India making pilgrimages to important Buddhist sites. In articles for the journal of the British Buddhist Society, *Buddhism in England*, he wrote vividly of one pilgrimage to Bodh Gaya, 'taking with me only a blanket, my begging bowl and a razor', where he spent three weeks in prayer and contemplation

seated under the Bodhi tree, where the Buddha attained enlightenment.
He described how

> Buddhagaya produces some remarkable mental effect. Memory and
> perception become more acute, and the solution of problems that had
> long perplexed me now became clearer.
>
> I remember sitting under the tree early one beautiful morning when I
> thought of a similar morning some years before when we were 'over the
> top' at Ypres, and I saw some of the glorious youth of Europe perish in an
> avalanche of fire and steel. There, and here. Memories too sad for tears.[22]

The life of a bhikku, he suggested, would not suit everyone: 'When the
aspirant dons the Yellow Robe he becomes a homeless beggar without
money or possessions. In the burning sun or pouring rain he must beg
his food from house to house, eat his one daily meal before noon, and
live apart from the world.' Such a life was particularly difficult for a
European. While some monks were 'very kind and spiritual men', others
were definitely not, 'and it is often with this latter kind that he has to live'.

Monasteries were frequently dirty and infested with insects. There
was officialdom to contend with, opposition from Christian missionaries,
an enervating climate and unsuitable food, as well as the difficulty of
observing the 227 Rules of the bhikku. But it was a life, he wrote, that he
would not exchange for any other:

> So once more the high road, Yellow Robe, and shaven head, the earth for
> bed, the sky for home, the beggar's bowl for food, as even as our Lord
> carried it. This is Life, Freedom, Rapture. The true Bhikku owns nothing
> yet possesses everything; the beggar becomes the royal Prince, a Saviour,
> helping all suffering life to reach the final Peace.
>
> As the little Mahayana hymn says —
>
>> 'When I went forth from home to homelessness
>> Neither comfort nor rest did I expect to find.
>> But the hope that I one day a Buddha may be
>> And men and Gods convey across Samsara's sea.'[23]

* * *

Throughout his time in India, Fletcher had continued to correspond with
his old friend Paul Brunton. And it is likely that he stayed with Brunton and
his family on his short-lived return to England, during his abortive attempt
to resume civilian life. Brunton's son Kenneth Hurst records that 'Bud'
was at one time a guest in the Brunton home until Brunton's wife, Karen,

apparently distressed by Bud's barrack-room language (to be expected in a former sergeant major, perhaps, but an unusual characteristic for a Buddhist monk), asked him to leave.

Having failed firstly as a bookseller and then as a publisher, and struggling to make ends meet by writing reviews and articles on psychic and occult matters, Brunton could not fail to have thought longingly about his friend's adventures in the world's largest emporium of supernatural mysteries—India. Freed of any domestic or professional ties, in 1930, a year before the publication *Are You Upward Bound*, he booked a passage for Bombay and set off on the journey that would result in his book *A Search in Secret India* (1934).

Written in the florid, purple-hued style of a Victorian adventure novel, *A Search in Secret India* is an account of Brunton's journey across the subcontinent in search of yogis and swamis. From the outset Brunton adopts two poses for his readers. In one, he characterises himself as the enquiring but sceptical journalist, 'trained ... to become ruthlessly critical in separating wheat from chaff', and determined to establish the 'real facts' about the sages and miracle workers of India—'even if they are to be facts of a strange, uncommon kind'. In the other, he is a masterful storyteller, exciting the reader's curiosity in strange tales of sages, adepts and miracle workers—spiritual supermen who, as he writes, 'struggle to wrest from Nature a mastery over forces invisible and intangible'.[24] Brunton's claims to clairvoyance and his childhood mystical experiences are not mentioned. Nor is his Samuel Smiles 'success' journalism.

*A Search in Secret India* begins in London, in a bookshop specialising in 'rare and recondite subjects' (we can assume Brunton had his friend Michael Houghton's Atlantis bookshop in mind) where the author encounters a mysterious Indian wearing 'a magnificent turban, the front of which is adorned with a sparkling jewel', who fills his head with stories of Oriental sages and miracle workers—'my friend, they know, they *know*'— and tells him that his destiny lies in the East. This introduction bears an uncanny resemblance to the beginning of one of Brunton's formative books, Bulwer-Lytton's *Zanoni*, in which the narrator enters a bookshop in Covent Garden—no ordinary bookshop, but 'the most notable collection, ever amassed by an enthusiast, of the works of alchemist, cabalist, and astrologer'—and meets a mysterious stranger who sets him on the path to the hermetic wisdom of the Rosicrucians.

In Brunton's case, duly enthralled by his chance meeting, he sets sail for India. No sooner has he stepped off the boat in Bombay than he is encountering yet another mysterious figure, an Egyptian magician, Mahmoud Bey, whose ability to apparently read his mind leaves Brunton speechless. Serendipitous meetings, a magical mind-reader ... the reader is left in no doubt that Brunton has a distinct predisposition to signs and wonders. The veneer of journalistic scepticism is only skin-deep. Schooled in the esotericism of Blavatsky and Leadbeater, with their stories of ascended Masters and journeys on the astral plane, Brunton was on the hunt, above all, for supernatural experience. It was with this expectation that in November 1930, within a few days of arriving in Bombay, Brunton set off to meet his first authentic Indian holy man.

\* \* \*

Meher Baba is one of the most extraordinary religious figures of the twentieth century, yet in the West he is probably best known—if at all—as the guru of The Who guitarist and songwriter Pete Townshend, several of whose songs, including the pop-opera about the 'deaf, dumb and blind boy' Tommy, were inspired by Meher's teachings. Oddly, probably the guru's most widespread legacy was his motto, which has appeared on a million gift cards and provided the title for a popular song by the jazz singer Bobby McFerrin: 'Don't Worry, Be Happy'.

Meher Baba was born Merwan Sheriar Irani in Poona, India, in 1894.[25] As a young man, his father, Sheriar, had roamed Persia as a dervish, before coming to India in search of work and then again following the life of a renunciate, travelling the country for ten years with only a robe, staff and begging bowl. Failing to find the spiritual enlightenment he had been seeking, under pressure from his family he took a wife. Sheriar was thirty-four, his new wife fourteen.

Meher was the second of six children. He was a happy child, noted for his gentle, unselfish nature, whose favourite haunts were the Muslim burial grounds and the Parsi 'tower of silence' where the dead would be brought to be devoured by vultures, and where, it is said, the young boy would often sit for hours alone. He attended a Roman Catholic high school and at the age of seventeen was enrolled at Deccan College—where thirty years earlier Edwin Arnold had served as Principal—where Meher's main interests were literature and poetry. He also loved to sing.

Up to this point—his predilection for burial grounds aside—there seems to be nothing to indicate that Meher was any different from any other young boy. But at the age of eighteen his life underwent a radical change.

Cycling home one day, he noticed an old woman sitting under a neem tree who beckoned him over to her. She was Hazrat Babajan, a Muslim woman who since childhood had dedicated her life to meditation and prayer, and who at the time of their meeting had been seated under the neem tree for some five years, in all weathers, the recipient of prayers from those who believed her to be a saint and insults from those who thought her mad. 'I was drawn to her,' Meher would later recall, 'as steel to a magnet.'

He continued to visit her each night, for the most part simply sitting with her in silence. One night, after six months of this, something remarkable occurred. At the end of his visit, Babajan kissed Meher on his forehead. Returning home, he went straight to bed. But after ten minutes he began to experience profound sensations of joy and pain, like an electric shock passing through his body, until losing consciousness altogether. The next morning, his mother found him lying in bed with wide-open, vacant eyes, and unable to speak. For three days, he lay in this condition without moving, before finally appearing to recover some consciousness and movement.

Over the next nine months he behaved as if in a dream. If he sat, he would remain in the same position for hours, seemingly unable to move; if he walked, he would do so for hours without stopping. Doctors were consulted. He was given morphine injections and sleeping draughts, to no effect. Eventually, he began to regain some semblance of normal consciousness, albeit behaving, it was said, 'like an automaton possessing intuition'.[26]

His education had been abandoned and he resisted his parents' exhortations to find work, and in 1915 Meher began to lead the life of a wandering mendicant. At length he came to the village of Shirdi, where he met the Muslim ascetic Sai Baba. Sai lived in the grounds of a mosque, begging for food and oil to keep a lamp burning there at all times. He drew thousands to his discourses, and in time would become one of the most revered of all Indian saints.

When Meher prostrated himself in front of Sai Baba, the ascetic is said to have acknowledged him with the word 'Parvardigar'—'God-Almighty-Sustainer'. On Sai Baba's instruction, Meher made his way to Sai's most famous disciple, a Hindu swami named Upasani Maharaj, who according to legend had been brought to God-consciousness by Sai Baba, and then settled in a place called Sakori, where he built a temple, open to all religions and castes.

Even by the eccentric standards of the guru, Upasani acted oddly. When Meher came to him for the first time, Upasani greeted him by throwing a stone, which struck him with some force on the head. Meher, it is said, recognised instantly that this was not an act of aggression, but intended to bring him to a state of self-realisation as 'the Ancient One'. He remained with Upasani for two days before returning to Poona, where he resumed his practice of visiting Babajan each night and spending time at the Parsi tower of silence, where he would sit banging his forehead against the stones, wrapping his head in a handkerchief to conceal the bruises from his worried parents.

Bowing to their demands, he also took on work doing several odd jobs. Eventually, with his friend Behramji, who would become his first disciple, he opened a shop selling toddy, or palm alcohol, although he would frequently urge his poor customers to drink less or to abstain altogether, and the business eventually closed. Meher, we are told, showed a strong desire to do the lowliest work he could find—almost as if to deliberately abase himself. One day in 1920 he shut himself up in an attic belonging to Behramji, with a bucket of refuse that he had got from a street-sweeper. He remained there for thirty-six hours, finally emerging smeared from head to toe in filth. Behramji took it upon himself to clean up his friend.[27]

In July 1921 Meher returned to Upasani Maharaj at Sakori. Each day, he and Upasani would spend several hours together, when nobody else was allowed to approach them. After six months, Upasani summoned his disciples and told them: 'I have given my charge to Meherwanji [Meher]. He is the holder of the key.' To Meher himself he added: 'Meherwanji, you are *adi-shakti* (primal power); you are Avatar.'[28]

With Upasani Maharaj's benediction, and now believing himself a Perfect Master, the 27-year-old Meher returned to Poona, where he established a small ashram. Followers of all religions—Hindu, Muslim and Parsi—began to gather around him, and he became known as Meher Baba.

His new disciples were given strict instructions that he demanded they follow without question. They were required to rise at 4am, to take a cold bath between 4 and 5am, and to retire at 9pm. They were to abstain from intoxicants and sexual intercourse. And under no circumstances, 'except when ordered', was any member of the group to leave Baba, 'even if the whole world turns against him'.[29] If any orders were intentionally broken, he threatened, he would lock himself in his room for a number of days without food. Whatever demands he made of his followers, he made more of himself, frequently going for long periods without food or rest, and performing the most menial tasks in the ashram. These things, he told his followers, were all part of his spiritual working on the higher planes of cosmic consciousness for the benefit of all humanity.

In 1924, Meher established a larger ashram, which he called Meherabad, on the site of an abandoned military camp at Arangaon, a few miles from the town of Ahmednagar in Maharashtra, 160 miles from Bombay. He opened a school for all the children in the village, regardless of their caste or creed. Beginning with 20 boys, the pupil body quickly grew to 150 boys and girls, the sexes taught separately.

Soon hundreds of people were appearing each weekend for *darshan*— the 'seeing' of the guru. Among them was Meher Baba's first Western follower, an Anglo-Indian named Lewis Charles Nelhams, who arrived at the ashram in June 1924. Nelhams was thirty-five, a Christian who had reputedly been drawn to Meher after praying in a cathedral, when on looking up at an image of Christ he had seen Meher's face before him. Nelhams bent himself to the austerities of ashram life, always the first to volunteer for the heavy work of lifting and carrying. But after only a month he contracted a slight wound on his leg, and a few days later he died.

On 4 June 1925, Meher announced that he would soon be retreating into silence, and on 9 July he spoke for the last time, explaining that his silence was necessary, partly for intensive spiritual working in view of the impending death of his first guru, Hazrat Babajan, and partly because of the wars and disturbances that he said were coming to the world. These warnings of global chaos and war and his own emergence as the world saviour, would become a recurring theme in his pronouncements thereafter.[30]

He would not speak another word before his death forty-four years later. The morning after his announcement, he began communicating with his followers by means of writing on a slate. In 1927 he changed to the method of communicating that he would use for the rest of his life, spelling out his thoughts on an alphabet board. This was the man that Paul Brunton would meet in November 1930.

\* \* \*

Brunton had first heard of Meher Baba from Meredith Starr (real name Herbert Close), the son of a wealthy industrialist, and a minor poet with an interest in the occult, who, like Brunton, was a contributor to *The Occult Review* and to Aleister Crowley's magazine, *Equinox*. Starr was also a member of Crowley's Order of the Silver Star, taking the name *Superna Sequor* ('I follow the gods').

In 1917, Starr married the Honourable Mary Grey, the daughter of the 8th Earl of Stamford—a drunken ne'er-do-well who had ended up living in South Africa and marrying his housekeeper, the daughter of a freed slave, who became the mother of Mary Grey. Starr and his wife Mary moved to Cornwall, settling in the village of Treveal, near St Ives, where they planned to establish an artists' colony. D. H. Lawrence and his wife Frieda had rented a cottage nearby and were introduced to the Starrs. 'There are some herb-eating occultists,' Lawrence wrote to his friend Lady Cynthia Asquith,

> a Meredith Starr and a Lady Mary ditto: she a half-caste, daughter of Earl of Stamford. They fast, or eat nettles: they descend naked into old mine-shafts and there meditate for hours, upon their own transcendent infinitude; they descend on us like a swarm of locusts, and devour all the food on shelf or board: they even gave a concert, and made most dreadful fools of themselves in St. Ives: violent correspondence in the *St Ives Times*.[31]

Starr had first learned of Meher Baba in 1928, when the guru despatched an emissary, Rustom Irani, to England on the curious mission of attempting to find English pupils for his boys' school at Meherabad. With help from Starr, Irani was able to find three children whose poverty-stricken parents were prepared to entrust them to Meher's care; but the India Office refused to grant the necessary permissions to travel. Irani was obliged to return to India without the children. Travelling with him, however, was Meredith Starr, along with his mistress Margaret Ross (the marriage to Lady Mary having hit the rocks) and her sister Esther.

Starr travelled to India in the expectation of remaining permanently, but after six months at Ahmednagar, Meher Baba—apparently finding the occult poet as tiresome as D. H. Lawrence had done—sent him packing, with instructions to spread the word of his work in the West. Following orders, Starr founded a centre for meditation and 'spiritual exercises', which he called 'The Retreat', in the tiny village of East Challacombe, on the edge of Exmoor in North Devon. The Retreat would become a focal point for Meher Baba's first followers in Britain.

Brunton, meanwhile, had also been corresponding with a disciple of Meher's, Khaikhushru Jamshedji Dastur, who edited a newsletter called *The Meher Message* and who wrote the first English-language account of Baba's life. Even before departing for India, Brunton seems to have embraced Meher as his guru. In August 1930, *The Meher Gazette* published a short article by Brunton announcing the founding of the Meher League in Britain, in which he wrote: 'There are only a few of us so far who have placed our complete faith in our beloved master; but there are several people who are becoming interested in Him and His teachings ... We firmly believe that He alone can save the West, or indeed the whole world.'[32]

In October, Brunton wrote to Meher's ashram, giving notice of his arrival: 'It is unnecessary for me to write further how much I have been looking forward to this visit, and what the gracious permission of the Master to stay at the ashram means to me.' On his arrival in Bombay, Brunton was met by two disciples from Meher's ashram. He had also arranged to meet his old friend Frederick Fletcher—Bhikku Prajnananda (a fact that Brunton would curiously omit in *A Search in Secret India*)—and, on 22 November, after journeying by train and car from Bombay, Brunton and the Bhikku arrived at Meherabad.

Meher was in retreat and received his visitor with some reluctance. But when at last Brunton was granted an audience, his high expectations appeared to come crashing down—or, at least, so his account in *A Search in Secret India* seemed to suggest. Meher's eyes, he recounted in the book, were 'unimpressive' and 'do not penetrate me'. His facial expression 'lacks strength', his white robe 'looks ludicrously like an old-fashioned English nightshirt', while the 'soft, silky texture' of his hair 'is remarkably like the hair of a woman'.[33]

And nothing Meher said improved Brunton's opinion. Gesturing for Brunton to stop taking notes, the guru tapped out on his alphabet board the names of Jesus, Buddha, Mohammed and Zoroaster, telling Brunton 'God has given me a mandate', and adding that the time was coming for mankind to be given 'a universal spiritual belief which shall serve all races of people and all countries. In other words, the way is being prepared to enable me to deliver a world-wide message.' The world, he continued, would soon be engulfed in a great war, to be followed by an 'era of unique peace, a time of world tranquility' when racial and communal strife would cease. 'I shall travel widely throughout the world and the nations will be eager to see me. My spiritual message will reach every land, every town, every village even.'

When Brunton expressed some scepticism about the West's readiness to recognise Meher Baba as its saviour, the guru pressed on:

Once I publicly announce myself as a messiah, nothing will be able to withstand my power. I shall openly work miracles in proof of my mission at the same time. Restoring sight to the blind, healing the sick, maimed and crippled, yes, even raising the dead—these things will be child's play to me. I shall work these miracles because through them people will everywhere be forced to believe in me, and then believe in my message.

The interview, Brunton wrote, had 'reached the boundary of common sense' and was 'entering the region of Oriental fantasy'. Meher brought the meeting to an end. But at a second interview Brunton challenged him, 'How do you know that you are a messiah?' Meher, he wrote, 'moves his bushy eyebrows' and dictating from his spelling board responded:

I know! I know it so well. You know that you are a human being, and so I know that I am a messiah! It is my whole life. My bliss never stops. You never mistake yourself for some other person; so I cannot mistake who I am. I have a divine work to do and I will do it.

His task on earth, he added, would last for (a distinctly biblical) thirty-three years, when he would suffer a tragic death. 'My own people, the Parsees, will be responsible for my violent end. But others will continue my work.'[34]

Meher then urged Brunton to 'go to the West as my representative!', assuring him that he would confer 'advanced powers' on him to spread Meher's name 'as that of the coming divine messenger'. 'The world,' Brunton wrote, 'will probably scout me as a madman.' Nothing short of working a series of miracles would convince the West that anyone was a spiritual superman, let alone messiah, 'and … since I cannot perform miracles I cannot undertake the job of being his herald'. 'Some men are born great,' Brunton concluded, 'Some achieve greatness, and others appoint a press agent. Meher seems to favour the latter course.'

The time had come for Brunton to leave the ashram. But Meher urged him to visit him again at his other ashram at Nasik, promising, 'I will give you wonderful spiritual experiences and enable you to know the real truth about me. You will be shown my inner spiritual powers. After that you will have no more doubts.' From Meherabad, Brunton, Fletcher and a disciple of Meher's travelled across southern India, being accommodated by a number of Meher's disciples before arriving at Madras in December, where they were greeted at the Meher Asramam in Saidapet, and where Brunton was welcomed as 'the founder of the Meher League in England'.

If Brunton's encounter with Meher had proved disillusioning, as his account in *A Search in Secret India* would later suggest, he evidently kept his reservations to himself. *The Meher Gazette* noted that 'Bro Raphael Hurst (English journalist) and Bro Bhikkhu Prajnananda (Buddhist monk)— both Baba's ardent disciples', were 'simplicity and sincerity personified'.[35]

On 30 December, Brunton wrote to Meher, saying that the Bhikku had become 'ill and irritable' and was resting while he continued the tour on his own. He had met with the assistant editor of *The Hindu* newspaper, who had shown some interest in meeting Meher. But it was proving hard to get people to commit to making financial donations unless they were already devotees: 'In the West it would naturally be easier for me because I am known there, but here I am a stranger.'[36]

In February 1931, Brunton and the Bhikku, apparently restored to good health, arrived at Meher's Nasik ashram. Brunton seemed to have finally made up his mind about Meher. 'The cold serpents of doubt have firmly coiled themselves around my mind,' he wrote in *A Search in Secret India*, 'and a strong inner feeling tells me that my proposed stay near him will be a waste of time, and that Meher Baba, though a good man and one living an ascetic life, is unfortunately suffering from colossal delusions about his own greatness.'[37]

Perhaps Meher sensed his scepticism, for instead of being given special consideration as he had at Meherabad, Brunton's meetings with the guru were brief, and he was instead brushed off with some diaries of Meher's followers, which Brunton dismissed as having 'clearly been compiled in a spirit of blind faith'. Meher, he concluded, was 'a fallible authority, a man subject to constantly changing moods, and an egotist who demands complete enslavement on the part of his brain-stupefied followers'.[38] Nor, it seemed, were the miracles or 'wonderful spiritual experiences' that Meher had promised forthcoming: 'Nothing unusual happens nor do I see anything unusual happening to the other men.' Brunton left Nasik on 8 February 1931 a disappointed man, his expectation of signs and wonders comprehensively dashed.

C. B. Purdom, an English devotee and biographer of Meher Baba, would later write: 'When the writer, then known as Raphael Hurst, came to see me in London some time after his visit [to India] he said he had no doubt Baba was false, as he, Raphael Hurst, had asked him to perform a miracle but Baba could not.'[39] Brunton returned to England in 1932. But laid low by blackwater fever, a severe form of malaria that he contracted in India, he did not start writing *A Search for Secret India* until 1933. The book was published in 1934. By then, Meher Baba had come to the West.[40]

6

# MEHER BABA COMES TO THE WEST

On 17 July 1931, Meredith Starr received a cable from Meher Baba's ashram: 'Love calls Me to the West,' it read, 'Make preparations.'

Two months later, in the company of two Indian disciples, Ali and Chanji, the guru set sail from Karachi under the name 'M. S. Irani' on the steamship *Rajputana*, en route for Marseilles. Among his fellow passengers was Mohandas Gandhi. The man who as a young barrister in London had shared duties as a committee member of the Vegetarian Society with Edwin Arnold, and who had been inspired by Arnold's translation of the Bhagavad Gita, was now 61 years of age and the leading figure in India's struggle for independence from British rule, whose policy of peaceful 'non-cooperation' had proved an inspiration to millions of Indians.

In 1930, Gandhi led a 240-mile march from his retreat near Ahmedabad to the village of Dandi on the coast of the Arabian Sea, in protest against the British tax and prohibition on the villagers' production of salt from the seawater. The 'salt march', as it became known, had led to mass protests and the arrest of some 80,000 people, including Gandhi himself. Now, released from jail, he was travelling to London to represent the Congress Movement at the Indian Round Table Conference.

Gandhi had received a telegram from Jamshed Mehta, the mayor of Karachi, who had met and been deeply impressed by Meher Baba, suggesting that Gandhi too should meet him. Along with his secretary, Gandhi presented himself at the guru's cabin, intending to stay for just a few minutes. He remained for three hours, during which time he urged Baba to break his silence and 'let the world hear, since I feel within me that you are something great'. Gandhi added that he had visited Baba's mentor, Upasani Maharaj, and been distinctly unimpressed. Upasani, he told Meher, was wearing a piece of rag around his loins which he removed to expose his private parts, saying to Gandhi, 'You may be a great man;

123

what is that to me? Why have you come here?' Gandhi, not surprisingly perhaps, was shocked. When Meher Baba assured him that Upasani was indeed 'a Perfect Master', Gandhi replied: 'No, Baba, I do not understand it at all.'[1]

Gandhi would later meet Meher Baba again in London, at a public meeting in the East End, but he was at pains to stress that he had no interest in Meher as a putative spiritual master for himself: 'I have never felt like being disciple to anybody in a spiritual way, though I am still, and have always been, in search of a Guru, as I hold every seeker of God should be.'[2]

* * *

When Meher Baba arrived in London, Meredith Starr was waiting to greet him. Starr had arranged for Baba to stay at the family home of Kitty Davy, at 32 Russell Road, Kensington. Kitty was a young music teacher who had first learned of Baba when she had visited Starr's Devon retreat with her brother Herbert, hoping that the spartan regime of cold baths, meditation sessions and energetic walks across the moors would help her recover from an attack of pleurisy.

Kitty would later recall that at first sight she was 'a little disappointed' at the slight, moustachioed figure who arrived on the doorstep of her home, dressed in 'a pink turban and white robe with a chinchilla jacket'.[3] But in a private interview later that day, Meher's 'long hair and kindly face and manner' evidently made a deep impression on her. 'My eyes,' she wrote later, 'filled with tears.' Kitty shared her fears with the godman about her brother Herbert, who was soon to depart for China. Baba, displaying his customary facility for telling people what they most wanted to hear, reassured her that it was actually he who was sending Herbert to China for 'His [Baba's] work.'[4]

A friend, Margaret Craske, was also staying at the Davy home. In the middle of the night a tearful Kitty came to her room and shook her awake. When Margaret asked why she was crying, Kitty replied, 'He is so wonderful, so lovely.'[5] This tendency to copious tears on first meeting Meher Baba would prove a marked characteristic of his female devotees in the West.

From London, Meher travelled to Meredith Starr's retreat in Devon, where a small group had gathered to greet him. Among them was Katherine 'Kim' Tolhurst, a student of martial arts, who had initially gone to the retreat at the suggestion of her judo teacher. Tall, strikingly beautiful, and the mother of two children, Tolhurst would later record that her first reaction on meeting Meher Baba at East Challacombe was to cry, 'as I think I had never cried before':

> The tears were streaming down my face. I don't think I was happy—I don't think I was unhappy. Perhaps the tears seemed to wash away all that happened to me in the past, all that I had regretted. I was empty, in a sense, yet filled with lightness and new dawn—fresh life. I felt clean and light. I don't know how long this weeping lasted, I couldn't tell you—it was timeless. Baba dictated on the board, which I heard Chanji interpret, 'She is to stay near me.'
>
> Somebody picked me up. I was put to bed, and fell into a deep slumber. I can't explain what happened.[6]

What was it about Meher Baba that proved so powerfully attractive for these people? Clearly it was not his powers of oratory. Nor did he offer to teach yoga or meditation or any other practical path to self-illumination. He simply said 'follow me'. And they did. What is clear is the powerful, almost hypnotic, effect that he had on those who met him. For Katherine Tolhurst, he seemed to touch some deep, atavistic chord in her childhood. Meher, she wrote,

> was like the Jesus I had known as a child in the paintings depicting him. I felt this tremendous love, this tremendous compassion. Although there was a great deal to criticise in me, and even be stern about (I most certainly had not always been as good or nice a person as I should have been), in his eyes there was nothing but understanding and compassion, and no condemnation at all.[7]

Christmas Humphreys, the Buddhist barrister, who met Baba in London in 1931, was equally smitten. 'He literally radiated love,' Humphreys wrote,

> It was a physical sensation of warmth and I have never experienced anything like it. The effect on visitors varied from garrulous chatter to silence, from halting questions to healing tears. And what fascinated me, who am not an emotional person, is that love was far above the emotional plane, nearer to the divine compassion which is the supreme quality of Mahayana Buddhism at its best.[8]

Charles Purdom was an economist, drama critic and author, who was working as the editor of *Everyman*, a weekly magazine of the arts, politics and culture with a progressive bent, when he first met Meher Baba in London. He would remain a follower until his death in 1965, writing two biographies of Baba—*The Perfect Master: The Early Life of Meher Baba* (1937) and *The God-Man: The Life, Journeys and Work of Meher Baba with an Interpretation of His Silence and Spiritual Teaching* (1964). Purdom wrote in *Everyman* after his first meeting with Baba:

> He has no doctrine; he is living truth. Therefore, it is not what he says that matters. That is why the fact that he does not speak seems of such small consequence. Always it is the power of the realized truth that convinces, not the mere utterance of the truth. I have never before met a man of whom I could say that with such certainty.[9]

Echoing Vivekananda's sentiment, Meher Baba told his followers that in the East it was men who were spiritual, but in the West it was women. Christ, he explained, had turned mankind 'from instinct to reason', but it was now time to turn from reason to intuition, and in 'the feminine incarnation' intuition functions better than it does in a male incarnation.

This was a message that naturally held a strong appeal to those Western women who came into his orbit. Like Vivekananda and Krishnamurti before him, Baba had a particularly bewitching effect on women of a certain age and social background, and it is notable that in the West it was women who constituted his largest and most devoted following.

In the first weeks of his stay in Britain, a group began to gather around him that he would call 'Kim & Co', which was shortened to 'Kimco'. All were middle class or upper middle class, comfortably off, cultured, artistic, on the fringes of bohemia—women of a certain social standing and sensibility, with the time and wherewithal to pursue their spiritual enthusiasms. The group would include Kim Tolhurst, Kitty Davy and her friend Margaret Craske, Mabel Ryan and Delia De Leon. Craske was a ballet dancer who had performed with the Diaghilev Ballets Russes and the Royal Ballet before opening her own studio in London; Mabel Ryan, another dancer, was her partner in the studio.

Delia De Leon was Panamanian, an actress who first met Meher Baba in the unlikely setting of a box at the Coliseum Theatre, where he had been taken to see a production of the musical comedy, *The White Horse Inn*. Seated next to him, De Leon described feeling 'as if someone had taken a hammer and knocked me on the head ... During that week I went about like one in a dream: I was stunned with the wonder of Baba, nothing else existed for me.'[10]

At Meredith Starr's retreat centre, where Meher would remain for ten days, life fell into an established pattern. In the mornings, he would give private interviews. A supplicant would be ushered into a room where he was sitting with one of his Indian disciples, his alphabet board on his knee. He would look at the visitor and smile, but usually ask no questions. He would then touch the visitor on the hand or arm and spell out on his board: 'I like you and will help you.' If the visitor had nothing to say—and many, it seems, were too bemused or overcome to say much, if anything, at all—the interview would be brought to a close. If the supplicant did have a question, the answer would be spelled out on the board. The 'conversation', such as it was, seldom lasted more than a few minutes.

In the afternoons there would be impromptu games of cricket, or long walks across the moor. It was on one of these walks, according to his biographer, Bhau Kalchuri, that the godman revealed to his new followers that for 'the first time in the history of the world' an avatar was 'consecrating the soil of the Western hemisphere by his presence', and that whereas in India his devotees were still referring to him as a Sadguru—a Perfect Master—he was in fact the Messiah, the Christ for whom the world had long been waiting.[11]

The response of those around Meher to this declaration was not recorded. That evening, as on every other, the gathering passed the time listening to music and playing parlour games, interrupted only by Meher occasionally asking one or other of the company on his spelling board: 'Are you happy?'

After ten days in Devon, Meher returned to Kitty Davy's home in London. Over the next two weeks there were excursions to the theatre, the zoo and to musical concerts. In the evenings, Meher sat with his closest disciples in the drawing room, often in silence. 'We lived only in the light and love of his wondrous being,' Kim Tolhurst wrote, 'And the silence was fuller than any music, any poem, any scripture—silence filled with love and light, revealing the true meaning of life. Love made flesh was dwelling among us.'[12]

Meher had been introduced to the recordings of the singer of spirituals, Paul Robeson, and on the last night of his stay, a group gathered in the drawing room including Tolhurst, Kitty Davy and her sister May, Delia De Leon, Margaret Craske, Charles Purdom and Quentin Tod—an American actor, living in England, who had been introduced to Meher by Craske, and who would later become Meher's secretary. The evening passed with the group listening to Robeson's deep, sorrowful voice, and, as was now the customary practice, weeping copiously. 'Baba looked so beautiful and they were so sorrowful at his departure', Kalchuri reported.

The next morning, the godman left for Turkey 'for spiritual reasons'. The atmosphere there, he explained, was 'very bad and the people are leaning more and more toward materialism. It is necessary for me to go there to change this.'[13]

\* \* \*

In November 1931, Meher Baba arrived in New York for his first visit to America. His trip had been arranged by friends of Meredith Starr, the poet Malcolm Schloss and his wife Jean Adriel, who ran the North Node bookshop in New York which specialised in occult and metaphysical titles. Adriel (who had been born Jean Robinson, changing her name for numerological reasons) had arranged accommodation for Meher in a private house in the town of Harmon, a 40-mile drive north of New York city along the Hudson River.

In her 1947 memoir titled *Avatar*, Adriel wrote that meeting Meher Baba for the first time, she found herself rendered incapable of speech: 'I felt that in an inexplicable way He was the reason for my very existence; that I have never really lived until this moment; that He was deeply familiar and precious to me, even as I was no stranger and very dear to Him.'[14] For 'five wonderful minutes' Adriel sat silently with the godman; then he spelled out on his board: 'What are you thinking about?' She recalls in her memoir how

> I could not put my thoughts into words. In truth, they were, I told Baba, too abstract even to recall. He replied: 'You need not try. I know what you were thinking. I know what you thought yesterday, what you will think a year from now.' For a long moment I was speechless. Never before had I encountered such egoless omniscience. Yet I accepted his statement naturally, without question. The force of his pure integrity lay behind it. Then I found my voice: 'Is it because you see things whole—unfettered by time?' He nodded his confirmation. Again, I sat silent for a few moments before replying: 'This seems so familiar, to be sitting here with you like this, Baba. I feel as if I had always done it.' He assured me it was so: 'You've been with me for ages.'

In response, Adriel—following the established pattern—left the room weeping 'purifying tears in which joy and pain strangely mingle; unashamed tears which both humble and exalt one'.[15]

Looked at dispassionately, one might interpret this exchange as further evidence of Meher's skill at telling his followers exactly what they wanted to hear ('You've been with me for ages'). He had a rare facility in his references to their past lives, or their future ones, of paying them the great compliment of appearing to know something about them they didn't know themselves. It was a flattery that most people found hard to resist, and which lent him a peculiar power over them.

Through Adriel, a small coterie of women began to gather around Baba, strikingly similar to the 'Kimco' group in Britain—a group that might have been arranged to reinforce the sceptic's suspicion that spiritual salvation was the sole prerogative of the elite, the educated and the well-to-do. Murshida Ivy Oneita Duce was the wife of James Duce, an American geologist who later became an executive for the Arabian American Oil Company (Aramco). Elizabeth Patterson was from a wealthy Chicago family and, unusually for a woman at the time, worked as an insurance broker on Wall Street. Nadine Tolstoy was the wife of Count Ilya Tolstoy, son of the author Leo. She had studied kriya yoga and meditation with Swami Yogananda, but with apparently unsatisfactory results, so she became disenchanted. She would describe meeting Meher Baba at Harmon in 1931 as 'the fulfillment of a long-awaited meeting, the climax of my life', continuing:

> I saw Christ before me, as He was seated on the couch, in the expression of all His figure and His divinely lit-up face, in His eyes beaming love … I declared as loud as I could: 'Jesus Christ!' with all the solemnity of those great words. Something within me recognized in this dear shape of Meher Baba, the incarnation of Jesus Christ of Nazareth.[16]

Norina Matchabelli was an actress, who at one time had been hailed as 'one of the six great beauties of Europe'. Born Eleanora Gilli in Florence in 1880, the daughter of a wealthy Italian businessman, as a teenager she suffered from a severe case of tuberculosis that required treatment in a Swiss sanatorium. Convalescing at home, she was introduced to the Austrian theatre and film director Max Reinhardt, who, impressed by her ghostly pallor and aura of suffering, cast her in the role of the Madonna in Karl Vollmöller's pantomime-play Das Mirakel (The Miracle; 1911). Matchabelli had never acted or even walked on a stage before, but playing the role, she recounted later, 'I was filled with divine illumination. I understood and became the Madonna. Playing the part cured me of galloping consumption.'[17]

Under the name Maria Carmi, she would go on to perform the role more than a thousand times in Europe and America, as well as featuring in twenty-five silent films. An early marriage to Vollmöller ended in divorce, and in 1917 she married Prince Georges Matchabelli, the first ambassador to Italy of the newly independent state of Georgia. In 1923, following Georgia's annexation by the Soviet Union, the couple moved to America, where the Prince, an amateur chemist, founded the perfume company Prince Matchabelli.

Her years performing the role of the Madonna had instilled in Norina a deep interest in spiritual matters. She studied the writings of the Russian esotericist P. D. Ouspensky, and claimed to have psychic abilities herself. Meeting Meher Baba for the first time at Harmon gave full theatrical vent to her spiritual aspirations. Jean Adriel would describe how 'momentarily blinded by the intensity of radiance that emanated from his person', Matchabelli staggered across the room with the help of one of Baba's Indian disciples and fell to her knees beside him, pleading, 'Take me out of this. Oh, take me away from it all!'[18]

'Oh, how I was weeping!' Matchabelli wrote, 'But I also began to laugh, and the streams running down my cheeks and the outbursts of laughter were one. I was resting my head on Baba's hand, and my whole body was shaken with the terrific sobs of liberation.'[19] Baba, she recounted, looked her in the eyes and then tapped out on his message board, '"I am man and woman and child. I am sexless." He then paused for a while, brought his face nearer to mine, and said: "Have no fear." An incredible joy went through me.'[20]

Baba told Matchabelli that in previous lives she had been his mother twice and his father once. He would later add that she had also been Joseph, the father of Jesus. Prince Georges, who did not share Matchabelli's passion for her new guru, was apparently unimpressed by the news that his wife had once been the father of the World Saviour. The couple divorced in 1933, and following the Prince's death two years later, Norina sold the perfume company named after him for $250,000—an ample amount for her to follow her spiritual enthusiasms in the years to come.

A decade earlier, Krishnamurti had been surrounded by young girls who became known in Theosophical circles as 'the gopis', after the milkmaids reputed to have served Krishna in Hindu mythology. Meher Baba referred to his coterie of female followers as his 'lovers'.[21] All appeared to have accepted the claims of his messiah-hood unquestioningly; most would remain faithful devotees for the rest of their lives.

From Harmon, Meher Baba moved on to Boston and then New York, returning after a few days to Harmon. One night, Meher asked to be driven to Sing-Sing prison, in the nearby town of Ossining. On arrival, the car drove around the prison while Meher gazed up at the walls, blowing kisses. Stopping at the heavily fortified main gate, he tapped out on his board, 'There is a man in this prison who is my agent—an *abdal*. He is doing good work for me. When I speak, I will free him.'[22] Nonplussed, the party drove back to Harmon.

On 5 December 1931, along with Meredith Starr and his two Indian disciples Ali and Chanji, Meher left America for France, en route to India. After landing at Le Havre, the party travelled to Paris. 'Kimco'—Margaret Craske, Delia De Leon, Kim Tolhurst and Kitty Davy—had travelled from England to greet them. Over the next week, there were excursions to the Eiffel Tower, the Louvre, Notre-Dame and to Versailles in a Rolls-Royce. Kim Tolhurst offered a rhapsodic description of the 'lovely, lovely atmosphere' of the Paris sojourn:

> We would curl up his hair and poke it up under his hat before going out. I don't say we didn't revere him; of course, we did. But perfect love does cast out fear and to us, he was just love and somebody we could tease and say, 'Oh, Baba, you look silly in that hat,' and so forth …
>
> It was a love-feast. You were in love. Baba was love and this was all that mattered.[23]

On his last night in Paris, Meher called the women to his room and spelled out a message on his alphabet board: 'I am Life Eternal. I was Krishna, I was Buddha, I was Jesus and I am now Meher Baba.'[24] The next day he left by train for Marseilles with Ali and Chanji and Margaret Craske, who was acting as his French interpreter.

In Marseilles, Craske took Baba to a small church on a hill, overlooking the town, where there was a statue of the Pietà. When Craske wondered aloud whether Baba too would be crucified, he spelt out on his alphabet board, 'It will not happen this time, but I will have mental persecution.' That afternoon, they paid a visit to a cinema where they watched a French-language version of the film *The Big House*, with Craske translating for the guru's benefit. At one point she noticed that he had slumped in his seat and seemed not to be listening. After a while he sat up and spelt out: 'I have been to Vienna.'[25]

Later that evening, Craske set off for London while Baba and his disciples boarded a ship for India. For Kim Tolhurst, the pain of separation was almost intolerable. Her adoration of her guru was beginning to take a toll on her marriage. 'Coming home was extremely hard for me, because one had really been in another world,' she wrote, in a letter to Baba's Indian disciple Chanji,

> It was difficult for me to pick up the threads and do what I had to do, which was to look after my husband and family, and come down to earthly, daily life. But Baba had told me how I must do my duty, and so I tried as best I could. Though it was not easy, I know it was right. I had to stay at home and work through the problems of life.

To console her, Baba cabled a message: 'Trying to please her Lord, poor Mary Magdalene's heart is breaking.'[26]

\* \* \*

Among some of his Indian followers, Meher Baba's interest in the spiritual welfare of privileged, wealthy and, to outward appearances, frivolous Western women was a cause of some bemusement. What exactly was the Sadguru up to? But perhaps there was no finer example of altruism than to seek out the spoiled, the superficial, the privileged and to bring them to God. In India, he once said, he had people's worship; in the West, he had their love.

Meher maintained that it was 'absolutely impossible' for 'an ordinary man' to understand him. His disciples talked of his 'inner work', but the nature of that work was never exactly clear. He travelled extensively, but often to no apparent purpose. He addressed no public meetings—although, admittedly, his vow of silence would have made this difficult. He prescribed no particular techniques or methods. He enjoyed excursions to museums, zoos, notable sights—including, on one occasion in Paris, to the Folies Bergère—but if there was a spiritual purpose to these outings it remained resolutely inscrutable. 'I visit places, see different sights, or go to plays, films, and do a hundred and one other things,' he said, 'but I don't enjoy movies or plays as you do, I make them the medium of my inner spiritual work. My every breath does this work constantly, while outwardly you find me doing nothing special. You cannot grasp the internal mystery.'[27]

In an interview with the journalist and author Rom Landau, Norina Matchabelli offered the explanation that Baba 'acts upon physical things as they actually are. He directs maya.' She provided an example:

> Let's assume that a friend of Baba's is in danger of being drowned in a lake. Baba, though hundreds of miles away, knows of the imminent danger. He

will ask his pupils to bring a basin of water; he will put his hands into it, and by doing it he will influence the water of the lake, thus producing there certain conditions that will save his friend. He always employs equal elements for his actions.

'And you really believe all that?' an obviously stupefied Landau asked. 'Of course, I do', Matchabelli replied. 'She answered with such determination,' Landau wrote, 'that I no longer felt like opposing her with my intellectual criticism. My hostess was, in a way, nothing but Baba's mouthpiece, almost more explicit than Baba himself.'[28]

Matchabelli elaborated on how the godman passed his days. He always rose early, before the rest of the household, took a hot bath and then attended to the important business of his appearance—'No-one can imagine the amount of time spent over the washing, combing and brushing of his beautiful hair.' He would then go from room to room stopping for a while in front of each bed, looking at the sleeping person, and so 'directs in his own way the life of the disciple for the rest of the day'. Days would be spent in interviews, tending to his correspondence and reading newspapers, which served simply as a medium for him, 'directing the daily destinies of the world'.

Actually, Baba did not *read* the papers, Matchabelli went on, 'He just goes over the headlines. But while doing this he places his hands and fingers on the printed words and through such a contact with the print he affects the results of events described in the article.' Nor did he ever read books, 'but he knows everything'. Baba, she continued, 'spiritualizes the world by creating certain spiritual centres in various parts of the world'. These, she explained, 'serve as transmitting stations for Baba's spiritual radiation'. 'I could not have wished for a more perfect source of information,' Landau wrote, 'And it was not for me to decide whether she was suffering from self-delusion or to what extent the admiration of such a fascinating woman had turned Baba's oriental head.'[29]

Meher Baba was to remain in India for barely three months before returning to the West for a second time. Accompanied by six of his Indian disciples, he disembarked in Venice, travelled through Italy and France, and arrived at Dover on 7 April 1932. His first visit had passed virtually unnoticed by the press, but now his arrival in Britain was heralded on the front page of *The Daily Mirror*, alongside news of two other recent arrivals—the industrialist and race-horse owner John 'Lucky' Dewar, and Andrew Mellon, 'one of the richest men in the world' and the new American ambassador to the Court of St James's.[30]

Kitty Davy arranged for Baba to be filmed by the Paramount Company for their weekly newsreel. He was shown seated on a divan, dressed in his white sadra, beside Charles Purdom, who read out the guru's address, which talked of Meher Baba's mission to bring together 'all religions and cults like beads on one string and revitalise them for individual and collective needs'. The clip was shown in cinemas throughout Britain.[31]

Describing him as India's 'Miracle Man', *The Daily Mirror* took a particularly keen interest in Meher Baba's supposed supernatural abilities. '"I can perform miracles if necessary," was one of his communications,' the paper reported, 'But he added that miracles were unimportant and "child's play to anyone who has reached my state of consciousness".'

'He has a gentle, affectionate manner and welcomed me with a graceful inclination,' the paper's 'Special Correspondent' went on, 'His large, lustrous, black eyes, very observant, lit up with a pleasant expression as his thin brown finger moved swiftly across an alphabet board.' Asked if he could raise the dead, Meher reportedly replied 'if necessary', adding that he did not think he would be performing any miracles in Britain, although perhaps in America he would.[32]

*The Mirror* developed a particular fascination for the 'Miracle Man'. Two days later, under the headline 'Baba Wears a Paper Hat', the paper was reporting his attendance at a children's party at the home where he was staying, where 'it seemed strange to see him groping in the bran to emerge holding a toy elephant or a doll's tea set'; and where his Indian disciples provided a recital of 'strange intoxicating music which one of them produced from a multi-stringed sort of banjo fashioned from a gourd' (an early sighting of a sitar in London).[33]

On 13 April, the paper carried yet another report, about a girl suffering from what doctors had described as an incurable condition in which she was unable to speak, and whose father—'the commander of a destroyer'—had appealed to Meher to meet her, in the hope of a miracle cure. One of his disciples, the paper reported, had 'telephoned to *The Daily Mirror* and assured them the girl would be speaking within four months, whether she saw him or not'.[34] Sadly, following a long tradition in newspapers, *The Daily Mirror* did not appear to follow up the story, and the fate of the poor child is lost to history.

In an interview with James Douglas, the editor of *The Sunday Express*, in April, Baba was characteristically cryptic. 'Are you a Mahatma?' Douglas asked. 'What is a Mahatma?' Meher replied, 'I know the truth. You live in London. You know it, I know.'

Nonplussed, Douglas pressed him further, asking, 'Are you divine?' to which Meher replied, 'I am one with God. I live in Him, like Buddha, like Christ, like Krishna. They know Him as I know Him. All men can know him.' When Douglas asked, 'What is your secret or special advice?' Meher replied, 'The elimination of the ego.' He slept for just three hours a night, he continued, 'Sex for me does not exist.' 'He is serenely certain he can redeem mankind,' Douglas concluded, 'I wonder.'[35]

If the overall tone of the press coverage was a mixture of the bemused and the sensationalist, one publication was undisguised in its antagonism. *John Bull* was a periodical that specialised in sensational and scurrilous stories, and in 1932 it published a series of disparaging articles about the man it sardonically referred to as 'the New Messiah'. These repeated a series of allegations that had appeared in Indian newspapers made by K. J. Dastur, the editor of *The Meher Message*, and the man who had served as Paul Brunton's original intermediary with Meher. Dastur had a slightly unhinged devotion to Baba, referring to him as 'His Holiness' and to himself as 'the Disciple of His Divine Majesty'; but, apparently taking umbrage at not being invited to join Baba on his world travels, he had turned against his guru, writing a series of articles attacking him for a variety of misdemeanours, including 'non-fulfillment of various prophesies', 'monkey-tricks practiced upon disciples' and 'throwing disciples as well as outsiders into Maya', by making them work in the Circle Cinema (a movie theatre in which Baba supposedly had an interest and where, according to Dastur, 'vulgar and sensual films' were being exhibited). 'My conscience tells me,' Dastur wrote, 'that Meher Baba is a humbug and a fraud.'[36]

The articles in *John Bull* followed in a similar vein, alleging that Baba accepted exaggerated titles—'His Divine Majesty' [*pace* Dastur] and 'the Blessed Lord'—and revelled in the company of 'beautiful young white girls'. Furthermore, they went on, Baba owned a cinema, a motor garage, used to own a toddy shop (a reference to the business in which he had been involved before his mission) and 'kept hired women companions'.[37]

Meher Baba, at least, was in no doubt who was responsible for the articles. It was Paul Brunton, he told his followers—an 'ignorant man' who had been made 'a fool and a tool' by Dastur. He accepted that 'It is an aspect of my game and I am happy to face this situation. This opposition has been deliberately created by me to give greater force and effect to my work in the West, and to the spiritual earthquake and upheaval that is also to take place.' Dastur, he added, 'loves me, but he is playing Judas' part'.[38]

From London, Meher travelled to Meredith Starr's retreat in Devon. Where his visit the previous year had passed largely unnoticed, the area around Combe Martin was now consumed with a feverish curiosity about his impending arrival. A local newspaper reporter was on hand as Meher made his way down the muddy path to Starr's retreat, wrapped in an overcoat, his hair blowing wildly in the wind, his disciples at his side, and to the accompaniment of the sound of skirling bagpipes played by Starr's brother-in-law:

> The spectacle as the procession neared the farm almost beggared description, being more reminiscent of a biblical scene than of the surroundings of a sleepy Devonshire farm … Never in all the long centuries of its history had East Challacombe farm seen such a strange person enter its portals.[39]

Ever since his arrival in Europe, Meher had dropped tantalising hints that it would be in the West that he would finally break his seven-year silence. 'Avatars,' he explained, 'usually observe a period of silence lasting for several years, breaking it to speak only when they wish to manifest the truth to the entire universe. So, when I speak, I shall manifest the Divine Will, and world-wide transformation of consciousness will take place.'[40] Among his disciples, excitement began to mount when word leaked out that this momentous event would take place in his next destination, America.

On 19 May 1932, Meher arrived in New York on the steam ship *Bremen*, his arrival preceded by a fanfare of hyperbole in the popular press announcing that 'the Messiah of India' had chosen America, 'land of talkies and loudspeakers', to at last speak himself. 'Holy Man of the Hindu Yogis Who Hasn't Spoken A Word For 8 Years [*sic*] and Claims He Can Perform Miracles, Will Try To Start A Colony of Mystics in America', trumpeted a story in *The Milwaukee Sentinel*—a publication more usually concerned with stories of dairy yields and beer sales than with silent Indian mystics. The fact that Meher Baba was neither a Hindu nor a yogi was by the by.

Accompanying the article was a photograph of Meher's head, pasted on a crudely drawn white robe, surrounded by sundry pictures of Indian yogis contorting themselves in a variety of tortuous positions. In fact, in a concession to Western sartorial convention Baba had now dispensed with the sadra in favour of a double-breasted suit, which with his luxuriant hair and moustache made him look less like a Messiah in search of a following than a pavement violinist in search of an orchestra.

The article reflected the mixture of fascination, suspicion, misinformation, scepticism and barely concealed humour with which Indian mysticism in general, and Meher Baba in particular, was generally regarded. The 'self-styled Messiah', it reported, had announced his intention to 'break down all religious factors, destroy American materialism and amalgamate all creeds into a common element of love'. It continued:

> In India a holy man's fame depends largely on how long he can go without eating, or whether he has lived for years without having spoken any words, or can hold himself down on a pole, or remain for many days buried in the ground with only his head showing. Meher Baba can do many of these tricks, and in addition is supposed to be able to perform miracles.
>
> The ignorant simple-minded natives of India are greatly impressed by 'holy men' and it is expected that the credulous-minded in America will also take Meher Baba seriously and chip in liberally when those who are promoting the holy man pass around the hat. But when it comes to performing miracles, men of science or real intelligence will want it to be shown.

Taking note of his 'long silk hair which falls in waves to his shoulders and gives him a very "holy" look' and the alarming fact that 'his eyes beam with a light that is supposed to have a magical effect', the article moved on to describe the various miracles that had supposedly been claimed for Baba. These included stopping a runaway car from hurtling over a precipice by 'touching the side of the auto and lightly snapping his fingers' and conjuring rain clouds on demand after weeks of drought:

> He admitted that he could perform all sorts of miracles because, as he said, anyone who becomes 'one with truth' can accomplish anything. But he was reticent as to which particular miracles he would perform. If Meher Baba undertakes miracles in the United States he will be watched very carefully. He has been advised that not all Americans are easily fooled.

The article continued:

> The Yogis perform no useful, practical service to mankind. If, down through the ages, everybody had been a Yogi, sitting in contemplation of spiritual matters there would have been very little practical progress of mankind; things would be somewhat as they were in cave-man days. Disease, famine and misery would still sweep the world as it did in the

137

earliest ages and as, indeed, it does now in India, which is known as the most backward and unenlightened country in the world.[41]

On 25 May, after a few days staying in Boston, attended by a small coterie of his Indian disciples and several of his inner circle of female 'lovers'—among them Norina Matchabelli and Elizabeth Patterson—Meher Baba left by train, bound for California. It had been announced that on 7 July he would finally break his silence—in Hollywood. What more appropriate place could there be?

\* \* \*

Drawn by its balmy climate, fertile soil and gushing oil, more than 2 million people, from every corner of America and beyond, settled in Southern California between 1920 and 1930—1.27 million in Los Angeles county alone. California was the state of boomers and boosters, lured by the promise of a new life and new freedoms—a utopia that offered fertile ground for religious proselytisers, cranks, self-styled prophets, crackpots and frauds of every denomination and none.

To the author Louis Adamic, writing in the 1920s,

> The people on the top in Los Angeles, the Big Men, are the business men, the Babbits ... the high priests of the Chamber of Commerce whose religion is Climate and Profits. And trailing after the big boys is a mob of lesser fellows, thousands of minor realtors, boomers, promoters, contractors, agents, salesmen, bunko-men, office-holders, lawyers, and preachers—all driven by the same motives of wealth, power, and personal glory ... They exploit the 'come-ons' and one another, envy the big boys, their wives gather in women's clubs, listen to swamis and yogis and English lecturers, join 'love cults' and Coue clubs in Hollywood and Pasadena, and their children jazz and drink and rush around in roadsters.[42]

Los Angeles' abundance of religious eccentrics almost qualified as one of the city's principal characteristics. As early as 1895, the author Mrs Charles Steward Daggett was writing, 'I am told that the millennium has already begun in Pasadena and that even now there are more sanctified cranks to the acre than in any other town in America.'[43] Swami Vivekananda would visit Pasadena four years later in 1899, although it would be another thirty years before his disciple Swami Prabhavananda, who would later attain celebrity as the guru of Christopher Isherwood, arrived in Los Angeles to found the Vedanta Society of Southern California in 1930.

138

One of the most celebrated gurus of the early twentieth century, Paramahansa Yogananda arrived in Los Angeles in 1925 to establish his international centre for the Self-Realization Fellowship, describing the city as 'the Benares of America', supposedly because he sensed something of the same spiritual energy that permeated India's holiest city.[44] In *The Secret Doctrine*, Madame Blavatsky, with her evolutionary taxonomy of 'root races' and sub-races, had talked about California as the cradle of the next civilisation—a prophecy that was taken up by Charles Leadbeater, who talked about the establishment of a colony in Baja, California, in the twenty-eighth century, for the intensive selective breeding of 'the sixth root race'.[45]

But the Hollywood where Meher Baba arrived in June 1932 already had its own gods and goddesses; it was a place where the young, the talented and the beautiful flocked in search of fame, approbation and riches in the movies. As the Great Depression tightened its grip on America, upwards of 60 million Americans each week filled movie theatres across the country to forget their troubles in the dreams spun by Hollywood.

Notwithstanding his claim that he did not enjoy films in the same way as ordinary mortals, Meher Baba loved the cinema. His secretary, Quentin Tod, wrote that it was 'his greatest relaxation' to go to a theatre or movie-house and 'be amused', and in his travels around Europe and America the guru sometimes managed to find the time to visit lunchtime, matinee and evening performances in one day. Fittingly, perhaps, for a man who was bound by a vow of silence, he was particularly fond of the silent-movie comedians Charlie Chaplin and Harold Lloyd.

Meher was fascinated by the power of motion pictures, and the hold they exercised over their audience, and fascinated too with those whom fame had made, on their own terms, gods. He would be the first Indian guru to realise the possibilities of film to influence and to persuade; the first guru to properly understand the power of mass media.

Meher's journey by train across America had provoked much curiosity among the press. There were reporters waiting to interview him when the train stopped at Chicago and at Kansas City, apparently fascinated by the prospect of the guru finally breaking his silence. 'Baba To Give Up His "Uh"' ran a headline in the *Kansas City Evening Star*:

A Few More Months and 7-Year Silence Will End!
– He'll Become a Messiah in Hollywood Then
– And His Fingers Will Get a Rest

The tone was heavily ironic:

> He who has transcended the world illusion and is of God and heaven walked in the flesh today at the Union Station under a depression suit worth probably $15 with an extra pair of pants, and smiled timidly under a mustache the size of Buffalo Bill's and black as the ace of spades.
>
> Shri Sadguru Meher Baba, this Holy One, Perfect Master and Compassionate Father, is on the way to Hollywood, California, to break a seven-year silence and thereby lead all men to happiness and peace. July 13th at 7 o'clock at night, Baba will cease pointing, snapping his fingers and grunting 'uh' to reporters in response to questions. Then he will break forth in the full bloom of his messiahship and through his speech transform the consciousness of the whole of humanity.

Unable to talk with the putative Messiah himself, the reporter was obliged to make do with the ever-attentive Meredith Starr. 'His is the tremendous radiation of divine love,' Starr enthused, 'He is universal, like Jesus, Buddha, Zoroaster and Krishna.' 'Baba,' the report went on, 'is 38 years old, not married, a stranger to sex experience. He has not sat contemplating his navel for years, as have many Indian mystics, but believes in long fasts and silences.'[46]

In a report in the *Los Angeles Times*, a local physician speculated that atrophied vocal cords, from his years of silence, might prevent the mystic from uttering any words at all. But Meher's intimates reassured reporters that the Master 'hemmed' and 'hawed', cleared his throat and otherwise exercised his larynx frequently, so speaking would not be a problem.

On his arrival in Los Angeles, Meher was installed in the home of an astrologer called Marc Jones—a friend of Malcolm Schloss. Norina Matchabelli and Quentin Tod had been calling on their social and professional connections to oil the wheels of the guru's visit. Eager to become acquainted with the new 'Messiah', Hollywood—the place of dreamers, sex sirens, cocaine fiends and self-made tyrants—welcomed him with open arms. Over the next six days he was thrown into a frenetic whirl of studio visits and meetings with actors, directors and writers.

On a conducted tour of the Paramount Studios, he was introduced to Tallulah Bankhead, Charles Laughton and Gary Cooper, who along with Cary Grant were making *Devil and the Deep*, before moving on to the Fox and Universal Studios where the godman met the cowboy actor Tom Mix. That evening a reception was held in his honour at the Hotel Knickerbocker, attended by several hundred people. Seated on a raised dais, with two harpists plucking softly behind him, Meher smiled and shook hands as men, women and children processed past him.

The next day, the party moved on to the Metro-Goldwyn-Mayer (MGM) Studios, where Meher was introduced to Marlene Dietrich and the director Josef von Sternberg, who were making *The Blond Venus*. (Meher liked Sternberg, but did not much care for Dietrich's 'offhand' manner.) That evening, the reigning deities of Hollywood, Douglas Fairbanks and Mary Pickford, hosted a gathering in his honour at their mansion, Pickfair, set on a 56-acre estate in Beverly Hills. Guests included Dietrich, Talullah Bankhead, Charles Laughton, Gary Cooper and his lover, the Countess Dentice di Frasso (née Dorothy Caldwell Taylor). Pickford seated Meher Baba on a velvet sofa and sat at his feet, gazing up at him adoringly as a prepared message was read out to the assembled throng:

> The whole universe and its structure I have created. The universe is my cinema. But just as an audience becomes absorbed in witnessing a drama on the screen, and the film engages their emotions and sways their feelings by its influence, causing them to forget that it is not real—in the same way, the spectators of the world are charmed by this worldly film show, forgetting themselves and taking it to be real.
>
> So I have come to tell them that this worldly cinema in which they are absorbed is not real. I have come to turn their focus toward Reality. Only God is real, and everything else is a mere motion picture![47]

Later, he expounded at greater length on the power of cinema, the responsibility of the movie industry to use it for good rather than ill, and how film might contribute to man realising his true 'divine self'. Love, romance and adventure, he said, were themselves fundamental, and should be portrayed 'as thrillingly, as entertainingly and as inspiringly as possible. The wider the appeal the better.' Even the love that expresses itself through physical desire was good, 'to the extent that it frees one from the thralldom of personal likes and dislikes and makes one want to serve the beloved above all other things'. Real spirituality was best portrayed in stories of 'pure love, of selfless service, of truth realized and applied to the most humble circumstances of our daily lives'. To portray such circumstances on the screen, he concluded, would help people realise that the spiritual life was something to be lived, not simply talked about, and that it 'and it alone will produce the peace and love and harmony which we seek to establish as the constant of our lives'.[48]

141

So enamoured was Meher with what he regarded as the spiritual possibilities of film—and of spreading the word of his own mission— that he instructed his followers to begin work immediately on preparing a motion picture according to his direction. The film, which was to be called 'A Touch of Maya', would be based on a fanciful plot about three characters being reincarnated over several lifetimes, and would include cannibalism, torture and torrid love affairs set in locations ranging from Africa to Persia to China.

Norina Matchabelli's first husband, Karl Vollmöller, was tasked with devising a script. Matchabelli approached another friend, Gabriel Pascal, the Hungarian who would later be known for his film adaptations of George Bernard Shaw's plays, *Major Barbara* and *Pygmalion*, to act as the film's producer. Pascal proposed a new title: 'The Slippers of a Perfect Master'. Thus began one of the longest-running sagas in Hollywood history. The film would never be made.

There is a photograph of Meher Baba and Tallulah Bankhead together on the day that he visited the Paramount Studios. It is clearly posed, yet its subjects appear to be drowning in each other, oblivious to all else. With his lustrous hair and moustache, dressed in an immaculate white, double-breasted suit, the guru looks disconcertingly like a matinee idol. He is gazing deeply into Bankhead's eyes, a smile playing at the corners of his mouth; in his hands he holds his alphabet board; he is pointing—arbitrarily perhaps—to the letter 'M'.

Was Meher aware of Bankhead's reputation as one of the most unabashedly sensual of all the Hollywood actresses, notorious for her predatory sexual appetite for both men and women? (She would later explain that the main reason for her taking the part in *Devil and the Deep* was 'to fuck that divine Gary Cooper!') In the photograph she is returning Baba's gaze in a defiantly flirtatious manner, as if to say that celibacy is vastly over-rated.

Later that same day, Bankhead was given a private interview with Baba. In the course of their talk she mentioned that she was on her way to see her friend Greta Garbo. She would tell Garbo about him and arrange a dinner where they might meet. The prospect galvanised Meher. Of all the stars in Hollywood, Garbo was the most alluring and the most enigmatic, with an appearance that looked as if she had been sculpted from ice, and an aura of unattainability that made her irresistible to both men and women. While Tallulah Bankhead described her mystery as being 'as thick as London fog', Meher Baba told his followers that she was 'the most spiritual' of all the Hollywood stars.

Arrangements had been made for the godman to visit San Francisco, but these were now cancelled to accommodate Bankhead's invitation to dinner. But at the last minute, Garbo telephoned to say she was too unwell to attend. Meher would leave Hollywood without meeting her. But they were yet to play a significant part in each other's lives.

\* \* \*

Among his followers, excitement continued to grow in anticipation of Meher breaking his silence. This momentous event, it was announced, would now take place at the Hollywood Bowl on 13 July, and be broadcast across America over the radio, introduced by Meher's new friend Mary Pickford.

To mark the impending worldwide transformation of consciousness, some of his 'lovers' had been visiting the best couturiers in Hollywood to have special 'God-Realization gowns' made at extravagant cost. But first, Meher announced, it was necessary for him to visit China, where, it seemed, there was work to be done before the great revelation. On 4 June he set sail from Los Angeles for Honolulu. It was from there that his followers received the fateful message: the godman had changed his mind; he would not be breaking his silence after all.

He would later explain his change of heart: 'Did you think I would speak on a definite date in a large hall before a crowd of people? I went into Silence without giving warning and I will speak in the same way— who knows when? But when I speak, the whole world will know and realize who I am!'[49]

It was to be the first in a series of false dawns. There was speculation that Meher would break his silence in London when he visited the following February. But that too did not come to pass. Rather than seeing this as evidence of his fallibility—or his capriciousness—his disciples came to regard the guru's constantly changing mind as a test of their faith. It was the disciple's familiar dilemma; for if the guru is fallible, so it follows, how much more fallible they must be in following him. So it was that the declaration of the ending of silence would be glossed over, and in time forgotten about.

But not all Meher's followers were so sanguine. Relations between Meher and Meredith Starr had become increasingly strained. Meher had grown weary of Starr's proprietorial devotion and his insistence on wanting to be at his side at all times, while for his part, Starr had evidently been growing increasingly disillusioned with his guru. In December 1932, he finally broke with Meher altogether. In a letter written the following year to one of Baba's 'mandali', Starr outlined a series of accusations:

(1) Baba is not a Perfect Master, nor a desirable teacher.

(2) Baba makes promises like an irresponsible child, and it is quite impossible to trust his word. For example, he did not speak in America last July.

(3) He has made all kinds of promises to me and others without attempting to keep them.

(4) According to Western standards, his conduct with women has been extremely undesirable. He deliberately encourages hysteria in women.

(5) He traveled in China with a European boy [Carl Philipp], which gave rise to scandal. He has become the laughingstock of the newspapers. His Western followers are mainly hysterical women; he has practically no appeal to serious men; and frankly, he is regarded in America as an undesirable adventurer.

(6) I have rarely seen a person more restless than Baba.

(7) I have repeatedly seen him flattering the most impossible people, just because he wanted to get money or other help from them ...

To my mind, these are serious personal charges. Baba claims that he intends to do all sorts of wonderful things. In spite of all these journeys, he has done practically nothing and has spent some seven thousand (nearer ten thousand) pounds.

Starr's allegations ended on a plaintive note: 'He owes me four hundred pounds. He has frequently promised to repay it by definite dates, but he has not done so. It was all I had! If you see him, please ask him to repay it.'[50]

Starr went so far as to lodge an official complaint with the English police against Baba, but when an investigating officer met with Margaret Craske, he admitted that they could find no evidence against him. Bitter and disillusioned, Starr closed down his Devon retreat and sold the property. He later organised 'nature cure and scientific relaxation' courses at Frogmore Hall in Hertfordshire, before moving to Cyprus. He died in 1971 at the age of eighty-one.

\* \* \*

Of all the women who became devotees of Meher Baba on his journeys to the West in the 1930s, none was more improbable than Mercedes de Acosta. An exotic ornament to Hollywood, de Acosta was a novelist, poet and playwright, who would attain greater notoriety for her lesbian conquests. She was the lover of, among many others, Isadora Duncan, the actresses Alla Nazimova, Ola Munson and Pola Negri, and the ballet dancer Tamara Karsavina. Isadora Duncan claimed she would 'follow her to the ends of the earth'. For Marlene Dietrich, she was 'mon grand amour'. As Alice B. Toklas observed, 'Say what you will about Mercedes de Acosta, she's had the most important women of the twentieth century.'

De Acosta defied conventional standards of beauty. She affected black silk capes, mannish pants, buckled shoes and tricorn hats. Her chalk-white face, coal-black eyes, blood-red lipstick and short hair, slicked back with brilliantine, prompted Tallulah Bankhead—another of her conquests (or was de Acosta one of Bankhead's?)—to call her 'Countess Dracula'. Yet such were her powers of seduction that she boasted, 'I can get any woman from any man.'

So prolific was her sex life that Truman Capote devised a card game called the International Daisy Chain, similar in principle to six degrees of separation, in which players would try to link people sexually using as few beds as possible. The best card to hold, Capote joked, was de Acosta: 'With one lucky stroke you could get from Cardinal Spellman to the Duchess of Windsor.'[51]

De Acosta was born in New York on 1 March 1893, the youngest of eight children of Ricardo de Acosta, the wealthy executive of a shipping company, who had come to America from Cuba in the 1850s. Mercedes liked to tell the story that her father was a fighter for Cuban independence, who, in a daring escape from a firing squad, had been forced to dive off the ramparts of Morro Castle into the bay of Havana, where he had been picked up by a passing American ship. According to an alternative account, he was a snitch working on behalf of American commercial interests who had to be spirited out of the country when his cover was blown.

De Acosta's mother, an orphaned Spanish heiress, married him when she was just 16 years old. The family combined fabulous wealth—de Acosta grew up in a large family house on 47th Street with Vanderbilts and Roosevelts for neighbours—with a morbidly devout Catholicism. As a child, she would often kneel for hours with her arms extended in the form of a cross and put stones in her shoes and walk until her feet bled.

Physically fragile, and by her own description 'nervously high-strung', from an early age she was afflicted with a curious condition that she called 'moaning sickness', where she would come awake with a sense of 'painful bewilderment' and 'acute fear' that meant she would have to lie still,

145

incapable of movement. Finally pulling herself from her bed, she would then stand in a corner with her face to the wall, moaning loudly. In later life, she came to believe that these attacks were caused by having 'gone so far on the astral plane [during sleep] that it has been hard for me to find my way back, so that when I woke up I was dazed and lost'. She would note: 'I discovered that whenever I discussed mystical or spiritual subjects with someone who understood them, for some days and even weeks afterwards these attacks failed to appear.'[52]

Her state of mind was hardly helped by her mother, who dressed the young Mercedes in boys' clothes and told her that her real name was 'Rafael'. Mercedes' sense of personal disorientation would sometimes induce suicidal feelings—exacerbated, perhaps, by her father killing himself when she was fourteen—setting a pattern of thoughts that would haunt her throughout her life.

As a young woman she acquired a small revolver, ostensibly for self-protection, but at the same time taking comfort from the fact that if life became too much she could always 'pop myself off this baffling planet'. Her sister, Baba, discovered the gun in a drawer, and fearing that Mercedes might use it in a vulnerable moment to kill herself, threw it in the East River.

Her highly strung temperament found its outlet in literature. De Acosta would write three volumes of poetry, a novel and ten plays, although her work never received the success or recognition that she felt it merited. Her friend the Indian dancer Ram Gopal put this down to antagonism by impresarios and producers: 'They did not want to work with a strong woman who loved women. Men found her too overpowering.'[53]

An ardent feminist, a vegetarian and an incorrigible snob, much of de Acosta's time was devoted to frantic socialising in artistic and bohemian circles in America and Europe. Large swathes of her autobiography, *Here Lies the Heart*, published in 1960, read like nothing so much as a social diary as she progresses from one glittering dinner party to the next fashionable opening, scattering famous names like confetti along the way: John Barrymore, Auguste Rodin, Anatole France, Noël Coward, Cecil Beaton, the odd count and prince ... In de Acosta's life there were 'notable people'—artists, poets, the socially connected—and 'little people', who were not notable at all.

But all her artistic enthusiasms and frantic socialising could not alleviate a pervasive feeling of unhappiness and spiritual vacancy. Her first steps on the spiritual path were prompted by a meeting in New York with

Khalil Gibran, the Lebanese writer, painter and philosopher, who pressed upon her a copy of the *Bhagavad Gita*, telling her to come back and see him after she had read it. 'I drank in the words somewhat like a parched camel who suddenly comes upon a spring at which he can quench his thirst', she wrote—in not one of her happiest similes.

On finishing the book, she dutifully rushed back to Gibran, who gave her a copy of the Upanishads and a crash course in Indian philosophy. Her childhood Catholicism melted in an instant: 'By nature I was too sensitive, impressionable and melancholy to have been raised with a religious belief that so emphasizes the agony of suffering and punishment. I need a joyful approach to God and not one that stressed my own morbidity.'[54] Reading the Gita and Upanishads, she wrote, 'it became clear to me that I must identify myself with great saints and mystics of every religion, but never again with any creed. I knew then as I know now that in seeking mystical truth I must look for it, ultimately, only within myself.'[55]

So began a programme of promiscuous spiritual self-improvement. From the great Vedic texts, she moved on to the lives of Ramakrishna and Vivekananda, and the teachings of the Buddha; she plunged into Theosophy, claiming to have achieved what so few were able to do— actually to have read Madame Blavatsky's *The Secret Doctrine* from cover to cover—moving on to Lao Tzu, Meister Eckhart, *The Tibetan Book of the Dead* and 'quantities of other spiritual books'. Mystics, she concluded, were in a sense artists transformed to a higher level:

> Of all the things in life I would like to have been a great poet or a great saint. But there is no 'becoming' either of these. For each of these states one must be born 'in perfection'. They are not unsimilar, because both poet and saint are unable to see the world as it is (if anyone can truly say what it is, or what it is not).[56]

Neither poetry nor the yearning for sainthood, however, could quite pacify her turbulent private life. In 1920 she married Abram Poole, a society painter, but they were to lead largely separate lives. Within a few months of the wedding de Acosta had embarked on a lengthy affair with the actress Eva Le Gallienne, for whom she would write her best-known play, *Jehanne d'Arc*. Their affair would last for five years, until Le Galliene left de Acosta for Alice DeLamar, a Colorado gold mine heiress who had promised to bankroll DeLamar's own theatre company in New York.

In 1931, de Acosta arrived in Hollywood to work as a screenwriter on a film titled 'East River', putatively starring her friend Pola Negri.

The film was never made—a setback that would characterise de Acosta's largely unhappy time in the film colony. De Acosta loathed Hollywood—a place, she wrote, of 'stupidity, vulgarity and bad taste'—and she particularly loathed what she dismissively called 'film people', jumped up arrivistes and philistines, one and all. 'Because of my profession I was forced to go to the studios, but obviously found it distasteful, preferring the company of "artists"', she wrote.[57] Hollywood enjoyed a reputation for libertine hedonism and depravity. But de Acosta would claim that her own life there 'passed as though I were living in a monastery'. This was not quite true.

She became friends with Salka Viertel, the actress and screenwriter who had arrived in Hollywood in 1928 with her husband, the Austrian film director Berthold Viertel. The Viertels were at the centre of Hollywood's European Jewish intelligentsia. They also conducted an open marriage, which allowed Salka to pursue her sapphic enthusiasms. It was at a dinner party hosted by Salka that de Acosta was introduced to the woman who would dominate her thoughts for the rest of her life. 'As we shook hands and she smiled at me I felt that I had known her all my life; in fact, in many previous incarnations', de Acosta wrote. 'I have been looking for you', Greta Garbo said.

An obsession was born. As de Acosta's friend Ram Gopal observed, 'Once Mercedes met Garbo, all she did was dream of Garbo.'[58] But the infatuation was soon to evaporate into prolonged bouts of doubts, recrimination and anguish.

Garbo was every bit as capricious and self-dramatising as de Acosta herself. Like de Acosta, she loathed Hollywood, and filmmaking, which she believed was beneath her. Faddish about diets, she would bore de Acosta with long descriptions of all the food that she was unable to eat. She also had a streak of casual cruelty. De Acosta, who was passionate about all animals, was appalled by her habit of striking a match and burning any insect that she happened to find in the garden or the house. After haranguing Garbo, she was gratified to receive a telephone call late one night from the actress, saying that she had found a spider on her bed and carefully picked it up and put it out of the window. De Acosta congratulated her: 'Now you are learning not to be a murderer.'[59]

Sometimes Garbo would welcome de Acosta avidly with open arms; but increasingly, she turned her away. When de Acosta tried to bring equilibrium to her life by meditating, Garbo dismissed her as 'a crazy mystic Spaniard'. 'I was more tortured within myself during those years than at any other time in my life,' de Acosta later wrote, 'But this suffering taught me much.'

In March 1932, Garbo left Hollywood for a trip to Sweden. In the months she was gone, de Acosta consoled herself by having an affair with Marlene Dietrich, but her obsession with Garbo could not be assuaged.

In a bid to bind Garbo closer to her and to revive her own waning career, de Acosta began work on a screenplay of her stage play *Jehanne d'Arc*, with a view to Garbo playing the lead role. For the nine months that she worked on the script, the characters of Jehanne d'Arc and Garbo became 'inseparable in my consciousness'. Irving Thalberg, the head of MGM, loved the script, but when Thalberg showed it to Garbo, she told him she had no interest in making the film. So intimidated was de Acosta by her inamorata that it seems she never discussed this rejection with her personally.

When Garbo began an affair with Rouben Mamoulian, who had directed her in *Queen Christina* (1933), de Acosta's old feelings of morbidity and depression began to return with a vengeance. On arriving in Hollywood, she had acquired another pistol, which she carried with her everywhere for self-protection. Now, 'as I held it in my hand,' she wrote in her autobiography, 'I felt again the old sense that it was a way of escape.' One day, 'in a morose frame of mind', she went for a drive with a companion, Rose. Approaching a crossroads she turned to Rose and said: 'I wish to God a car would hit us and kill me.'[60] The words had barely left her mouth when another vehicle approached the crossroads at speed, hitting their car. Both de Acosta and her friend survived the crash, but de Acosta was badly injured and spent several weeks in hospital.

It was in this despondent state that one day in December 1934 she received a telephone call from her friend Norina Matchabelli, telling her that there was someone she should meet. De Acosta told her she had no wish to meet anyone, but Matchabelli finally persuaded her to come.

Meher Baba had returned to Hollywood for the principal purpose of hastening the film project about his life. Karl Vollmöller had been struggling fruitlessly to write a script that incorporated all the themes of creation, reincarnation and God-Realisation demanded by Meher. Meetings were being conducted on a daily basis between him and Matchabelli. But Matchabelli persuaded the guru that de Acosta was a soul in torment. She might also have mentioned that de Acosta happened to be a screenwriter.

When de Acosta first set eyes on Meher Baba she was smitten. 'What I felt overwhelmingly was the warmth that radiated from him and seemed to flood the whole room', she wrote. When she asked, 'Who are you?' Meher put his fingers to his lips to indicate that he was unable to speak and tapped out on his alphabet board that he had taken a vow of silence. Again, de Acosta asked, 'Who are you?' He spelled out his answer: 'I am You.' Then, to her evident astonishment, he added: 'Go and bring me your revolver.' De Acosta had told no one that she carried her gun in her car.

Returning with the weapon, she handed it to Meher, who, proving to be surprisingly adept with a firearm, took out the bullets one by one and handed the gun back to her. 'Suicide,' he told her, 'is not the solution. It only entails rebirth with the same problems all over again. The only solution is God Realization—to see God in everything. Then everything is easy. Promise me you will put this revolver away and never again think of suicide.'[61]

De Acosta then raised the subject that was always uppermost in her mind—Greta Garbo. If Meher registered any surprise, or pleasure, at hearing the name of the actress he considered 'the most spiritual' in Hollywood, he evidently showed no sign of it. Instead, he told de Acosta what she most wanted to hear: that she and Garbo had indeed been linked in previous incarnations. 'You both were husband and wife in a past life in Italy. That is why there is such love between you', he told her. Garbo, he went on, 'was a yogi in a previous life and died suddenly. She has latent yogic powers in her in this life, too, but no spiritual elevation. She both suffers and enjoys simultaneously. She will be in the pangs of such agony one day that she may commit suicide.' He proposed that de Acosta should make an introduction: 'She needs my contact. If she sees me, all this will change.'[62]

A few days later, Meher accepted an invitation to tea at de Acosta's house, where once again Garbo was the main topic of conversation. On leaving, Meher instructed his driver to go to Garbo's house, circling it three times. He did not, it seems, feel it necessary to knock on the door and see if she was in.

De Acosta would see Meher Baba several times before he left Hollywood. Inevitably, she had been inveigled into working on the ongoing project of Baba's film, agreeing to write the story continuity in collaboration with another new follower, Garrett Fort, a well-known screenwriter whose previous work on such films as *Dracula*, *Frankenstein* and *The Invisible Man* appeared to make him an improbable candidate for a script that was concerned, as Meher would put it, with the purpose of creation and the spiritual journey.

When the time came for Meher to leave Hollywood, de Acosta presented him with a phonograph. In return, he gave her a handkerchief, instructing her never to give it away. She vowed that she would always sleep with it under her pillow. On his return to London, she called him on the telephone. Bound by his vow of silence he simply cooed at her down the line.

Garbo had once again left for Sweden, leaving de Acosta in a state of desolation. She wrote to Meher, who replied on 31 December 1934, warning her that 'the extreme of agonies' of her present state could 'grow so terrible at times that they may lead to excesses of mad behavior or even insanity'.[63]

The roles of spiritual guide and agony uncle were fast becoming inseparable. On 16 January 1935, Meher wrote to de Acosta again, consoling her over Garbo's refusal to commit to *Jehanne d'Arc*, but leaving her in no doubt about what he regarded as the best remedy for her ongoing emotional *crise*:

> I want you to work for me and in my cause as much and as best you can. That will help your spiritual advancement a great deal, and will, besides, bring you closer to me in love, which you so desire ... As for your apprehension re: Garbo, as I already told you, she will come to the real thing in time, I know, and you needn't at all feel anxious about that anymore. This phase of her life will pass off too—it has to—and then you will find her a changed being—her real self that will express itself beautifully in the story you have written—and the world will see a real Garbo, and a real picture too.[64]

In June 1935, Meher Baba went into retreat at Mount Abu in the Himalayas. For six weeks he stayed in a small, remote cave, in which ascetics and sadhus had meditated for hundreds of years, living mostly on milk brought by his disciples. Yet de Acosta, it seemed, was never far from his thoughts. On 10 July 1935 he wrote to her about her suffering for love:

> I don't want you to be so intensely nervous, despondent and depressed as to give up all hopes and drown yourself in sorrows to feel so miserable ... These difficulties and anxieties in life that one has to face are only apparent and transitory—mere passing phases that throw a temporary gloom and dismal aspect to everything for the time being, but like the clouds they are all carried away by the winds of time, with the beautiful sunshine of happiness and bliss which alone exist behind all this, for ever.[65]

Once again, he encouraged her to continue working on the film about his life and work: 'You will do it as I want you to do it, even in spite of disappointment all around, and in this very disturbed state of mind, and even if Greta has gone away without seeing you.' He urged her to 'Go to Sweden to see her without fail,' adding the significant caveat, 'But at the present moment, my work is more important.'

Despite Garbo's evident coolness towards the idea, de Acosta followed his advice. On 19 October, Baba cabled her at the Grand Hotel in Stockholm: 'Cheer up, Dearest, be brave, am helping you. Love.'

De Acosta spent two days with Garbo, then cabled Meher Baba again to share her news. Perhaps tiring of indulging her romantic dramas, he replied: 'Now that you have seen her, let it cheer you up to go on with the work of writing my story. Thinking and working on MY story would be BEST if you would just try to persevere.' De Acosta left Stockholm on a cloud, believing that she had won back her recalcitrant lover. (Garbo saw things differently. She wrote to Salka Viertel: 'I was a wreck after she went and I told her she must not write to me. We had a sad farewell.'[66])

But doubts were beginning to creep into de Acosta's mind about Meher Baba. Her biographer, Robert Schanke, writes that she came to the conclusion—somewhat belatedly, it seems, given their correspondence—that Meher's constant urging to work on his film suggested that it was his needs rather than hers that were uppermost in his mind. One might also conclude that she was beginning to suspect that the godman was also using her in the hope of making the world's most famous film actress his disciple.

De Acosta was going through a pattern of behaviour as common in guru worship as it is in romantic love—the early infatuation; the heady, all-consuming passion; the gradually dawning disenchantment; and, finally, the search for another object of love and affection. In 1936, a few months after her visit to Stockholm, at a dinner party in Hollywood given by the dress and costume designer Adrian, she was introduced to Paul Brunton, which led to de Acosta reading his *A Search in Secret India*.

'It had a profound influence on me', she wrote. Brunton's scepticism about Meher Baba reinforced de Acosta's own growing disenchantment. But it was his enthusiasm for another guru that he had met on his travels in India that was to change Mercedes de Acosta's life.

# 7

## RAMANA MAHARSHI

Having left Meher Baba's ashram in a state of frustration and disappointment, Paul Brunton and the Bhikku, Frederick Fletcher, continued on their journey. Brunton was exhausted and ill, and quickly coming to the realisation that would dawn on successive generations of spiritual seekers in India: that the ranks of yogis, swamis and putative godmen are also filled with charlatans, skivers and scroungers, and that saints are very rare indeed.

Even the most sincere of holy men proved frustratingly opaque when it came to offering a path to enlightenment. To the same question repeatedly asked, Brunton found only the same answer: 'Seek your own self, and you shall know the Truth which is deep hidden therein.'

What to do?

Then, finally, in January 1931, in the small Tamil Nadu town of Tiruvannamalai, 120 miles south of Madras, Brunton found the saint he was looking for.

\* \* \*

There was nothing in the first sixteen years of the life of Venkataraman Iyer to suggest that he would be in any way remarkable, still less that under the name Sri Ramana Maharshi he would become one of the most revered religious figures in Indian history.

Venkataraman was born on 30 December 1879 in the small village of Tiruchuli, about 30 miles from the town of Madurai, the site of one of the largest and most important religious sites in southern India, the Meenakshi temple. His father, Sundaram, was an uncertified pleader in the local magistrate's court—something like a solicitor. Sundaram died when Venkataraman was twelve, and with his mother Algammal and his two brothers and a sister, the young boy moved to Madurai to live with an uncle.

He was an unremarkable boy, fonder of wrestling and boxing than of school, who showed no particular religious inclinations and displayed only one—minor—peculiarity: he was an exceptionally heavy sleeper—so much so that on one occasion, after shouting and banging on the door of his room, friends had to break it down in order to wake him.

When he was aged sixteen a relation came to visit the family. When Venkataraman asked where he came from, the relation replied 'From Arunachala'—a hill close to the town of Tiruvannamalai, which is revered by Hindus as a manifestation of Lord Shiva, and as one of the holiest sites in India. On hearing the name, Venkataraman was said to have been filled with awe and joy. A few months later came the defining experience in his life. Alone in his room, he was suddenly seized by a deep and unshakeable fear of death.

This fear—or perhaps 'realisation' is a better word—immediately prompted a series of questions: What is death? What is it that is dying?—that led him to the understanding that while the body might die, what he knew to be 'the "I" within' is imperishable. 'The material body dies,' he wrote later, 'but the spirit transcending it cannot be touched by death. I am therefore the deathless spirit.' With this realisation, the fear of death 'had vanished once and for ever'. Thus began what he called his 'Absorption in the Self'.

An English disciple, Major A. W. Chadwick, who took the name Sadhu Arunachala, would write in his biography of Sri Ramana that 'In this one short hour in the room upstairs Venkataraman had become a fully realized soul. He was now God-realized.'[1] From that moment, we are told, the old identity of 'Venkataraman' died to the world.

His mother still called him by his old name, he went to school and ate his meals, but the real 'he' did not associate 'himself' with any of this: 'he observed it all as one might watch a cinema show, but knew it as the show it was'.[2] He left home shortly afterwards, leaving an unsigned note telling his family of his departure, and made his way to the town of Tiruvannamalai, close to the holy hill of Arunachala.

The Sanskrit word Arunachala means 'red mountain'. The hill rises from the plain, visible from miles around, thickly wooded on its sides and with a forbidding outcrop of rock at its summit. The sage Shankara is said to have stated that Arunachala is Mount Meru, in Indian mythology the axis of the world and the dwelling place of the gods.

Since time immemorial, ascetics and renunciates have lived in the numerous caves on the eastern slope of the mountain, and pilgrims from all over India continue to make their way to Arunachala to circumambulate the mountain. At its foot stands the Arunachaleswara temple, one of the most sacred places in southern India. It was here, in the temple's great thousand-pillared hall, that Venkataraman, in a state of ecstasy, offered himself to the God. He shaved his head—the symbol of renouncing the world—and tore his clothes to pieces, keeping only a thin strip to serve as a loincloth. It was the only garment he would ever wear. He then installed himself in the great hall, absorbed in meditation. He would not speak for another seven years, communicating only by sign language and occasional written notes.

His presence soon attracted the attention of local urchins, who would tease and throw stones at him, obliging him to retreat to a windowless vault under the hall. There, in front of a Shiva lingam, he sat in a state of *samadhi*, or bliss. Ants, wasps and scorpions attacked his body, but he noticed nothing. Since he no longer associated with his body, it was said that he had come to regard pain and suffering with complete indifference—'as a dream,' as Chadwick put it, 'which could be regarded objectively'.[3]

Drawn by his saintly renunciation, people would bring him water and food, placing it in his mouth since he seemed incapable of or indifferent to the act of eating. At length, one visitor, alarmed at his physical condition, moved him to a quiet shrine where he could meditate undisturbed. When his fame grew and more pilgrims began to gather, he moved again to a neighbouring temple, and finally to a cave in the sacred hill Arunachala.

Two years had passed with his family hearing no news of him, but at length word came to them of a young saint living at Tiruvannamalai. His mother, Algammal, made her way to the town and climbed the hill to the cave where Venkataraman was living. Shocked by his matted hair and filthy body, she pleaded with him to come home. When he refused, a distraught Algammal returned to Madurai.

With the passing of time, more followers began to gather around Venkataraman. It was one of these disciples, Ganapathi Muni, himself revered as a great sage, who decreed that Venkataraman should be known as Bhagavan Sri Ramana Maharshi (great seer Ramana). His disciples referred to him simply as 'Bhagavan'. They would bring food—which he ate with complete indifference, claiming that, to him, all food tasted exactly the same—and money, which he refused to accept.

From time to time Algammal would come to visit her son, eventually remaining at his side as his disciple. On her death in 1922, she was buried on the plain at the foot of the hill. Sri Ramana would visit the grave almost every day; but after six months he simply stayed there. His disciples built a hall to act as his permanent abode, which would become the centre of the ashram that grew up around it.

Just as Sri Ramana himself had not studied under any other teacher, nor learned any particular system of yoga, so he would tell his disciples not to waste their time with yogic practices, 'going the long way round, when they could go direct by the practice of Self-enquiry'.[4] His prescription was, in a sense, straightforward. To free the binds of the Ego, with all its attendant traps and delusions, one must simply concentrate the mind on the single question 'Who am I?' In so doing, the seeker would come to know that he was not the body, which he temporarily inhabited, but the Self, which was eternal.

Sri Ramana was presenting a traditional Advaita, or non-dualist, view about the essential unreality of the world, which to the Western mind can appear intensely fatalistic and solipsistic. Asked by a disciple how he could help others, Sri Ramana replied, 'Who is there for you to help? Who is the "I" that is to help others? First clear up that point and then everything will settle itself.'[5] Self-realisation was the best possible help that one could give to others, 'but in fact there are no others to help'. 'There was no good and no bad for him, only actions and attachment to actions,' Chadwick wrote, 'Know the actor and rest there, then all else had absolutely no importance.'[6]

Sri Ramana lived a life of utter simplicity. He dressed only in a simple loincloth, and his sole earthly possessions were a gourd-shell, a water jug and a bamboo staff. He would pick vegetables and tend the cows in the ashram. Each day, he would walk on the Hill, which he said was 'God Himself'. Arunachala is about 2,600 feet high. In his younger days, Sri Ramana would climb from Skandahsram, the smaller ashram building, about 600 feet up the mountainside to the summit and back in about one hour. A normal, healthy adult would take twice as long. Sri Ramana's speed was even more remarkable given that he never wore shoes or sandals.[7] But mostly he sat—at first on the ground, and later, when his disciples seemed to insist on it—on a divan covered in a tiger skin. Sometimes he would give instruction or answer questions. But much of his time was spent in silence.

An American devotee, Robert Adams, who as a young child growing up in New York had had visions of Sri Ramana, made his way to India in 1946, when he was just eighteen, to meet him. He described entering the hall, and seeing Sri Ramana seated on his couch, a guardrail in front of him 'to prevent fanatics from attacking him, with love':

And then I sat down in front of him. He looked at me and smiled, and I
smiled back. I have been to many teachers, many saints, many sages. I was
with Nisargadatta, Anandamayi Ma, Papa Ramdas, Neem Karoli Baba and
many others, but never did I meet anyone who exuded such compassion,
such love, such bliss as Ramana Maharshi.[8]

Such was his presence, wrote another witness, 'that by staying with him
some time a person may change his life habits and instincts, and that by this
grace one can receive faith in God as tangibly and certainly as one receives
a fruit or a book'.[9] He made no claims for himself. Everything he said and
did seemed designed to eviscerate any sense of self-regard. Rather, he
simply *was*—a luminous, mysterious exemplar of non-attachment.[10]

Paul Brunton and the Bhikku Frederick Fletcher arrived at
Tiruvannamalai in January 1931. In *A Search in Secret India*, Brunton
offered an evocative description of his first encounter with Sri Ramana.
He was ushered into the hall, where Sri Ramana sat in 'pin-drop silence'
and 'as steady as a statue', apparently not noticing his visitors at all.[11]
Brunton wrote that for almost two hours they sat in silence, in the course
of which time his own conceptions, thoughts and preoccupations began
to fall away, until a single question came to occupy his mind: 'Does this
man, the Maharishee, emanate the perfume of spiritual peace as a flower
emanates fragrance from its petals?'

A disciple interrupted his reverie, asking if he wished to ask any
questions.

Brunton writes that he looked into Sri Ramana's eyes, and discerned
in them 'another question, albeit unspoken. Can it be—is it possible—
that you are still tormented with distracting doubts when you have now
glimpsed the deep mental peace which you—and all men—may attain?'

In fact, this deep mystical communion that Brunton describes seemed
to be the result of a misunderstanding. According to a disciple of Sri
Ramana who was taking notes of the meeting, when first ushered into
the sage's presence Brunton and Fletcher were asked if they wished to ask
any questions; 'they were however not in a mood to do so'. Rather than
Brunton waiting for Sri Ramana to break the silence, the latter seemed to
be waiting for Brunton.

The following day Brunton and Fletcher had a second meeting with
the sage, in which Brunton asked whether Sri Ramana might assist him
in attaining enlightenment. Sri Ramana pondered the question for ten
minutes. 'You say I,' he said at last, '"I want to know." Tell me who is that
I?' Brunton pointed at himself and said his name. Sri Ramana continued:

'But that is only your body. Again I ask "Who are you?" ... Know first that "I" and then you shall know the truth.'

The discussion moved on to whether a master is necessary for a seeker to attain enlightenment. 'It might be,' Sri Ramana replied. And is it necessary to be in contact with a master, and if so for how long? It depends on the maturity of the disciple, Sri Ramana said, for 'The gunpowder catches fire in an instant, while much time is needed to set fire to the coal.'[12]

What Brunton does not mention in his book, but which the disciple of Sri Ramana who was taking notes of the meeting recorded, was that Fletcher then asked Sri Ramana whether he had heard of Meher Baba.

'Yes.'

'He says that he will become an avatar in a few years,' Fletcher said.

'Everyone is an Avatar of God,' Sri Ramana replied, '"The kingdom of heaven is within you". Jesus, Mohammed, Buddha, Krishna, all are in you. One who knows the Truth sees everyone else as a manifestation of God.'

Fletcher persisted. 'Will the Maharshi make a statement about Meher Baba?'

'What statement?' Sri Ramana replied. 'That is a question which seekers of Truth need not consider.'[13]

Reading Brunton's account, it seems that it was less what Sri Ramana said that touched him so deeply than what he exemplified. Simply being in Sri Ramana's presence was enough to lead Brunton to the conclusion that here was the living embodiment of holiness and sanctity. 'There is a mysterious property in this man,' he wrote,

> which differentiates him from all others I have met. I feel, somehow, that he does not belong to us, the human race, so much as he belongs to Nature, to the solitary peak which rises behind the hermitage, to the rough tract of jungle which stretches away into distant forests, and to the impenetrable sky which fills all space.

Looking in Ramana's eyes, he went on,

> strange sensations begin to arise in me. Those lustrous orbs seem to be peering into the inmost recesses of my soul. In a peculiar way, I feel aware of everything he can see in my heart. His mysterious glance penetrates my thoughts, my emotions, my desires; I am helpless before it.[14]

In *A Search in Secret India*, Brunton wrote that 'not one Englishman in a thousand is prepared to prostrate himself before a brown, half-naked figure'. In Ramana Maharshi, Brunton had found his brown, half-naked figure—and he prostrated himself before him. Brunton remained in the ashram for two weeks, on most days sitting in the hall with Ramana. While he was unable to engage the sage in conversation, in that time, he writes, a single thought took possession of his mind: 'This man has freed himself from all problems, and no woe can touch him.'[15]

By the time of his last meeting with Sri Ramana, Brunton had convinced himself that in his silence Maharshi was 'definitely linking my own mind with his', causing Brunton too to experience 'that state of starry calm which he seems perpetually to enjoy':

> In this extraordinary peace, I find a sense of exaltation and lightness. Time seems to stand still. My heart is released from its burden of care ... What is this man's gaze but a thaumaturgic wand, which evokes a hidden world of unexpected splendour before my profane eyes?[16]

Leaving Tiruvannamalai, Brunton continued on his travels. By now he was succumbing to the vicissitudes of the Indian food and climate, his body 'a weary burden flung on a bed of pain'. But so taken was he by Ramana, that when a 'silent voice' instructed him to 'Go back to the Maharishee', he heeded its call and returned to the ashram. There Ramana reiterated his message: 'You must find the master within you, within your own spiritual self.'

Pondering Ramana's quietude, and his apparent indifference to the world, Brunton posed the obvious question: 'Not a few Western minds will inevitably consider this life of the Maharishee's a wasted one,' he writes, but 'perhaps it may be good for us to have a few men who sit apart from our world of unending activity and survey it for us from afar.' He would later come to a somewhat different conclusion. But Brunton left Tiruvannamalai convinced that 'in this quiet and obscure corner of Southern India' he had encountered 'one of the last of India's spiritual supermen'.[17]

On its publication in 1934, *A Search in Secret India* would become a *succès d'estime* and establish Paul Brunton as a celebrated author. Inspired by Brunton's book, a steady stream of Western visitors began to make their way to Ramana's ashram, their encounters with Sri Ramana chronicled in the ashram records.

In January 1935, Douglas Ainslie (Grant Duff), a retired diplomat, poet and author, described as 'an aristocratic English gentleman', 70 years of age, arrived bearing a letter of introduction from Brunton. Over two days he sat silently in the hall with Sri Ramana. 'His habits are abstemious,' the records note of Ainslie,

> He remains without food of any kind till 1 p.m. and then lunches; he is said to have coffee and biscuits in the evening and retires without any further food.
>
> He has been a bachelor all along, walks a few miles a day on an empty stomach, speaks little and is very graceful in his movements. His voice is low and soft and his words appear to come from the heart.

One day, a letter arrived with questions for Sri Ramana on the existence of departed souls and how best to serve them—a subject on which, coincidentally, Ainslie had been seeking advice. Sri Ramana's reply was read to Ainslie, the records continue, and Tamil songs from Maharshi's 'Truth Revealed' and the Vedas were repeated in his presence:

> [Ainslie] considered the recitations magnificent. He came the next afternoon and to the wonder of others, had an experience on the previous night which he repeated to Maharshi. It was that he had seen something like an electric light within himself in the centre on the right side. And he added further that he had seen the sun shining within.[18]
>
> Maharshi smiled a little and then had a translation of 'Atmavidya' (Self-Knowledge) read out to him wherein there is the cryptic saying that realisation consists in reaching the Atman (Self) which is the expanse of consciousness (*chidvyoman*) as distinguished from the mind, which is the expansion of *chittavyoman*. This explanation appealed to him.

Speaking of him later, Maharshi remarked:

> Just think of an old man of 70 not choosing to live peacefully in his own house on the income he had earned! How intense has been his earnestness that he has left his native land, dared a sea-voyage of 6,000 miles, and faced the hardships of long railway journeys in a foreign land, ignorant of the language, undergoing the vicissitudes of a lonely life, submitting to the inclemency of a hot climate, in surroundings uncongenial and unaccustomed to him. He could have been happy in his own house. It is his longing for internal peace that has brought him here.[19]

Ainslie was followed shortly afterwards by Walter Evans-Wentz, the American anthropologist who had compiled and edited the first English translation of *The Tibetan Book of the Dead*, and who again arrived bearing a letter of introduction from Brunton. The ashram records note that Evans-

Wentz (no doubt referring to the tiger skin on which Ramana sat) asked if it was right to kill animals such as tiger and deer and to use the skin for 'Yoga posture (asana)'. 'The mind is the tiger or the deer,' Ramana replied. 'If everything be illusion, then one can take lives?' Evans-Wentz asked. 'To whom is it illusion? Find that out! In fact, everyone is a "killer of the Self" (*atmahan*) every moment of his life,' Ramana replied.

Another visitor who had made her way to the ashram, an English lady called Mrs M. A. Piggott, questioned Ramana on what diet he would prescribe for a spiritual practitioner. The answer was 'Satvic food'—bread, fruits, vegetables and milk—'in limited quantities.' When Mrs Piggott asked whether one might eat fish, the ashram records state: 'No answer was made by the Maharshi.'[20]

In 1935, Paul Brunton himself returned to the ashram. His visit coincided with the arrival of Swami Yogananda, who, remarkably, living as he was in America, had first learned of Sri Ramana through Brunton's book. Sri Ramana, Yogananda and Brunton were filmed together on 29 November. Ramana sits on a bench, dressed only in his loincloth. To his left stands the portly figure of Yoganada, dressed in a flowing robe, alongside the diminutive Brunton, looking like a minor colonial official in suit, tie and pocket handkerchief, and clutching an outsize topee in his hand. Yoganada and Brunton exchange pleasantries and shake hands, painfully conscious of the camera. Sri Ramana stares into middle space, apparently blissfully oblivious, or indifferent, to their presence.[21]

On 26 December 1936, a Swiss visitor described to Sri Ramana a luminous apparition she had witnessed. While sitting with her eyes wide open, she explained, she saw his face becoming cherub-like and draped in glorious flowers, and 'She was drawn in love towards that child-like face.' 'The vision is in your mind,' Sri Ramana told her, 'Your love is the cause. Paul Brunton saw me as a giant figure; you saw me like a child.' He cautioned her: 'Do not be deceived by visions ...'[22]

A few months later, an American woman named Mrs Jennings visited the ashram and recited some lines by the English Romantic poet Percy Bysshe Shelley:

> Within a cavern of man's trackless spirit
> Is throned an Image, so intensely fair
> That the adventurous thoughts that wander near it
> Worship, and as they kneel, tremble and fear
> The splendour of its presence, and the light

Penetrates their dreamlike frame
Till they become charged with the strength of flame.

Was Shelley, Mrs Jennings enquired, a realised soul? 'Yes,' Ramana replied, 'The lines are excellent. He must have realized what he wrote.'[23]

Major Chadwick tells a story of an American couple named the Taylors, who arrived with a party of tourists, who had been persuaded to part with a small fortune to come to India on a peculiar tour, led by a man named Baird Spalding, in search of the mythical group of Masters (Blavatsky, again) who were supposed to live in caves buried deep in the mountains of the Himalayas.[24] When the Masters proved mysteriously reluctant to show themselves, the tour party threatened mutiny, and to placate them, after a visit to the Aurobindo ashram in Pondicherry, Spalding led them to Ramana's ashram.[25]

It seems that Mrs Taylor became particularly attached to the Maharshi. Sitting with him one day, she suddenly burst out: 'Bhagavan, I want Self-realization.' 'Wait,' replied Ramana, 'it will come in due time.' 'No,' she insisted, 'that's no good. I want it here and now.' Ramana said nothing, but gazed into her eyes for five minutes, at which Mrs Taylor burst into tears and fled from the hall. She would never tell anybody what had happened.[26]

The search for self-realisation could also lead to despair. Arthur Osborne, an English writer and journalist, who had read *A Search in Secret India* and became a devotee of Ramana in the 1940s, after being interned by the Japanese in a prison camp in Thailand, describes loaning a fellow internee—'a very sociable, good-hearted man, a complete extrovert one would have said'—a copy of Brunton's book in order to read about Sri Ramana. On returning the book to him, the man said: 'Yes, well, when one reads about something like Ramana Maharshi one either does nothing about it—or else ...' Soon afterwards, the war ended and the camp was broken up. Osborne, who would spend his life at Ramana's ashram, later learned that his fellow internee had committed suicide.[27]

When Mercedes de Acosta read Brunton's account of Sri Ramana, it was, she wrote, 'as though some emanation of this saint was projected out of the book to me':

> For days and nights after reading about him I could not think of anything else. I became, as it were, possessed by him. I could not even talk of anything else. So much so, that as a joke, Adrian made a drawing of me peering out from behind a group of Indians and wrote under it A SEARCH IN SECRET INDIA.[28]

From that moment on, de Acosta wrote, the whole direction of her life turned away from Hollywood and towards India: 'I felt that I would meet the Maharshi and that this meeting would be the greatest experience of my life.' Inspired by Brunton's book, she acquired a volume of Ramana's teachings, reading and re-reading it, and marking particular passages in red pencil:

– The mind must be used both to illuminate the path and to destroy itself, once this purpose is effected.
– Know thus that the quest for this ego amounts to wholesale renunciation.
– Clear away all mental dispositions by steady and incessant meditation in the Heart.

Not only did reading Brunton's book sow the seeds of de Acosta's enthusiasm for Sri Ramana Maharshi; it also exacerbated her growing doubts about Meher Baba. But she was not ready to give him up for good just yet.

\* \* \*

In 1937 Meher returned once more to Europe. Travelling with him was a group of his 'lovers', who had been staying at the Nasik ashram for some months undergoing 'training'. Among them were the tirelessly faithful Norina Matchabelli, Elizabeth Patterson and Ruano Bogislav, a statuesque actress and singer with a passion for smoking Cuban cigars, who had once been married to the opera singer Ricardo Martin, and who was known among Meher Baba's circle as 'the Eagle'. Under Baba's instructions, all the women stayed in strict seclusion throughout the voyage to Europe, with Matchabelli sleeping on the floor outside the cabin, keeping guard.

On 13 August the group docked at Marseilles, then travelled to Cannes, where in the last week of October they were joined by Baba's quixotic follower, Mercedes de Acosta. Baba had continued to correspond with de Acosta, encouraging her to work on his film—at the same time his desire to meet the elusive Greta Garbo was growing ever more obvious. Early in 1937 he wrote to de Acosta: 'You must come to India next year as soon as you can, and if possible Greta to come with you. I am with you. You have my love.'[29] De Acosta eagerly put his proposal to Garbo. She turned it down. Heaping agony on de Acosta's distress, Garbo had embarked on an affair with the conductor Leopold Stokowski (whom Meher had met in New York on his first visit to America). She was as far from de Acosta as she had ever been. And as far from Meher Baba.[30]

Now Meher summoned de Acosta to join him in Cannes. Desperate for advice and spiritual consolation, she set sail on the SS *Normandie* from New York, sharing the journey with her friend Noël Coward and arriving in Cannes in the last week of October. She found Meher installed in customarily agreeable accommodation at the Villa Caldana, in the hills behind Cannes, where he had been joined by a number of his 'lovers' including Kitty Davy and Delia De Leon. The men's 'mandali' was housed in another villa.

Meher had also summoned from India a young man named Mohammed, one of those whom Meher called '*masts*'—men and women who to all outward appearances seemed mentally disturbed, but whom Meher described as actually being 'intoxicated with God', and on a spiritually elevated plane (one immediately thinks of Ramakrishna).[31] According to Meher, *masts* were mostly to be found in India, where levels of devotion went far beyond that of most places, although they could also be found in Iran, Tibet, China, Egypt and parts of Arabia.

Beginning in the 1920s, Meher devoted a great deal of his time to seeking out and caring for *masts*, including opening a special ashram for them. He evidently had a particular gift, not only for discerning between the genuinely 'God intoxicated' and the merely mad, but for sniffing out the enlightened from those who wished to pass themselves off as such. In 1948 he visited the Kumbh Mela, the largest religious gathering in the world, in Allahabad, when tens of thousands of sadhus from all over India congregate to bathe in the Ganges. Having spent the day walking through the sadhu encampment, he reported back to his followers that of the 4,000 or so sadhus he had encountered there were no more than seven 'advanced souls'.

Charles Purdom tells the extraordinary story of one such *mast* named Karim Baba, to whom Meher Baba devoted his attentions for a number of weeks in 1940. Meher had first encountered Karim in Calcutta, sitting on a pavement against a wall. He was clad in filthy rags, with skeins of steel wire around his neck, his hair and beard thick, dirty and matted, but with eyes 'that shone like burnished swords'. He was said to have sat at the same spot for six years.

Sometime later, Meher dispatched a disciple, known as Kaka, to Calcutta to bring Karim to his ashram at Ranchi, where Meher was staying. Kaka found the *mast* seated at his customary spot, but when Kaka asked him to come with him Karim simply laughed. Kaka went to buy a tunic and loincloth and returned to the spot, where he enlisted the help of two interested Muslims and hailed a Victoria cab. When he invited Karim to exchange his rags for clothes, the *mast* rose without a word and allowed himself to be dressed in the street. By this time a small crowd had gathered, for Karim, we are told, was locally venerated as a holy man. Kaka feared a disturbance, but the *mast* allowed himself to be led to the cab and carried to the railway station. There, Kaka found a third-class compartment and installed his prize.

As the train was leaving, Karim spoke for the first time, saying: 'The ticket is taken and the train has started.' But he soon became restless, putting one leg out of the window and saying nothing. Kaka assumed he wished to visit the toilet. This was the case, and when the *mast* had relieved himself, he 'picked out three or four coins of one or two annas, and an odd copper piece, from his ordure, washed them thoroughly under the tap, tossed them in his mouth and swallowed them'.[32] It later became apparent that this was a regular practice of his.

At Ranchi, the *mast* was lodged in a special room, where Meher Baba would go several times a day to feed him and sit alone with him. The *mast* was usually silent, but from time to time would utter some short phrase 'with the sudden vigour of a lid blowing off a boiling kettle'. Sometimes, as Meher sat with him, Karim would laugh and sing, and sometimes he could be heard in the dead of night, singing to himself.

A few weeks later, Meher returned to his ashram Meherabad ('Meher flourishing') at Ahmednagar, taking Karim with him. The *mast* was installed in a special hut with a bamboo lattice screen. After two weeks, Meher announced that his work with Karim was over, and Kaka was instructed to return him to his pavement in Calcutta. There was a dispensary nearby, and the doctor undertook to feed Karim regularly, sufficient money being left for the purpose. Meher Baba would visit Calcutta on several occasions after that, but he did not see Karim again.

\* \* \*

In Cannes, Meher had been provided with a convertible, and one day he decided to go for a drive along the Côte d'Azur, taking Mohammed and de Acosta with him. In Nice, as the car slowed to a crawl in traffic, Mohammed began to shout out loudly. A policeman waved the car over to the kerb and asked what was going on. Meher Baba put his hand over his mouth to indicate that he was unable to speak; Mohammed continued to shout at the top of his lungs and then burst into song. It was left to de Acosta to explain that one of the men had taken a vow of silence, and the other was a 'mentally ill Hindu' who was undergoing treatment and was totally harmless. Bemused, the policeman shrugged and waved them on their way.

That night, Meher visited the casino at Monte Carlo with Matchabelli and de Acosta, dressed in a cape belonging to Norina and a beret belonging to Mercedes. But no amount of distraction could allay Mercedes' underlying feelings of unease and unhappiness.

On 29 October 1937, after only a few days in France, de Acosta left to return to America. Meher Baba set sail for India. He would not return to the West for another fifteen years. Although she continued to correspond with him, unlike her friend Norina Matchabelli, de Acosta evidently felt no great calling to become one of Meher's 'lovers'. Not only had he fallen short in providing what she wished for from a guru, but his counsel had done nothing to bring Greta Garbo closer to her. The object of de Acosta's life-long obsession remained obdurately at arm's length.

She would later write in her autobiography that her relationship with Meher Baba had 'greatly lifted my spirits'. But her comments in a passage in the original manuscript, seen by her biographer Robert Schanke, that was subsequently deleted, are more revealing: 'At this time Baba had an influence on me. I was pathetically seeking some kind of spiritual guidance and I blindly seized onto him.'[33]

De Acosta was in the throes of a recurring syndrome of guru worship— deep enamouration followed by a slowly rising disenchantment, and the eventual transference of affection to another guru. Her new enthusiasm for Sri Ramana Maharshi, inspired by Brunton's book, was further fuelled in 1938, when she met the dancer Ram Gopal.

Meher Baba, he told her, was 'a small man spiritually', who meant well but was 'too interested in self promotion'. Gopal had met Sri Ramana, and his sister was a devotee; he assured de Acosta that he was much more the genuine article. Determined to travel to India to meet Sri Ramana herself, in the summer of 1938 de Acosta set sail for Europe in the company of Gopal.

Europe was hovering on the brink of war. De Acosta was in Paris on the day the Munich Pact was signed on 29 September, promising 'peace in our time'. A few days later she travelled to Genoa, and booked passage on an Indian steamship, the SS *Victoria*. She had been joined by her friend Consuelo de Sides, a Manhattan socialite who had become a devotee of Meher.

Consuelo was married to an art dealer, Alfredo de Sides. Mindful, perhaps, of the destructive effect which devotion to the God-man had wreaked on Norina Matchabelli's marriage, Alfredo made de Acosta promise that she would keep a vigilant eye on his wife and bring her back safely. The plan was for Consuelo to disembark in Bombay and for de Acosta to continue on to Colombo in Ceylon. From there, de Acosta would cross over to southern India and make her way to Ramana Maharshi's ashram at Tiruvannamalai. She also had plans to meet with Mahatma Gandhi. But when the *Victoria* docked in Bombay, Norina Matchabelli came on board, bearing a message from Meher: de Acosta was to disembark with Consuelo, and they were to come immediately to his ashram Meherabad. Reluctantly, de Acosta agreed.

A large group of the God-intoxicated *masts* had taken up residence at Meherabad. De Acosta arrived to find 'five thousand of these mad people' living there.[34] (This figure is surely an exaggeration.) Already put out at having her travel plans disrupted, de Acosta was even more upset to be told that instead of having her own room, as Meher had always promised her if she ever visited, she would have to stay in a women's dormitory. Baba, she reflected, was possibly teaching her a lesson, 'but I felt that a man who was a spiritual teacher should not break his word'. De Acosta was not accustomed to staying in dormitories. She passed an uncomfortable and sleepless night, kept awake by the sounds of her fellow residents snoring and employing the pots placed under the bed.

When, next morning, Norina Matchabelli told her that Meher expected her and Consuelo to remain at the ashram for the next five years, de Acosta exploded: 'Five years! Are you mad? I came to see the Maharshi and I am leaving today.' She confronted Meher, who was apparently put out that de Acosta was ready to throw him over for Sri Ramana Maharshi. 'Do you consider the Maharshi a Perfect Master?' he asked her. De Acosta replied that she was no judge of Perfect Masters, or even of whether such beings existed, 'I only know that I long to see the Maharshi with all my heart, and I must go to him.'[35]

When she told him she was leaving that day, Meher shrugged; there were no cars going to Bombay, he replied; she would need to stay another night, and Consuelo must stay for five years. De Acosta protested that Alfredo had put Consuelo in her care and that she would be leaving with her.

That night Matchabelli tried to persuade de Acosta to stay, telling her that by refusing Meher's instructions she would face 'ten terrible incarnations'. De Acosta told her she would take her chances. Matchabelli railed at her: 'Surely you are not thinking of going back to that horrible

Western world and to that terrible Hollywood!' De Acosta replied that after she had seen Ramana Maharshi, it was quite likely that she would. Matchabelli threw her hands up in disgust: 'There is nothing to be done with you. You are lost.'[36]

The next day de Acosta had a furious argument with Consuelo. Matchabelli had been working on her and had persuaded her to stay. But de Acosta prevailed on her friend to change her mind and leave with her. They bid farewell to Meher Baba. He was 'very gracious', de Acosta wrote. But in a curious request, that seemed to indicate the need to exercise his waning power over her, he extracted a promise that they would not go to see either Sri Ramana or Gandhi, before taking a sightseeing tour of India. De Acosta agreed—later coming to regret it, she would note, as it caused her to miss meeting with Gandhi. She and Meher Baba kissed farewell. She would not see him again for eighteen years.

From Meherabad, de Acosta and Consuelo made an excursion through India's most celebrated sights and beauty spots—Jaipur, Agra, the *ghats* of Benares, the caves of Ellora. On 21 November, they arrived in the French colony of Pondicherry, on India's eastern seaboard, hoping for an audience with one of India's most revered spiritual teachers, Sri Aurobindo.

Born Aurobindo Ghose in Calcutta in 1872, the son of a senior civil servant and committed Anglophile, Aurobindo was educated in Britain at St Paul's, an elite public school in London, and at Cambridge. Returning to India, he worked in the civil service and then as a professor at Baroda College, where he developed two passions—yoga and campaigning for an end to British rule. For Aurobindo, the politics of nationalism were inseparable from the renaissance of Hinduism embodied in the lives and teachings of Ramakrishna and Vivekananda: 'Mother India' and the 'Divine Mother'—the animating force of all life—were inextricably linked.

In 1908 Aurobindo was arrested following an explosion in which two British women were killed by a bomb that had been thrown at a British magistrate, but had missed its target. Aurobindo was charged with plotting the attack. He spent a year in prison before coming to trial and being acquitted of the charge. A year before his imprisonment, Aurobindo had his first experience of what he described as 'silent Brahman', in which all sense of self, 'impersonal or other', disappeared, 'and there was only an awareness of That as the sole reality, all else being quite insubstantial, void, non-real'.

In jail in Alipur, he had his second decisive spiritual experience, seeing 'God present in all things' and understanding 'what Sri Krishna demanded of Arjuna … to be free from repulsion and desire'. On his release from jail, Aurobindo withdrew from politics, and in 1910 moved to Pondicherry, at that time still under the control of the French, where he founded an ashram, based on his teachings on what he called 'Integral Yoga', a physical and spiritual system which he believed would transfigure man into 'Superman'—a cosmic being, conscious of the unity of all existence, acting free from the ego in harmony with universal laws.

His most devoted disciple was Mirra Alfassa. Born in Paris in 1878 into a Sephardic Jewish family, the daughter of an Egyptian mother and a Turkish banker father, Mirra would claim that as a child she had been gripped by profound psychic and spiritual experiences, convincing her of the existence of God, and to have been visited often in her sleep by a series of teachers, including one whom she knew as 'Krishna'.

Trained as a painter—she exhibited several times at the Salon in Paris— Mirra followed her esoteric enthusiasms, studying the Kabbalah with the occultist and erstwhile associate of Madame Blavatsky, Max Théon, and joining an esoteric group in Paris called Le Mouvement Cosmique, which also included among its number the Tibetologist Alexandra David-Néel, who in 1924 became the first European woman ever to set foot in Lhasa.

She married the artist Henri Morisset and gave birth to a son named André. But the marriage failed, and in 1914 Mirra travelled to Pondicherry with her second husband, Paul Richard, a lawyer and aspiring politician with an interest in Vedanta, who had met Sri Aurobindo on an earlier visit to India. Meeting the Indian sage for the first time, Mirra would later write, she experienced a deep pang of recognition. Here was the 'Krishna' who had inhabited her dreams as a child.

In 1915 Mirra and Richard returned to France, the following year travelling to Japan. In 1920 the couple returned to Pondicherry, but Richard had grown disillusioned with Aurobindo and left for France. Mirra took up permanent residence at the ashram, at Aurobindo's right hand. Together, they built an ashram community, based in a handsome colonial house on Marine Street in the 'white' quarter of the town, from where they could almost hear the waves of the Bay of Bengal slapping against the rocks at the foot of the promenade.

Aurobindo had declared that he had created his ashram not with the usual objectives of such institutions, for renunciation from the world, but as the 'centre and field of practice' for his theories about developing a new kind of man embodying a higher spiritual consciousness. But in 1926 he adopted something that looked very much like renunciation, withdrawing to his private quarters to concentrate on his spiritual work in virtual isolation. For the next twenty-four years, until his death in 1950, he lived in complete retirement and total silence, entrusting the affairs of the ashram and his mission to Mirra. He declared her 'the Mother', maintaining that she was an avatar—an embodiment of the divine feminine principle. Under the Mother's direction, the activities of the ashram took a singular bent: she encouraged physical and sporting activities—she was particularly partial to tennis herself—and taught flower arranging according to the spiritual qualities she claimed to discern in each bloom.

Devotees from both India and Europe flocked to the ashram.[37] Among them was Margaret Wilson, a friend of Mercedes' and the eldest daughter of the American President Woodrow Wilson, who had made her way to Pondicherry in October 1938 after falling rapturously upon a copy of Sri Aurobindo's *Essays on the Gita* (1922) in the New York Public Library. *The Washington Post* reported her arrival at the ashram with the headline: 'Daughter of Wilson Turns Hindu'.

When de Acosta arrived in Pondicherry, she sought out Wilson, and requested a personal audience with Aurobindo. She was told this was impossible; Aurobindo had retreated into seclusion, and only appeared before his disciples for *darshan* four times a year. Happily, de Acosta's arrival coincided with one of these *darshans*. But she took an immediate dislike to the ashram: 'To me it seemed like another convent and I have always wanted to forget my convent experiences.' Women in 'nun like' costumes whispered in corners and the atmosphere was 'deadly'. But Margaret Wilson told de Acosta she was happy there and hoped to remain there until her death.[38]

Early next morning, Wilson was able to secure a place for de Acosta and Consuelo at the front of the line for Aurobindo's *darshan*. But as the faithful filed into the room and took their places in a mood of feverish expectancy, a disciple suddenly appeared and announced that Aurobindo had sprained his ankle and was in too much pain to give *darshan*; 'Mother' would give *darshan* instead. 'I could hardly believe my ears,' de Acosta wrote,

> Thousands of poor people who had traveled hundreds of miles, many of whom had been journeying for months, were to be disappointed because of a sprained ankle. There was a hush, and a wave of depression ran through the crowd that was almost staggering. Many people wept, but I was angry. 'If a spiritual leader can disappoint so many people how can one find fault with a government leader or a politician?' I asked out loud—but no one answered me.[39]

Eventually the Mother appeared and mounted the platform: 'Made up within an inch of her life, her lips scarlet and her hair brightly dyed, she wore a trailing chiffon dress, and as she took her place on the chair I wondered if anyone in that crowd could experience darshan', de Acosta recounted. Dutifully, de Acosta joined the devotees trailing past her, and placed a garland of flowers at her feet. 'I felt,' she would write later, 'like a first-class hypocrite.'[40] The next day, wondering 'how such a great man as Aurobindo could have allowed himself to be so exploited', she left for Tiruvannamalai.

# 8

# MERCEDES AND SOMERSET

The day before Mercedes de Acosta arrived at Sri Ramana Maharshi's ashram in November 1938, his disciple Ganapati Sastri showed the sage a letter the ashram had received from her requesting a meeting. 'See the trouble to so many because I am here ...', Ramana remarked with a sigh.

Travelling on the train to Madras, de Acosta and Consuelo shared a carriage with a young, besuited lawyer and an elderly man clad only in a loincloth. At some point a conductor appeared and began to talk excitedly in Tamil. Perplexed, Mercedes brandished her ticket. The elderly man leaned forward and in perfect English offered to translate: the inspector, he explained, had no problem with the ticket. He was merely asking whether she believed in 'the unity of the Divine and the individual soul'.

Acting as if this was the most natural enquiry in the world from a railway conductor, de Acosta replied that she was of the opinion that there was indeed no separation between the Divine Source and the individual soul. The elderly man conveyed her opinion to the conductor who nodded and bowed, indicating that he too held these views. The conductor moved on to inspect tickets elsewhere in the train, but presently returned, settling himself down for a lively philosophical discussion until the train eventually reached Madras.

On arrival, de Acosta hired a car and driver for the long journey to Arunachala. Approaching the ashram, the road became a track, rough and dusty, rutted from the wheels of heavy ox-drawn wagons. At length, the driver said he would go no further and that she must proceed by foot. 'As I ran those two miles up the hill,' de Acosta later wrote, 'deeply within myself I knew that I was running toward the greatest experience of my life.'[1] She was to stay just three days, but later wrote that these were the three most significant days of her life.

De Acosta offered a characteristically dramatic description of her first encounter with Sri Ramana. Walking into the hall where he passed his days, she wrote, 'I felt overcome by some strong power in the hall as if an invisible wind was pushing violently against me.' She was greeted by an American disciple of the Maharshi's, Guy Hague, who took her hand and led her to a place against the wall from where she could observe the sage. He was sitting absolutely straight on his divan, in the Buddha posture, looking directly in front of him.

'As he sat there he seemed like a statue, and yet something extraordinary emanated from him', she wrote. 'I had a feeling that on some invisible level I was receiving a spiritual shock from him although his gaze was not directed toward me. He did not seem to be looking at anything, and yet I felt he could see and was conscious of the whole world.'[2] Hague explained to her that the Maharshi was in a state of *samadhi*, in which he had been sitting for the past seven hours.

De Acosta sat for some time, 'lost in a sort of inner world'. Then Hague suggested she should go and sit near Sri Ramana. Shortly afterwards, the sage came out of *samadhi* and opened his eyes. 'He moved his head and looked directly down at me, his eyes looking into mine,' de Acosta wrote,

> It would be impossible to describe this moment and I am not going to attempt it. I can only say that at this second I felt my inner being raised to a new level—as if, suddenly, my state of consciousness was lifted to a much higher degree. Perhaps in this split second I was no longer my human self but the Self. Then Bhagavan smiled at me. It seemed to me that I had never before known what a smile was. I said, 'I have come a long way to see you.' He said, 'I knew you were coming and I have been guiding your steps.'[3]

Mercedes asked a series of questions, about whom or what she should follow. Sri Ramana answered as he always did: 'You should follow the Self. There is nothing or no one else to follow.' It is only by 'diving deep into the Spiritual Heart that one can find the Self,' he told her. 'He placed his right hand on my right breast and continued, "Here lies the Heart, the Dynamic, Spiritual Heart".'

De Acosta sat in the meditation hall with the Maharshi for two days and two nights. She wished to stay longer, but towards the end of the third day he told her that she should leave. 'There will be what will be called a "war", but which, in reality, will be a great world revolution,' he said. 'Every country and every person will be touched by it. You must return to

America. Your destiny is not in India at this time,' he continued. Sadly, de Acosta packed her bags. As she was leaving, Sri Ramana told her: 'You will return here again.' She never did.

Reflecting on her meeting with Sri Ramana, de Acosta would later write that it would be 'presumptuous' to say he changed her life: 'My life was perhaps not so important as all this. But I definitely saw life differently after I had been in his presence, a presence that just by merely "being" was sufficient spiritual nourishment for a lifetime.' There was, she wrote, 'a transformation of my entire consciousness. And how could it have been otherwise? I had been in the atmosphere of an egoless, world-detached, and completely Pure Being.'

One begins de Acosta's *Here Lies the Heart* irritated at her snobbery and superficiality, but ends the autobiography touched by her spiritual sincerity, her deep yearning for truth and meaning. It is as a lesbian—a heroine of gay liberation—that de Acosta is now known, but surely it is for her spiritual quest that she would rather be remembered.

De Acosta's screen-writing career had come to an end; in New York she worked as an associate editor on a magazine called *Tomorrow* that was devoted to mystical and parapsychological subjects. In 1944, Greta Garbo finally broke off their relationship, instructing de Acosta to stop sending her letters and poems. De Acosta's health was deteriorating rapidly, and she suffered a nervous breakdown.

In July 1956, Meher Baba returned to America for a tour. In New York, de Acosta visited him at the Hotel Delmonico, and complained to him of her worsening health and failing eyesight. Meher asked her to repeat his name 7,000 times every day, beginning at 7 o'clock that evening. How effective this treatment proved to be is not recorded.

In 1960, in need of money, de Acosta published her autobiography, alienating some of her friends who were mentioned in the book because of their implied homosexuality. She died in 1968 at the age of seventy-five, virtually penniless, alone and living in a tiny two-room apartment in New York. At her bedside was a Bible. Inside were six snapshots of Garbo. On the title page was an inscription in de Acosta's handwriting, dated 1922. It was from Matthew 10:39: 'He that findeth his life shall lose it: and he that loseth his life shall find it.'[4]

Greta Garbo died in 1990 at the age of eighty-five. She never met Meher Baba, but she dabbled in Eastern philosophy all her life, and in the 1960s became a practitioner of Transcendental Meditation. Among her personal items auctioned after her death was a collection of thirteen books that

175

included *Inspired Talks: My Master and Other Writings* by Swami Vivekananda (with an inscription in an unknown hand to Greta Garbo); *Autobiography of a Yogi* by Paramahansa Yogananda, with an inscription on the end paper that reads 'Presented with Compliments of the author, in remembrance of your visit to our hermitage in Encinitas'; *Science of Being and Art of Living* by the Maharishi Mahesh Yogi; *Hatha Yoga* by Yogi Ramacharaka; and *The I Ching*. The books were sold at auction in 2012 for $1,280.

\* \* \*

A few months before de Acosta's short sojourn at Arunachala, another visitor had come in search of Maharshi—the English novelist William Somerset Maugham.

At the time he walked into Sri Ramana Maharshi's ashram in 1938, Maugham's uncluttered prose and formidable skill as a storyteller had made him the most popular author in the English-speaking world—'in the very first row of the second-raters,' as he put it. He might also have been one of the least contented.

Maugham was sixty-three, and in a career spanning some forty years he had written more than thirty books and plays. He lived in regal splendour on Cap Ferrat, on the French Riviera, in the Villa Mauresque (a Moorish fantasy that had been built by the famously dissolute Leopold II, King of Belgium, to house his priest confessor). Here, tended by a platoon of servants, Maugham entertained such visitors as Winston Churchill, T. S. Eliot, Noël Coward and Jean Cocteau. An evil eye was painted on the outside wall to repel malign spirits—and, presumably, unwanted guests.

Maugham's biographer Ted Morgan would note that there were four categories of persons who had easy access to the Villa Mauresque: the titled, the wealthy, the famous, and attractive young men. Yet success had done little to alleviate a sense of restlessness and dissatisfaction that had shadowed Maugham for all his life.

Maugham was born on 25 January 1874 in the British Embassy in Paris, where his father, Robert, was the solicitor in charge of the Embassy's legal affairs. Maugham was one of only three children ever to be born in the Embassy; in his case it was to avoid a situation whereby being born on French soil he would automatically have French citizenship, and thereby be eligible for conscription in the French army. (Another of the three, and born in the same year as Maugham, was Lady Emily Lutyens.)

His mother, Edith, died of consumption on Maugham's eighth birthday. Her death would scar him forever, robbing him, he would later note, 'of the only love in the world that is quite unselfish'. Two years later his father died of stomach cancer, and the young Maugham was packed off to live with his strict uncle Henry, a clergyman in Whitstable in Kent.

Maugham loathed his life there. He was sent to the King's School, Canterbury, where his short stature, shyness and stammer made him the butt of relentless teasing by his fellow pupils. At sixteen he demanded to leave the school, and his uncle allowed him to escape to the University of Heidelberg, where he studied literature and philosophy.

Maugham had made up his mind to be a writer, but in need of a more secure profession and to appease his guardian, he went on to study medicine at St Thomas' Hospital in London. His years as a medical student, ministering to the impoverished slum-dwellers of Lambeth, confirmed his belief in a Hobbesian view of the world, and destroyed any faith he might have had in a merciful and loving God. 'I'm glad I don't believe in God,' he wrote as a young man, 'When I look at the misery of the world and its bitterness I think that no belief can be more ignoble.'[5] But behind the youthful bravado, the search for faith or for meaning in life in the absence of faith, would be a recurring theme in Maugham's work throughout his life.

Maugham's first book, *Liza of Lambeth*, which drew heavily on his experiences at St Thomas', was published in 1897. Its success gave Maugham the confidence to abandon medicine, but further success as a novelist and a playwright would elude him until 1907, when a play called *Lady Frederick* dramatically changed his fortunes.

Two years earlier, Maugham had been living in Paris. It was there, in a cafe in Montparnasse called Le Chat Blanc, that he first met Aleister Crowley. 'I took an immense dislike to him, but he interested and amused me', Maugham wrote later. Crowley, he thought, was 'a fake, but not entirely a fake ... He was a liar and unbecomingly boastful, but the odd thing was that he had actually done some of the things he boasted of.'[6]

Maugham was sufficiently interested and amused to write a thinly disguised *roman-à-clef*, *The Magician* (1908), in which Crowley was renamed Oliver Haddo. Haddo is described as a tall, fleshy man, who styles himself as 'The Brother of the Shadow' and is much given to flamboyant bragging and absurdly orotund phrases. 'Marie, disembarrass me of this coat of frieze!' he calls, on entering a restaurant called Le Chien Noir, 'Hang my sombrero upon a convenient peg.'[7]

After being ridiculed by an English doctor called Arthur Burdon, Haddo takes his revenge by casting a spell on Burdon's fiancée Margaret, which causes her to become sexually obsessed with Haddo. A slave to her passions, powerless to resist, she leaves the unfortunate Arthur and marries Haddo, who spirits her back to his castle, 'Skene' (a clear reference to Crowley's Scottish manor house 'Boleskine'), where ..e makes her the object of demonic magical rituals. Arthur follows them to Skene, where Haddo is ultimately defeated, although Margaret dies.

The book is probably the worst Maugham ever wrote and he would later dismiss it as 'dull and stupid' and the subject of magic as 'moonshine. I did not believe a word of it. It was a game I was playing.' While acknowledging that Crowley served as the model for Haddo, Maugham maintained that he had made his character 'more striking in appearance, more sinister and more ruthless than Crowley ever was'.[8]

Nonetheless, Crowley was quick to see himself in Haddo. 'My old and valued friend', he wrote, had shamelessly plundered the details of his life, his marriage, his explorations, his ambitions, exploits and 'magical opinions', adding:

> I was not in the least offended by the attempts of the book to represent me as, in many ways, the most atrocious scoundrel, for he had done more than justice to the qualities of which I was proud ... The Magician was, in fact, an appreciation of my genius such as I had never dreamed of inspiring.[9]

When next they met by chance, Crowley told Maugham, 'I almost wish that you were an important writer.'[10]

The saga of Maugham's dealings with Crowley has an intriguing coda involving Gerald Haxton, the reprobate and drunk who for thirty years was Maugham's secretary, travelling companion and lover. Robin Maugham, the writer's nephew, whose relationship with him was almost that of father and son, told the story of how Haxton, deep in his cups, had told him that he had often wondered whether Crowley hadn't made a pact with Maugham: "'If you give me your soul, I'll make you the most famous writer alive this century." And I believe that somehow Willie accepted,' Haxton told Robin.[11]

By 1907, Maugham had written five plays, but none had been produced and he was growing increasingly despondent over his career. Lady Frederick, which he had been struggling to place for three years, had been turned down by seventeen managers. Then Maugham was introduced to Otho Stuart, the manager of the Court Theatre in London. By a remarkable stroke of good fortune—for Maugham at least—a play that had been running at the Court had closed at short notice, leaving Stuart with an empty theatre to fill.

*Lady Frederick* is a light comedy about a fashionable woman of a certain age, who, in an attempt to cool the ardour of a young suitor who has fallen hopelessly in love with her, lets him watch as she makes up her face, revealing to him the artificial nature of beauty. Stuart liked the play, but told Maugham he doubted that any actress would compromise her public image by playing the scene. However, on reading the play, Ethel Irving, a leading light on the London stage, then aged thirty-seven, agreed to take the part. *Lady Frederick* was a roaring success, and the making of Maugham as a playwright. Within a year he had four plays running simultaneously in London.

Maugham later told his nephew that he had made up his mind that if *Lady Frederick* failed he would give up writing as a career and sign on as a ship's doctor: 'And I suppose I might never have been heard of again.'[12] According to Robin Maugham, the man who introduced his uncle to Otho Stuart was ... Aleister Crowley. Robin writes that he often wondered whether Haxton's 'drunken maunderings' about Crowley did not possess some odd element of truth: 'I felt that something was haunting Willie— something evil.'[13]

Haunted or not, Maugham suffered from a weary pessimism about the human condition that threaded its way through his life and books. 'We're the product of our genes and chromosomes,' he told his nephew, 'And there's nothing whatever we can do about it. We can't change the essential natures we're born with.'[14]

He found no great happiness in his emotional life, lamenting that he had 'never experienced the bliss of requited love. I have most loved people who cared little or nothing for me and when people have loved me I have been embarrassed.'[15]

Maugham lost his virginity at the age of sixteen to a homosexual aesthete named John Ellingham Brookes. As a young man, Maugham married out of a sense of duty rather than love in 1917, after the woman with whom he had been having an affair, Syrie Wellcome (the daughter of Thomas Barnardo, the founder of Dr Barnardo's children's homes) became pregnant. But the marriage was unhappy. Women, going all the way back to his mother, were 'a disappointment, an unreliable species'.[16] In later life he was almost exclusively, and promiscuously, homosexual.

His two closest relationships were with the men who were successively employed as his secretaries and companions: Gerald Haxton—a man with an indefatigable enthusiasm for sailors and rent-boys, and whom the Hollywood film director George Cukor described as being 'wonderful for Willie. He kept him in touch with the gutter'—and Alan Searle, who following Haxton's death in 1944, faithfully served Maugham for the last years of his life.

As Christmas Humphreys observed, Maugham was 'Not an easy man to know.'[17] Maugham's biographer likened him to the man in Max Beerbohm's *The Happy Hypocrite*, who has worn a mask for so long it becomes his face—'a façade person' to whom appearances, manners and propriety were everything. Maugham went to the right tailor, belonged to the right club and was scrupulously—and opaquely—courteous. But he was also 'gratuitously cruel ... extremely judgmental and extremely thin-skinned'.[18] The mask was cold, aloof, the mouth downturned in a permanent rictus of reproval; the manner was imperious, designed to keep the rest of the world at bay.

The default critical position on Maugham as a novelist was that he took an unforgiving view of human nature, but that he was always preoccupied by the essential questions: 'what is the value of life, how he should live and what sense he can ascribe to the universe'.[19] He had the faithless man's fascination with the power of faith. In his early twenties, whilst living in Spain, he became an admirer of the 'Spiritual Exercises' of St Ignatius Loyola, the founder of the Jesuit order (to give them their full title—'Spiritual Exercises for overcoming oneself and for regulating one's life without being swayed by any inordinate attachment'). And throughout his life he read extensively on philosophy, from Plato to the Christian saints. 'It may be that my heart, having found rest nowhere, had some deep ancestral craving for God and immortality which my reason would have no truck with,' he would write somewhat wistfully in his memoir, *The Summing Up* (1938).

Maugham was also an indefatigable and endlessly curious traveller. And by the late 1930s, his search for experience—and for material as a writer—had taken him to virtually every corner of the world—every corner, that is, but one: India. That was to change in 1937.

\* \* \*

The India that Maugham was drawn to was not the India of the British Raj, of Kipling, of polo tournaments and hill station summers. His travels in the colonies of the Far East had inculcated in him an abiding scepticism about the effects of British rule and the character of British rulers. Maugham planned an itinerary that would take him not to 'British' India, but to the Princely or 'Native' states of southern India. These were governed by local rulers under a form of indirect rule, subject to the paramount authority of the British Crown, but where British influence was at its least pervasive.

It was India's spiritual life that truly interested Maugham, and in which he intended to immerse himself, visiting temples and meeting holy men, scholars and teachers. Along with Gerald Haxton, in December 1937 Maugham set sail from Genoa to Bombay, not only furnished with introductions to various Maharajahs from his Cap Ferrat neighbour, the Aga Khan, but with his steamer trunk laden with copies of Charles Eliot's *Hinduism and Buddhism*, Radhakrishnan's *History of Indian Philosophy* and L. D. Barnett's translation of the *Upanishads*. Maugham was clearly in search of something more than just material.

From Bombay, the pair travelled first to Goa then on to Madurai, where Maugham spent a rapt day exploring the labyrinthine corridors and gloomy halls of the Meenakshi temple, where he sensed something 'secret and terrible', before moving on to Madras. When, at a cocktail party, he expressed his interest in seeking out Indian holy men, Christina Austin, the wife of a senior British civil servant called Thomas Austin, offered to take him to meet Sri Ramana Maharshi.

After a hot, tiring drive along dusty, rutted roads, Maugham and Mrs Austin arrived at the ashram at midday. They were met by Ramana's English disciple Major Chadwick, who had been living at the ashram for the past two years and had taken the name Sadhu Arunachala.

Alan Chadwick was the son of an Anglican vicar and grammar school headmaster from Basingstoke, and had an early vocation to follow his father into religious orders. As a student at Oxford, however, he suffered a crisis of faith. Leaving university without having graduated, he worked in a series of jobs before making his way to Canada, where he worked as a land surveyor. At the outbreak of the First World War, he returned to England, enlisting in the Hampshire Regiment and rising to the rank of major.

After the war, Chadwick came into a modest inheritance, which would afford him financial independence for the rest of his life. When a friend gave him a copy of the *Bhagavad Gita*, he also found the spiritual direction that had been lacking in his life since his abdication from Christianity.

Chadwick was living on the Balearic Island of Majorca and practising meditation when he read Paul Brunton's *A Search in Secret India*. Determined to meet the Maharshi, he immediately set about settling his affairs, leaving his home and possessions in Majorca. After a visit to England for a short stay with his sisters, and where he also met Brunton, he set off for India, arriving in Tiruvannamalai in November 1935.

Walking through the gate of the ashram, Chadwick prostrated himself at the feet of the first person he saw, believing it was Ramana. In fact it was another ashramite, Annamalai Swami, who gestured to the Englishman to get to his feet and led him to the main hall where he pointed out Ramana seated in his customary position on the sedan.

Chadwick would remain at the ashram for the next fifteen years until Ramana's death in 1950 (Chadwick died in 1952). 'To try and describe my reactions when I first came into the presence of Bhagavan is difficult,' Chadwick wrote,

I felt the tremendous peace of his presence, his graciousness. It was not as though I were meeting him for the first time. It seemed that I had always known him. It was not even like the renewal of an old acquaintanceship. It had always been there though I had not been conscious of it at the time. Now I knew.[20]

Photographs of the Major from the period show a tall, erect, cheerful-looking man, with neatly parted dark hair, smartly dressed in white *kurta* pyjamas. He was allowed to build his own hut at the ashram, furnished with a bed, a table, an armchair and a bookshelf, lined with volumes on the Vedanta. Behind the hut was a small kitchen, where his own cook prepared curries, supplemented by a regular supply of tinned goods sent from Madras.

On arriving at the ashram, Maugham and Mrs Austin were asked by Chadwick to wait until Ramana was ready to see them. They had taken the precaution of packing a picnic lunch, which they ate while Maugham questioned Chadwick about his life, apologising for his inquisitiveness. 'He had an expression of peaceful happiness,' Maugham noted later,

He spoke slowly but fluently, in a rather loud voice. He smiled a great deal and laughed frequently. His manner was cheerful. He was very polite and anxious to do what he could to be pleasant. It was hard to tell if he was intelligent or a little stupid.[21]

Chadwick told Maugham that he considered Ramana to be the greatest spiritual figure that the world had known since Christ, and described how he passed his days in the ashram. He spent many hours sitting in the hall with the Maharshi, though he seldom spoke more than a few words to him in a week. The rest of his time was spent reading, riding his bicycle for exercise, and in meditation. He told Maugham he was endeavouring 'to realize the self in him in communion with the universal self, to separate the I that thinks from the self, for that, he said, is the infinite'. When he had achieved that, Chadwick said, and really felt that the divine in himself was part of the infinite divine, then he would have reached enlightenment. His answer left Maugham bemused. 'He was certainly very happy,' he wrote, 'I had thought to discover something of the truth about him from what he looked like and from what he said, but I came away completely puzzled.'[22]

Maugham and Chadwick had been talking for some time when something curious happened: Maugham suddenly fainted. He was carried into Chadwick's hut and laid on a pallet bed. At length he recovered consciousness, but felt too unwell to move. Hearing of what had happened, Ramana, accompanied by Chadwick and an attendant, came to the hut where the writer was resting. 'His mien was cheerful, smiling, polite,' Maugham wrote later, 'he did not give the impression of a scholar, but rather of a sweet-natured old peasant.' For a few minutes, Ramana gazed with a 'gentle benignity' at Maugham, then shifted his gaze and sat in motionless silence for perhaps a quarter of an hour, before asking Maugham whether he wished to ask him any questions. Maugham replied that he felt too unwell to say anything, whereupon Ramana smiled and said: 'silence is also conversation'.[23] Ramana turned his head away and resumed his concentrated meditation, 'looking, as it were, over my shoulder'. No one spoke. After another quarter of an hour, Ramana turned to Chadwick and said he should leave, as people would be looking for him. He got up, bowed to Maugham, smiled farewell and left the room.

Whether as a consequence of having rested or of the Maharshi's meditation, Maugham wrote, after a little while he felt well enough to go into the hall where Ramana was seated. He watched as two visitors offered a basket of fruit and prostrated themselves before him, and the Maharshi then went into *samadhi*: 'A little shiver seemed to pass through those present. The silence was intense and impressive. You felt that something strange was taking place that made you inclined to hold your breath. After a time, I tiptoed out of the hall.'[24] (Major Chadwick would offer a somewhat different account. Because Maugham was wearing a heavy pair of boots, Chadwick wrote, he did not enter the hall, but instead looked through a window into the hall, 'taking mental notes'.[25] If this is true, quite why Maugham could not simply have removed his boots is not made clear.)

Word of Maugham's fainting fit quickly spread far and wide throughout India, with people ascribing it either to Maugham being overcome with awe at the prospect of being in the presence of the holy man, or of the Maharshi having somehow caused the Englishman to be 'rapt for a while in the infinite'. The truth was more prosaic. As Maugham later explained, he had been subject to occasional fainting fits throughout his life, due to an irritability of the solar plexus, which pressed the diaphragm against the heart.

This was not the explanation that those Indians who wished to see the great Englishman as the beneficiary of Ramana's special grace were inclined to believe. As Maugham wrote:

> How do I know, they ask me, that I was not rapt in the infinite? To that I do not know the answer, and the only thing I can say, but refrain from saying for fear it will offend them, is that if it was, the infinite is an absolute blank.
>
> The idea of theirs is not so bizarre as at first glance it seems when one remembers their belief that in deep, dreamless sleep consciousness remains and the soul is then united with the infinite reality which is Brahman.[26]

Maugham had been touched by Ramana's humility and dignity, and by the palpable reverence of his disciples, but he had experienced nothing of the rapture that had overcome Brunton and Mercedes de Acosta, nor the feeling of deep recognition and of 'coming home' that had made its mark on Chadwick. Maugham had not been stopped in his tracks. He was not devotee material.

Nonetheless, the Maharshi left a sufficient impression for Maugham to use him as the model for the sage 'Shri Ganesha' in his novel *The Razor's Edge*, published in 1944, and to return to the subject in a lengthy essay titled 'The Saint', published in 1958, which leaves the reader in no doubt that a saint is exactly what Maugham believed Ramana Maharshi to be.

In this essay, Maugham describes his visit to the ashram and gives a detailed account of Ramana's life, an explanation of the philosophy of Advaita, and teachings on the Atman, karma and the theory of reincarnation—'as plausible an explanation of the existence of evil in the world as has been devised by human wit'. Ramana, he concluded, was 'a fatalist', whose message to his followers was that the most important thing was 'to realize the Self in themselves', and that since nothing happens except by divine dispensation, nothing they might do could affect it. 'It was natural that the question should be put to him,' Maugham wrote, 'If what is destined to happen will happen, is there any use in prayer or effort? It does not seem to me that he answered the question.'[27]

One person who was not impressed by Maugham's observations was Major Chadwick, who damned 'The Saint' as 'indifferent and uninspired'. Maugham, Chadwick complained, had clearly not understood Advaita and had singularly failed to grasp the meaning of Ramana's teachings, not least in his observation that 'to the Maharshi the world was a place of suffering and sorrow'. 'What absolute rubbish!' Chadwick wrote, 'Bhagavan always insisted that there was nothing wrong with the world. All the trouble lay with us.' Maugham, he went on, had attributed words and thoughts to Sri Ramana that he 'could never have uttered in his life. But such is the habit of famous authors, to put their own opinions into the mouths of others.' On reading 'The Saint', Chadwick went on, 'one comes to the conclusion that he has again succeeded as a first-class writer of fiction'.[28] Perhaps he was smarting over Maugham's uncertainty over whether he was 'intelligent or a little stupid'.

Leaving Tiruvannamalai, Maugham continued on his travels round India, visiting Hyderabad, Calcutta, Benares, Agra and New Delhi, before returning to Bombay. On a roadside outside Hyderabad, he encountered a sadhu who was said to have healing powers and was surrounded by a large group of supplicants. Maugham was initially fascinated, and then embarrassed when the sadhu asked him for a blessing. He protested that he was not the proper person to bless anyone, but the sadhu insisted. Maugham obliged, 'feeling hypocritical and very foolish, with all those people looking on'.[29]

He experienced moments of quiet, personal rapture. Walking one day at dusk in the Taj Mahal, he was struck by an 'eerie, mysterious sense of its emptiness' and seemed to hear 'the noiseless footfall of the infinite'.[30] But he grew tired of different holy men telling him the same thing he had heard from others twenty times before, and repeating 'like parrots' the same similes and metaphors for Reality, illusion and enlightenment: 'Your heart sinks when you hear again the one about the snake and the rope.'[31]

The spiritual illumination that others had spoken of, and that he perhaps yearned for himself, remained tantalisingly out of reach. Under instructions from a yogi, who promised him that with perseverance he would have 'extraordinary experiences', he attempted to meditate; convinced that he had far exceeded the suggested fifteen minutes, he glanced at his watch and saw that just three minutes had passed: 'It had seemed an eternity.'[32] 'As for getting any insight into the intense spiritual life that one finds here, there & everywhere,' he wrote, 'well, it is like seeing the Himalayas at night only in one flash of lightning.'[33]

Later, he would write that when people asked him what sights had most impressed him in India, he would give the answers that they expected. But in truth, it wasn't the Taj Mahal, the temple at Madurai or the *ghats* of Benares that had most moved him; it was the Indian peasant, clad only in a rag around his waist, terribly emaciated, shivering in the cold of dawn and sweating in the heat of noon, 'toiling as he had toiled from father to son, back three thousand years when the Aryans had first descended upon the country, toiling for a scant subsistence, his only hope to keep body and soul together'.[34] It was India's suffering that affected him most deeply.

\* \* \*

In March 1938, Maugham set sail from Bombay, resolved to return to India the following year. In fact, he would never go back. He returned to his home on Cap Ferrat. But on the outbreak of the Second World War, he was forced to flee France, undergoing a harrowing voyage on a coal barge to England. In October 1940 he travelled to America, where he was to see out the rest of the war.

In need of somewhere to live, Maugham's American publisher Nelson Doubleday offered to build him a house on his plantation, Bonny Hall in South Carolina, and provide him with staff. It was there that Maugham wrote his novel of India, *The Razor's Edge*.

*The Razor's Edge* tells the story of Larry Darrell, a First World War fighter pilot who returns to America traumatised by the experience of war and the death of a friend who has died in the act of saving his life. Larry is engaged to Isabel, a beautiful but shallow girl from an haute-bourgeois family. Social connections have secured him a job in a thriving brokerage firm. But he is undergoing an existential *crise*. Bent on a life of the mind, his sole aim, he announces, is to 'loaf'. When Isabel tells him to stop 'shirking' and 'do a man's work', Larry protests that 'it would be the betrayal of my soul'. 'That's the way hysterical, highbrow women talk,' Isabel responds, 'What does it mean? Nothing. Nothing. Nothing.'[35]

So that's the end of that.

Larry sets off to tramp his way across Europe, and eventually finds his way to India. Arriving in Bombay, he is struck by the realisation that has afflicted seekers throughout the ages, 'an intense conviction that India had something to give me that I had to have. It seemed to me that a chance was offered to me and I must take it there and then or it would never be offered me.'[36] He makes his way to Kerala, and the ashram of a famous swami named Shri Ganesha, who bears more than a passing physical resemblance to Ramana Maharshi: 'He wasn't tall, neither thin nor fat, palish brown in colour and clean-shaven with close-cropped white hair. He never wore anything but a loincloth and yet he managed to look as trim and well-dressed as a young man in one of our Brooks' Brothers' advertisements.'

Larry is invited to stay at the ashram and is given the shack where Shri Ganesha himself once lived. After two years, he moves to a forester's bungalow on the hill above the ashram, where he has an experience of *samadhi* while meditating—an experience 'of the same order as the mystics have had all over the world through all the centuries, Brahmins in India; Sufis in Persia, Catholics in Spain, Protestants in New England' (an observation that reflects Larry's—or rather Maugham's—acquaintance with William James' book, *The Varieties of Religious Experience*).

Infused with a certainty about the state of the Absolute, Larry leaves the ashram and returns to Europe. It is at this point in the tale that he recounts his experiences to the book's narrator. Asked what attracted him to the Swami, Larry replies:

> 'Saintliness. We've read all about the Saints, St Francis, St John of the Cross, but that was hundreds of years ago. I never thought it possible to meet one who was alive now. From the first time I saw him I never doubted that he was a saint. It was a wonderful experience.'
>
> 'And what did you gain from it?'
>
> 'Peace.'[37]

Shri Ganesha, Larry goes on,

> taught that it is not essential to salvation to retire from the world, but only to renounce the self. He taught that work done with no selfish interest purifies the mind and that duties are the opportunities offered to man to sink his separate self and become one with the universal self. But it wasn't his teaching that was so remarkable; it was the man himself, his benignity, his greatness of soul, his saintliness. His presence was a benediction. I was very happy with him. I felt that at last I had found what I wanted.

Larry tells the narrator that he is now resolved to go on, living with 'calmness, forbearance, compassion, selflessness and continence' because 'I know by personal experience that in nothing are the wise men of India more dead right than in the contention that chastity intensely enhances the power of the spirit' (a statement that falls intriguingly from the pen of Maugham, a writer for whom chastity was not so much a foreign land as a distant galaxy). Larry's plan is to become a taxi-driver in order to earn a living: 'My taxi would be merely the instrument of my labour. It would be an equivalent to the staff and the begging bowl of the wandering mendicant.'[38]

Thus, Maugham concludes, has Larry found the happiness he is seeking.

In Larry's disenchantment with materialism, his search for a more meaningful life, Maugham was not only echoing the frustrations of the post-war 'lost generation', but anticipating the yearnings of the 1960s hippies on their migratory trail east in search of escape or illumination.

The problem with *The Razor's Edge* is that rather than being the sympathetic figure he should be, Larry comes across as an earnest and tiresome prig. The most vivid and entertaining character in the novel is Elliott Templeton—a suave, wealthy aesthete and art dealer (based on Maugham's close friend Henry 'Chips' Channon, the American-born Tory politician and incorrigible social climber), whose refined tastes, vaulting snobbery and unshakeable footing in the material world provide a counterpoint to Larry's rejection of materialism and his inner search. The pair could almost be seen as the two conflicting sides of Maugham's own character—the anguished seeker and the world-weary, jaundiced dilettante.

Incidents from Maugham's own visit to India find their way into the book. To illustrate the point that whatever miraculous powers a yogi might develop are intrinsically worthless, Larry recounts a story that Maugham was told, of how a yogi came to the bank of a river, but did not have the money to pay the ferryman to take him across. The ferryman refused to take him for nothing, so the yogi stepped on the water and walked on its surface to the other side. Maugham wrote that 'The Yogi who told me shrugged his shoulders rather scornfully. "A miracle like that," he said, "is worth no more than the penny it would have cost to go on the ferryboat."'[39]

Maugham also drew on material that he had requested from the Ramana ashram. Larry's musings on the Advaita teachings, the Absolute, reincarnation and his philosophical *aperçus*, all have the ring of Ramana's teachings. 'Shri Ganesha,' Larry tells the narrator, 'used to say that silence is also conversation': exactly the words that Ramana had used to Maugham.

Maugham also turned for advice to his friend the English novelist Christopher Isherwood. At the age of thirty-four, having written three novels and lived for some years in Berlin, Isherwood had moved to

America in 1939, determined not to become embroiled in the impending war with Germany—a decision largely influenced by his resolution that he could not take any part in a war in which his German lover, Heinz Neddermeyer, could possibly be killed.

Isherwood was not looking for God. Quite the opposite. To Isherwood, religion was a word that 'made me wince and grit my teeth with loathing'.[40] But in spite of his best intentions, he had found himself succumbing when introduced to Swami Prabhavananda—a monk at the Ramakrishna ashram in Madras who had come to America in 1923 to assist at a Ramakrishna centre in San Francisco, and who in 1930 had founded his own Vedanta centre in Hollywood.

Among the visitors to the centre were Aldous Huxley and his friend Gerald Heard, a brilliant *littérateur* whose books ranged from *Narcissus: An Anatomy of Clothes* (1924), a study of the relationship between architecture and dress, to a study of evolution titled *Pain, Sex and Time* (1939) and a series of macabre horror stories including *The Black Fox* and *Doppelgangers*. It was Heard who introduced Isherwood to Prabhavananda.

The Swami was a small, smiling figure with an affectation for dapper dress—he wore expensive, pointy shoes under his monk's robe. An avowed ascetic, he displayed a remarkably accommodating attitude to the failings and foibles of his disciples—in Isherwood's case, his promiscuous homosexuality, a cause of torment for Isherwood himself, who oscillated guiltily between the austerities of the ashram and frenetic sex with a variety of different partners. In Vedanta, Isherwood found a belief system that not only reinforced his pacifism and answered his intellectual needs; it also tolerated his homosexuality.

It was Isherwood, after consulting with Swami Prabhavananda, who provided Maugham with the translation of a verse from the Katha Upanishad for the epigraph to *The Razor's Edge*, which Maugham paraphrased to read: 'The sharp edge of a razor is difficult to pass over; thus the wise say the path to Salvation is hard.' Isherwood disapproved of Maugham's interpretation, complaining that he had explained to the author that the image of the razor is used to describe a path that is both very painful and very narrow. Therefore, one should not say that the path is 'difficult to cross' as many translations have it, since nothing is easier than to step across a path—or a razor—from one side to the other. What is difficult is to *tread* the razor's edge and the path to enlightenment. 'To Swami and me, it seemed that "pass over" is nearly if not quite as ambiguous as "cross"', Isherwood complained.[41]

Later, when Maugham came to write his essay on Ramana, 'The Saint', he again consulted Prabhavananda on the Maharshi's teachings, sending him a copy of the text before it was published. 'All the philosophy in it was wrong!' Isherwood lamented in his diary, 'Now we have to concoct a tactful reply.'[42] Maugham duly incorporated Prabhavananda's corrections into the finished text. Evidently these were not sufficient to satisfy Major Chadwick.

It is common for novelists to draw their characters from real life. But Maugham did it more than most, and not always with the greatest subtlety—as the numerous people who extended their friendship and hospitality to him over the years, only to find themselves, and their lives, depicted in his short stories with the merest fig-leaf of a pseudonym, discovered to their cost.

Maugham habitually employed the device of the detached narrator in his novels, but *The Razor's Edge* was the only book where he called that narrator by his own name. It is the only novel, too, which contains the declaratory line in the introduction that in writing the book, 'I have invented nothing.' Indeed, Maugham's desire to suggest that Larry Darrell had a life beyond the book is emphasised on its very first page:

> The man I am writing about is not famous. It may be that he never will be. It may be that when his life at last comes to an end he will leave no more trace of his sojourn on earth than a stone thrown into a river leaves on the surface of the water. But it may be that the way of life that he has chosen for himself and the peculiar strength and sweetness of his character may have an ever-growing influence over his fellow men so that, long after his death perhaps, it may be realized that there lived in this age a very remarkable creature.[43]

At the book's conclusion, Maugham goes even further in lending credence to the idea that Darrell was something more than just a figment of the author's imagination:

> He is without ambition, and he has no desire for fame; to become anything of a public figure would be deeply distasteful to him; and so it may be that he is satisfied to lead his chosen life and be no more than just himself. He is too modest to set himself up as an example to others; but it may be he thinks that a few uncertain souls, drawn to him like moths to a candle, will be brought in time to share his own glowing belief that ultimate satisfaction can only be found in the life of the spirit, and that by himself following with selflessness and renunciation the path of perfection he will serve as well as if he wrote books or addressed multitudes.[44]

Almost from the moment of its publication, *The Razor's Edge* prompted much speculation about whom, if anybody, Larry Darrell was based upon. Christopher Isherwood was dismayed to find himself being put forward as the model in an article in *Time* magazine, and wrote to *Time* to complain: 'I can stand a good deal of kidding from my friends, but this rumor has poisoned my life for the past six months, and I wish it would die as quickly as possible.'[45]

Another candidate for Darrell was Guy Hague—the American who had greeted Mercedes de Acosta when she first arrived at the Ramana ashram, just a few months after Maugham's visit. De Acosta offered a sketchy description of Hague as an American from Long Beach, California, who had been honourably discharged from the US Navy in the Philippines and then worked his way to Bombay, where he had taken up the study of yoga. Hearing of Ramana Maharshi, he had made his way to Tiruvannamalai. 'When I met him he had already been with the Maharshi for a year,' de Acosta wrote, 'sitting uninterruptedly day and night in the hall with the sage.'

The researcher Dennis Wills put more flesh on Hague's bones. Rather than being a sailor, as de Acosta suggested, Hague had actually served in the US Army Signals Corps, stationed on the Mexican border.[46] Following the death of his wife, Hague travelled to South America, working in the copper mines in Mexico and Peru, before making his way to the Philippines and then to India. Rather than him having been at the ashram for a year, as de Acosta suggested, Hague had arrived only a few weeks before de Acosta herself. This means he would not have been at the ashram when Maugham visited, and Maugham makes no mention elsewhere of having ever met or heard of Hague. Hague remained at the Ramana ashram until 1941, acting as the emissary and passing a series of letters back and forth between de Acosta and Ramana, before returning to America and his work as a miner. He and de Acosta continued to correspond for some years after his return.

Paul Brunton's son Kenneth Hurst wrote that his father had told him that Maugham conceived the character of Larry Darrell after sitting next to Brunton at a Hollywood dinner party, where he had first told Maugham about the Maharshi. In fact, there is no evidence that Brunton and Maugham ever met, although Brunton maintained that Maugham had once attempted to contact him. Brunton was dismissive of *The Razor's Edge*. The descriptions in the book, he wrote, were 'fanciful', the events 'unreal':

Maugham is a newcomer to these things, anyway, and cannot get even a quarter of an inch below appearances, while often soaking in clouds of self-deception. Nevertheless, he has come out of agnosticism to this higher standpoint; it is good to know that he wrote this novel instead of concentrating exclusively on sex, as in his other stories.[47]

Perhaps the most likely model for the background detail of the time that Darrell spends at the ashram of Shri Ganesha—if indeed there was a model at all—was the redoubtable Major Chadwick, whom Maugham had questioned so assiduously on his arrival at Tiruvannamalai.

In his 2001 novel *Half a Life*, V. S. Naipaul playfully proposes an alternative source of inspiration for the guru Shri Ganesha. *Half a Life* tells the story of Chandran, an impetuous young Brahmin from a long line of 'foolish, foreign-ruled, starvling priests'. It is the 1930s, and following Mahatma Gandhi's call to rise up, fight the caste system and 'live a life of sacrifice', Chandran makes the grand gesture of courting a young girl from the so-called backward caste. But the gesture gets out of hand; pursued by the principal of his school and the girl's 'firebrand' uncle, he takes refuge in the temple where he sits in silence, adopting the pose of a holy man.[48]

The silence that Chandran adopts is very different from the state of silence that Ramana Maharshi described as *mouna*, whereby the mind as well as the tongue becomes silent and free from thought. 'It is this state,' Ramana wrote, 'where there is not the slightest trace of the "I" thought, that is the true Being of oneself.' And it is in this silence, in 'Heart to Heart' teachings, that the teacher can most effectively communicate with the receptive disciple. As Ramana told Maugham, 'Silence is also conversation.'

But Chandran's silence is neither illumination nor 'conversation'; it is an act of escape, a con trick. But it is a successful one. People bring offerings, and he begins to win a certain amount of respect, even renown.[49]

In Naipaul's novel, after Chandran has been sitting in the temple for three months, an English writer happens upon him. It is Somerset Maugham. Taking Chandran at face value, the gullible Maugham asks him: 'Are you happy?' 'With perfect seriousness' Chandran writes down his answer: 'Within my silence I feel quite free. That is happiness.' Maugham dutifully writes it down in his notebook. 'There were a few more questions like that,' Chandran reflects, 'Quite easy stuff, really, once I had got into it.'[50]

In the novel, Maugham returns to England and writes up the encounter. As a result, Western visitors begin to make their way to see Chandran, and his stock grows still further when Maugham publishes *The Razor's Edge* and critics see Chandran as the spiritual inspiration for the novel. Bathed in the light of Maugham's naivety, the fraud becomes a celebrity. He is able to take his place back in society, his union with the backward caste girl is blessed; but secretly ashamed he takes a private vow of sexual abstinence, *brachmacharya*, like Gandhi. But unlike Gandhi, he fails—twice—giving birth to a son and a daughter. He names the son William (or Willie) Somerset Chandran—after Maugham.

Willie, who comes to recognise his father as a fraud and a coward, is sent to a Christian school and sets his heart on moving to the West. Chandran writes to Maugham, seeking his help, but the writer fobs him off with a pro-forma reply: 'Dear Chandran, It was very nice getting your letter. I have nice memories of the country, and it is nice hearing from Indian friends. Yours very sincerely.' It is 'as though the old writer hadn't understood what was being asked of him,' Chandran observes.

The benediction of being named after the great writer does not serve Willie well. He journeys to London, 'a stranger here with the nerves of a stranger', where he too tries to make a life as a writer. He publishes a volume of short stories, but it is a failure. A meeting with one of his few readers, Ana, leads to him following her to colonial Mozambique, where he idles his life away on her estate, visiting prostitutes and indulging in a stale affair until his marriage finally collapses.

*Half a Life* touches on familiar themes in Naipaul's work about the postcolonial experience, cultural dislocation and the religious life as a form of escape or charlatanry. In this, the fictive Somerset Maugham plays an interesting role. Maugham was a writer whom Naipaul greatly admired; in 1961 Naipaul was the recipient of the Somerset Maugham Award, which had been instituted by the writer in 1947. The place of Maugham as the catalyst in the bogus Chandran's life may be taken as part compliment, part joke; but it contains a cautionary meaning for those looking to India for spiritual illumination. We might adapt the metaphor of the snake and the rope: a person who, to outward appearances, looks like a guru might be something else entirely.

Asked about the origins of *The Razor's Edge*, Maugham said that he had had the idea of writing a book about a man turning his back on the world in search of spiritual fulfilment in mind for twenty years—but it was his visit to India that had revived the idea and given it a geographical context. He told his friend Karl Pfeiffer that writing *The Razor's Edge* had given him 'great pleasure. I do not care if people think it good or poor. I have got it off my chest & that is all that matters to me.'[51]

In writing *The Razor's Edge*, Maugham, like Hermann Hesse, was remarkably prescient, anticipating an embrace of Eastern culture by a younger generation of Americans and Europeans decades before it happened. The book was one of Maugham's most successful, selling more than 3 million copies and spending almost a year on the bestseller lists. In 1946 it was turned into a successful Hollywood film starring Tyrone Power, and in 1984 into an unsuccessful one starring Bill Murray. ParamahansaYogananda inscribed a copy of his 1946 *Autobiography of a Yogi* to Maugham, thanking him for 'spreading the seed of India's teachings'.

But despite its theme of spiritual search, *The Razor's Edge* did not become a handbook of the 1960s counterculture in the way the novels of Hesse did. The social milieu that Maugham describes Larry Darrell escaping from—rich, snooty, entitled—was already unrecognisable in the 1960s. And Maugham himself—stiff-necked, remote, fabulously wealthy, and in so many ways a product of Edwardian England—was highly improbable material for a cult hero. Hesse was suitably exotic and safely dead.

But of all Maugham's novels, *The Razor's Edge* is the one that most directly addresses the questions that exercised Maugham throughout his life, the yearning for faith, meaning and peace of mind in life. All of this was Maugham's wish for himself, and for all his wealth, success and acclaim, he would never find it. In 1941, on a visit to Hollywood, he met with his friends Christopher Isherwood and Gerald Heard. 'I'm getting an old man,' he told them. All he wanted to do was return to India and write a last serious book about Shankara, the Hindu philosopher who consolidated the doctrine of Vedanta, and spend his last days in a monastery. Isherwood wrote later:

> I was much moved on hearing this, until news reached us through [John] van Druten and others that Willie had made fun of Gerald, albeit quite affectionately, at a cocktail party the next day, and had deplored my wasting my time with mysticism when I ought to be writing novels. But then he's like that; a mass of guilt and contradictions. I doubt if anybody really understands him.[52]

Towards the end of his life, his nephew Robin asked Maugham what was the happiest memory of his life. Maugham replied: 'I can't think of a single one.'[53]

# 9

# THE LIFE AND DEATH OF PAUL BRUNTON

In 1935, following the phenomenal success of *A Search in Secret India*, Paul Brunton published *The Secret Path*, a short manual on meditation and self-enquiry, explicating Ramana Maharshi's 'Who Am I' method. Brunton did not actually mention Ramana by name, instead cryptically referring to the guru as a 'wise man of the east' whom he had met 'unexpectedly'. 'There in that seated being was a great impersonal force that read the scales of my life with better sight than I could ever hope to do,' he wrote.

Over the next fifteen years, Brunton, the journalist who had once sought out sages in search of enlightenment, would write a series of books in which he assumed the mantle of sage himself, espousing his own theories of Mentalism and what he called the 'Overself' and the 'Universal Mind'. In Brunton's teaching it was the 'Universal Mind' which had brought the world into being—'a Mind which is perennially benevolent, unfathomable, wise and eternally peaceful'.[1] The 'Overself' was the presence of the 'Universal Mind' in the individual—the place 'where man may become conscious of God'.

Brunton emphasised that the 'Overself' was not a metaphysical concept, but a living presence. He used the metaphor of the guardian angel in Christian teaching, 'a felt presence,' as he put it, 'ever with us and never deserting us. It is our invisible saviour. But we must realize that it seeks primarily to save us not from suffering but from ignorance which is the cause of suffering.'[2] He even went so far as to specify its location— 'hidden away in the human body on the right side of the physical heart'[3]—a physical position that exactly matched Ramana Maharshi's location for the centre of spiritual awareness.

But Brunton's relationship with the Maharshi was to prove short-lived. The catalyst was Ramana's brother Nagasundaram—known to all as Chinnaswami—who acted as the ashram manager. Chinnaswami was a difficult, autocratic and suspicious man, who apparently saw the success of *In Search of Secret India* as a potentially lucrative source of income for the ashram, and who accused Brunton of 'using' the Maharshi and his teachings to build his own reputation.[4]

In March 1939, Brunton returned to Arunachala, expecting to stay for three months. But no sooner had he arrived than he found himself confronted by Chinnaswami. Brunton, the ashram manager claimed, had been writing about Ramana without permission, and given nothing that he made from his books to the ashram. He demanded that Brunton should write nothing more about Ramana in the future, nor ask him any questions.

Brunton appealed directly to Ramana, arguing that he was writing about the sage 'for the benefit of the world'. Ramana replied: 'If you ask Chinnaswami, he will also say "I am doing good for the world." You are saying that you are doing good for the world. What can I say?' Emboldened by Ramana's words, Chinnaswami told Brunton to leave, threatening to call the police if he refused.[5]

The ashram records note that Brunton left after eight days, adding that he had given an assurance that he would not speak or write about Ramana thereafter, and that he would be content with seeing Sri Maharishi in his heart: 'Sri Bhagavan said that Dr Brunton was obliged to leave the place by the play of the higher power. He could not stop here a moment longer than was allowed by that power; nor can he stay away from here when drawn again by the same power.'[6]

But Brunton would never see Ramana again. He would subsequently attribute the falling out to intrigues within Ramana's inner circle. He wrote that it had become 'painfully evident' to him that the ashram had become mired in politics, over which Ramana's 'ascetic indifference' rendered him temperamentally disinclined to exercise the slightest control. The ashram had turned out to be 'a miniature fragment of the imperfect world I had deserted,' he wrote, 'I had no alternative but to bid it an abrupt and final farewell.'[7] Ramana was the Indian mystic who had inspired him most, he wrote, the sage whom he most revered. But the 'clear guidance' that Brunton hoped the Maharshi would provide never came:

> With all the deep respect and affection I feel for him, it must be said that the role of a teaching sage was not his forte.
>
> This explained why his open disdain for life's practical fulfillment in disinterested service of others had led to inevitable consequences of a disappointing kind in his immediate external environment ... The question of the significance of the universe in which he lived did not

appear to trouble him. The question of the significance of the human being did not trouble him, and he had found an answer which satisfied him.[8]

Brunton now revised the opinion he had arrived at early on in his meetings with Ramana and expressed in *A Search in Secret India*, that it may be good for the world to have 'a few men who sit apart from our world of unending activity and survey it for us from afar'.[9] Instead, he came to the view that the person who merely meditated was 'a complacent recluse' and nothing more, that meditation apart from experience was 'inevitably empty', and that 'a monastic mysticism which scorned the life and responsibilities of the busy world would frequently waste itself in ineffectual beating of the air'.[10] He had 'over-idealized' mystics, he wrote, mistaking

> their attainment of yogic peace for the true self-realisation ... I discovered in the end that the yogi is afraid of action and consequently indifferent to the troubles of the world and unconcerned about mankind's well-being; that his society and presence does not radically change human character for the better, as is claimed, but merely lulls its worst qualities into semi-quiescence to spring up again, however, at the first release from his immediate influence.[11]

The West, he cautioned, should guard against believing that India held the monopoly on spirituality, and the seeker should not turn to 'ancient Hinduism and become its ill-fitting proselytes, nor to contemporary Hindu mysticism and become its blind followers, nor to yogic ashrams and become their escapist inmates'.[12]

The 'worship of human idols', the segregated life of the ashram, or the 'mere wandering' around India, 'whose outward degeneration is an apt symbol of its inward ignorance', could only lead to the 'temporary titillations' of the emotions, he wrote, 'but never to that sublime knowledge which releases man forever from all quests and all hankering and alone confers the realization of what we are here for and alone bestows immortal benefit to himself and all creatures'.[13]

Ramana himself appeared indifferent to the falling out with Brunton, and often recommended to visitors that they should read his books. But for Brunton the banishment would haunt him thereafter. He wrote that in the years afterwards, whenever he was travelling in the vicinity of the Maharshi's ashram, 'a lump would come into my throat and a choking sensation would seize me as I thought how close we were in spirit and yet so harshly separated by the ill-will of certain men and by the dark shadows of my own karma'.[14] While they would never meet again, he claimed that

197

he remained in touch with Ramana 'telepathically' until the guru's death in April 1950.

By then, Brunton's reputation as an author was firmly established. With *A Search in Secret India* he had been the first writer to bring Indian spiritual life to a popular audience. He had proved an important link between Eastern ideas and the West—even if it was not quite as important as his more ardent champions, who have credited him with the introduction of meditation and yoga to the West, would maintain. He had published more than twenty books that had sold in their hundreds of thousands around the world. To his readers he was Paul Brunton, the gentle sage. To his friends, and a growing number of followers, he was 'PB'.

'PB' was a shy, retiring man, who gave very little away about himself. To outward appearances, he led a restlessly peripatetic life, with no fixed abode. He always insisted that he was not a guru, nor a spiritual teacher—a label he claimed to dislike 'so much that a chill would creep over me at the thought'—and insisted too that he did not actively seek a following. Yet over the years a circle of people gathered around him whom he called friends, or 'questers', but who tended to behave more like disciples, hanging on his teachings and occasionally accommodating him as he travelled around the world.

Among these was a prosperous Los Angeles jeweller named Jacques Masson, whose son Jeffrey would later write a diverting account of his family's association with Brunton called *My Father's Guru* (1993). Jacques had been introduced to Brunton's teachings in the early 1940s by his brother Bernard, who had met Brunton and became convinced that he was an avatar with tremendous occult powers.

In 1945, determined to meet Brunton, Jacques travelled to India, where Brunton had spent the war years, staying with his patron the Maharajah of Mysore. Brunton told Jacques that the jeweller was the reincarnation of a medieval Kabbalist named Althodas (the name actually came from a book by the Victorian novelist Marie Corelli, whose purple fictions about mysticism were a huge popular success, and had enthralled Brunton as a boy), and that he had had a vision of Jacques at the age of forty having developed occult powers and become a seer whom people would come to consult 'from all over the world'.[15]

Duly flattered, Jacques became a close friend and one of Brunton's most devoted 'questers'. Over the course of some fifteen years, Brunton would often stay with the Massons at their homes in California and, later, Hawaii, and for a brief period the young Jeffrey was given over to Brunton's guidance and groomed as his spiritual student, for a time working as his secretary.

For Jeffrey, Brunton was a source of constant wonder and mystery, with his tales of Indian swamis and miracle workers and his claim that he could read people's auras. Masson was enthralled when Brunton told him that he was a teacher at the 'Astral University', and that he would one day take Masson there; and even more enthralled when Brunton told him that he had actually come from the planet Sirius. Masson later came to think that this was simply an entertaining fantasy spun to amuse a young boy. But Brunton repeated the claim in his *Notebooks*, adding that the inhabitants of Sirius were infinitely superior to the miserable creatures inhabiting earth: 'In intelligence, in character, in creative power and in spirituality we are as slugs crawling at their feet.'[16]

Masson describes Brunton as a man who deliberately cultivated the air of the all-knowing sage: 'He'd have this strange, faraway look in his eyes, so he always looked kind of dreamy. And he would smile mysteriously—that was his favourite thing, to smile to himself—not a chuckle, but a real smile, like "I know something you don't know."' If ever visitors came to the house, Brunton would tell the Massons to introduce him as 'Philo', for Philo S. Opher—philosopher: 'He thought this was hilarious. But he would kind of lurk in the background, as if he didn't want to be recognised or known.'[17]

Brunton would go to considerable lengths to preserve his anonymity, often using a pseudonym. Replying to a quester who had written to ask Brunton if he would agree to meet him and his wife, Brunton gave exacting instructions about meeting in a vegetarian restaurant in Kensington: 'If your wife is coming alone on Tuesday then you will of course describe me to her as I shall be seated. My name in public is "Mr Brown".'[18]

Masson recalls an occasion when Brunton was visiting the Masson family in Rome and went with Jeffrey and his sister to the cinema:

> As we went in he put on dark glasses. I said, why would you do that? And he said, I don't want to be recognised. I thought to myself, who the hell is going to recognise him in Rome? And wouldn't you know, ten minutes later someone came up to him and said, aren't you Paul Brunton?

Masson writes that Brunton took pains to avoid what he called 'psychic contamination'. He disliked shaking hands, claiming to 'feel ill' when he touched anybody he sensed was 'lowly evolved'. He cautioned the young Masson to 'refrain from associating with anyone who is a failure'.[19] But he was also possessed of a lively, and sometimes wicked, sense of humour. 'I think that was one of the reasons my parents liked him,' Masson says,

> My father had a very louche sense of humour himself, and PB loved making fun of all kinds of people and things, other gurus—usually if they were being pretentious. He'd make fun of himself. He would say something to prick the balloon, and my father would collapse with laughter; they would just egg each other on, and literally fall off their chairs. He was very entertaining.
>
> My parents thought they were privileged to be close to him. They were wealthy and he had a very nice life with us. He would get a beautiful room and good vegetarian food and so on. But I don't think he did it out of greed, I really don't. He could at some point have said to my father, look I need money. And my father would have given it to him. But as far as I know he never did.

Brunton maintained that his teachings were the distillation of a universal wisdom which he had accrued over his years of travelling to the furthest corners of the world—'not only in India but on the limitless sands of the Sahara Desert, on the canyon-sides of the mountain-girdled Yangtze River, in the steaming hot jungles of Siam and Malaya, and on the snowy heights of Tibet'.[20] Tibet, of course, was held to be the very crucible of esoteric knowledge. Brunton told Jeffrey Masson that he had taken teachings from 'a highly advanced yogi' of the Kagyu school, 'a direct descendant of Milarepa', but when the Chinese discovered their meetings he had been forced to flee, leaving behind a cache of manuscripts that was going to be *A Search in Secret Tibet*.

Did Brunton ever visit Tibet? In 1936, he applied to the government of India asking it to make representations on his behalf to the government of Tibet for permission to visit the holy pilgrimage site of Mount Kailash, but two British botanists, Captain Frank Kingdon-Ward and Ronald Kaulback, had inflamed Tibetan sensitivities at the time by entering the country without permission, and Brunton's request was refused.

Brunton tried to short-cut the bureaucracy by appealing directly to the British government's Secretary of State for India, Lord Zetland. But Zetland rebuffed his request in a sharp memo sent to the Indian government: 'Please inform Brunton, with whom I have some slight personal acquaintance, that I have received his telegram but can only concur in the decision.'[21] The permission was never granted.

In recent years, photographs have emerged, ostensibly taken by Brunton, of Mount Kailash and Lake Manasarovar in Tibet, suggesting that he penetrated the interior of the country clandestinely, although there is nothing in his books or notebooks to prove it. Brunton's *A Hermit in the Himalayas* was written during a stay in the small principality of Tehri Garhwal in the foothills of the Himalayas ('There are unexpected things in this book by an Occidental who sits cross-legged under the shadow of the mountains and finds himself full of Power derived from the One', wrote *The Daily Telegraph* in a review).

Brunton had an unusual relationship with his son. Kenneth was raised by his mother, Karen Tottrup, and Brunton's constant travelling meant that he played little direct part in the boy's upbringing. Kenneth was nonetheless clearly in awe of his father, and his book about Brunton is an adoring hagiography—less the work of a son than of a *chela*, or disciple—the term that Kenneth says Brunton used to describe him. Kenneth gives numerous examples of what he regarded as Brunton's teachings—some of them distinctly eccentric. When Kenneth fell in love with a girl and wanted to marry her, he arranged a dinner to introduce her to his father for his blessing. Brunton was late arriving at the restaurant and then maintained total silence throughout the meal, completely unnerving the unfortunate woman. When, the following day, Kenneth questioned him on his behaviour, Brunton replied that in order to ascertain whether the girl was suitable, 'I had to go within to the deeper part of my being and contact her intuitively.'[22] His conclusions were clearly unfavourable; the marriage, perhaps inevitably, never happened.

Brunton was a man of abstemious habits. He was teetotal, ate only vegetarian food and had strong views about sexual purity and the dangers of dissipating what he considered the life-force through lax sexual activity. He told Kenneth that if, when walking down the street, he saw an attractive woman, he would consciously avoid looking at her: 'I do not want her to feel, "Oh dear, here's another of those men ogling me and looking at my breasts".'[23]

Following the dissolution of his first marriage, Brunton appeared to lead a celibate life. So, it was a matter of some astonishment to his friends and 'questers' when in 1952 Brunton married a strikingly beautiful 19-year-old opera singer named Evangeline Young. Brunton was 54. Evangeline had been raised in a small town in Ohio and had developed an early passion for Eastern philosophy. She was writing a high school graduation thesis on yoga when she discovered Brunton's books in the local library. 'When I read them it was as if I could hear his voice speaking inwardly to me, and I knew he had the truth about these very complicated things,' she remembers. 'He spoke to me like a friend and a mentor.'[24]

She wrote to him, beginning a correspondence that would last two years, until they eventually met in California. Meeting Brunton confirmed Evangeline in her belief that he was a 'great spiritual being. And I never changed my mind about that, in all the years we were married and afterwards.' Evangeline describes the marriage as a deep spiritual friendship: 'It was a teacher-pupil relationship in the sense that I greatly respected and looked up to him and I was in awe of his great spirituality, all my life. It was a relationship that had deep affection and humanity in it.'

Brunton's 'spiritual work', meditating and writing, was the most important thing to him, she remembered, 'But we weren't just sitting looking at our navels all day. He loved opera, ballet, he loved reading great authors. He was not a hermit. He was a very normal, sane person.' The marriage had the effect of alienating Brunton from many of his friends and 'questers', Evangeline recalled:

> The majority of people around him were very negative and there was this terrible jealousy. PB was extremely kind and very loving, but he guarded his privacy and his right to be who he was and to live the way he wanted to. And these people couldn't accept that. It was almost unbearable at times, not only with these so-called 'questers', but sneering people, when we would travel, going into hotels, this very distinguished older man and the young woman that I was ... But we overcame a great deal of that, because our basic relationship was a highly spiritual one, and it was based on how we could help each other and be of service to each other.

Brunton published his last book, *The Spiritual Crisis of Man*, in 1952. But the royalties from his work, and his modest habits, afforded him the opportunity to lead a peripatetic life. It was his vocation, he wrote, to delve into the spiritual and mystical traditions of whichever country he visited, and to seek out those he regarded as mystics and 'unusually gifted and spiritually advanced individuals'. He spent time with Carl Jung and the Danish mystic Martinus Thomsen; visited the young Dalai Lama in India; and travelled to Italy to meet the Catholic priest, stigmatist and mystic Padre Pio. 'PB had thousands of people who wrote to him,'

Evangeline remembers, 'and we would travel around with huge trunks full of letters for him to answer. He felt whoever wrote to him he had a duty to answer them.'[25]

'PB had a certain target audience for his books,' says Melody Talcott, the daughter of Evangeline Glass, who knew Brunton well in later life:

> His audience was the materialistic Western mind, and he felt if he could reach people of influence and power, they in turn would be able to reach a lot of people. Sometimes he and Mother went to some really magnificent places, and he would say to Mother, 'this is much more trouble than it's worth'. It sapped his energy. He had to be present with these people and share spiritual things with them. He thought of it rather as a job. He said to Mother, 'it's not all fun and games you know'.[26]

His connections were often surprising, and he was a shameless name-dropper. In a letter to one 'quester' he talked of the Shankaracharya of Kanchi[27] as 'the Pope of the South'—'but with the difference that he is fully enlightened, whereas the Pope, whom I met in Rome a few years ago is not, although a good man within his personal limitations'.[28] In another letter, he wrote: 'My final advice to you cannot be better than to quote what was carved over the entrance to that temple in Delphi where I sat in deep meditation: "Man Know Thyself", and which I repeated, during our long, earnest talk later, to the King and Queen of Greece.'[29]

In fact, this was no idle boast. Queen Frederica of Greece was a passionate admirer of Brunton's work. When her husband King Paul fell ill, Frederica summoned Brunton to the royal residence in Athens. According to a newspaper report at the time, Brunton—described as 'suave, discreet, and, above all, secretive'—was even admitted to the operating room during a procedure on the King. 'I thought he was a prominent foreign physician observing the operation,' one of the doctors performing the operation said, 'Yet he did absolutely nothing but stand intensely silent in the background absorbed in deep thought. We dubbed him the mystery man.'[30]

Following King Paul's death in February 1964, Queen Frederica increasingly turned to Brunton for solace and spiritual guidance, to a degree that began to cause consternation to the Greek Orthodox Church and members of the court, recalling the controversy that had blown up in the Netherlands a few years previously when Queen Juliana had fallen under the influence of a spiritualist. Brunton was quietly urged to depart 'temporarily'. 'Now,' the newspaper reported, 'he has returned and in a chauffeur-driven limousine is being whisked in and out of the palace gates as unobtrusively as before.'[31]

Brunton's marriage to Evangeline would come to an end after six years, when she travelled to California to study with the celebrated operatic singer Lotte Lehmann and fell in love with Lehmann's accompanist, a concert pianist named Beaumont Glass. In 1958, Evangeline and Brunton divorced, but she and Beaumont, whom she would later marry, were to remain friends with Brunton for the rest of his life. In Evangeline's words, 'PB loved me forever and I will love him forever. That never changed.' She went on to have a highly successful career in the world of opera, singing lead soprano roles at some of the most important opera houses in Europe, including Cologne, Geneva and Naples and at the Salzburg Festival. She remained married to Beaumont Glass for fifty-four years, until his death in 2011.

Throughout the 1950s, as the Cold War between Russia and the West intensified, Brunton became increasingly fearful that the world was on course for destruction. He began to warn his 'questers' that nuclear holocaust was inevitable, and furthermore that it would probably occur in 1962. He advanced a plan, which he called 'Operation Shield', which suggested that South America would be the safest place to take refuge from the nuclear fallout. Acting on this advice, a number of 'questers' packed up their lives and relocated to South America. Among them were the Massons, who liquidated the family business and moved to Uruguay. But in 1961, Brunton dramatically revised his opinion, suggesting that South America would not, after all, offer any particular sanctuary from the impending holocaust. Rather than following his friends to South America, Brunton himself moved to Australia and later New Zealand.

For Jacques Masson it was the final straw in his growing disenchantment with Brunton. Ever since his first meeting with him in 1945, Masson had been waiting patiently for the enlightenment he believed Brunton had promised he would experience around his fortieth birthday. But enlightenment had stubbornly declined to arrive. By the age of fifty, Masson was in a state of despondency, and while his son notes that 'he never abdicated his long and unceasingly hopeless and lonely vigil', his relationship with Brunton came to an end.[32]

Evangeline Glass believes that if there was disillusionment among some 'questers', it owed more to their misunderstanding than to anything Brunton had said. Those who went to South America went of their own free will, she says:

But when the war didn't come they were furious. And PB was all to blame. But PB always told me, and everyone else including the Massons, that nothing can be predicted. Many people recognised this global terror of annihilation; it wasn't just PB's fantasy world. But he never told people what to do. And he never, ever said that they should all get together like a cult.

Brunton now began to withdraw from his circle of 'questers'. He circulated a document, 'The Message', announcing that he would be going into 'deeper retirement' and would no longer be available to answer spiritual or personal questions, and explaining that henceforth his activities would be concentrated on the serious business of saving the world from annihilation. Referring to himself in the third person, he wrote: 'He has to be outwardly away and free to attend to his personal assignment which involves the fate of millions. He cannot allow himself to be distracted by the few and they [his followers] should not be so selfish as to expect him to.'[33]

He told his son Kenneth that he was working in league with a group of 'celestial beings' around the globe whose mission was to concentrate mentally during meditation on world leaders, in order to help their own 'higher selves' to restrain any war-like actions. Brunton claimed that he had been concentrating his personal efforts on Mao Zedong, and told Kenneth that his intervention had been instrumental in Mao not taking advantage of the Cuban Missile Crisis in 1962 by pressing China's territorial designs on the borders with Russia.

Jeffrey Masson was experiencing his own feelings of disenchantment. Inspired by Brunton with a fascination for the East, and a belief that he too should follow the spiritual path, Masson went on to study at Harvard, where he attained degrees in Sanskrit and Indian Studies. In learning Sanskrit himself, Masson writes, he realised that Brunton, rather than being fluent in the language as he had claimed, could not read 'a single sentence':

> I felt I had been taken in, duped. It was all a trick. PB knew no Sanskrit, knew no texts, invented things, lied, cheated and stole, intellectually speaking. How could I have been so stupid? In spirit, PB might have been like the Indian sages he idolized. His ideas may have been similar to theirs. But he did not really represent any tradition, any body of knowledge, any other person—in fact anything at all.[34]

To Masson, the man he had once idolised, who had enthralled him with stories of astral travel and the mystic East, was 'a phony, a charlatan, a mountebank, an imposter, a quack ... I couldn't find enough words to describe my disappointment.'[35]

Paul Brunton spent his last years in Switzerland, living in a series of modest rented apartments in Lugano, Montreux and, finally, Vevey near Lake Geneva. He painted his homes in warm reds and oranges and hung Oriental paintings on the wall. He had few possessions—religious objects he had collected on his travels around the world; books of spiritual teachings.

He worked on a series of diaries, *pensées* and philosophical musings that would be published posthumously under the title *The Notebooks*, and corresponded with friends—practical advice on diet and spiritual growth ('how valuable are those few minutes prized from the day's routine for mental quiet!'), thanks for gifts—biscuits, socks, gloves, nail-clippers and the skull-caps he took to wearing in old age—and quirky asides: 'Lobsang Rampa is not authentic. He acknowledged under pressure that his books were written mediumistically as he never visited Tibet.' 'You mention the young Prince of Wales,' he wrote to one friend in 1968, 'I suggest you watch his unfoldment. He is marked for spiritual enlightenment.'

Increasingly his letters contained intimations of his own mortality, of ailments minor—a request for acne cream—and not so minor: 'It seems I have to undergo an operation on the blood supply to the brain', he wrote to a friend in 1966.

When Evangeline and Beaumont Glass moved to Switzerland, they would see Brunton regularly. Their daughter Melody remembers him as 'a princely figure—regal in his energy', who radiated a spiritual aura, 'on the same level of enlightenment as any of the great spiritual teachers he encountered or wrote about'.

Jeff Cox, an American student who had read and been deeply impressed by Brunton's books—and who would later go on to found the publisher Snow Lion—visited him in Switzerland in 1975. They passed the time talking and meditating, occasionally walking to the lake to feed the pigeons. Cox would shop for provisions. Brunton was particularly partial to Marmite—a yeast spread much loved by the British, but which is a mystery to the rest of the world. 'He was a proper English gentleman,' Cox says,

> He had a very quiet presence. Many people had mystical experiences in his presence, or through their connection with him. What I felt was

this very strong, deep presence of silence and stillness. He was like a wise grandfather who would watch and intuit what you needed and then convey something that might be helpful. We all need models and for me he represented the wisdom of a great sage.[36]

Brunton's principles remained steadfast to the last. As his health declined, he refused his doctor's suggestion of drugs on the grounds that their testing had involved the death of animals. In the *Notebooks*, he wrote that on his death 'I shall be carried away to my own star, to Sothis of the Egyptians, Sirius of the Westerners. I shall at last be happy.'[37]

He died peacefully in hospital on 27 July 1981, at the age of eighty-two, with his son Kenneth and a friend at his bedside. Shortly before his death, Brunton told a friend that a new manager at the Ramana Maharshi ashram had contacted him, holding out an olive branch and offering Brunton a place to stay for the remainder of his life. He had considered the offer, and politely declined.

\* \* \*

Brunton's old friend Frederick Fletcher never gave up his bhikku's robes. In the early 1930s he travelled to Britain for a short lecture tour, before returning to 'the English monastery' in Rangoon. In 1941, an inquisitive reporter from the Australian newspaper *The Age* found him there.

The reporter described Fletcher: 'He had low sunken eyes, hollow cheeks and almost luminous skin. In the begging bowl which he set down on the floor, was some rice and a few bananas.'[38] In his room was a small Buddhist shrine, 'set amid paper flowers and a few bits of tinsel'. Hanging on the wall were a few photographs, some paintings of the Buddha, the bhikku's war medals and the certificate stating that Frederick Charles Fletcher had in 1913 been made an associate member of the Institution of Mechanical Engineers. 'If, as Diogenes maintains, a man's happiness may be computed by the number of things with which he can do without,' the reporter wrote, 'Prajnananda must be truly happy—and in fact he maintains that he has found true happiness in simplicity, meditation and study.'[39]

The following year, the Japanese Army occupied Burma. According to Christmas Humphreys, who corresponded with him, Fletcher was three times arrested for spying and twice condemned to death, being spared only by the intervention of the Japanese High Commander, a Zen Buddhist, who recognised that Bhikku Prajnananda was a genuine practitioner and renunciate. Having survived two world wars, Frederick Fletcher died in Rangoon on 28 December 1950. He was accorded a full Buddhist funeral, conducted by the Latvian Buddhist Archbishop, and attended by several hundred people.

Over the years, Fletcher, as well as maintaining his friendship with Paul Brunton, had also corresponded intermittently with Brunton's son Kenneth. In 1959, Kenneth happened to be in Rangoon. Curious to learn more about the bhikku's life, he was led to the quarters of the Latvian Buddhist Archbishop, who informed him that Fletcher's last wish had been that half his ashes should be buried in the flower garden of the English monastery—which had been done—and the other half preserved in the headquarters of the Buddhist Society in London.

When Christmas Humphreys visited Rangoon shortly after Fletcher's death, the Archbishop asked him to take the remainder of the ashes to London in order to fulfil Fletcher's last wishes. But according to the Archbishop, Humphreys had demurred, ostensibly on the grounds that it was bad luck to carry a dead man's ashes on a plane.

Kenneth Hurst, showing no such qualms, agreed that he would take the ashes with him and deliver them to the Buddhist Society when he was next in London. With a tin containing the ashes packed in his suitcase, he flew to Jakarta, en route to Perth, where his father was staying—preparing for his work to save the world. Arriving at customs, Hurst was questioned about the contents of the tin. When he replied that it was a dead man's ashes the tin was confiscated, and he was told to collect it a few days later.

Finally arriving in Perth, and unpacking his suitcase, Hurst discovered that the lid had not been screwed firmly back on the tin and that some of the Bhikku Prajnananda's ashes were scattered among his clothing. Together, he and Brunton carefully vacuumed the suitcase, gathered the ashes and scattered them around the flowers in the garden.

Some months later, with the remainder of the ashes tightly fastened in the tin, Hurst flew to London, intending to honour Fletcher's last wish. On arrival he wrote to Christmas Humphreys, asking whether he could place the ashes in the shrine at the Buddhist Society's headquarters. But according to Hurst, Humphreys replied that it would not be possible. Hurst wrote a stiff letter of complaint, threatening to broadcast the Society's 'discourtesy' to 'a gallant officer and an outstanding Buddhist monk' if it did not comply.

208

Word came back that the Society would be happy to accept the ashes after all, and in 1961 Hurst delivered them to the Society's headquarters in Eccleston Square, where they were put in a suitable urn and placed in a niche in the shrine. In April 1975, the ashes were finally interred in the rose garden at another Buddhist centre, Wat Dhammapadipa in Hampstead. Thus were the last earthly traces of Frederick Fletcher, engineer, soldier and monk, distributed in Rangoon, Perth and London.

1. Sir Edwin Arnold: 'He knows India better than any living Englishman knows it'.

2. Swami Vivekananda: 'Purposeful, virile and strong ... a man among men'.

3. Allan Bennett with members of the Buddhasasana Samagama in Burma, circa 1903.

4. Aleister Crowley, the Beast, in ceremonial regalia:
'I will endure to the end'.

5. Jiddu Krishnamurti:
Groomed as the Messiah.

6. William McGovern,
scholar and adventurer.

7. Meher Baba: Devotees were prone to tears.

8. Meher Baba, centre. Left to right, unknown, Margaret Craske, Margaret Starr, KimTolhurst and Meredith Starr.

9. Mercedes de Acosta: 'I can get any woman from any man'.

10. Ramana Maharshi, Paul Brunton, disciples and calf, 1930s.

11. Somerset Maugham: 'I doubt if anybody really understands him'.

12. Timothy Leary: 'Playing out the ancient role'.

13. The Beatles meet the Maharishi in 1967.
'We thought there was more to him than there was'.

14. Maharishi Mahesh Yogi at a press conference at the Royal Festival
Hall, London, on his world tour to usher in the Age of Enlightenment.

15. Shrine to 'the Mother', Mirra Alfassa, 'an embodiment of the divine feminine principle', in the house in Kolkata where Aurobindo Ghose was born.

16. John McLaughlin, Carlos
Santana and Sri Chinmoy:
Love, devotion, surrender.

17. Rajneesh (centre) and his personal secretary Ma Anand Sheela,
leaving the Immigration and Naturalization Services building in
Portland, Oregon, 1982.

# SECOND WAVE

# THE SACRAMENT

*None are more hopelessly enslaved than those who falsely believe they are free.*

Goethe

# 'WE ARE ALL HINDUS IN OUR ESSENCE'

In the spring of 1962, Timothy Leary, a Harvard psychologist who had recently begun conducting experiments with the psychedelic drugs psilocybin and LSD, visited a Ramakrishna ashram in Boston run by a former Air Force major, turned Vedanta Hindu monk, named Fred Swain.

Leary, a rambunctious Irish-American, whose colourful CV included being court-martialled whilst a cadet at West Point Military Academy, had been introduced to magic mushrooms while on a trip to Mexico in 1960. Through intensive use and experimentation, he had become convinced that psilocybin—the active ingredient of magic mushrooms—and the hallucinogen LSD, opened the door to the enlightenment experience that mystics and seers in all religions had described for millennia. Fred Swain had also ingested magic mushrooms in Mexico with the anthropologist R. Gordon Wasson, and after taking LSD with Leary at his home, Swain invited Leary to visit his ashram, with a view to leading some of his students through an LSD session.[1]

On the appointed day, Leary arrived at the ashram. In a mood of sacramental reverence, LSD was placed in chalices on an altar adorned with incense and flowers. The LSD was then mixed with holy water from the Ganges, blessed and drunk. As the drug took hold, the group moved to the shrine room, sitting 'Indian style' on cushions and chanting Hindu mantras, the pungent aroma of incense perfuming the air.

Swain had already acquainted Leary with the teachings of Ramakrishna and what Leary would describe as 'the psychedelic pantheon of gods' in Hinduism. Now, 'as the Holy folk got high', the shrine room began to take on the aspect of a living *purana*, or Hindu mythological text. Leary felt himself transforming into the god Shiva; a Vedanta nun crawled into his lap, whom Leary, naturally, saw as Shiva's consort Shakti. 'The incense smoke rose', Leary wrote, essence of Holy India, reek of Khaligat temple Calcutta, holy scent of Ram Mandir, Benares and Jaganath Puri and Konarak. Ramakrishna's statue breathed and his eyes twinkled the message. Vivekananda's brown face beamed and winked. Christ grinned to be joined again by his celestial brothers. The rare wood walls breathed. The sacred kundalini serpent uncoiled up the bronzed candelabra to the thousand-petaled lotus blossom. This was the fulcrum moment of eternity. The exact second of consciousness, fragile, omniscient. God was present and spoke to us in silence.

Leary maintained that he was 'a Hindu from that moment on':

> No, that's not the way to say it. I recognized that day in the temple that we are all Hindus in our essence. We are all Hindu Gods and Goddesses, Laughing Krishna, Immutable Brahma. Yes, and Asiatic-sensual Siva. Stern Kali with bloody hands. Undulant flowering Laxmi. Multi-armed Vishnu. Noble Rama. That day in the temple I discovered my Hindu-ness.[2]

For Timothy Leary, 'The slow, invisible process of becoming a guru, a holy man,' as he put it, had begun.

*  *  *

What had brought Timothy Leary to a Hindu ashram? Leary's father was a dentist, who dreamed of his son pursuing a military career and enrolled him at West Point, where Leary's strong anti-authority streak quickly emerged. From the minute he set foot in West Point he was being carpeted for various infractions. Asked to resign, he refused. After being accused of going on a drinking-binge he was court-martialled. The charge was subsequently dropped, but it was the end of his time at West Point.

Leary went on to serve in the army, but after the Second World War decided to pursue an academic career. He studied for a degree in psychology and took work as research director of the psychiatric clinic at the Kaiser Hospital in Oakland, California. He married Marianne Busch in 1944, who gave birth to a son and a daughter.

Leary would describe himself during this period as 'an anonymous institutional employee who drove to work each morning in a long line of commuter cars and drove home each night and drank martinis ... like several million middle-class, liberal, intellectual robots'. Furthermore, his marriage was quickly going to hell, marked by multiple infidelities and alcohol abuse on both sides. In 1955, Marianne committed suicide.

214

Unmoored, Leary drifted with his two children, taking teaching fellowships in Spain, Denmark and Italy.

In 1957, he published *Interpersonal Diagnosis of Personality*, which advocated an existential approach to psychology, whereby rather than being the dispassionate scientific observer the psychologist should be a participant, interacting with patients in real-life situations—a hands-on philosophy that would later mark his approach to psychedelics. The book was praised by *The Annual Review of Psychology* as 'the most important book on psychotherapy of the year'. But despite this success, Leary was growing increasingly frustrated by what he perceived as the failure of clinical psychology to tackle the big problems of human nature—unhappiness, stupidity and conflict.

In January 1960 he returned to America and joined the Department of Social Relations at Harvard, in search of a physiological stimulus that could, in his words, 'loosen neurological bonds'. In the spring of that year, on a trip to Mexico, he was introduced to the sacred mushrooms— 'divinatory fungi', as he put it—used in shamanistic rituals by native Indians. 'In four hours by the swimming pool in Cuernavaca,' he would later write, 'I learned more about the mind, the brain and its structure than I did in the preceding fifteen years as a diligent psychologist.'[3]

Here, at last, was the answer to those big questions about unhappiness, stupidity and conflict that psychology had failed to provide. These mind-altering substances—psychedelics, as they would later be called—would radically remake one's relationship to the world, Leary believed, jolting one into the awareness that what we conventionally accept as 'reality' is really 'just social fabrication'. Here was a ticket to the roller-coaster ride to the god realms experienced by mystics from time immemorial.

With his Harvard colleague Richard Alpert, Leary established a research programme called the Harvard Psilocybin Project. In keeping with his belief in the importance of the psychologist's role as participant rather than observer, Leary wasted no time in diving in and joining the experiments himself.

Alpert was himself ready for transformation. The youngest of three sons of George Alpert, a lawyer who went on to become president of the New York, New Haven and Hartford Railroad, Richard had failed to satisfy his parents' ambitions for him to become a doctor by being turned down for medical school. Instead, he studied psychology, gaining a doctorate at Stanford University. Moving to Harvard, he taught and conducted research at the Department of Social Relations and the Graduate School of Education.

When Leary walked into his life, Alpert was 29 years old—ten years younger than Leary—and by any purely material measure, a success. He lived in an apartment in Cambridge, Massachusetts, filled with antiques, where he gave charming dinner parties. He owned a Mercedes sedan, an MG sports car, a Triumph 500cc motorcycle and a Cessna 172 airplane. He scuba-dived in the Caribbean. In short, as he would put it, he was living as a successful bachelor professor was supposed to live in the American world of 'he who makes it'.[4] He was also depressed, anxious, dissatisfied with his work and confused about his sexuality—a medley of discontents that five years of psychoanalysis at $20 an hour had done nothing to dispel.

In March 1961, at Leary's home, Alpert took psilocybin for the first time. Writing of the experience later, he described how he had watched as each of the social roles he had played in his life appeared before him as if on a stage—the little boy eager to please his parents by becoming a brain surgeon, the successful professional, the sophisticated cosmopolite—and then disappeared. Looking down at his body, he was shocked to see that his arms, legs and torso were all disappearing. Fearing that he was on the verge of total extinction, Alpert was reassured to hear a small voice in the back of his mind that asked:

> 'who's minding the store?' When I could finally focus on the question I realized that although everything by which I knew myself, even my body and life itself was gone, I was still fully aware! ... I had just found that 'I', that scanning device—that point—that essence—that place beyond.[5]

Leary and Alpert were following a well-trodden path of investigation into mind-altering substances among Western intellectuals and artists. In 1897, the English physician and writer Havelock Ellis ingested peyote buttons, which had been supplied to him by a Philadelphia physician named Weir Mitchell, who was said to be the first ever white man to write an account of 'peyote inebriation'.[6] Ellis wrote of experiencing a series of intense visions including 'a vast field of golden jewels, studded with red and green stones, ever changing', writing up his reflections in an article tellingly entitled 'Mescal: A New Artificial Paradise'.[7] His friend W. B. Yeats was similarly impressed, describing visions of 'the most delightful dragons, puffing out their breath straight in front of them like rigid lines of steam, and balancing white balls on their breath'— although Yeats later wrote that he preferred cannabis. But the most famous witness to the transformative effects of mescaline—the active agent of the peyote cactus—was the English writer and philosopher Aldous Huxley.

Huxley came from a line of distinguished rationalists. His grandfather Thomas Huxley was a zoologist, who coined the term 'agnostic' and whose fierce championing of the theory of evolution earned him the nickname 'Darwin's Bulldog'. Aldous' brother Julian and half-brother Andrew were both biologists.

Uncommonly tall, elegant, diffident, bespectacled and betweeded, Huxley had the appearance and manner of the quintessential English intellectual. He made his early name as a novelist writing waspish social satires, but became increasingly interested in broader philosophical and social issues, in particular the pacifist cause.

In 1937 he moved to California to work as a screenwriter, with his wife Maria, son Matthew and his friend Gerald Heard. He became close friends with Jiddu Krishnamurti, who had been taken up by some members of the film community, and through Heard he became part of a Vedanta circle, based around Vivekananda's disciple and emissary Swami Prabhavananda. It was Huxley who introduced his fellow writer Christopher Isherwood to Prabhavananda—although unlike Isherwood and Heard, Huxley resisted becoming a disciple himself.

In 1945 Huxley published his book *The Perennial Philosophy*, an anthology of thoughts and writings from saints, teachers and philosophers, from Thomas Aquinas and St Augustine to Rumi, Shankara and the Upanishads, with a commentary by Huxley, designed to illustrate the commonality of wisdom and mystical experience through the great religions.

Huxley had long been interested in the social effects of drugs. In 1932 he published his dystopian novel, *Brave New World*, describing a society in which social and spiritual needs are answered, and insurrectionary instincts are pacified, by a drug called 'soma'—a name Huxley had borrowed from a mind-altering substance mentioned in the Rig Veda ('All the advantages of Christianity and alcohol; none of their defects,' as Huxley wrote). The man who invents such a substance, he wrote in an article for the Los Angeles *Herald-Examiner*, 'will be counted among the greatest benefactors of suffering humanity'.[8]

Huxley's personal introduction to mind-altering drugs came through an English psychiatrist, Humphrey Osmond, who had been researching the possible use of mescaline in the treatment of schizophrenia.[9] Reading of Osmond's work, Huxley wrote to the psychiatrist, inviting him to visit if he should ever find himself in Los Angeles, and suggesting that he would be willing to try mescaline himself. By chance, Osmond was scheduled to attend a conference in Los Angeles. So it was that 'one bright May morning' in 1953, Huxley sat down in the lounge of his home, and with Osmond on hand to supervise and record the experience, swallowed four-tenths of a gram of mescaline, dissolved in half a glass of water, and waited expectantly to observe the results.

With his extensive knowledge of mystical experiences in both Eastern and Western religious traditions, it was perfectly natural for Huxley to interpret the experience that unfolded over the next few hours in precisely that light. Writing of his experience in *The Doors of Perception* (1954), Huxley described how pondering a bunch of flowers, 'shining with their own inner light and all but quivering under the pressure of the significance with which they were charged', he saw the 'Istigkeit—or "Is-ness" that the Christian mystic Meister Eckhart had described, and too the Dharma-Body of the Buddha'. The four legs of a bamboo chair in the middle of a room were

> like Wordsworth's daffodils, they brought all manner of wealth—the gift, beyond price, of a new direct insight into the very Nature of Things, together with a more modest treasure of understanding in the field, especially, of the arts. A rose is a rose is a rose. But these chair legs were chair legs were St Michael and all angels.[10]

Mescaline, Huxley concluded, was not enlightenment itself or the Beatific Vision, but rather—in the words of Thomas Aquinas—'a gratuitous grace'. Acknowledging, as it did, the powerful potential of psychedelics to transform consciousness and to offer a way of seeing the world that radically differed from the quotidian, *The Doors of Perception* would be a founding text of the drug culture that burgeoned through the late 1950s and 1960s.

In 1960, Huxley arrived in Boston to take up a position as the Carnegie Visiting Professor at the Massachusetts Institute of Technology (MIT). It was there he met Timothy Leary for the first time over lunch (dining, appropriately enough, Leary would note, on mushroom soup). Afterwards they adjourned to Leary's home to take psilocybin together. Listening to recordings of Bach, Mozart, African drums and Ravi Shankar, together they mapped out the conditions that would best aid a fruitful voyage into the psychedelic realms—the 'set and setting', as it became known.

Huxley advocated a patrician view of psychedelics, suggesting they should be confined to those of a refined and cultivated sensibility—artists, philosophers, poets, musicians, rich bohemians—who in turn could educate 'the intelligent rich'. According to Leary, Huxley told him, 'Your role is quite simple. Become a cheerleader for evolution.' It was a role he would play with evangelical fervour. 'Pursuing the religious life today without using psychedelic drugs,' said Leary, in one of his most famous utterances, 'is like studying astronomy with the naked eye.'[11]

To those of a mind to see it that way—and Leary certainly was—the psychedelic experience seemed to be a mirror of the Eastern philosophical teachings of immanence, the indwelling nature of God. The sense not that God is out there, but *in here*. Time, space, the separation between the see-er and the seen, become as nothing. The world is as it should be. As William Blake had it (and Huxley had confirmed), a rose is a rose is a rose, and perfect in its utter *rose-ness*. Thou art that ... The psychedelic traveller could feel he had journeyed to the very Godhead itself.[12]

Even if it meant coming back down to Earth with a bump. As the philosopher Arthur Koestler, who took psilocybin with Leary, observed: 'I solved the secret of the universe last night, but this morning I forgot what it was.'

While Aldous Huxley could see the mind-expanding potential of psychedelics, he was under no illusions about their limitations. Such insights as drugs afforded, he knew, were not in themselves enlightenment, nor were they a path that should be followed indiscriminately. Huxley believed drugs could be a complement to meditation and should only be taken under carefully controlled conditions. He particularly recognised the dangers of quietism that psychedelics carried. Mescaline, he wrote,

> opens up the way of Mary, but shuts the door on that of Martha. It gives access to contemplation—but to a contemplation that is incompatible with action and even with the will to action, the very thought of action. In the intervals between his revelations the mescaline taker is apt to feel that, though in one way everything is supremely as it should be, in another there is something wrong. His problem is essentially the same as that which confronts the quietist, the *arhat* and, on another level, the landscape painter and the painter of human still lives. Mescaline can never solve that problem; it can only pose it, apocalyptically, for those to whom it had never before presented itself. The full and final solution can be found only by those who are prepared to implement the right kind of *Welranschauung* by means of the right kind of behavior and the right kind of constant and unstrained alertness.[13]

For Leary, it was much simpler. Psychedelic drugs had revealed a self-evident truth: 'The Hindu Bibles read like psychedelic manuals. The Hindu myths were sessions reports.'[14] Leary's ecstatic discovery of his 'Hindu-ness' and his assertion that the ancient Vedic texts were actually 'psychedelic manuals' might well have bemused such emissaries of Vedanta and Advaita thought as Vivekananda, Ramakrishna and Sri Ramana Maharshi. Neither Vivekananda, Ramakrishna nor Sri Ramana had any recorded experience of hallucinogenic drugs and had nothing to say about them, but Vivekananda's disciple—and Gerald Heard and Christopher Isherwood's guru—Swami Prabhavananda disapproved violently of drug taking, considering it dangerous and illusory—'a deadly heresy', as Isherwood put it.

This did not stop Heard experimenting with mescaline. And Isherwood was also keen to weigh up the effects for himself. He asked Huxley and Heard to provide some for him. They prevaricated, Isherwood eventually learning from a mutual friend that they considered him 'too unstable emotionally'. Nonetheless, he was able to obtain some himself, and with his companion Don Bachardy acting as a sober observer, tried it one day in London. Under the influence, Isherwood asked to be taken to the Catholic Westminster Cathedral, 'to see if God was there'. Apparently, He wasn't. 'His absence was so utter that it made me laugh,' Isherwood recalled, 'So we went on to Westminster Abbey. Here the situation appeared even more comic to me. I had to go into a dark corner and stay there until I could control my giggles.'[15]

While Leary would become probably the world's most famous—or infamous—proselytiser for LSD, he had actually come rather late to the party. The drug had first been formulated in 1938 by Albert Hofmann, a Swiss biochemist working for the pharmaceutical-chemical department of Sandoz Laboratories in Basel, Switzerland, who, in search of a respiratory and circulatory stimulant, synthesised d-lysergic acid diethylamide tartrate (or LSD, as it became known), compounded from a constituent of a rye fungus known as ergot.

Hofmann put his work on LSD to one side for a few years, and it was not until 1943, when re-examining the compound, that he happened to touch his hand to his mouth, inadvertently ingesting a small amount. Feeling woozy, he decided to take the rest of the day off. Returning home he lay down, to be overcome, as he would later note, by 'an uninterrupted stream of fantastic images of extraordinary plasticity and vividness and accompanied by an intense kaleidoscopic play of colours'.[16] Concluding that the visions had been brought on by his accidental ingestion of LSD, Hofmann returned to his laboratory three days later, on 19 April 1943, and ingested 250 micrograms of the substance, commencing the first intentional acid trip.

Sandoz initially made the drug available on a limited basis for clinical and research purposes, and by the early 1950s a handful of psychiatrists in America had begun tentatively using LSD in the treatment of anxiety states and obsessional neuroses.

Among the first to recognise the extraordinary potency of the drug were the military and intelligence services in both Britain and America, who ran tests on military personnel exploring its potential properties as a truth serum. There is no record of any of these patients seeing the experience as being in any way equivalent to the bliss of enlightenment or *satori* talked about in Buddhist or Vedic texts. When Herman Kahn, an analyst for the RAND Corporation, took LSD as part of an investigation carried out by the psychiatrist Sidney Cohen, he claimed to have spent much of the session reviewing bombing strategies against mainland China.[17]

Timothy Leary first took LSD in the autumn of 1961, turned on by a fast-talking Englishman named Michael Hollingshead. Contemporary descriptions of Hollingshead vary from 'prankster' to 'fabulist' to 'no-good, two-bit, English con-man'. Richard Alpert described him as 'the closest to evil of most of the people I've ever met. I have this distinction between a rascal and a scoundrel. Timothy always stayed a rascal. Hollingshead was certainly a scoundrel.'[18]

Tall, in his mid-thirties, with prematurely receding hair and an English accent that he exaggerated to Wodehousian levels, at the time he met Leary, Hollingshead was living in New York and working as the executive secretary for an organisation called the Institute of British-American Cultural Exchange, the principal *raison d'être* of which seemed to be to gain Hollingshead entrée into American social and academic circles.

Hollingshead had already sampled psilocybin before he and a doctor friend, and a fellow drugs connoisseur, John Beresford, secured a gram of pure LSD from the Sandoz laboratories in Switzerland. Beresford and Hollingshead diluted the substance in water, adding confectioners' sugar to create a thick white paste which filled a 16-ounce mayonnaise jar— the equivalent of 5,000 spoonfuls of acid. Licking off the sticky residue, Hollingshead set off on a trip that lasted fifteen hours. 'What I had experienced,' he wrote later, 'was the equivalent of death's abolition of the body. I had literally "stepped forth" out of the shell of my body, into some other strange land of unlikeliness, which can only be grasped in terms of astonishment and mystery, as an *état de l'absurde*, ecstatic nirvana.'[19]

In search of someone who might help him make sense of this experience, Hollingshead contacted Aldous Huxley, who had himself already experimented with the drug, concluding that, by comparison, his experiences with mescaline were a mere sideshow to LSD's main event. Huxley in turn recommended that he contact Leary—'a splendid fellow', as Huxley put it. In September 1961, Hollingshead travelled to Cambridge to meet Leary, carrying his mayonnaise jar filled with LSD with him.

Leary first took the drug in his home with Hollingshead and his friends the jazz musician Maynard Ferguson and his wife Flo. Flo dropped it first. Her reaction, Leary noted, was distinctly and oddly … well … *Hindu*:

> She looked at me and began to talk. It was pure advaita Vedanta. She was Krishna lecturing Arjuna. She was reciting in chuckling, hip Manhattanese the essence of Hindu philosophy. Maya. Non-duality. Reincarnation. And this, mind you, coming from little Flo Ferguson, who hadn't finished high school and had never read a philosophy book in her life.[20]

For Leary, LSD was quite simply 'the most shattering experience of my life'. As it would be for hundreds of thousands of other people—if not all in the benign way that Leary experienced it. Five years after his first trip he wrote:

> I have never recovered from the shattering ontological confrontation. From the date of this session it was inevitable that we would leave Harvard, that we would leave American society and that we would spend the rest of our lives as mutants, faithfully following the instructions of our internal blueprints and tenderly, gently disregarding the parochial social inanities.[21]

LSD would accelerate the transformation in Leary's idea of himself, from professor to high priest. Visiting the Hindu ashram in Boston ('a serene, rhythmic life of work and meditation all aimed at getting high'— apparently), the handful of monks and nuns, he wrote, had treated him as a guru: 'To them it was obvious. I was not a Harvard psychologist with a staff of research assistants. Come off it, please. I was, like it or not, playing out the ancient role.'[22]

The 'ancient role' was not quite what the Harvard authorities had envisaged when they hired Leary. He was intensely charismatic, with a klieg-light smile and a roguish Irish charm. He made friends and attracted followers wherever he went. Leary soon had students queuing up to enrol in his research programme. The Psilocybin Project had initially been greeted with a mixture of indifference and mild alarm by most of his colleagues at Harvard, but the results had been remarkable. Under Leary's guidance, experiments with the inmates at a local prison had seen hardened criminals suddenly waxing lyrical about peace and love and talking of quasi-religious experiences.

In April 1962, Walter N. Pahnke, a graduate student in theology at Harvard Divinity School, devised an experiment under the supervision of Leary and Alpert to administer psilocybin to ten students from Andover Newton Theological School, along with a control group of another ten students who were given an active placebo of vitamin B3. Known as 'the Good Friday experiment' after the day on which it took place, nine of the ten students who had taken the psilocybin reported having a deep religious or mystical experience.[23] The results confirmed Leary in his conviction that 'spiritual ecstasy and religious revelation and union with God' were now 'directly accessible' by swallowing a tablet, and that 'mystical experience could be produced for and by those who sought it'.[24]

Three years into his research, this view was being shared by a growing number of students at Harvard. The genie had escaped from the bottle, and rather than signing on for Leary's research, many had started sourcing their own supplies of psilocybin and LSD, or cooking up the stuff themselves in home laboratories. Some students quit college altogether, and, in search of a deeper experience of enlightenment, journeyed eastward—early pioneers on what over the next few years would become the mass migration of the hippie trail. 'Not necessarily a bad development from our point of view,' Leary observed, 'but understandably upsetting to parents, who did not send their kids to Harvard to become buddhas.'[25]

Upsetting, too, to the Dean of the university, who was obliged to field an increasing number of complaints from parents that their children were phoning home to tell them they'd found God. Leary's days at Harvard were numbered, and in 1963 the Psilocybin Project was closed down by the college authorities and Alpert and Leary were dismissed.

Founding a new organisation, the Castalia Foundation (a name taken from Hermann Hesse's 1943 novel, *The Glass Bead Game*), dedicated to promulgating psychedelic revelation as the new religion of the twentieth century, they retreated to a rambling mansion in Millbrook, upstate New York, provided by the heiress Peggy Hitchcock, which quickly became a gathering place for avant-garde painters, musicians, hipsters, well-heeled bohemians and intellectuals such as Alan Watts and the Beat poet Allen Ginsberg. A visiting reporter for *Time* magazine described it as 'a strange mutation of Thoreau's Walden and a Tantric Buddhist temple'.[26]

In rooms perfumed with incense and decorated with Buddhist mandalas and images of Hindu gods, visitors would be led step-by-step through the psychedelic process, following Leary's exhortation to 'turn on, tune in, drop out'.[27] Having dispensed with his tweed sports jackets and shirts in favour of dashikis and Nehru-style shirts, the high priest of Millbrook set about producing new sacred texts for the psychedelic religion. The most significant, written in collaboration with Alpert and another Harvard psychologist called Ralph Metzner, was *The Psychedelic Experience: A Manual Based on the Tibetan Book of the Dead* (1964). It was a book that would be critical in LSD paving the way for Eastern ideas to become popular currency in the burgeoning drug culture of the 1960s.

*The Tibetan Book of the Dead* was an ancient funerary text that had originally been published by the American anthropologist and Theosophist Walter Evans-Wentz. 'The Great Liberation by Hearing in the Intermediate State' (*Bar do thos grol chen mo,* to give the text its proper Tibetan name), elaborates the Tibetan Buddhist teaching on the journey of the consciousness through the three stages, or *bardos,* of dying: the moment of death, the intermediate state between death and rebirth, and the process of rebirth itself. Central to the text is the belief that death presents the greatest opportunity to gain liberation, and so to step off the endless wheel of suffering that is held to characterise worldly existence.

The text was supposedly composed by the Indian yogi Padmasambhava, who is said to have introduced Buddhism into Tibet in the eighth century and is regarded as the founding father of the esoteric tradition. Like hundreds of his teachings, the text was transcribed in a cryptic language and secreted as a *terma,* or 'treasure text', to be discovered at a time when it was appropriate to be transmitted to the general populace.

It was supposedly then found in the fourteenth century, hidden in a mountain, by the *terton* ('treasure seeker') Karma Lingpa, who deciphered the text and passed on the teaching orally to his son. Several generations were to pass before it was finally written down, becoming one of the central teachings in the Tibetan Buddhist canon.

The first English translation appeared in 1927, edited by Walter Evans-Wentz. Born in 1878, after studying religion, philosophy and history at Stanford, Evans-Wentz attended Jesus College, Oxford, where he studied

Celtic mythology and folklore, publishing his degree thesis, *The Fairy-Faith in Celtic Countries*, in 1911. Living on money from real-estate investments in California, he made his way via Greece and Egypt to India, 'seeking', as he put it, 'wise men of the East'. In 1919, he acquired a collection of Tibetan texts from a British army officer in Darjeeling who had recently returned from Tibet. Evans-Wentz took the texts to a Tibetan called Kazi Dawa-Samdup, who was working as the English teacher at the Maharajah's Bhutia Boarding School for boys in Gangtok. Dawa-Samdup had been with the 13th Dalai Lama during the years the spiritual leader had been in exile in India, and had also worked as a translator for Alexandra David-Néel, the intrepid French explorer and Buddhist convert. Over the course of two months, Evans-Wentz met with Dawa-Samdup each day as he translated the texts. In fact, Evans-Wentz had stumbled upon only a small portion of the *Bar do thos grol chen mo,* but it was the translation of this small fragment that would form the basis for the numerous adaptations that have appeared since.

Aldous Huxley referred to *The Tibetan Book of the Dead* in *The Doors of Perception*, describing how at one point, under the influence of mescaline, he had felt himself on the verge of panic, comparing his fear of total personal disintegration to that of a dead Tibetan man who could not face the 'Pure Light of the Void', instead preferring rebirth and 'the comforting darkness of selfhood'.

After listening to the record of this part of the experiment, Huxley wrote, he reached for his copy of Evans-Wentz's edition of *The Tibetan Book of the Dead*, and opened it at random: '"O nobly born, let not thy mind be distracted."That was the problem—to remain undistracted. Undistracted by the memory of past sins, by imagined pleasure, by the bitter aftertaste of old wrongs and humiliations, by all the fears and hates and cravings that ordinarily eclipse the Light.' Might not the modern psychiatrist do for the insane what those Buddhist monks had done for the dying and the dead? he pondered:

> Let there be a voice to assure them, by day and even while they are asleep, that in spite of all the terror, all the bewilderment and confusion, the ultimate Reality remains unshakably itself and is of the same substance as the inner light of even the most cruelly tormented mind.[28]

When Huxley's wife Maria died in 1955, he sat with her for her last hours, with tears streaming down his face, reading to her from *The Tibetan Book of the Dead* as the ancient texts prescribed.

Leary—inevitably—interpreted the book through the prism of acid trip—or rather, interpreted the acid trip through the prism of the book, and in a fit of evangelical enthusiasm set about translating Evans-Wentz's text, as he put it, 'from Anglo-Buddhist to American psychedelic'. *The Psychedelic Experience* sought to strip the Tibetan text from its mortuary associations, depicting the acid trip rather as a kind of psychedelic voyage through the experience of ego death, and being reborn anew. 'The concept of actual physical death was an exoteric façade adopted to fit the prejudices of the Bonist tradition in Tibet', Leary wrote—offering an interpretation that fitted neatly with prejudices of his own. 'Far from being an embalmer's guide,' he continued, 'the manual is a detailed account of how to lose the ego; how to break out of personality into new realms of consciousness; and how to avoid the involuntary limiting processes of the ego; how to make the consciousness-expansion experience endure in subsequent daily life.'[29]

Every mystical religious tradition has taught that the abnegation of the self, or ego, is a condition of union with God, or Godhead. 'Only when I become as nothing,' as William James wrote, 'can God enter in and no difference between his life and mine remain outstanding.'[30] Hinduism and Buddhism both saw the play of the ego as an obstacle to spiritual progress: the bull to be caught, the tiger to be tamed, the monkey-mind to be controlled. Both proposed a tradition of sustained contemplation and meditation to bring the ego under control. But rather than the slow, dripping-water erosion of spiritual discipline, Leary saw LSD as the gelignite to blow up the ego in one cataclysmic explosion.

'You must remember that throughout human history, millions have made this voyage,' he wrote in the introduction to *The Psychedelic Experience*:

A few (whom we call mystics, saints or buddhas) have made this experience endure and have communicated it to their fellow men. You must remember, too, that the experience is safe (at the very worst, you will end up the same person who entered the experience), and that all of the dangers which you have feared are unnecessary productions of your mind. Whether you experience heaven or hell, remember that it is your mind which creates them. Avoid grasping the one or fleeing the other. Avoid imposing the ego game on the experience.

With your ego left behind you, he reassured his readers, 'the brain can't go wrong'.

In 1963, as Aldous Huxley lay dying of throat cancer, it was Leary's book that Huxley's second wife, Laura, read to him at his bedside. On the morning of 22 November 1963—as President John Kennedy, on a campaigning visit to Dallas, set off on the motorcade that would lead to his death—Huxley scribbled an instruction to Laura: 'LSD—try it. Intermuscular. 100mm [sic].' Following his instruction, Laura went into her husband's room, prepared a syringe and injected him with the requested 100 micrograms of the drug. An hour later she administered a further 100 micrograms. At twenty past five that afternoon, Aldous Huxley died, tripping on LSD.

# 11

## ALLEN GINSBERG'S VISION

On a warm summer's evening in 1948, a young law student named Allen Ginsberg was sitting in his cramped apartment in East Harlem, New York, idly masturbating while reading William Blake's poem 'Ah Sun-flower' (1794):

> Ah Sun-flower! weary of time,
> Who countest the steps of the Sun:
> Seeking after that sweet golden clime
> Where the traveller's journey is done.
>
> Where the Youth pined away with desire,
> And the pale Virgin shrouded in snow:
> Arise from their graves and aspire
> Where my Sun-flower wishes to go.

Rapt in the poem, Ginsberg heard a voice that he immediately recognised as Blake's, but which then transformed into the voice of God Himself, resounding 'with all the infinite tenderness and anciency and mortal gravity of a living Creator speaking to his son'.[1]

In an instant Ginsberg knew with utmost certainty that the 'sweet golden clime' that Blake described was existence itself, and that 'This was the moment I was born for. This initiation, this consciousness of being alive unto myself. The spirit of the universe was what I was born to realise.'

Overcome by an urge to share the good news, Ginsberg crawled out of the window onto the fire-escape and tapped on the window of the neighbouring apartment, which was occupied by two girls. The window opened: 'I've seen God!' Ginsberg screamed excitedly. The window slammed shut. 'Oh,' Ginsberg later lamented, 'what tales I could have told them if they'd let me in!'

Psilocybin, mescaline, LSD, the Amazonian drug ayahuasca, even laughing gas dispensed by his dentist—in his search for illumination over the years to come, Allen Ginsberg—poet laureate of the Beat generation, antic cheerleader of the nascent hippie movement and America's greatest visionary poet since Walt Whitman—would try them all. But none would have the effect of returning him to the vivid, divinely revelatory experience that he had experienced in his cold-water East Harlem apartment in 1948.

Ginsberg was twenty-two at the time, studying law at Columbia University, derelict in his studies, leading his 'solitary vegetarian contemplative life' and consorting with the motley group of putative writers, thinkers, delinquent philosophers, junkies and petty criminals—including Jack Kerouac, William S. Burroughs, Neal Cassady and Herbert Huncke—who would go on to constitute what would be known as the Beats.

Ginsberg was born into a Jewish family, and grew up in Paterson, New Jersey. His father, Louis, was a high school teacher and poet. His mother, Naomi, was a member of the Communist Party, who sometimes took the young Allen and his brother Eugene to party meetings. Naomi suffered from a mental illness that was never properly diagnosed, but manifested in paranoid delusions about being spied on, including a belief that the President had planted listening devices in the family home. On one occasion she attempted to kill herself by slitting her own wrists. She would spend much of Ginsberg's youth in mental hospitals, and the strain of madness that he feared ran in his family would haunt Ginsberg for years to come.

His early ambition was to become a labour lawyer—at the age of seventeen, travelling on the ferry to Manhattan, he had fallen to his knees and vowed to devote his life to the working oppressed. But his central preoccupation was poetry as a key to understanding the unknowable universe, and the poetic pursuit of what he and Kerouac called the 'Great Vision'—a new vision for literature, in Ginsberg's case, considerably vivified by his experiments with marijuana and Benzedrine, inspired by Arthur Rimbaud's insistence that a poet becomes a seer 'by a long, involved and logical *derangement of all the senses*'.[2]

His Blakean experience was Ginsberg's epiphany. He had glimpsed heaven, and to recapture that vision, to realise once more the absolute certainty of his place in the universe, became his *raison d'être*, his grail:

My first thought was this was what I was born for, and second thought, never forget—never forget, never renege, never deny. Never deny the voice—no, never *forget* it, don't get lost mentally wandering in other spirit worlds or American or job worlds or advertising worlds or war worlds or earth worlds. But the spirit of the universe was what I was born to realise.[3]

Less than a year later, Ginsberg was admitted to the Columbia Presbyterian Psychiatric Institute in June 1949 for an eight-month stay in the hospital, which he had accepted in lieu of a prison sentence for allowing his Harlem apartment to be used for storing stolen goods, heisted by his junkie friend Huncke and his criminal associates. Ginsberg had a font of human kindness that would never be exhausted, no matter how much he was taken advantage of.

On his first day on the ward he encountered an overweight, bespectacled Jewish youth named Carl Solomon, still shaking from the effects of an insulin shock treatment. Two years younger than Ginsberg, Solomon— like Ginsberg's mother—had joined the Communist Party as a teenager, before making his way to France. Settling in Paris, he immersed himself in the work of the existentialists and surrealists—André Gide, Jean-Paul Sartre, Louis-Ferdinand Céline—and encountered the man who would become his hero and inspiration, the poet and dramatist Antonin Artaud. Artaud had spent many years in psychiatric institutions, arriving at the conclusion that madness was the honourable choice in a society devoid of principle, and that psychiatry was nothing but the invention of a sick society 'to defend itself against the investigations of certain visionaries whose faculties of divination disturbed it'.[4]

Returning to New York, Solomon decided that like Artaud he too should follow the path of the 'professional-lunatic saint'—a vocation that would eventually lead him to the gates of Columbia Presbyterian requesting a prefrontal lobotomy. The request was declined; instead, Solomon was subjected to an intensive course of insulin shock treatment. Ginsberg was fascinated by Solomon, and in the months that he was hospitalised spent much of his time meticulously noting down the history of what Solomon called his 'adventures and pseudo-intellectual deeds of daring'.

Five years later, on a warm August afternoon in 1955, Ginsberg sat down at his typewriter in the one-room cottage where he was living in San Francisco, and began crafting what would become the most instantly recognisable line in twentieth-century American poetry: 'I saw the best minds of my generation destroyed by madness, starving hysterical, naked, dragging themselves through the negro streets at dawn looking for an angry fix ...'

The broad theme of 'Howl, for Carl Solomon' is the struggle of the individual in the face of the crushing conformity of President Eisenhower's United States, 'Moloch'—the sun god of the Canaanites to whom firstborn children were sacrificed—'the heavy judger of men', as 'Howl' has it—and 'the narcotic tobacco haze of Capitalism'. But its references are specifically personal—incidents drawn from Ginsberg's life as a student and penurious poet, and the lives of his friends and acquaintances, the 'angel-headed hipsters' of the poem, foremost among them his fellow inmate at Columbia Presbyterian.

'Carl Solomon!' Ginsberg wrote, 'I'm with you in Rockland/ where you're madder than I am .../ where fifty more shocks will never return your soul to its body again from its pilgrimage to a cross in the void'.[5] But if the prevailing mood of 'Howl' is one of righteous anger and lamentation, its closing passage, or 'Footnote to Howl', is pure religious ecstasy:

> Holy, Holy, Holy ...
> Everything is holy! everybody's holy! everywhere is holy! ...
> ... the madman is holy as you my soul are holy! ...
> Holy Peter holy Allen holy Solomon holy Lucien holy Kerouac holy
>   Huncke holy Burroughs holy Cassady ...
> Holy my mother in the insane asylum! ...
> Holy the supernatural extra brilliant intelligent kindness of the soul!

The inspiration, of course, was William Blake's line in 'The Marriage of Heaven and Hell': 'For everything that lives is holy, life delights in life'.

'Howl' was published in 1956. The following year, Jack Kerouac published *On the Road*. The Beats—those 'angel-headed hipsters'—had become public property and Ginsberg (Carlo Marx in *On the Road*, as the cognoscenti recognised him) the most famous young poet in America.

The poet Michael McClure described the Beat movement as a 'spiritual occasion', and Jack Kerouac, more than anyone, came to interpret the term in explicitly religious terms, 'beat' as in run-down, for sure—but also, he wrote, as in 'beatific, to be in a state of beatitude, like St Francis, trying to love all life, trying to be utterly sincere ... practicing endurance, kindness, cultivating joy of heart'.[6] Of the Beats, it was Ginsberg, Kerouac and the poet Gary Snyder who had delved most deeply into Eastern philosophy.

William S. Burroughs had studied books on Theosophy in the New York Public Library, and found Madame Blavatsky's stories about a hierarchy of Masters ridiculous. He had dabbled in yoga and Zen Buddhism, but Buddhism, he wrote in a letter to Kerouac, 'is only for the West to study as history', not to practise. He had little time for Vedanta, and even less for Christopher Isherwood, Gerald Heard and the followers who had gathered around Swami Prabhavananda and Swami Yogananda: 'I have seen nothing from those California Vedantists but a lot of horse shit, and I denounce them without cavil as a pack of frauds.'[7] Burroughs was never going to embrace Eastern mysticism—although he did for a while embrace Scientology.

Gary Snyder's interest in Buddhism had been awakened while studying Asian languages at the University of California, and in 1956 he travelled to Japan to study Zen Buddhism, becoming a disciple of the Rinzai Zen master Oda Sesso Roshi, the head abbot of Daitoku-ji in Kyoto. Zen philosophy would become the backbone of his writing.

Kerouac's engagement with Buddhism had characteristically romantic, and melancholic, beginnings. Following the break-up of a love affair, he went to a library to read Henry David Thoreau, determined to 'cut out from civilisation and go back and live in the woods like Thoreau'. Reading Thoreau talking about Hindu philosophy led Kerouac to 'accidentally' pick up *The Life of Buddha*—or the *Buddhacharita*—composed in the second century CE by the Indian philosopher and poet Ashvaghosa.[8]

Kerouac took it upon himself to become Ginsberg's instructor in the matter, drawing up a reading list for his friend's 'beginning studies of Buddhism'; instructing Ginsberg in the basics of Buddhist philosophy; and 'crooning' the Buddhist vows to his friend—'I take refuge in the Buddha, the dharma (teachings) and the sangha (community),' Ginsberg wrote, 'like Frank Sinatra in a beautiful way.'[9]

Kerouac's Buddhism came filtered through his French Catholic gloom and guilt, and marinated in his growing alcoholism. He wrote extensively on Buddhism, notably a biography of the Buddha called *Wake Up*, and a translation of Buddhist scriptures from French into English with accompanying notes called *Some of the Dharma*, neither of which were published in his lifetime.[10] But he never abandoned his cradle Catholicism. He told one TV interviewer that each night he prayed to Christ, the Virgin Mary and the Buddha—'a *Catholic*-Buddhist', as Burroughs acidly described him, whose ecumenism was vividly expressed in Kerouac's recitation of Christian and Buddhist saints in *Mexico City Blues* (1959):

I believe in the sweetness
    of Jesus
And Buddha—
    I believe
In St Francis,
    Avoloki,
Tesvara,
    the Saints
Of First Century
    India A D
And Scholars
    Santidevan
And Otherwise
    Santayanan
    Everywhere[11]

While Snyder devoted his life to Zen, Kerouac was drawn more to Mahayana Buddhism, believing it to be more in tune with a compassionate (and perhaps Christian) view of the world. 'All those Zen masters throwing young kids in the mud because they can't answer their silly word questions,' Kerouac's alter ego, Ray Smith, complains to Japhy Ryder (Snyder) in *The Dharma Bums* (1958), 'Compassion is the heart of Buddhism.' Compassion, in fact, is the heart of everything. 'Who knows, my God, but that the universe is not one vast sea of compassion actually, the veritable holy honey, beneath all this show of personality and cruelty', Kerouac wrote in an essay on the Beat movement in *Playboy* magazine.[12]

All his life Kerouac had dreamed of recognition as a writer, but he was grievously ill-equipped to handle the fame—or rather, notoriety—that came with the publication of *On the Road*. Suddenly he found himself feted as 'the king of the Beats'—the avatar of a new generation of restless youth. To Kerouac it was a farce. In 1954, in an unpublished notebook, he outlined his plans to attain Nirvana by the year 2000:

1954—No chasing after women. No more drunkenness or alcohol, no more 'sipping'

1955—No more rich or/& expensive foods—elementary diet of salt pork, beans, bread, greens, peanuts, figs, coffee (and later grow everything & pick acorns, pinyon nuts, cacti fruit myself)

1956—Finally (after 5-volume LIFE) no more writing for communicating and other SKETCH books of wilds, no more writing or I art-ego of any kind, finally no I-self, or Name; no shaving of beard.

1970—No possessions, finally, but wilderness Robe, no hut, no mirror, begging at houses of village

2000—Nirvana and willed death beyond death.[13]

There is something unbearably touching about Kerouac's aspirations for sainthood. In 1958, a year after publication of *On the Road*, Kerouac became embroiled in a conversation about the Beats and mysticism in an interview with Mike Wallace. 'What do Beat mystics believe in?' Wallace asked. 'Oh, they believe in love ... and ... all is well ... we're in heaven now, really', Kerouac replied. 'You don't sound happy', said Wallace. 'Oh, I'm tremendously sad. I'm in great despair.' 'Why?' 'Oh, it's a great burden to be alive', Kerouac said.[14]

Kerouac's sweetness and holy aspirations were undermined by his drinking and his unreliability. One girlfriend, Helen Weaver, complained that Kerouac would show up three hours late for dinner or not at all. 'Nothing matters—it's all a dream', Kerouac would say. Weaver wrote: 'I was beginning to feel that his Buddhism was just one big philosophical rationalization for doing whatever he wanted.'[15]

What Kerouac most wanted to do was escape 'from everything'. He wrote to his friend Philip Whalen that he planned to found a monastery in the high country outside Mexico City, dedicated to 'Pure essence Buddhism ... That would be, I spose, NO RULES'—a prescription that would have made it unique among Buddhist monasteries throughout the world, which generally have more rules than the British civil service—but then Kerouac had evidently never been in a Buddhist monastery. And he never would.[16]

\* \* \*

As well the list of Buddhist works supplied by Kerouac, Allen Ginsberg had read extensively in Eastern philosophy—Krishnamurti, Yogananda, *The Bhagavad Gita*, translations by Christopher Isherwood and Swami Prabhavananda of the Upanishads, *The Gospel of Sri Ramakrishna*—a collection of the guru's conversations and 'table talk'—and, of course, *The Tibetan Book of the Dead*.

His Blakean glimpse of heaven haunted Ginsberg, firing in him a determination to explore whatever consciousness-expanding methods he could find to recapture the visionary experience of that summer Harlem evening. And over the years he experimented assiduously with the entire smorgasbord of psychotropic drugs—psilocybin, peyote, ayahuasca, mescaline and LSD ...

After sampling psilocybin with Timothy Leary at Harvard in 1960, Ginsberg became a fully signed-up member of Leary's mission to turn on America. Canvassing his friends and acquaintances, he drew up a list of people who agreed to take the drug and report back on its effects—among them the artists Franz Kline and Willem de Kooning, and the musicians Dizzy Gillespie and Thelonious Monk. Monk was given fifteen pills to take in the privacy of his own home. Five hours into the allotted time, Ginsberg called to check that everything was okay. Monk reported that he felt fine. A few weeks later Ginsberg visited the musician to get a more detailed account of the experience. 'Well I took 'em,' Monk said, 'but ain't you got anything stronger?'[17]

But it was LSD that brought Ginsberg closest to the taste of enlightenment he had experienced all those years ago in Harlem. He first took the drug in 1959, as part of an investigation being conducted by the anthropologist and social scientist Gregory Bateson at the Mental Research Institute in Palo Alto. Like Leary, Ginsberg saw something distinctly Hindu in the experience. He wrote to his father:

> It was astounding. I lay back, listening to music and went into a sort of trance state (somewhat similar to the high state of Laughing Gas) and in a fantasy much like Coleridge world of Kubla Khan, saw a vision of that part of my consciousness which seemed to be permanent and transcendent and identical with the origin of the universe—a sort of identity common to everything—but a clear and coherent sight of it. Rather beautiful images also, of Hindu-type Gods dancing on themselves. This drug seems to automatically produce a mystical experience. Science is getting very hip.[18]

But LSD also took him on what he called

> the horror trip, because I was trying so hard to get back into that Eternity that I'd seen before; so that every time I got high, when the first doubt came that I might not see 'Eternity' ... or the fear came that I might get eaten alive by 'God,' then the trip immediately turned into a hell.[19]

For Ginsberg, drugs had brought ecstasy—and terror—but they had not brought illumination. And, hung on the Harlem God, Ginsberg remained in search, as he put it, of some way 'of making it more permanent, or mastering it or getting clearer about in my own mind'.[20]

So it was that his thoughts turned to the East. 'I was interested,' he would remember, 'in what that older culture still had as a living transmission of spiritual and visionary energy because in the West there didn't seem to be one.'[21] In 1961, following in the footsteps of Charles Leadbeater, Paul Brunton and countless others, Ginsberg and his lover Peter Orlovsky set off for India in search of enlightenment. Travelling to Paris, then Tangier, Israel and finally by ship from Kenya, they set foot in Bombay in February 1962—Ginsberg preparing for his arrival by smoking grass scored from a shoeshine boy in Mombasa and reading *A Passage to India*, the Ramayana and Rudyard Kipling's *Kim*.

From Bombay, the pair made their way across India to Delhi, on the way seeking out Indian poets, indulging in morphine, opium and copious amounts of hash, and steeping themselves in the vividly colourful pageant of Indian religious life. Even Ginsberg was astonished at just how deeply devotion permeated every aspect of existence. He wrote to Jack Kerouac: 'Everybody in India is religious, it's weird, everybody ON to some Saddhana (method) and had family guru or Brahmin priest who knows all about how the universe is a big illusion; it's totally unlike the West—it really is another Dimension of time-history here.'[22]

In Delhi, Ginsberg and Orlovsky were joined by Gary Snyder and his wife, the poet Joanne Kyger, who had been travelling in Japan. The party headed for Rishikesh on the banks of the Ganges, a holy town with gurus of all types and persuasions, and the ashram of Swami Sivananda. A former physician, Sivananda had taken up the life of a sannyasin following encounters with Aurobindo and Ramana Maharshi, developing a form of yoga called the Yoga of Synthesis, and going on to found a mission called the Divine Life Society and to write more than 200 books on yoga and spiritual teachings.

Ginsberg and his companions ate the parsimonious portions in the ashram dining hall, followed the pilgrim custom of feeding the fish in the Ganges, and took yoga lessons from the ashram's resident teacher. At an audience with Sivananda, the elderly guru fielded questions about the nature of dualism and the self with cryptic, non-committal grunts and presented Ginsberg with 5 rupees and a book called *Raja Yoga for Americans*.

Ginsberg wrote to Kerouac that Sivananda was

[a] charlatan of mass-production international nirvana racket—but actually quite a calm holy old man ... I rather like him. Next day I asked where can I get a Guru? And he smiles and touches his heart and says the only Guru is in your own heart dearie or words to that effect and adds—you'll know your Guru when you see him because you'll love him, otherwise don't bother. Well not quite that funny but that was the message.[23]

Ginsberg's off-hand description disguised the fact that it was advice that struck him deeply, awakening his abiding reverence for what he would call the 'sacred heart' of humanity.

A few miles from Rishikesh lies Haridwar, where, serendipitously, India's holiest festival, the Kumbh Mela, was about to commence. Held in four holy sites—Haridwar, Allahabad, Nashik-Trimbak and Ujjain—at three-year intervals, each site hosting it once every twelve years, the Kumbh Mela is one of the most extraordinary spectacles on earth. Millions of pilgrims make their way to the banks of the Ganges, led by the massed ranks of sadhus and *Naga babas*, their naked bodies dusted with ash from the charnel grounds, who pitch their tents and pavilions in specially designated camps. On the first day of the festival, they stampede in their thousands into the Ganges, risking life and limb—not least of anybody who happens to get in their way.

Ginsberg wandered through the sadhu camps entranced, wondering whether he too could give up the world with all its temptations and follies and follow the path of renunciation. Watching the groups of old ladies, high on faith, who followed the *Naga babas* into the Ganges, holding on to each other for support and chanting spiritual songs, he wept at the memory of his dead mother Naomi.

What Ginsberg loved about India was its tolerance. He wrote to Kerouac about how things that would be considered outrageous or strange in America were in India quite normal. Nobody batted an eyelid at someone walking around the streets in their undershorts, or even appeared to notice when a naked *Naga baba*, covered in ashes and carrying a trident, walked down the street, and sadhus were to be found smoking hashish in every temple. Compared with India, everything about America seemed constrained, authoritarian, uptight.

With every teacher and guru he encountered, Ginsberg shared the story of his Harlem vision; the glimpse of the divine which he yearned to repeat and which no drug had ever properly returned him to. In Brindaban (now known as Vrindavan), a town in Uttar Pradesh that is believed to stand at the place where the god Krishna spent his childhood, 'a lady saint', Sri Mata Krishnaji, advised him to embrace the vision and 'take Blake for your guru', on the grounds that the figure he worshipped was less important than the process of uncovering the love inherent in feeling such devotion. It was advice, he later noted, that put the nineteenth-century English visionary poet 'in the context, oddly, of the Indian transcendental scene'.[24]

Ginsberg moved on to Sikkim, in search of a Buddhist lama who might give him initiations. In Kalimpong he met Dudjom Rinpoche, the head of the Nyingma, the oldest school in Tibetan Buddhism. Ginsberg again raised the matter of drugs, telling Dudjom about his fear of the hallucinations caused by LSD and ayahuasca. Ecstatic visions were no different from more mundane thoughts, Dudjom advised him, equally transient and ephemeral. Ginsberg should treat everything with detachment and equanimity: 'Watch the wheels within wheels, but don't get attached to anything you see. Let it pass into you, but be inactive and not grasping nor rejecting. If you see anything horrible, don't cling to it. If you see anything beautiful, don't cling to it.' It was advice, Ginsberg would later remark, that finally 'cut the Gordian knot that I'd inherited from too rash and untutored experiments with psychedelics'.[25]

From Kalimpong he headed north to Gangtok and to Rumtek, the monastery of the 16th Karmapa, the head of the Kagyu school of Tibetan Buddhism, who had fled from Tibet in 1959. Ginsberg watched the Karmapa perform the traditional Black Hat ceremony, during which the lama dons a crown dating from the fourteenth century, representing an 'ethereal' crown said to have been woven from the hair of dakini spirits, and is believed to become the embodiment of Avalokiteshvara, the bodhisattva who embodies the compassion of all the Buddhas.

The Karmapa was revered among Tibetans as a great miracle worker. He kept a large aviary of birds at Rumtek, many of whom, he maintained, were reincarnated bodhisattvas; there were stories of birds dying but remaining on their perches in a state of *tukdam*—meditative luminosity—for days afterwards. When the Karmapa himself died of cancer in hospital in Zion, Illinois, in 1991, at the age of fifty-seven, the doctors treating him were astonished to discover that the area around his heart remained warm and his skin pliable for forty-eight hours after his death.

The Karmapa warmed to Ginsberg, likening him to Manjushri, the bodhisattva of wisdom. He invited him to stay at Rumtek, but Ginsberg had only been given a three-day visa for Sikkim and regretfully turned the invitation down. By now Ginsberg had spent more than a year in

India, searching for, and failing to find, the Harlem God or any single teacher whom he believed could lead him to enlightenment. A mood of disenchantment gripped him. 'I wanted to be a saint', he wrote in his *Indian Journals*:

> But suffer for what? Illusions? ... Next the rest of India & Japan, and I suppose later a trip: England, Denmark, Sweden & Norway, Germany, Poland, Russia, China & then back home again. And that'll be the end of that world, I'll be about 50, the relatives'll all be dead by then, old ties with the boys of yore be loosed or burnt, unfaithful, in so many decades it's best to let it all go—is Jack drunk? Is Neal still aware of me? Gregory yakking? Bill mad at me? Am I even here to myself? I daren't write it all down, it's too shameful & boring now & I haven't the energy to make a great passional autobiography of it all ... I guess I have nothing to contribute to general edification by this vague haphazard slow motion death.[26]

In March 1963, Ginsberg left India for Vancouver, where he had been invited to teach a poetry course at the University. His journey took him by air to Bangkok, then on to Vietnam, where America was becoming ever more deeply embroiled in propping up the corrupt regime of President Ngo Dinh Diem.

Ginsberg moved on to Cambodia and then Japan, where he had arranged to meet Gary and Joanne Snyder. Spending time in Kyoto, meditating with Snyder, walking the clean streets and delighting in the idiosyncrasies of Japanese society, he realised just how much India, in its chaos, squalor and poverty, had depressed him. Riding the train from Kyoto to Tokyo, where he would leave Japan for America, a deep feeling of clarity and serenity descended on him. India had intensified his desire for enlightenment, through either drugs or finding a teacher, but now he suddenly realised that the search was an obstacle in itself—that he no longer felt the burning need to search for or become anything, and that it was enough simply to *be*.

'I had a very strange ecstatic experience then and there, once I had gotten that burden off my back,' he wrote later,

> because I was suddenly free to love myself again, and therefore love the people around me in the form that they already were. And love myself in my own form as I am ... And nothing more to fulfil, except to be willing to die when I am dying, whenever that be. And be willing to live as a human being in this form now. So I started weeping, it was such a happy moment.[27]

It was the moment of release from his pursuit of the Harlem God, and the Blakean vision that had obsessed him. He said later, 'The remarkable thing is that I stupefied myself from 1948 to 1963. A long time—that's fifteen years preoccupied with a single thought.'[28] And with one train journey he was free.

\* \* \*

In the winter of 1964, following in his friend Allen Ginberg's footsteps, Timothy Leary finally set off for the East. Travelling with his new wife Nanette, an erstwhile model whom he had met at a Fourth of July party at Millbrook, Leary went first to Japan, visiting 'karate dogens, Shinto temples, Buddhist temples and department stores', before moving on to Calcutta. Following Ginsberg's instruction, Leary made his way to the burning *ghats*, where he sat getting high, 'the sweet odor of cannabis mingled with the sweet odor of burning corpses. Breathe deeply. What's death but the end of breath?'[29]

Plentiful hashish, trippy sadhus, ragged, bearded saints, mystics and yogis, then Varanasi, the holiest city of the Hindus—or, as Leary put it, 'the site of a non-stop hippie festival for the last 5,000 years'—here was the 'oh wow!' vision of India that had somehow escaped previous travellers, from William Jones to Paul Brunton to Somerset Maugham, but that would establish the motif for a coming generation of seekers.

In Varanasi, a curious thing happened. Wandering, high as a kite, along the *ghats* lining the Ganges, Leary noticed that while the Western bank of the river was crowded to bursting point with temples, shops and a teeming mass of humanity, the Eastern bank seemed quite deserted, cursed, he was told, by evil spirits. After much negotiation he was able to find a Muslim boatman who would ferry him under cover of the gathering dusk across the river. Arriving there, Leary paddled ashore and sat down, looking back across the river at the flickering lights on the Western bank. Suddenly he heard something moving behind him and was shocked to see an old man with long white hair, dressed only in a dhoti, materialising out of the darkness.

Leary was terrified. Then he understood:

> He was some special ancient teacher who had been waiting for me all my life. I wanted to run forward and throw myself at his feet. But I was paralyzed with fright, thinking at the same time that he could be a crazed fanatic. He might attack me, a profaner of holy ground.[30]

Leary babbled to the old man in English, who babbled back to him in a language Leary was unable to understand. His heart pounding, Leary made his way back to the shore, where the boatman, equally terrified, was gesticulating furiously that they must leave. Leary scrambled aboard the boat and fell to the floor weeping uncontrollably: 'I was convinced that I had met the Buddha and had run away.'

In Delhi, Leary and Nanette met up with Ralph Metzner, his former Harvard colleague and collaborator, who had spent three months in Almora, in the Himalayan foothills, studying with the Tibetan Buddhist philosopher Lama Anagarika Govinda.

Govinda was not actually Tibetan; he was German. Born Ernst Lothar Hoffmann in Waldheim in 1898, he developed an interest in Eastern religion and philosophy from an early age, publishing his first book, *The Basic Ideas of Buddhism and its Relationship to Ideas of God* (1920), when he was just twenty-two. In 1928 he travelled to Ceylon where he studied meditation and Buddhist philosophy with a German-born Theravada monk named Nyanatiloka Mahathera, who gave him the name Govinda. Adopting the life of a mendicant monk, he travelled through Ceylon and India, before settling into a life of writing and teaching.

In 1942, he was interned by the British authorities at Dehra Dun. And following the war, he married a Parsi woman, Ratti Petit, who changed her name to Li Gotami. Together they travelled in Tibet, where Govinda claimed to have been initiated into the Kagyu order, of which the Karmapa is the spiritual leader. As the scholar of Buddhist and Tibetan studies, Donald Lopez, has pointed out, there is no 'initiation' as such into the Kagyu, or any other order in Tibetan Buddhism. But as Frederick Fletcher and Paul Brunton had demonstrated, Eastern mysticism offered bountiful opportunities for reinvention. Govinda adopted the term 'lama' and the maroon and yellow robes of the order.

In the 1950s, Govinda and Li Gotami settled in the small hamlet of Kasar Devi near Almora, in the Himalayan foothills, in a house rented to them by Walter Evans-Wentz. Almora was a magnet for spiritual seekers, travellers and bohemians from Europe, to the point that it was known locally as 'Crank's Ridge'. It was the end of winter when Leary, Nanette and Metzner arrived at Almora. They rented a cottage, hired a Muslim cook named Abdul and arranged for fresh provisions to be delivered each day.

Each afternoon they made their way to Lama Govinda's house for Buddhist instruction and meditation, and to listen to the elderly German expounding his theory on the necessity of spreading Eastern wisdom to the West. The power of Oriental religions, Govinda told Leary, historically lay in the importance of the oral tradition, in which knowledge was passed from master to disciple in an unbroken line. But in recent years, according to Govinda, many of the guardians of the old philosophic traditions had come to the conclusion that the evolution of the human race depended upon establishing a unity between 'the outer science' advanced by the West and the inner yoga advanced by the East.

Many teachers, Eastern and Western, Govinda went on, from the Theosophists to Krishnamurti to George Gurdjieff, had attempted to awaken the West from its mechanistic sleepwalking. Evans-Wentz's translation of *The Tibetan Book of the Dead* had been part of this 'plan'. But when word came to 'the philosophic community of India' that a group of Harvard psychologists was using the ancient Buddhist text 'as a manual for drug-induced satoris', there was great interest.

'You are the predictable result of a strategy that has been unfolding for over fifty years,' Govinda told Leary, 'You have done exactly what the philosophers wanted done. You were prepared discreetly by several Englishmen who were themselves agents of this process. You have been an unwitting tool of the great transformation of our age.'[31]

(At this point it is necessary to pause and point out that we have only Leary's word that this conversation, putting him at a pivotal place in history, unfolded as he described it—or indeed took place at all. Who exactly were this 'philosophic community of India' that had been keeping a watchful eye on the world's spiritual evolution? One is reminded of Madame Blavatsky's mythical 'Masters'. And who were the 'several Englishmen' who had discreetly prepared Leary to be a 'tool of the great transformation of our age'? Presumably Aldous Huxley and the acid hustler Michael Hollingshead. Leary does not tell us.)

But that was not all. In keeping with this unfolding of a preordained plan, Govinda had a proposition to make. For decades he had been engaged in a study of personality types, across centuries and cultures, in search of meaningful correspondences between classification systems such as the Zodiac, the Tarot, the I Ching and the myths of Olympian gods and goddesses and their Hindu counterparts. A successful demonstration of correspondences among the great systems of 'human mentation', Govinda went on, 'would help harmonize East and West, science and yoga, past and future'. Would Leary be prepared to work on this problem?

'I was interested in the task,' Leary wrote, 'but despaired of finding the time for such arcane research. One would have to live like the Lama, withdrawn from the world, like a mediaeval scholar in a monastery.'[32] And Timothy Leary was not about to do that.[33]

After four months in Almora, Leary and Nanette's romantic honeymoon was turning sour. Making enquiries locally about where they could find a guru who could teach them the mysteries of tantric sex, they were directed to the dwelling of a man named Sri Krishna Prem. In fact, Krishna Prem was the last person who could offer any useful advice on the subject. Prem was a celibate monk, born in England and originally named Ronald Nixon. But he was the closest that Leary would come in India to finding himself a guru.

Ronald Nixon was born in Cheltenham in 1898, the son of a businessman father and a Christian Scientist mother. In 1916—two years into the Great War—and aged eighteen, he enlisted in the Royal Air Corps and trained as a pilot, going on to fly missions in France. On one occasion, pursued by enemy aircraft, he narrowly avoided death due to a miraculous escape that he attributed to a 'power beyond our ken'. Like many we have already met in this book, the brutality of war left Nixon with a profound sense of 'futility and meaninglessness', and a yearning to find some deeper purpose in life.

After the war, he enrolled at King's College, Cambridge, where he became friends with fellow student Christmas Humphreys and immersed himself in Theosophy and the study of Vedanta and Buddhism. In 1921, Nixon left England for India to teach English at Lucknow University. There he came under the influence of the wife of the university's vice-chancellor, Dr Gyanendra Nath Chakravarti—a well-known socialite named Manika Devi. Manika was a powerful, magnetic character, whose air of self-assured worldliness disguised a deeper spiritual calling.

Dr Chakravarti was a Theosophist, who had known Madame Blavatsky. When Dixon once asked him what sort of woman Blavatsky was, he replied: 'I have known only one woman like her,' and nodded towards his wife who was sitting a few feet away.

In 1928 Manika Devi turned her back on her marriage and all worldly things, shaved her head, and taking the name Sri Yashoda Ma, retired to an ashram at Mirtola, a small village near Almora. Nixon followed as her disciple, adopting the name Sri Krishna Prem.

Among their earliest followers were Sri Yashoda Ma's youngest daughter, Moti Rani, and another Englishman, Major Robert Dudley

Alexander. Dixon and Alexander had first met as students in a Cambridge bookshop, looking for books by Madame Blavatsky. 'At that instant,' Alexander recalled, 'I felt I had met a man I could follow for the rest of my life.'[34] He followed Dixon to Lucknow, where Alexander became Principal of the Lucknow Medical College before abandoning his career to live at the ashram at Mirtola.

Life in the ashram was hard. Krishna Prem slept on the floor on a single blanket beside Yashoda Ma. They took only a single meal a day, and observed strict celibacy. Winter or summer, ashramites bathed in cold water, and no leather was allowed on the premises. Krishna Prem's sole vice was smoking an old clay pipe, which he filled not with tobacco but matches.

In 1944 Yashoda Ma died and Krishna Prem succeeded her as head of the ashram. Over the next twenty years he would leave Mirtola just once, in 1948 travelling to southern India to visit the ashram of Ramana Maharshi, and then on to Pondicherry to meet Sri Aurobindo and 'the Mother'. He published two books on yoga and spiritual practice, *The Yoga of the Kathopanishad* and *Yoga for the Westerner*, and became widely known and admired, both as a teacher and a vivid example of renunciation.

By the time Leary arrived at Mirtola in 1965, Krishna Prem was aged sixty-four. His old friend Robert Alexander had died, but Krishna Prem had been joined by another Englishman, Alexander Phipps, a former RAF engineer, who had arrived at Mirtola shortly after the war, taking the name Madhava Ashish.

Mirtola was deserted when Leary and Nanette arrived. They waited by Krishna Prem's house until the sound of barking dogs alerted them to the arrival of the guru, emerging from the forest—a tall, athletic Englishman, dressed in a saffron robe, with open-toed sandals on his 'enormous beat-up feet'. Madhava Ashish was by his side, a 'tall rugby type', according to Leary, who proved surprisingly *au courant* with the latest developments in American academic circles. 'Aren't you the chap that got bounced from Harvard for giving Huxley's satori pills to prisoners and Episcopalians?' he enquired of Leary.[35]

A lengthy discussion followed, in which Leary described his struggles against the scientific and academic establishment and what he described as the 'Reckless Cerebral Courage' of the young in embracing psychedelics. Leary noticed that Krishna Prem, 'this 67-year-old philosopher [*sic*], niched in the foothills of the Himalayas, seemed to understand Harvard and Millbrook exactly: our confusions, our aspirations, our need for guidance'.

Over the course of their stay, Krishna Prem offered to show Leary a mandala that provided the key to illumination in the twentieth century. He unfolded a standard map of the world, and then turned it so that west was up and east was at the bottom—the past, and the future. For thousands of years, Krishna Prem said, the experience of spirituality in the East had been determined by the lack of any possibility or change in people's lives. Even Ramana Maharshi, 'the great master', had never left 'the stone of India'. Krishna Prem went on: 'Since the philosophers of the past couldn't migrate in their bodies, they invented a theory of migrating souls.' The wisdom of our age, he said, is 'movement and change'.

Drugs, he warned Leary, were among 'the most influential and dangerous powers' available to man: 'They open up glorious and pleasurable chambers in the mind. They give great power. Thus they can seduce the searcher away from the Path.' It was time, Krishna Prem said, for Leary to return to the West, 'and there you will meet difficult challenges and be forced to pass many arduous tests'.[36]

Leary and Nanette packed their bags to return to America. Before departing they had one more LSD session, in a deserted Shiva temple close to Lama Govinda's home. In the gloomy surroundings, with battered stone lingams 'sticking up like rotting mushrooms', Leary was overcome with feelings of panic and paranoia. They made their way back to their house. Reaching out to touch Nanette he was horrified to find she had turned to stone. The marriage, both realised, was over. Borrowing $100 from a local Methodist missionary, they made their way to Delhi and back to America.[37]

It is notable that in his time in India, the teachers that Leary sought out were not Indian but Westerners. He would later describe Krishna Prem as 'the wisest man in India'. Ralph Metzner would say that it was his impression that Krishna Prem was the closest that Leary ever came to accepting a guru.

Leary may have been 'Hindu' as he said—as we all are—but his Hinduism proved somewhat provisional. He was less interested in exploring traditional paths to enlightenment than in seeking affirmation that psychedelics was the way, the truth and the life; too absorbed in his own mission as an acid evangelist to become anyone's disciple. It would be his close friend Richard Alpert who would do that.

* * *

Leary returned from India to discover that in his absence Millbrook had descended into chaos, Alpert's administrative capabilities somewhat hampered by his consumption of industrial quantities of LSD. While struggling with the complexities of realising enlightenment, nobody at Millbrook seemed to have answered the eternal conundrum that would undermine so many utopian attempts at communal living: who does the washing-up? Irreparably at loggerheads, Leary and Alpert parted company.

The genie was now out of the bottle. Leary's psychedelic revolution had spread, vivifying a growing revolution in behaviour, mores and consciousness, rooted in a disillusionment with the American military-industrial machine, consumerism and a way of life that seemed to value material success and competitiveness over happiness and spiritual fulfilment.

The epicentre of this revolution was San Francisco, where Ginsberg had ushered the Beats into public awareness ten years earlier, on 7 October 1955, with his reading of the first part of 'Howl' at the Six Gallery, featuring a cast of West Coast poets (and seminal Beat figures) including Michael McClure, Gary Snyder and Philip Whalen ('Remarkable collection of angels all gathered at once in the same spot', as the flyers that Ginsberg prepared for the event put it).

Now, San Francisco—specifically Haight-Ashbury, 'the Haight', a neighbourhood of run-down Victorian wood-frame houses, close by Golden Gate Park—had been colonised by a new generation of bohemians, whom the media christened 'hippies'—musicians, artists and a growing legion of runaways from around America, lured by the promise of the new freedoms of drugs and sexuality.

The Victorian gingerbread houses accommodated communes and crash-pads, and the main drag of Haight Street was lined with 'head shops' selling drug paraphernalia, hippie threads, the new underground newspapers, samidzat pamphlets and bookshops crammed with the works of Hermann Hesse, Alan Watts' writings on Zen, The Tibetan Book of the Dead, Hindu philosophy and the occult. Even Madame Blavatsky and Aleister Crowley had made a comeback.

Allen Ginsberg—'the secretary-general of the world's poets, beatnicks, anarchists, socialists, free-sex/love cultists', as Timothy Leary affectionately described him—was the self-anointed Pied Piper for the movement,[38] proselytising about the revolution in consciousness in newspaper and magazine interviews and television appearances, ever the astute observer and the fluent communicator, providing a helpful guide for those mystified by the behaviour of the young by explaining 'this turning to East' as the evolution of 'the new consciousness' first explored by the Beats.

'These young people are forming a community, which has escaped the electronic hypnosis of stereotype mass media conditioning,' Ginsberg wrote, 'Eastern religions and LSD being the specific anti-brainwash medicines.'[39] By 1966, when it was made illegal, it was estimated that more than 2 million Americans had taken LSD, most of high school and college age.[40]

Richard Alpert remained in the vanguard of proselytising about the 'anti-brainwash medicines'. Irrevocably alienated from a conventional academic career, since leaving Millbrook Alpert had earned a living by writing and lecturing on the LSD experience to everyone, from the government Food and Drug Administration to the Hells Angels.

But he was also experiencing LSD's law of diminishing returns: no matter how high you got, at some point you would have to come down. 'It was a terribly frustrating experience,' he wrote,

> as if you came into the kingdom of heaven and you saw how it all was and you felt these new states of awareness and then you got cast out again, and after two or 300 times of this, began to feel an extraordinary kind of depression set in—a very gentle depression that whatever I knew still wasn't enough![41]

Alpert's erstwhile associates, Leary and Ralph Metzner, and Ginsberg, had all been to India in search of a greater truth, Alpert reasoned; but no matter how enriched they might have been by the experience, they were all still in search of something. Alpert was looking for something too, and he had no great expectation that going to India would lead him to find it. But such was his desperation that when a wealthy friend urged Alpert to join him on a journey 'to look for holy men', he agreed to go. After all, what did he have to lose?

On 14 January 1967, Alpert, Leary and Ginsberg—draped with Indian necklaces, flowers in their hair—were among 30,000 people gathered in San Francisco's Golden Gate Park for what was billed as 'A Gathering of the Tribes for the First Human Be-In'. The tribes included political radicals from across the bay in Berkeley, unreconstructed Beat generation survivors, Hells Angels, and the hippies and acid heads from the Haight. In keeping with the spirit of the times, the poster advertising the event, designed by local artist Stanley Mouse, showed a bearded Indian sadhu, with a pyramid imposed over his forehead, an expression of divine benediction on his face. In what was effectively a curtain-raiser to the forthcoming 'summer of love', local rock bands including the Grateful Dead, Jefferson Airplane and Quicksilver Messenger Service provided a throbbing, clamorous soundtrack.

On stage, Leary, barefoot and dressed in his now habitual white holy man uniform, a marigold behind each ear, told the crowd that Western man needed to get 'out of the cities and back into tribes and villages. The only way out is in,' adding his familiar mantra, 'Turn on, tune in, drop out'; while Allen Ginsberg led the audience in his repertoire of Hindu chants. At the height of the proceedings, as the atmosphere reached fever-pitch, Ginsberg leaned over to Lawrence Ferlinghetti, who was seated next to him, and whispered, 'What if we're all wrong?'[42]

The following month a gathering of the movement's 'elders' was held on the Sausalito houseboat of the English Zen Buddhist Alan Watts, and included Ginsberg, Leary and Snyder. At issue, as Watts put it, was the question of whether to 'drop out or take over'. Ginsberg pointed out to Leary that while he might have dropped out of his job as a psychology teacher at Harvard, he had multiple safety nets that would never be available to the vast majority of teenagers who were taking acid and trying to figure out how to function in the world while 'staying true to their new selves'. What, Ginsberg asked, can I drop out of? 'Your teaching at Cal,' Leary snapped back. Ginsberg chuckled: 'But I need the money.'[43]

The meeting moved on to discuss the emergence of 'an ecological conscience' and how the new version of humanity would abandon the cities for the countryside. 'There will be deer grazing in Times Square in forty years,' Leary prophesied, with characteristically fanciful inaccuracy.

A few weeks later, Richard Alpert left for India. Packed in his bag was a cache of premium-quality 'White Lightning' LSD, manufactured by the Haight's foremost 'underground chemist', Owsley Stanley. Alpert's plan was that he would meet holy men along the way and give them the drug, 'and they'd tell me what LSD is. Maybe I'd learn the missing clue.'[44]

Alpert's friend had arranged for a Land Rover to be shipped to Tehran. From there, they followed what was by then becoming the hippie trail, through Afghanistan and Pakistan into India. By the time they reached Nepal, they had visited Kashmir, seen the Dalai Lama and the burning *ghats* of Varanasi and smoked copious amounts of hash, and the only thing Alpert was feeling was depressed. In Kathmandu, sitting in a cafe called

The Blue Tibetan, a Westerner with shoulder-length hair and dressed only in a dhoti approached Alpert's table. His name was Kermit Michael Riggs, a 6-feet-4-inches blonde-haired surfer from Laguna Beach in California who had arrived in India in 1964, taken the name Bhagavan Das and was living the life of an Indian sadhu.

Alpert was smitten. After five days in Alpert's hotel room, eating peach melbas and getting high on hash and mescaline, Bhagavan Das took Alpert on a prolonged tour of monasteries and spiritual sites, teaching him holy songs and hatha yoga postures. At length, the erstwhile surfer led Alpert to a remote mountaintop ashram in Uttarakhand, where he was introduced to a little man in his sixties, wrapped in a blanket.

The first question Neem Karoli Baba asked Alpert was whether he was rich. When Alpert replied that he did okay, Karoli Baba immediately asked him to buy him a Land Rover. 'I had come out of a family of fund-raisers for the United Jewish Appeal, Brandeis and the Einstein Medical School,' Alpert later wrote, 'and I had never seen hustling like this.'[45]

The guru then told Alpert that Alpert had dreamed of his mother last night, and that she had died of a stomach ailment. Alpert was flabbergasted. The previous night he had indeed dreamed of his mother, and she had died of a stomach ailment.

Alpert passed a restless and confused night. He had no idea what to make of Neem Karoli Baba, but perhaps he was the man who could tell Alpert about LSD. He resolved to ask him. The next morning Baba summoned him, but before Alpert could say a word, the guru asked, 'You have a question?' Taken aback, Alpert hesitated. 'Where's the medicine?' Neem Karoli prompted him.

The penny dropped: the guru had apparently read his mind, and was referring to Alpert's cache of LSD. Alpert handed him the bottle. To his alarm, the guru swallowed three 305 microgram tablets—some ten times the normal dose. At the end of the day, Alpert reported, the little man's eyes were still twinkling as if absolutely nothing had happened.

Alpert was to remain at the ashram for a year, coming under the guidance of one of Neem Karoli Baba's disciples named Hari Dass Baba. Hari Dass was 48 years old, weighed 90 pounds, and had been silent for fifteen years, communicating by writing on a chalkboard. He slept for two hours a night and lived only on two glasses of milk a day. His faeces, Alpert reported, were 'like two small marbles each day', but his one-pointedness of mind enabled him to lift heavy rocks that no one else could move.

Alpert returned to America a man reborn, now bearing the name given to him by Neem Karoli Baba—Ram Dass. In 1971 he published a memoir, *Be Here Now*, describing his transformation from 'neurotic Jewish over-achiever' to bearded mystic. It would go on to sell more than 2 million copies. They were all Hindus now.[46]

# 12

## LOVE IS ALL YOU NEED

### THE MAHARISHI AND THE BEATLES

In April 1966, the Beatles, the most successful and influential pop group in the world, went into the Abbey Road studios in London to record the first song for a new album, *Revolver*.

The architect of the song was John Lennon. The Beatle had first taken LSD a year earlier, and his investigations into the drug had led him to Timothy Leary and Richard Alpert's book *The Psychedelic Experience*. Intent on following its instructions, Lennon read passages of the book onto a tape-recorder, dropping a tab of acid and playing back the recording as the drug took effect.

So enthralled was he by the results that he committed key lines of the text to the song 'Tomorrow Never Knows', including a reference to the state that Leary and Alpert's book called 'the Void'—what in Tibetan Buddhism is known as *sunyata*, or 'emptiness', the limitless condition, free from self, from which all things arise.

Recording the song, the producer George Martin—to whom the very mention of drugs was anathema—shaped a vivid evocation of the LSD trip by over-dubbing tape-loops of organ, mellotron, guitars, George Harrison's sitar and Lennon's vocals—treated, according to the singer's specifications, to make his voice sound like 'a Dalai Lama singing from the top of a mountain'. The song would be the first introduction—if unknowingly—to Timothy Leary and the LSD experience for millions of Beatles fans around the world.

Lennon first took LSD in April 1965 along with George Harrison, turned on at a dinner party at the London flat of George's dentist, John Riley, who unbeknown to the two Beatles had dropped sugar lumps saturated with the drug into their after-dinner coffee. For Lennon, the effects were earth-shattering. By the time he read *The Psychedelic Experience*—plucked from the shelves of Indica, the bookshop and gallery in Mason's Yard in London which stocked the Beat poets, editions of the Olympia Press and books on revolutionary politics and Eastern mysticism—Lennon had already become a fervent apostle for Leary's 'religion of the 21st century'. Leary hailed the Beatles as 'Divine Messiahs, the wisest, holiest, most effective avatars the human race has yet produced, prototypes of a new race of laughing freemen'.[1] But for Lennon, LSD was to prove anything but a laughing matter.

At his Weybridge home, he would retreat for days at a time, tripping. Such was his consumption that his grasp on reality became ever more tenuous, threatening to destroy him altogether, making him so paranoid that, as he would later recall, 'I could hardly move.'[2]

The notion of taming the ego, refined over millennia in Oriental philosophy, and condensed by Timothy Leary and acid evangelists into the span of a single trip, had entered popular currency. 'All over America young people are shedding their egos', John Garabedian and Orde Coombs pronounced, in a book published in 1969 called *Eastern Religions in the Electric Age: Why American Youth is Rejecting its Own Traditions and Seeking New Answers in the Ideas and Religions of the East*, a primer for bewildered and anxious grown-ups, which jogged through the teachings and beliefs of half a dozen Eastern faiths and creeds, from Buddhism to Jainism (not a creed, it has to be said, that was attracting many young Western converts).

The 'ego-trip' was held to be the ultimate social transgression in countercultural circles—an unseemly demonstration of individual power and control when the prevailing mood was supposed to be of communality and brother- and sisterhood. But Lennon carried Leary's prescription for evaporating the ego to hitherto unseen limits of self-abnegation and loathing. On one occasion at Paul McCartney's house, where McCartney's girlfriend, the actress Jane Asher, was entertaining some of her theatre friends to dinner, Lennon demonstrated his abject humility by crawling around the table on his hands and knees offering his open mouth to be used as an ashtray. Asher's admirably cool response was to extend one leg and push him over. In order to shake him out of his torpor and restore some sense of self-esteem in his friend, the Beatles' publicist, Derek Taylor, shared a trip with Lennon while playing a selection of his greatest compositions to convince him he was not entirely worthless.

The Beatles, as in most things, had been the first popular musicians of the era to be drawn to Indian spirituality, through a chance encounter in,

of all places, the Bahamas, where in 1965 the group were filming *Help!*
The film's nonsensical plot involves the group being pursued by a fictitious
Indian cult of Kali-worshippers, under the leadership of the nefarious
Swami Clang, who is bent on retrieving a ring worn by Ringo Starr. On
location on Paradise Island, George was approached by an authentic Indian
swami, Vishnudevananda (a disciple of Swami Sivananda), who had been
sent to the West to establish teaching centres, and would later open a yoga
retreat on the island.

Learning that the Beatles were filming there, Vishnudevananda made
his way to the set and pressed into George's hand a copy of his *Complete
Illustrated Book of Yoga* (1960). The seed was sown. During filming, George
had also picked up a sitar, used in a scene set in an Indian restaurant.
Intrigued by the instrument, he bought one for himself and began to take
lessons from an Indian musician in London, and in 1965 he used the sitar
for the first time on the Beatles' song 'Norwegian Wood'.[3] At the same
time, he was introduced to the recordings of India's virtuoso musician,
Ravi Shankar.

In June 1966, Harrison met Shankar in person at a dinner party in
London, where Harrison asked if Shankar would take him as his pupil.
Perhaps to temper Harrison's enthusiasm, Shankar, who confessed that
he had never heard 'Norwegian Wood'—indeed had barely heard of the
Beatles—described how there was much more to the sitar than 'exciting
the listeners with virtuosity and loud crash-bang effects'.[4] Mastering
the instrument, he told Harrison, was as much a spiritual discipline as a
musical one, requiring years of intensive practice. Harrison, who promised
Shankar that he would do his best, would later recall that the Beatles had
met prime ministers, celebrities and royalty, 'but I got to a point where
I thought "I'd like to meet somebody who could really impress me". And
that was when I met Ravi.'[5]

Shankar duly took his new pupil under his wing. In September 1966,
Harrison and his girlfriend, the model Pattie Boyd, joined Shankar on a
whistle-stop tour of India, visiting the Taj Mahal and the burning *ghats* of
Varanasi, before arriving in Srinagar, Kashmir, where the party rented
houseboats near a floating garden on Lake Dal.

Shankar had already introduced his protégé to *Autobiography of a Yogi*
(1948), Swami Paramahansa Yogananda's fantastical recounting of his
encounters with miracle-working swamis and saints, that would become
one of the handbooks of Western spiritual search. Now Harrison was
reading Vivekananda's *Raja Yoga* (1896). 'As soon as I read that I thought,

"That's what I want to know!'" Harrison later recalled, 'They tried to bring me up as a Catholic, and for me it didn't deliver. But to read "Each soul is potentially divine. The goal is to manifest that divinity"—and here's how you can do it—was very important for me.'[6]

Harrison's growing enthusiasm for Indian music and spirituality was consummated in March 1967, when he went into the Abbey Road studios to record a new composition, 'Within You, Without You', accompanied by a group of Indian musicians from the Asian Music Centre in London, with a string arrangement in the Indian idiom provided by George Martin.

Harrison had written the song following a conversation over dinner with his friend Klaus Voormann, on the topics that were now preoccupying increasing numbers of young Westerners—the aridity of Western life and the nature of impermanence.

'Within You, Without You' appeared as the last track on the Beatles' otherwise joyously celebratory *Sgt. Pepper's Lonely Hearts Club Band* album of 1967, 'the necessary sermon that comes with the community singing', as the music critic Ian MacDonald astringently observed.[7] For the album cover, each Beatle contributed their own choice of heroes (or villains) for the collage of characters, from film stars to comedians to philosophers. Harrison's choices included four Indian gurus—Sri Yukteswar Giri, Sri Lahiri Mahasaya, Paramahansa Yogananda and Yogananda's guru, Sri Mahavatar Babaji. Aleister Crowley was Lennon's suggestion.

It was Pattie Boyd—who had now become Harrison's wife—who first introduced him to Transcendental Meditation, after she had attended a lecture given by TM's founder, Maharishi Mahesh Yogi, and then been initiated into the meditation techniques. On 24 August 1967, at her instigation, Harrison, along with John Lennon and Paul McCartney, attended a lecture by the Maharishi at the Hilton Hotel in London. ('They seemed to do everything as a group,' Boyd remembered, 'If one of them did something, they would all want to do it.'[8]) 'We had all the material things,' Harrison would later recall, 'Fame and all that. But there was still something needed, you see. It can't be one hundred per cent without the inner life, can it?' And there it was: 'All of a sudden there was this man from India. Not in a flash of lightning or anything, but there in the Hilton Hotel.'

* * *

It was eight years earlier—on 29 January 1959—that a slight, bearded figure, with barely a penny to his name, dressed in a long white robe and sandals, dark, lank hair hanging to his shoulders, and carrying his few possessions wrapped inside a carpet roll under his arm, had landed at San Francisco airport on a flight from Honolulu. Accompanied by two companions, Maharishi Mahesh Yogi checked into a local hotel and sent word that he was ready to receive visitors.

Mahesh Prasad Varma, to give him his proper name, had been born in the Northern Indian state of Uttar Pradesh, the son of a local tax official. Various accounts give the year of his birth as 1911, 1917 or 1918—a confusion that, as the Maharishi, he would show no great inclination to clear up. Age, he maintained, was of no importance. The celebration of his eightieth birthday in 1998, however, made 1918 the official year for his followers.

According to his authorised biography, he studied physics at Allahabad University and earned a degree in 1942. While in college, he became a student of Swami Brahmananda Saraswati, known to his followers as Guru Dev—or 'divine teacher'—who was held to be in the direct lineage of Shankara, the philosopher credited with consolidating the doctrine of Advaita Vedanta in the eighth century BCE. Shankara is said to have established four great monasteries, or *mathas*—one in each corner of the Indian peninsula, North, South, East and West. The heads of these *mathas* were known as Shankaracharya. Guru Dev, who would travel about the local districts on a specially modified truck, seated on a throne amidst foliage and flowers, was the Shankaracharya of the North. After graduating from university, Mahesh took the *chela*'s vows of service and celibacy and a new name, Bal Brahmacharya Mahesh, and took up residence in the Shankaracharya's ancestral monastery in the holy town of Joshimath in the Himalayan foothills.

Shortly after Mahesh's arrival, Guru Dev instructed him to go as quickly as his feet would carry him to deliver an urgent message to a yogi who lived some miles away in the mountains. On arriving, the exhausted boy handed over the message, expecting the yogi to write a reply; but after reading the message the yogi simply nodded and instructed the boy to return to the Shankaracharya as quickly as he could. This same task was repeated several times, until one day, Mahesh, hurrying to honour his master's wishes, tripped and fell, dropping the message on the ground. Stooping to pick it up he sneaked a glance. It read: 'Please instruct this *brahmachari* to return immediately.' 'The disciple adjusts his likes and dislikes to the likes and dislikes of the Master,' the Maharishi later explained, 'thereby elevating his mind to the status of the master's mind. In this nothing matters except obedience.'[9]

In 1953 the Shankaracharya died, seated in the lotus position. His body was transported to Benares, where it was committed to the Ganges. Following instructions left by his guru, Mahesh took leave of the monastery, retiring to the caves of the 'Valley of the Saints' in Uttar Kashi, high in the Himalayas, where he remained for the next two years practising meditation.

Emerging in 1955, he travelled to Cochin in Southern India to address a gathering of disciples of the late Shankaracharya. It was there that he first expounded on the teachings of what would become known as Transcendental Meditation, bearing the glad tidings that it was not necessary to follow the monastic life to experience the highest of spiritual goals, but that peace of mind was available to all by following his prescription of meditating on a particular mantra, word, syllable or sound. This, Mahesh, specified, should be chosen 'to accord with the rhythms or impulses of the individual' and should be revealed to no one. By repeating the mantra, the initiate would resonate with the 'sound' to go 'beyond thought' and attain a state of fulfilment.

It was an idea that quickly caught on. Adopting the title Maharishi (or 'great seer') Mahesh Yogi, he travelled through India, holding meditation camps and lecturing to growing numbers of people. In 1958, at a 'Seminar of Spiritual Luminaries' held in the town of Mylapore, and attended by 'eminent saints and philosophers of all countries', the Maharishi announced the formation of his own Spiritual Regeneration Movement, to 'infuse this system of meditation in the daily life of everybody everywhere in earth'.

Over the next few months, twenty-five meditation centres would be opened in his name across India. In April 1958, the Maharishi boarded a plane to begin a whistle-stop tour to Rangoon, Bangkok, Kuala Lumpur and Hong Kong, opening meditation centres in each city. On 31 December 1958, the *Honolulu Star Bulletin* announced his arrival in Hawaii, reporting: 'He has no money; he asks for nothing. His worldly possessions can be carried in one hand. Maharishi Mahesh Yogi is on a world odyssey. He carries a message that he says will rid the world of unhappiness and discontent.'

Four weeks later he arrived in America. Addressing a press conference in Los Angeles at the Ambassador Hotel shortly after his arrival, he told reporters that he had 'brought from the land of ancient sages' to the modern man 'a simple technique of living in peace and happiness'. If just 1 per cent of the world practised Transcendental Meditation, he said, 'they will give off such vibrations that war will not be possible. Then mankind will embark on an age of peace.'

'Yogi Has Cure for World Ills', reported the local Los Angeles *Herald Express*, above a photograph of the Maharishi beaming beatifically, and clutching a bouquet of flowers—an image that would become ubiquitous in the coming years. In Los Angeles, his message that one could pursue a spiritual life without the need for renunciation—in other words, have your cake and eat it—fell on fertile ground. Among the first to take up the Maharishi were John Hislop, a land developer and erstwhile Theosophist, who had been a follower of Krishnamurti and Yogananda before discovering the Maharishi, and who would later become a devotee of Sathya Sai Baba; Charles Lutes, a former steel and concrete salesman turned clairvoyant and spiritual healer, who would become the Maharishi's right-hand man and later president of the Spiritual Regeneration Movement (SRM); and Roland Olson and his wife Helena, who had attended the Maharishi's first lecture in Los Angeles, and been so enamoured that they had invited him to stay in their home.

He quickly took over the household, upsetting the Olsons' daughter by insisting on using her bedroom rather than the guest room, and transforming the study into a shrine-room, filled with photographs of Guru Dev, incense and flowers. Within a matter of days, the Olsons were hosting lectures in their living room and greeting visitors for private interviews with the guru (as well as paying his soaring telephone bills).

Those wishing to be initiated into TM were asked to give an assurance that they were not using psychotropic drugs or undergoing psychoanalysis, and to bring six fresh flowers, two pieces of fruit, a clean white handkerchief and a financial donation roughly equivalent to a week's wages. This voluntary 'donation' would later be changed to a fixed fee. Serious meditators were encouraged to become instructors themselves, as part of the Maharishi's 'Three Year Plan' to train 25,000 teachers and establish an equivalent number of meditation centres.

Over the next two years, the Maharishi would travel the world, expenses paid by his followers in Los Angeles, establishing centres in Britain, Germany, Greece and Scandinavia. In 1961, the first international Teacher Training Course (TTC), attended by meditators from Britain, Denmark, India, America, Australia and Greece, was held in Rishikesh in India, where the Maharishi planned to construct a new ashram, grandly named the International Academy of Meditation.

The Maharishi was eased on his path by the American socialite Nancy Cooke de Herrera, who had at one time worked for the US State Department as a goodwill ambassador, travelling the world lecturing on fashion and cultural customs and socialising with the likes of King Hussein of Jordan and the Shah of Iran—a role that led to her being known as the 'US Ambassadress of Fashion'.

In 1955, following the death of her Argentinian husband, the racing car driver Luis de Herrera, Cooke had been given a copy of Yogananda's *Autobiography of a Yogi* by a friend, the Indian Ambassador to Washington, and in 1962 she travelled to India. Cooke was in search of a teacher, and in Rishikesh, where she had gone to meet Swami Sivananda, she was told of another swami 'who appeals to Western students'. Cooke made her way to the Maharishi's ashram, only to be told that he had just left for California.

She returned to America, and within a matter of months had been initiated into TM. Following a regime of intensive meditation, she was soon experiencing 'the golden glow'—the ecstatic feeling, the Maharishi told his students, that would be experienced in the 'Field of Pure Bliss Consciousness'. Utilising her extensive Rolodex of contacts, Cooke was soon taking care of the Maharishi's public relations, introducing the guru to her extended social circle. These were not hippies—the word had not yet been invented—and not even Beats or bohemians, but were for the most part society figures, professionals and people from the world of entertainment—such as the actor Glenn Ford and Efram Zimbalist, Jr., a popular television actor through his role in 77 *Sunset Strip*—much the same sort of people, in fact, who had been drawn to Meher Baba when he had visited Hollywood thirty years earlier.

When it came to Indian gurus, the Maharishi—with his white robe, beard and shoulder-length hair—looked, as a friend of Cooke's put it, 'straight from central casting'. To really garner column inches, Cooke realised, what was required were stories about notable, successful people coming to hear him speak—and to make the Maharishi's religious message palatable to a wider audience.

It was advice the Maharishi heeded. Decrying the fact that Vedic teachings had been, as he put it, 'shrouded in the garb of mysticism', he instead emphasised TM as a practical, systematic and 'scientifically proven' way of clearing the cluttered mind, relieving tension and finding happiness. Along the way would come a host of other benefits: increased energy, clearer thinking, success in business, improved relations with husband or wife. In fact, TM was the answer to pretty much everything except death and taxes. To a physician, he maintained that it was the 'new wonder drug. You will learn to cure your patients with meditation', while a physicist was informed that TM was 'the answer to physics; it gives us an understanding of matter'.[10]

Staying with the Olsons, one of his requests was for 'a dark room where scientists can measure light rays from the glow on the face that comes after practicing the technique'.[11] There was nothing miraculous to it. Asked by Glenn Ford, who seemingly had a particular interest in supranormal powers, whether he could levitate, the Maharishi joked that it was 'not necessary. There are so many airplanes to take one anywhere.'[12]

And it worked. There were clear benefits to TM. People *did* feel more alert, clear-minded, better able to concentrate, less stressed—even if it did not actually provide 'the answer to physics' or cure the sick, and few actually realised the 'cosmic consciousness' that the Maharishi held out as the ultimate result of his methods.

The Maharishi had not invented meditation, but he had developed a simple and effective variation on it, and also developed a way to market it to people who would have otherwise looked askance at anything that smacked of Indian spirituality. Like Henry Ford with the Model T, he had found a way to roll out meditation to the masses. Because of his rapidly expanding programme of meditators becoming teachers, it was not even necessary to be initiated into TM by the Maharishi himself.

Cultivating the rich, the powerful and people of influence was an integral part of this mission. In his book *The Science of Being and Art of Living* (1963) he wrote: 'If there is a fort, and the whole territory belongs to it, it is wise to go straight to the fort and capture it. Having captured the fort, all that is in the surrounding territory will naturally be possessed.'[13] Among the circle of friends and acquaintances that Nancy Cooke introduced to the Maharishi there was no one richer than Doris Duke, heiress to the American Tobacco Company fortune and once dubbed by newspapers 'the richest girl in the world'.

Duke was cursed by her fortune. Growing up distrustful of people trying to take advantage of her had proved no immunity to her twice making bad marriages—the first to an American diplomat, James Cromwell, the second to a Dominican diplomat, racing car driver and playboy, Porfirio Rubirosa. Both marriages ended quickly and for Duke, very expensively (Rubirosa emerged from the four-year marriage with a stable of polo ponies, several sports cars, a converted B-25 bomber and a seventeenth-century house in Paris).

Duke was also no stranger to Indian swamis. She had been a disciple and friend of Paramahansa Yogananda and a practitioner of kriya yoga for ten years. She agreed to try TM on the condition that she be initiated by the Maharishi himself. Unorthodox as this request was, the Maharishi, for reasons best known to himself, agreed.

At their first meeting, he offered his view that if you are born into wealth, you have been given a good opportunity, but you are also in danger of being ruined by it. 'That,' he told Duke, 'is why you must do something important with your money; otherwise it will control and ruin your life.' Because her fortune derived from tobacco, 'a life-destructive plant', he continued, which 'brings bad karma to those who sell it to others', it was necessary for her to perform 'life constructive acts' with her money 'to offset this bad karma'. 'I am asking nothing,' he told her, 'I only speak of universal law. That is why I warn you.' Instead, on her initiation, he suggested that as an offering to Guru Dev she should give 'some of your time. That is more valuable to me than your money, for then you will be giving of yourself.'[14]

As an example of soft-shoe salesmanship, it was hard to surpass. Duke, who claimed to have been transformed by the effects of TM, duly donated $100,000 (equivalent to about $900,000 in 2020) to the Maharishi, enabling him to complete the building of his International Academy of Meditation in Rishikesh, along with a new house for himself. The new buildings had only recently been finished when, in February 1968, and amidst a blaze of publicity, the Maharishi's most famous students came to stay.

John Lennon had initially been sceptical when Pattie Boyd told him about Transcendental Meditation: 'She said: "They gave me this word but I can't tell, it's a secret", And I said "What kind of scene is this if you keep secrets from your friends?'[15] But overcoming his reservations, along with George and Paul, and with much the same enthusiasm with which he had adopted LSD, Lennon quickly became a convert.

On 25 August 1967, the day after seeing the Maharishi for the first time at the Hilton Hotel, all four Beatles, along with Pattie Boyd, Jane Asher, Ringo Starr's wife Maureen, and their friends Mick Jagger and Marianne Faithfull, boarded a train at Euston station in London bound for Bangor in North Wales, where the guru was staging a ten-day 'Spiritual Guides' course at a teacher training college.

The encounter came perfumed with the sweet aroma of serendipity, for both the group and the Maharishi. After years of frenetic touring, the exhaustion of being the most popular group in the world, and the dawning realisation that fame and money were not the answer to everything, the Beatles were ready to be beguiled by the promise of bliss, peace and happiness—a high without drugs—to be found by simply meditating for half an hour each day; while the Maharishi, having been apprised of who the Beatles were, was quick to realise just how useful they could be for promoting his mission of global spiritual regeneration.

'You have created a magic air through your names,' he told them on their arrival in Wales, 'You have now got to use that magic influence on the generation that look up to you. You have a big responsibility.' As the *Daily Express* reported, 'The Beatles, all twiddling red flowers, nodded agreement.'[16]

The Bangor retreat would provide an opportunity for the group to be initiated into TM, preparatory to a longer retreat in India planned for the following year. But just two days into the course came the shocking news that the group's manager, Brian Epstein, had been found dead from a drugs overdose in his mews flat in London.

Over the previous six years Epstein had steered the Beatles' career, from lunchtime sessions in the scruffy surroundings of the Cavern Club in Liverpool, to becoming the most popular group in the world, as much surrogate elder brother as manager. Without him they were rudderless, bereft. All the Vedic teachings about impermanence had suddenly taken on a horrible reality. But meditation, it seemed, was already offering the soothing balm of consolation and acceptance.

'There is no such thing as death,' George Harrison told reporters as the group prepared to return to London, 'only in the physical sense. We know he's ok now. He will return because he was striving for happiness and desired bliss so much.' 'We all feel very sad,' Lennon added,

These talks on Transcendental Meditation have helped us to stand up to it so much better. You don't get upset when a young kid becomes a teenager or a teenager becomes an adult or an adult gets old. Well, Brian is just passing into the next phase. His spirit is still with us.

It was a somewhat different sentiment that Lennon would express some years later when asked about the Maharishi and Epstein's death: 'I was stunned, and we all were, I suppose, and the Maharishi, we went in to him, "What?", you know, "He's dead," and all of that. And he was sort of saying, "Oh forget it, be happy," fuckin' idiot ...'[17]

The Maharishi made no secret of regarding TM as a product to be rolled out to the masses, likening it to ice cream: 'So having manufactured the ice-cream, and having found a beautiful label and then advertised and accepted its value in the market, now I have to see that every generation receives those beautiful packets in their purity.'[18]

And no amount of money could have bought the promotional fillip that came with the Beatles' name. In 1965, as part of the programme of spreading TM, a Student International Meditation Society (SIMS) had been established with branches at Harvard, Yale, Berkeley and other colleges across America. With *The New York Times* hailing the Maharishi as 'Chief Guru of the Western World', enrolment in SIMS was growing exponentially.[19] A front-page article in New York's *Village Voice*, 'What's New in America? Maharishi and Meditation', suggested that with 2,000 students having signed up to the SIMS course at Berkeley, 'it now looks that Maharishi may become more popular than the Beatles' (a neat inversion on the furore that the Beatles had caused a year earlier, when Lennon had opined that the Beatles were bigger than Jesus).[20] *Time* magazine would later suggest that TM 'may be the most welcome mystique to attract a youthful following since ... the Boy Scout movement'.[21]

The Maharishi himself wasted no time in exploiting his connection with the Beatles, releasing a recording of his lectures on which he billed himself as 'the Beatles' spiritual teacher', and promising the American Broadcasting Corporation that the group would be appearing in a planned television special.[22] Paul and George, along with their aide Peter Brown, were obliged to fly to Sweden where the Maharishi was conducting a course, to gently explain that he was not to use their name in connection with his business affairs. 'The Maharishi just nodded and giggled again', Brown wrote later.[23] 'He's not a modern man,' George said forgivingly on the plane home, 'He just doesn't understand these things.'[24]

Allen Ginsberg took a beadier view. In December 1967, the Maharishi addressed a gathering of 3,600 people at the Felt Forum in Madison Square Garden, New York. Afterwards, Ginsberg visited him in his suite at the Plaza Hotel, finding the guru surrounded by a group of besuited devotees. Ginsberg taxed him on his views on the escalating war in Vietnam ('he said [President] Johnson and his secret police had more information and they knew what they were doing. I said they were a buncha dumbells ...') and on the subject of drugs. Had it not been for LSD, Ginsberg told the Maharishi, nobody would have come to see him. 'Devotees gasped,' Ginsberg wrote, 'He said, well LSD has done its thing, now forget it. Just let it drop. He said his meditation was stronger. I said excellent, if it works why not? I said I would be glad to try; can't do anything but good.'

The Maharishi then appalled Ginsberg by telling him that he had been visited by six hippies in Los Angeles and they had smelled so bad that he had to take them outside into the garden. 'I said WHAT? You must have been reading the newspapers. He said he didn't read newspapers ... He insisted that hippies smelled. I must say that was tendentious.'

But despite his reservations, Ginsberg concluded that the Maharishi's 'Pyramid club' of people meditating would certainly 'generate peacefulness' if it caught on 'massively and universally'. But 'his political statements are definitely dim-witted and a bit out of place'.[25]

\* \* \*

In February 1968, the Beatles fulfilled their promise and flew to India to join the Maharishi at his ashram in Rishikesh on a course designed to teach meditators to become initiators. With funding from Doris Duke, the International Academy of Meditation was taking shape. Set high on a hill, downriver from Rishikesh, the ashram comprised six long, whitewashed buildings, each accommodating five or six bedrooms, a scattering of smaller residences, a large lecture hall accommodating 200 people and a dining hall. The Maharishi's house was set off from the other buildings in a grove of trees on a promontory offering a commanding view over the Ganges. A barbed wire fence surrounded the property to keep out intruders.

Some sixty people were scheduled to attend the course: meditators from Europe, America, Scandinavia and Australia. A local tailor, who had set up shop in the ashram, turned out robes and kurta pyjamas for the visitors.

The Maharishi had appointed Nancy Cooke as his liaison with the students and visitors. He had flown to India accompanied by the actress Mia Farrow, whom he had met in Boston, following a talk at Harvard's Sanders Hall, along with her sister Prudence. Farrow had just finished filming *Rosemary's Baby* and had also recently been served divorce papers by her husband, Frank Sinatra.

The Maharishi had paid for Farrow's and her sister's plane tickets. Mia Farrow, he told Cooke, was good for publicity and should be treated 'as a special person'. She was allocated accommodation close to the

Maharishi's house, and he lavished all his attention on her, summoning her each afternoon for a private talk, and in his public lectures (to her considerable embarrassment) placing a paper crown on her head. Quickly tiring of the ashram and of the Maharishi's over-attentiveness, Farrow sent a telegram to her estranged husband, Sinatra: 'Fed up with meditation. Am leaving ashram. Will phone from Delhi.'[26]

Tipped off about the telegram, and anxious about the prospect of bad publicity, the Maharishi instructed Cooke to organise a tour to a tiger reserve to keep the actress occupied. She would come and go on the course, eventually leaving early.

The first members of the Beatles, John and George, arrived two weeks into the course, accompanied by their wives, the Beatles' road manager, Mal Evans. They were shortly joined by Paul and Jane Asher, Ringo and his wife Maureen, the folk singer Donovan, accompanied by his friend and manager Gypsy Dave, and Mike Love of the Beach Boys.

Love had first encountered the Maharishi a few months earlier, at a Christmas concert on behalf of UNICEF in Paris, where the Beach Boys had performed a close harmony version of 'O Come All Ye Faithful', and the Maharishi had been scheduled to give a talk. For Love, the Maharishi's message about integrating the practice of TM into everyday life struck a resounding chord. 'One of the greatest things [about TM] that interested me,' he would later explain, 'was that [the Maharishi] said, "You don't have to give up your Rolls-Royce and forsake all your pursuits of material pleasures to develop inner-spiritual qualities." That sounded real good to me.'[27]

At Rishikesh, newspaper reporters and television news crews from around the world had joined the beggars habitually camped at the ashram gates. Occasionally, the Maharishi, accompanied by a bearded monk holding an umbrella to shade him from the piercing sunlight, would descend the hill to move among them, clutching a bouquet of marigolds and offering spiritually elevating *pensées* about 'the ocean of happiness within', while brushing aside any untoward questions about his finances.

The Beatles and other famous visitors were accommodated in the best rooms in the ashrams, closest to the Maharishi, where they would meditate each day. John and George were particularly dedicated, but nobody applied themselves quite so assiduously as Mia Farrow's sister, Prudence, who spent so much time alone in meditation that even the Maharishi grew concerned for her well-being. When she finally emerged after one session lasting most of the day, he told her that she must meditate only in short bursts. Lennon wrote a song for her, 'Dear Prudence'.

Life at the ashram was to prove surprisingly conducive to song writing. More than half the songs that subsequently appeared on the group's *White Album* (1968), including 'Back in the USSR', 'Piggies' and 'Why Don't We Do It in the Road?' (as well as 'Across the Universe' which appeared on *Let it Be* in 1970—which includes the words 'Jai guru deva om', a phrase that translates roughly as 'I give thanks to Guru Dev') were written at Rishikesh. There is some irony that the album born in the place where the spirit of peace and love was ostensibly being cultivated, should have been employed by the era's anti-Christ, Charles Manson, as inspiration to foment his 'Helter Skelter' killing spree the following year.

Like Mia Farrow, the Beatles, Donovan and Love were afforded favourite status, being summoned for private meetings in the Maharishi's bungalow and occupying the reserved seats in the front row of the lecture hall where he spoke each evening and answered questions on such matters as 'God consciousness' and whether 'rapturous joy' always accompanied the descent into 'pure being'.

So congenial was the atmosphere that the Maharishi suggested to Nancy Cooke that she might invite his benefactress, Doris Duke, to join them: 'She'd enjoy the young people and their music. And I'd like her to see what her money had built.' But Duke could not be contacted.[28]

But the ashram regime did not suit everyone. Less than two weeks after arriving, tired of the food and missing their children, Ringo Starr and his wife Maureen left the ashram to return to Britain. Paul McCartney and Jane Asher departed two weeks later.

Reluctant to leave, George Harrison talked of a concert to raise funds for building a Maharishi academy in London. Meanwhile, John Lennon declared his intention to build a transmitter at Rishikesh that was powerful enough to transmit the Maharishi's teachings around the world, and suggested that he was ready to relinquish his life as a Beatle and bring his son Julian from England to join the Maharishi and continue their spiritual training in Kashmir.

The first rumblings of disquiet came with the arrival of a friend of the Beatles, Alexis Mardas, or as he was known among the group, 'Magic Alex'. The son of a major in the Greek secret police, Mardas was an electronics engineer who had arrived in Britain in 1965 on a student visa, and who ingratiated himself into the Beatles' circle after exhibiting his 'Kinetic Light Sculptures' at the Indica Gallery in London. Lennon was particularly enthralled by Mardas' 'Nothing Box', a small plastic box with randomly blinking lights, which the Beatle would stare at for hours while tripping on LSD.

Before long, Mardas had become a ubiquitous presence in the Beatles' lives, travelling with them to Greece to facilitate the purchase of their own island (soon dispensed with) and even appearing in the group's 1967 television film, *Magical Mystery Tour*. Lennon, who was particularly impressed by Mardas' ambitious plans to develop an X-ray camera and a force field that would surround the Beatles' homes, referred to him—not altogether facetiously—as 'my guru'. Mardas had his suspicions about the Maharishi. Fearful, perhaps, of seeing his own influence usurped, he told Lennon that the swami was nothing more than a confidence trickster. And arriving at the ashram, he immediately proved a subversive presence, smuggling in alcohol in defiance of the ashram rules and, on his walks with Lennon through the forest, musing loudly on how strange it was that the holy man always seemed to have an accountant at his side.

The final seed of doubt came to flower when Mardas gossiped to Lennon that the Maharishi had had sex with a young American student and made advances to Mia Farrow. After conferring with George Harrison, Lennon decided to leave, but not before confronting the Maharishi. 'I said, "We're leaving",' he explained later,

> He asked 'Why?' and all that shit, and I said, 'Well, if you're so cosmic you'll know why,' because he was always intimating, and there were all these right-hand men intimating, that he did these miracles, you know. And I said 'You know why,' and he said 'I don't know why, you must tell me,' and I just kept saying 'You ought to know,' and he gave me a look like 'I'll kill you, you bastard,' and he gave me such a look and I knew then, when he looked at me, you know, because I had called his bluff, because I said it all, you know.[29]

Lennon left, leaving behind a large photo of the Maharishi torn in half and thrown on the floor of his room. He would subsequently write the song 'Sexy Sadie', based on the incident, changing the Maharishi's name for fear of a libel action.

It would be some time before the allegations against the Maharishi became public, and they would continue to haunt him for years afterwards.

But were they true? When Charlie Lutes told him why Harrison and Lennon had left, he expressed shock and bemusement: 'But, Charlie, I am a lifetime celibate. I don't know anything about sensual desires.' It was a statement contradicted by several women who would later claim to have had intimate relations with him.

In June 1969, Lennon and McCartney appeared at a press conference in New York, where Lennon described their flirtation with the guru as 'a personal mistake we made in public'—'Meditation is good and does what they say. It's like exercise or cleaning your teeth—it works. But we're finished with that bit. We're as naive as the next person.' 'We thought there was more to him than there was,' McCartney explained, 'but he's human. And for a while we thought he wasn't, you know, we thought he was a ...' The sentence remained unfinished.

Despite the opprobrium heaped on the Maharishi over the years, George Harrison never abandoned his loyalty to him. Nor did he ever lose his sense of exasperation over the fact that people never quite understood his spiritual search—a fact that Harrison put down to 'ignorance'. 'They say ignorance is bliss,' he told me when I interviewed him in 1979,

> but bliss is not ignorance—it's the opposite of that, which is knowledge. And there's a lot of people who have fear. Basically I feel fortunate to have realised what the goal is in life. There's no point in dying having gone through your life without knowing who you are or what the purpose of life is.

Harrison's last public appearance in Britain was at a concert at the Royal Albert Hall in 1992 on behalf of the Maharishi's Natural Law Party. The following year he visited the Maharishi to ask for forgiveness over the events at Rishikesh, saying he now believed the allegations were false. According to Deepak Chopra—a student of the Maharishi, who later fell out with him—the Maharishi told Harrison that there was nothing to forgive; the Beatles, he said, were 'angels in disguise'.

* * *

The Maharishi supposedly said that if the Beatles meditated they would stay together, and if the Beach Boys meditated, they would become the most influential group in the world. Perhaps this is what accounted for the Beach Boys—at least some of them—becoming even keener meditators than the Beatles.

Brian Wilson, the group's creative genius, in the moments when he wasn't ingesting copious amounts of marijuana and psychedelics and fretting over the creative muse that seemed to have deserted him, took to meditating, seated in the purple and gold silk Arabian tent that he had erected inside his Beverly Hills mansion. He soon gave up, later explaining that 'I couldn't concentrate on my mantra.'[30] Mike Love and Al Jardine, however, became avid practitioners, and went on to train as instructors. 'My first impression was that it was so simple that anyone could learn it,' Love remembered, 'And if only everyone could learn it the whole world could be different.' What's more, he added, meditation helped him to 'compete and win'. Even Bruce Johnston, by his own description 'a pretty conservative guy', became a regular meditator. When Johnston first encountered the Maharishi he was sceptical:

> [T]o me it sounded a bit like turning water into wine, y'know.
>
> I thought singing music was the way I wanted to be connected in Beach Boy land; I didn't want to suddenly become an instant expert on how to spread love and peace throughout the world. And then all of a sudden there's people from India on the map, and there's Sammy Davis wearing beads and the Beatles on the train going to Bangor.
>
> Then Mike came back from India. And the Maharishi thing just consumed Mike Love. And *that* got my curiosity, because Mike was someone I knew—and talking to him I thought, wait a second, there is something to all this. For Mike, it just gave him a great focus. And eventually I was initiated—and to this day I meditate twice a day. I'm a Christian Presbyterian—and that hasn't changed.[31]

Inspired with the idea of spreading the word about the Maharishi, Love envisaged a series of concerts, under the rubric of 'World Peace', that would be staged throughout Europe and Asia in destinations as varied as Moscow and Bangkok. 'We are hoping to involve as many creative people in all forms of art and entertainment, as possible,' he told the *New Musical Express*, 'from Picasso to Hefner's bunny girls.'[32] Some of the most famous names in the pop world had already 'guaranteed their assistance', he claimed, adding that the Secretary General of the United Nations, U Thant, had met the Maharishi and said that the guru 'made more sense in 15 minutes than he had heard in 30 years'.

The 'World Peace' tour would be quietly abandoned, but in May 1968 the Maharishi joined the Beach Boys on a short tour of America. 'The emanation of vibrations is very important if the world is going to live harmoniously', Love told a reporter from *The Chicago Tribune* immediately prior to the tour, adding that practising meditation had 'shot our record sales up to three million dollars last year from around two and a half million'.[33]

The group chartered a plane for the tour, the Maharishi sitting in pride of place, surrounded by his entourage and enveloped in flowers. 'He was kind of like the Wizard of Oz, just this gentle, lovely soul, with this huge thing that people believed in,' Bruce Johnston remembered, 'and being with us was probably great on paper for him. 10,000 people every night? Fantastic! That's the way I'd have been thinking if I were him. But we were just like a little shooting star in the Maharishi world.'[34]

The tour began in Washington on 3 May. The following night, in Baltimore, the Maharishi took to the stage to address the audience before the appearance of the group. 'The kids wanted to hear "Fun, Fun, Fun",' Johnston said,

> and Maharishi's speaking, and he kind of giggled 'cos he sounds like he's on helium—so here he is doing this sweet, wonderful sharing that he believes people should be made aware of, and people were booing and shouting. The apples and oranges were definitely not working out on that tour.

After five concerts, Love was forced to admit that the plan had failed, and the tour was abandoned, with the announcement that the Maharishi had been 'taken ill'.

Twenty-four further tour dates, including a planned appearance at the Hollywood Bowl, were cancelled at an estimated cost to the band of $250,000. As Al Jardine remarked, 'the only people to make a profit were the florists'. Nor did the group's association with the Maharishi help their record sales. Their next album, *Friends* (1968), which included songs reflecting their enthusiasm for TM such as 'Wake the World' and 'Transcendental Meditation', was the worst selling in their career to date, reaching only 126 in the US charts.

But the indifference of the Beach Boys' audience was no setback for the Maharishi. By the early 1970s, his organisation was claiming to have more than 600,000 practitioners of TM around the world. In 1971, the Maharishi opened the Maharishi International University in Goleta, California (it relocated to Fairfield, Iowa, in 1974) and in 1975 his first European 'university' opened in Switzerland.

\* \* \*

The Maharishi was not the only guru to have come to the West in the wake of the rising interest in Indian spirituality.

Sri Chinmoy had arrived in New York in 1964, having spent twenty years living in Sri Aurobindo ashram in Pondicherry practising meditation and studying Bengali and English literature. Working initially as a clerk in the Indian consulate, he then began to give lectures on Hinduism, quickly establishing a reputation as a teacher and holy man. In 1966 he opened a Sri Chinmoy Centre in San Juan, Puerto Rico, followed by other centres in America and Europe. Chinmoy emphasised physical fitness as an integral part of the spiritual path. He was an avid runner, and in later life took up weightlifting. He was particularly fond of lifting public figures, and it is claimed that over the years, as his reputation spread, he lifted Nelson Mandela, Sting, Yoko Ono and Richard Gere, among others.

Chinmoy's most public disciples were the musicians John McLaughlin and Santana. In the 1960s, McLaughlin had experimented with LSD. 'I began asking myself the fundamental questions of my existence,' he remembered,

> These are questions such as 'What is God?', 'What is this infinite Universe?', 'What is religion and what does it mean?', and, of course, 'Who am I and what am I doing here?' These kinds of questions are not specifically addressed in the Western Christian religions, at least not to my knowledge at the time. I know differently now. However, at that time, I along with thousands of other seekers, found answers to these questions in Asia in general and India in particular.[35]

McLaughlin became a member of the Theosophical Society, was introduced to the teachings of Ramana Maharshi, among others, and joined a meditation group in London. In 1969, when living in New York, he attended a meeting where Sri Chinmoy was speaking:

> It was in a public meditation, and he asked for questions. I asked him a question about the relationship between music and enlightenment, and he answered that it was not important what one did. What was (is) important is the consciousness of the person. In short, a street sweeper can be enlightened through sweeping streets. I found this answer very interesting. That said, the first two years I spent with him, he never spoke once about meditation. However, I learned a great deal about myself.

McLaughlin became a follower of Chinmoy, adopting the name Mahavishnu given to him by his guru.

At the same time, the musician Santana had also become a follower, taking the name Devadip. Adopting all white clothing as a symbol of purity, both McLaughlin and Santana recorded albums of beautiful jazz rock improvisations inspired by Chinmoy and his teachings, including a joint album in 1973 named in honour of his central maxim, 'Love, Devotion, Surrender'. 'Those are the three most profound words in any language, and without living them, any way towards enlightenment and liberation is doomed from the start', McLaughlin told me,

> The teacher represents enlightenment and perfect interior freedom to the disciple, so of course he surrenders his/her will to the Guru since the disciple is seeking the same liberation and enlightenment. It is extremely difficult for a human being to 'Love, Devote and Surrender' to an abstraction such as 'divine'. What is 'divine'? It's an idea or ideal concocted in the mind of human beings.

McLaughlin ceased to be a disciple—'outwardly'—of Sri Chinmoy in the mid-1970s:

> There were fundamental propositions I could not agree with, and I felt the urge to assume responsibility for my own development. Inside I continue to revere him and thank him for the blessings he brought me. I continue to meditate to this day because it is an integral part of my life. We are all part of the infinite, and in meditation, we can experience this reality.

He was later followed by Santana, who in 2000 told *Rolling Stone* that he had become disenchanted with Chinmoy in the 1980s, adding that the guru had been 'pretty vindictive for a while' following the break: 'He told all my friends not to call me ever again, because I was to drown in the dark sea of ignorance for leaving him.'[36] In a later interview in 2017, Santana noted: 'I'm really grateful for those 10 years I spent with that spiritual master.'[37]

\* \* \*

The most extraordinary guru to come to the West at that time was the 'boy god' Guru Maharaj Ji, who arrived in London from India in 1971.

His birth name was Prem Pal Singh Rawat. He was born on 10 December 1957 in a small village on the outskirts of Haridwar, but

grew up in the former British hill station of Dehradun. His father, Shri
Hans Ji Maharaj (full title, Yogiraj [King of Yogis] Param Sant [First and
Supreme Saint] Satgurudev [True Worshipful Teacher]), was a revered
teacher who travelled extensively in the north of India, establishing the
organisation Divya Sandesh Parishad (later to be known as Divine Light
Mission) and building a following that at its height numbered in the tens
of thousands.

A precocious child, as a small boy Prem would accompany his father
to his talks, occasionally giving discourses himself. According to his
hagiography, at one such talk he was recognised by a Sikh sage as the
reincarnation of a seventeenth-century poet and Sant named Tukaram.[38]
He was known as Sant Ji from then on. At the age of eight, following
his father's death, he inherited the title Maharaj Ji—and the Divine
Light Mission.

By 1968, the first Westerners had begun to find their way to the guru's
ashram in Haridwar, and in 1969 an Indian disciple, Guru Charananand,
was despatched to London to prepare the ground for Maharaj Ji's first
visit to the West. He set up base in a cramped basement flat in West
Kensington, and began to harvest new followers, known as 'premies',
preaching Maharaj Ji's message about seeking out 'the Truth Within'.

In June 1971, the 13-year-old Maharaj Ji travelled to the West for
the first time. A Rolls-Royce, hired by his followers for the occasion
and festooned with flowers, awaited him at Heathrow airport. Within a
few days of his arrival, his followers had arranged his first major public
appearance, at the Glastonbury Fayre. The festival was to be held on the
summer solstice, 22 June, a propitious time, his followers reasoned,
for the world saviour to announce his arrival in the West to a new and
hopeful generation.

Michael Eavis, the farmer who staged the festival on his dairy farm in
the southwest of England, would remember receiving a telephone call
asking if he would agree to God appearing on stage. Being an agreeable
sort, Eavis replied, why not?

On the appointed day, the Maharaj Ji was driven in a Ford Zodiac
(the Rolls-Royce had been returned) the 100 miles from London to
Glastonbury, arriving shortly after dusk. The rock group Brinsley Schwarz
were in the middle of a performance on the newly erected Pyramid Stage.
A number of premies made their way on stage and demanded that the
group give way for the boy guru. 'There was no security in those days,' the
band's singer Nick Lowe remembered,

and when we wouldn't get off, the flower children became more and more nasty. We'd finish a tune, and they'd say, 'The Master is here!' Then huge chunks of metal started being dropped on us from the pyramid by his more enthusiastic followers, and eventually they drove us off the stage. He got on, asked the audience for money, got back in his car and cleared off.[39]

In fact, Lowe seemed to have misunderstood, so garbled was the Maharaj Ji's English. What he actually asked for was 'the money of love and devotion', but the crowd was in no mood to give it to him. (There was apparently further confusion when he instructed that there should be 'no more sects'; many thought he was saying there should be 'no more sex'.) After five minutes the crowd started shouting and heckling, the power was cut off and the Maharaj Ji left the stage and returned to London that night.[40]

Within a few weeks, he was on his way to America. When the first Guru Puja was held in Colorado the following year it attracted more than 2,000 devotees. Maharaj Ji's main selling point, and the pathway, or so it was said, to divine bliss, was something he called 'the Knowledge'. This was a four-part meditation technique that Maharaj Ji's father had been taught by his guru, and which he in turn had taught to Maharaj Ji when he was just 6 years old.

For the first technique, the devotee sat with eyes closed and placed the thumb and middle finger on each eyeball, squeezing hard. This was said to reveal 'The Divine Light'. The second technique involved blocking both ears with your thumbs. This supposedly gave rise to Divine Music. The third technique was the basic meditation practice of following the breath. The fourth involved rolling the tongue back as far as it would go, if possible, into the nasal cavity, with the object of tasting 'Divine Nectar'.

It was not enough simply to learn these techniques; they needed to be revealed by the Maharaj Ji himself or one of his accredited Mahatmas. Through this, it was said, the devotee was forging a direct connection to the Maharaj Ji's 'divine grace'. Nor was it enough simply to receive Knowledge. It needed to be strengthened constantly by practice—the giving and receiving of *satsang*, or testimony, to the guru's greatness; by 'service'—or work for his organisation; and, of course, by donations.

The very word 'Knowledge' bespoke some hermetic wisdom available only to the initiated. And those initiated in the techniques were obliged to take a vow not to reveal them to anybody. We have it—you don't. Smugness and arrogance masquerading as humility was a leitmotif of the times.

Under the direction of a devotee named Glen Whittaker, an Oxford graduate who had once been tutored by J. R. R. Tolkien, the Divine Light Mission grew rapidly, establishing its headquarters in a former Odeon cinema in Dulwich, South London, renamed the Palace of Peace. It boasted a merchandising arm, Divine Sales, that manufactured everything from clothes to cosmetics; a film production company called Shri Hans Productions; a publishing arm; and a service and security arm, the World Peace Corps. There was also a building division (Millennium Construction) and a clothing company (Mother Nature Fashions).

The Mission also established a network of ashrams throughout Britain and America, where residents were expected to perform a daily series of rituals binding them to the guru, while working in the outside world and contributing money to the organisation. It bore all the trappings of a cult.

In November 1973, the Divine Light Mission staged a three-day festival called Millennium '73, at the Houston Astrodome in Texas. Billed as 'the most significant event in the history of humanity', posters for the event promised it would be the prelude to 'a thousand years of peace for those who want peace'. The event coincided with the Maharaj Ji's sixteenth birthday.

Maharaj Ji's arrival at Houston would be heralded by a new, rather surprising, convert. Rennie Davis had been a prominent activist in student politics and the leader of Students for a Democratic Society (SDS). A vehement opponent of the war in Vietnam, he had twice gone to Hanoi, risking charges of treason, to draw attention to America's bombing of the country. He was one of the Chicago Seven, a group of political activists and radicals who in March 1969 were put on trial on charges of conspiracy and inciting to riot arising from the protests at the Democratic National Convention the previous September, when police had brutally put down anti-war demonstrations.[41]

But by the early 1970s, the energy of the New Left and student politics had begun to dissipate. The events in Chicago, and the shooting by the Ohio National Guard of unarmed college students at Kent State University, Ohio, protesting against President Richard Nixon's escalation of the Vietnam War in May 1970, resulting in the death of four students and the wounding of nine others, had sapped the energy from the movement, and sowed the seeds of a widespread disillusionment in the politics of protest.

Davis would later speak of how he had come to see all his political activity as merely the prelude to his meeting with Maharaj Ji.

In 1973, after reading Ram Dass' memoir, *Be Here Now*, Davis travelled to India with a political activist friend, spending a week in an ashram with a group of Americans, many of whom had participated in anti-war demonstrations that Davis had organised. Despite being sceptical when he was introduced to Maharaj Ji for the first time, Davis soon found himself warming to the boy's promise that 'I will show you a peace inside yourself.' Davis duly took 'Knowledge', describing an extraordinary 'light experience' that started in his brow and then filled him from head to toe with light:

> After that, there was only light. It is hard to explain although many poets and mystics have written about such light experiences through the ages. Pascal had a light experience and wrote a short poem about it that he carried in his pocket everywhere he went his entire life. That's how much it meant to him. His poem was discovered after he died.
>
> At the time of my light experience, I didn't really understand what had happened to me except that, like Pascal, it was the most extraordinary moment of my life.[42]

Davis became a fully-fledged believer. Returning to America, he wrote the introduction for a book edited by Charles Cameron, *Who is Guru Maharaj Ji?* (1973)—the 'authentic authorized story' according to the jacket blurb—in which he described Maharaj Ji as 'the greatest event in history,' adding, 'If we knew who he was we would crawl across America on our hands and knees to rest our heads at his feet.' An editorial in the *San Francisco Sunday Examiner* speculated on whether Davis had undergone a lobotomy, and suggested, 'If not, maybe he should try one.'

His conversion particularly bemused and infuriated his fellow radicals. Tom Hayden, Davis' close friend and one of the co-founders of the SDS, would write of feeling that he was 'almost going to be ill' when Davis told him his conversion story.[43] Echoing the suspicions that Allen Ginsberg had harboured about the Maharishi Mahesh, the journalist and radical Paul Krassner wondered whether Davis was working for the CIA, and whether the Maharaj Ji was either 'a conscious or unconscious agent of the Government', which was only too glad to see political activism dissipate in the passive devotion to an Indian guru.

But for Davis, the Maharaj Ji was the perfect manifestation of the millenarian mood of the time. The forces of student protest and revolution

277

had been predicated on the belief that mankind, driven by greed and self-interest, was hurtling towards destruction. But political protest had had no effect; the revolution had failed. The only solution was to seek change within. The political and cultural revolution, Davis enthused, was simply 'a warm-up for the greatest transformation in the history of human civilization. And it's going to be far out.'

According to *The New York Times*, at the time of Millennium '73 the membership of the Divine Light Mission in America numbered 40–50,000 people, in thrall, as the paper put it, to 'an Oriental Humpty Dumpty as round, bland and androgynous as an egg'. Of these, 4,000 were full-time premies, living in fifty-four ashrams across the country. Incorporated as a tax-exempt foundation in the state of Colorado, the organisation registered an estimated annual budget of $3 million. The executive financial director of the organisation, 27-year-old Michael Bergman, who had left his job as public information officer for the New York City Sanitation Department to join the guru, was quoted in the paper claiming that the Mission was 'the fastest growing corporation in America', with membership rising 800 per cent between January and June 1973.[44]

The Houston event was conducted in an atmosphere of millenarian hysteria. Rumours abounded that extra-terrestrials would seize the opportunity to make contact, and that plans had been laid to adapt the Astrodome car park as a landing space for alien craft. According to another rumour, NASA had been tracking the Maharaj Ji's movements because his energy level was stronger than anything ever encountered before. The belief that the Astrodome itself would levitate was widespread. In short, all the post-acid pathologies of the day were present and correct.

Organisers had predicted that more than 100,000 people would attend the event. But at the height of the Millennium celebrations, the stadium appeared to contain no more than 15–20,000 people— 'meagre,' *The New York Times* noted, 'when compared to the Astrodome record of 66,000, achieved by the evangelist Billy Graham'.[45] There was no arrival of extra-terrestrials and the Astrodome did not levitate. It was later estimated that the event had left the Divine Light Mission $682,000 in debt.

By the end of 1973, the Mission claimed to be active in fifty-five countries, with several hundred centres and dozens of ashrams. But the failure of Millennium '73 to meet expectations left the organisation heavily in debt and opened up new fissures in the organisation. With Maharaj Ji spending more time in the West, a family rift also began to appear.

Until now, the wheels of the organisation had been turned by Prem Rawat's mother and his elder brother, Bal Bhagwan Ji. Six months after Millennium '73, events took a yet more astonishing turn. In May 1974, Maharaj Ji married a 24-year-old American premie named Marolyn Johnson, a former TWA air stewardess. The marriage ceremony was conducted at a non-denominational church in Golden, Colorado. Rawat's mother, Mata Ji, was not invited. The relationship had been kept secret from his followers, with the guru's wife following him at a discreet distance during a North American tour, checking into different hotels, and with Maharaj Ji sneaking off after delivering *satsangs* for clandestine rendezvous.

The marriage brought the final break between Rawat and his mother, who now announced that she was stripping Maharaj Ji of his status as Perfect Master because of his 'unspiritual' behaviour, and appointing his brother Bal Bhagwan Ji in his place. After a protracted court case, Mata Ji and Bal Bhagwan Ji won ownership of the name and property of Divine Light Mission in India. The majority of the Mahatmas who had come to the West with Maharaj Ji now returned to India.

With his links to India severed, the Maharaj Ji now took up permanent residence in California, in a walled estate set in 4 acres of land on a hill above Malibu, with commanding views over the Pacific Ocean and the Santa Monica Mountains. And in 1979 he acquired a Boeing 707 jet to facilitate his travels around the world with his growing family—he now had three children—and staff. He took flying lessons and acquired the appropriate licences to pilot the plane himself.

By now, Maharaj Ji had begun to quietly shed the Hindu trappings that had surrounded him on his arrival in the West. In the UK, gatherings were no longer held at the Palace of Peace—in 1978 it was purchased by the London Clock Company and converted into offices and a warehouse. It was demolished in April 2001, and a housing project built on the site. Instead, such appearances as Maharaj Ji made were in conference centres and public halls. There was less talk of divinity, God-realisation and finding heaven on earth; the message had now become one of 'peace' and self-improvement. Nobody in the organisation now talked of him as God, and he strived to distance himself from any suggestion that anyone ever had. Any suggestion of divinity, it seemed, was entirely the fault of delusions on the part of his followers: 'People have always asked me if I was God, and I always say no. But they decided that I was God, because if I were not, I would say that I was. How do you win when someone's concepts are stronger than reality?'[46]

One by one, the ashrams began to close. By 1983 all of them had gone. In the same year, the organisation's name was changed from the Divine Light Mission to Elan Vital, and the guru instructed his followers he should no longer be known as 'Guru Maharaj Ji' but simply as 'Maharaj Ji'. The original Indian Mahatmas had long since been replaced by Western instructors; Elan Vital now offered structured courses in 'the Knowledge', advocating it as a secular experience 'which Christians, atheists and businessmen can enjoy'.

By 2000, Maharaj Ji had stopped calling himself by that name and reverted to his birth name, Prem Rawat. He was now described on his website and in his literature as a 'peace ambassador', a jowly, smartly suited figure in his fifties who looked less like a guru, and more like the managing director of an Indian engineering company. In 2001 he founded the Prem Rawat Foundation (TPRF), a non-profit organisation raising money for food and aid programmes, incorporating the Peace Education Program, a 'non religious and non sectarian' education project for use in schools, prisons and other institutions.

In 2010, Elan Vital was dissolved and replaced by a new organisation, Words of Peace International, Inc.[47] According to the Words of Peace Annual Report for 2017, Rawat attended 79 speaking engagements and interviews in the year. An estimated 547,976 people saw him speak at live events, and he had 88,534 followers on social media. The organisation received donations amounting to €1.3 million, 'mainly used to support the live engagements and other speaking engagements such as radio and TV interviews and special events'.

Rather than 'the Knowledge'—once hailed as the doorway to the divine—Rawat's website now offers a scheme called PEAK (Peace, Education and Knowledge), a ten-step programme offering 'unique perspectives on how to develop a true sense of yourself and realise the untapped inner resources available to you', covering a range of topics from 'Understanding' to 'Self-knowledge' (lower case K).

If the Guru Maharaj Ji was the strangest manifestation of the West's interest in Indian spirituality, perhaps the most enduring was the organisation established in a small storefront temple on the Lower East Side of New York in 1966 by the former owner of a small pharmaceuticals business in Calcutta. The Hare Krishna movement, more properly known as the International Society for Krishna Consciousness (ISKCON), had been founded by the 69-year-old A. C. Bhaktivedanta Swami Prabhupāda, who had renounced his business and family life to become a Vaishnava monk, and arrived in New York in 1965 after a 35-day boat journey from India. Penniless, he began his preaching mission by sitting under a tree in Central Park, chanting the mantra 'Hare Krishna'.

Prabhupāda was frustrated in his attempts to cultivate a following from what he called 'the intelligent class of men' that he believed would be most receptive to his message, but he found an appreciative audience among young hippies. In May 1966 he founded ISKCON, handing out leaflets that said: 'STAY HIGH FOREVER! No more coming down. Practice Krishna consciousness. Expand your consciousness by practicing TRANSCENDENTAL SOUND VIBRATION'. One of his favourite techniques when approached by hippies was to ask if they'd taken LSD, and then tell them to 'imagine a room full of LSD. Krishna consciousness is like that.'[48]

The organisation quickly spread across America to San Francisco and then to London, where shaven-headed disciples became a familiar sight on the streets, chanting the Hare Krishna mantra and pressing books on unsuspecting passers-by. George Harrison was particularly sympathetic to the movement and produced an album of chants by devotees under the name of the Radha Krishna Temple. One single, 'Hare Krishna Mantra', reached number twelve in the British charts in 1971, and led to the odd spectacle of the saffron-robed devotees appearing on the weekly chart show *Top of the Pops*, chanting a devotional Hindu song to the programme's bemused teenage audience.

One person was to prove particularly hostile to the spread of the Hare Krisha mantra and Krishna Consciousness—the Maharishi Mahesh: 'Whosoever advocated concentration, control, the need of detachment, renunciation for enlightenment, whosoever he was, he didn't know what he was talking about.'[49] He likened the Hare Krishna chant to

a monkey, jumping from branch to branch all the time ... Mind is a monkey, we want the mind to be not wandering, mind wants steady. What we do, give it such heavy work, one word keep on repeating, '*duun, duun, duun*', all the time. The tongue becomes tired, the lungs become tired, the mind becomes tired, the whole thing collapses.[50]

For anybody who was still in search of spiritual enlightenment, TM, he declared, was 'the soul of all yogas', which made redundant any other approach, teaching—or teacher.

As if to purge the last vestiges of any religious associations, God was now known as 'the source of creative intelligence', and Supreme knowledge as 'unity consciousness'; while TM was rebranded as the 'Science of Creative Intelligence'—a science that had the power to totally transform society and realise the elusive goal of world peace.[51] At the heart of this transformation lay what was now called 'the Maharishi Effect'—his insistence that if just 1 per cent of the world's population practised TM, crime would decrease and world peace would result. This utopian vision was enshrined in what Maharishi called 'The World Plan', announced in 1972, to develop the full potential of the individual, improve governmental achievements and 'eliminate the age-old problems of crime and all behaviour that brings unhappiness to the family of man'.[52]

Critical to the Plan was the training of more initiators to spread the message of TM. The Maharishi's original 'Three Year Plan', announced on his arrival in America, was to train 25,000 teachers and establish an equivalent number of meditation centres around the world. The new 'World Plan' was to extend TM to reach the entire world population of some 3.6 billion people. To reach that goal it was estimated that the organisation would need to train 3.6 million teachers. As of 1972, the total number of TM instructors was just 1,000.

The year 1973 was hailed as the 'Year of Action for the World Plan', and 1974, with growing optimism, as the 'Year of Achievement for the World Plan'. The 'Year of Fulfilment of the World Plan' was to be 1975. But, despite the Maharishi's optimism—and the multiplying number of plans—world peace remained as frustratingly distant as it had ever been.

This did not stop him declaring 1976 to be the 'Year of Government' and announcing the inauguration of the World Government for the Age of Enlightenment—'a global organization for administering the well-being and progress of society throughout the world'. The Maharishi inaugurated various ministries in the new government—the Ministry of Development of Consciousness, the Ministry of Prosperity and Progress, the Ministry of Health and Immortality—and allocated disciples to fill them. Sadly, the 'World Government' would never come to power.

As well as being the universal panacea for the world's ills, the Maharishi claimed that TM also provided a short-cut to the *siddhis*, or powers, described by Patanjali, the supposed author of the Yoga Sutras, which date back to the second century BCE. Patanjali listed sixty-four minor *siddhis* and eight major ones. These include the ability to be as small as one wants; the ability to be as large as one wants; the ability to become light to any degree, or as heavy as desired; and subjugation of everyone and everything, even to conquering death.[53]

The Maharishi inaugurated special 'siddhi courses' for a select group of long-term meditators, which eventually grew to comprise almost 1,000 people. Graduates, he promised, would be conferred with the status of 'executive governor of consciousness'. Even old, devoted Maharishi hands, such as Charlie Lutes, felt the inflated claims and the Ruritanian titles were a step too far. 'Just when he gets respectable, he comes out with something like this,' Lutes told Nancy Cooke, 'The press will eat him up.'[54]

The most highly touted of these siddhis was what the Maharishi called 'yogic flying'—or levitation. 'We teach our students that by concentration through meditation they can create an impenetrable field of energy between the ground and their bodies', he claimed, possibly forgetting what he'd told Glenn Ford about it being quicker by airplane: 'The greater the field of energy, the higher the meditating man can rise. It is simple QED.'[55]

Here was the promise of miracles that had enticed Westerners looking to the East since before Paul Brunton. But when 'yogic flying' was unveiled to the public, the response was largely one of bemusement: rather than levitating on an 'impenetrable field of energy' the 'yogic flyers' seemed merely to be hopping rather awkwardly, like frogs, on mattresses.

The simple holy man, his few possessions wrapped inside a carpet roll, travelling the world to dispense enlightenment, was now a far-distant memory. In 1974, Krishnamurti, on a visit to Delhi, found himself leaving the plane with the Maharishi, who, clutching a flower, moved to greet the older man. Krishnamurti quickly made his apologies and left. He later told friends that he would like to see the Maharishi's balance sheet.

It was looking healthier by the minute. Estimates of the wealth of the Maharishi's organisation fluctuated wildly, but at one time it was reported to have an annual income of more than £72 million. In 1970, trouble with the tax authorities had obliged the Maharishi to leave India. He established new headquarters firstly in the Italian resort of Fiuggi Fonte and then in Switzerland. He would eventually settle in a former Franciscan monastery in the small town of Vlodrop in the Netherlands.

A complex network of companies marketed such merchandise as Ayurvedic treatments, books and CDs, as well as TM courses—all trademarked in the Maharishi's name. All of this was largely immaterial to the Maharishi himself. As he grew older, his organisation passed into the hands of his senior students and lieutenants; he ceased travelling and seldom appeared in public, preferring to communicate with his followers via video and closed-circuit television. In 2008 he died at his home in Vlodrop at the reported age of ninety.

In many respects the Maharishi was a failed Messiah. TM did not bring world peace; there was no army of *siddhas* with miraculous powers to usher in a new age of enlightenment. But, albeit by dint of his association with the most famous pop group in the world, the Maharishi became the most celebrated Indian guru of the day. Hundreds of thousands of people around the world continue to practise TM, and by demystifying meditation and presenting it in a widely accessible form, he opened the doors to Eastern teachings for millions.

But it is not for himself that he remains most remembered. After the Maharishi moved to Europe in the 1970s, his Academy of Meditation in Rishikesh was closed down, and for years it remained deserted, falling into neglect and disrepair. But in 2015 it was opened to the public. Visitors can now wander around the overgrown compound, and discover the stone beehive meditation room, with number nine marked as 'the Beatles kave'. [In fact the room was built in the 1970s, after the Beatles' departure]. A mural on the wall of one building depicts a number of spiritual figures— Ramana Maharshi, Amma, Anandamayi Ma and the Zen master Maezumi Roshi—but not the Maharishi.

Visitors to Rishikesh nowadays seldom ask for directions to the Maharishi's ashram. They come asking for 'the Beatles' ashram'.

# 13

# RAJNEESH

## THE LAST GURU

By 1984, Bhagwan Shree Rajneesh, the most brilliant and most controversial guru of the age—a man who had compared himself variously to the Buddha and Pythagoras, and whom the novelist Tom Robbins would describe as 'the most dangerous man since Jesus'—was on his way to accumulating the largest private collection of Rolls-Royces in the world.

Nobody, it seems, could be sure of the exact number. Some said eighty-five, others said ninety, others still, ninety-three—sufficient, in any case, among the guru's numerous holdings, to be incorporated into a separate organisation, the Modern Car Trust. In the parking area of Rajneeshpuram, behind the large mobile home where the guru had his private quarters, a team of mechanics kept them polished and in good working order. His extensive collection of diamond watches was incorporated in a separate trust.

To the journalists and television crews that by then numbered some of the ashram's most frequent visitors, various reasons were given for Rajneesh's enthusiasm for the aristocrat of automobiles. The Rolls-Royces, it was said, were gifts from his disciples, a demonstration of their love for him—for how much more love could you give than eighty-five, or ninety, or ninety-three Rolls-Royces? Then again, they were a teaching on the emptiness of materialism—the object of so many people's desires, the very epitome of wealth and status, rendered meaningless by their sheer number and redundancy, for who could possibly drive eighty-five, or ninety, or ninety-three Rolls-Royces, and what possible prestige could be accrued by driving on empty roads with no passers-by to admire them? Then again, it was said, perhaps that was itself the point, and the cars were an act of absurdist theatre designed to attract media attention, in order to spread the message of Rajneesh as the prophet of a revolution in human thinking, the begetter of 'a New Man'.

Rajneesh remained, in public at least, inscrutable on the matter, as he was on all things. By 1984, he had been silent for three years. The brilliant lectures and philosophical expositions, the Zen koans, Buddhist sutras, the parables, aphorisms and the fortune-cookie gags were a thing of the past. To his disciples it was explained that silence was a necessary stage in his work; among his inner circle it was recognised more as a pragmatic decision to keep himself out of further trouble.

Most of his time now was spent in the large mobile home named Lao Tzu House, in honour of the sixth century BCE Chinese philosopher—another figure with whom Rajneesh often compared himself—where he had lived since arriving in America three years earlier. The windows looked out onto juniper scrubland and the rolling hills beyond. Arriving in Oregon, he could hardly believe the vast openness of the landscape, the boundless blue arc of the sky.

The surroundings, while comfortable, were neither luxurious nor stylish. Rajneesh had no perceivable sense of aesthetics. The floor was wood, with no rugs or carpets—one of the many precautions taken to protect him from the sundry allergies that assailed him for much of his life—and the furnishings were utilitarian. In the living room was a comfortable armchair where Rajneesh would sit. Visitors were expected to sit on the floor. It was not so many years since he had been just another university professor in a provincial Indian city, whom nobody took terribly seriously. Now his followers treated him as a king—more than that, a god.

Many believed that as an enlightened being, Rajneesh was impervious to vices and human failings, but no one could mistake his vanity: his robes were of the finest silk; his grey, wispy beard carefully combed; the woollen hats that he habitually wore disguised his hair loss. But the eyes that had once burned brightly and mischievously had grown rheumy. Copious amounts of Valium and hits of nitrous oxide now frequently dulled the once razor-sharp intellect.

Each afternoon, punctually at 2 pm, he would venture forth from his home to be driven along Nirvana Drive to *darshan*—the public viewing of the guru—in one of his innumerable Rolls-Royces. Accompanied by members of the ashram's security force, armed with semi-automatic weapons, and with a helicopter hovering overhead, his devotees applauded, genuflected and danced, chanting his name: 'We're going to sing it from the rooftops, we're going to shout it from the mountain. Bhagwan is the master, of love, life and laughter.'

Certainly, the Rolls-Royces were a useful tool of provocation. In the early days of the ashram, Rajneesh had taken to driving himself in one of his cars the 50 miles through open country down Highway 97 to the town of Madras, accompanied by a jeep carrying armed devotees. There he would be greeted by protesters, led by the Reverend Mardo Jiménez of the local Madras Conservative Baptist Church, who brandished banners proclaiming 'Bhagwan out of Madras' and 'Repent your Sins'. When Rajneesh's followers, who had been bussed from the ashram, mounted counterdemonstrations, things had threatened to get out of hand, but the tensions eventually simmered down.

Rajneesh drove—as with so many things in his life—with a blithe indifference to rules or safety. At length, when a Rolls-Royce he was driving collided with a concrete mixing truck, his closest aides felt obliged to intervene and revoke his driving privileges altogether.

By 1984, the bold experiment of Rajneeshpuram was visibly fraying at the edges. The liberal sexual freedoms that had been so central to Rajneesh's philosophy, and that in his early years as a teacher had led the Indian press to condemn him as 'the sex guru', were now notably curtailed. The arrival of a new global pandemic—Aids—had led to the introduction of stringent precautions governing sexual behaviour within the ashram, which included residents being supplied with condoms and rubber gloves, and being told not to share food, drink or cigarettes, and to carry a small bottle of alcohol to sanitise taps and toilet seats when they used the ashram's rest rooms.

The guru saw Aids as the beginning of the coming apocalypse, but it was a prospect that he appeared to be facing with equanimity. As his dream of building a new utopia crumbled around him, he would sit on his porch in a sulk, thumbing through the brochures from the local car dealership, picking the models he wanted, pondering on colours and specifications. As one devotee would later remember, 'It kept him occupied.'[1]

\* \* \*

Rajneesh was born Chandra Mohan Jain, the eldest of eleven children of a Jain cloth merchant in Kuchwada, Central India, in December 1931. As a baby he was said to be so beautiful that his besotted grandfather, Nana, named him 'Raja' (which would later become Rajneesh), believing he had been a monarch in a previous life.

For the first several years of his life he lived with his maternal grandparents, who thoroughly indulged him. His grandfather Nana in particular, Rajneesh would later recall,

> not only loved me but loved everything I did. And I did everything that you could call a nuisance. I was a continuous nuisance. The whole day he had to listen to complaints about me, and he always rejoiced in them ... He never punished me ... He simply allowed, absolutely allowed me to be myself.[2]

When Rajneesh was seven, Nana died. Rajneesh would date it as the defining moment of his life: 'Aloneness became my nature. His death freed me forever from all relationships. His death became for me the death of all attachments. Thereafter I could not establish a bond of relationship with anyone. Whenever my relationship with anyone began to become intimate, that death stared at me.' 'I became,' he said, 'a universe unto myself.'[3]

He moved to his parents' home in Gadarwara, but was unhappy in their company, and when his widowed grandmother settled nearby, Rajneesh moved back in with her. She continued to indulge him. At school he was an inattentive and troublesome pupil, who would frequently play truant, deploying his considerable powers of persuasion on teachers who, glad to be rid a troublemaker, would happily falsify his attendance records. Some years later, as a graduate student at the University of Saugar (now Sagar), he would manage to avoid two years of compulsory training at the institution by persuading a vice-chancellor to secretly doctor his records.[4]

What Rajneesh would later describe as 'the explosion' which transformed his life, occurred when he was twenty-one and studying philosophy at a college in Jabalpur. For a year he was plunged into a crisis of doubt, insecurity and what he would describe as 'utter darkness'. Suffering from chronic headaches, sleeplessness, sweating fits and a sense of dissociation from his own body, he would run for miles each day and meditate for hours at a time.

On 21 March 1953, meditating under a moulshree tree in a small public park, Bhanvartal Garden, Rajneesh claimed to have experienced a sense of complete ego-dissolution, or enlightenment. The mythopoeic setting for this experience might have been deliberately designed to evoke the story of the Buddha's enlightenment under the Bodhi tree. Rajneesh would later describe it as a moment of death and rebirth:

But the one that was reborn has nothing to do with that which died …
The one who died, died totally; nothing of him has remained.

For the first time I was not alone, for the first time I was no more an individual, for the first time the drop has come and fallen into the ocean. Now the whole ocean was mine. I was the ocean. There was no limitation. A tremendous power arose as if I could do anything whatsoever.[5]

This pattern of breakdown followed by breakthrough is a familiar one in the annals of gurus. One is reminded of Meher Baba's 'spiritual crisis' as a young man; of Ramana Maharshi's awakening; and Sathya Sai Baba's declaration of his own avatarhood as a child after being bitten by a scorpion.

Writing of Rajneesh, the clinical psychologist Anthony Storr puts a quite different interpretation on this critical experience, describing it more simply as a psychotic episode: 'It appears probable that Rajneesh suffered from a fairly severe depressive illness between the ages of nineteen and twenty-one which came to an end with a hypomanic state in the form of an ecstatic experience.'[6] Conventional Western psychology does not allow much accommodation for religious or mystical experience.

After graduating with a MA in philosophy in 1957, Rajneesh taught at Raipur Sanskrit College and then as an assistant professor of philosophy at the University of Jabalpur. In 1966 he gave up his university post and taking the title 'Acharya' (teacher), began conducting his own teaching groups and holding regular meditation camps in cities around India.

He soon began to gain a reputation as a provocative and original speaker on spiritual and philosophical themes—a controversialist, tilting at authority and the sacred cows of organised religion, attacking the moral conservatism and sexual puritanism that had characterised the teachings of the early Hindu reformers such as Ramakrishna and Vivekananda, and arguing that the primal force of sex was divine and 'the first step to superconsciousness'.

In 1969, when the country was celebrating the centenary of Gandhi's birth, Rajneesh took the opportunity to attack the father of India, saying that his sexual abstinence was a form of perversion and his fasting a form of masochism. His teachings scandalised many, but excited the Indian press, who quickly dubbed Rajneesh 'the sex guru', and he began to attract a following among educated, progressively minded professionals.

In 1970 he settled in Bombay. By now he had acquired a secretary, Laxmi Thakarsi Kuruwa (who would later take the name Ma Yoga Laxmi), who was secretary of the Bombay branch of the All-India Women's Congress and the daughter of one of his early followers, a wealthy Jain businessman. Laxmi had a gift for organisation and for fund-raising, which would be invaluable in helping to establish Rajneesh in the early years. She was the first of a number of powerful women that he would gather around him.

Rajneesh preached what he called 'a religionless religiousness'—a religious attitude to life, but without subscribing to any particular creed or dogma. His early teachings were a composite of Jain and Buddhist philosophy, with a heavy smattering of Tantra. But he would also cite passages from the Gospels and Lao Tzu, with a heavy side-serving of provocation. God, he taught, was 'the greatest lie invented by man'—a psychological projection of the lost child, searching for their father or mother, with no basis in reality:

> Man is the seed, the source, God is the flowering. When you flower, God comes into existence. It comes into existence and disappears. When Buddha was here, God existed. When Jesus was here, God existed. When Jesus disappears, God disappears, just as a flower disappears ... You carry him as a seed; it is up to you to allow him to grow and become a great tree.[7]

There were distinct overtones in his teachings of Krishnamurti's dictum that 'the truth is a pathless land'—but with none of Krishnamurti's austere intellectualism. Rajneesh had clearly read Gurdjieff and Wilhelm Reich. But his appeal lay less in any coherent philosophy than in his immense personal charisma, and in his ability to animate the desires and yearnings of his followers and to offer them a glimpse of release from the stifling disenchantments of Western convention and materialism. 'I am not going to give you any answers,' he told them, 'You have too many already. I am going to teach you to unlearn the answers you have already learnt.'[8]

In 1971 he dropped the title 'Acharya' and assumed a new one, 'Bhagwan' (meaning 'blessed one'), calling himself Bhagwan Shree Rajneesh. No longer simply a controversial philosophy teacher, he was now a guru.

He initiated his first disciples, including a handful of Westerners. Among these were Catherine Venizelos, the daughter of a Greek shipping magnate, who took the name MaYoga Mukta, and the young Englishwoman Christena Woolf, who had come to India on the hippie trail in 1967 when she was twenty-one, and found her way to Rajneesh. Woolf would take the name Vivek, and in time become Rajneesh's constant companion, 'caretaker' and lover.

Initiating his disciples, Rajneesh introduced the concept of neo-Sannyas, to distinguish it from traditional *sannyas*. *Saṃnyāsa* in Sanskrit means 'renunciation' or 'abandonment'. Historically, the term describes a person who has given up worldly or materialistic pursuits to devote their lives to spiritual contemplation. The traditional saffron robe of the sannyasin symbolises the purging fires of renunciation. Rajneesh instructed his 'neo-sannyasins' to dress in red or orange, 'the colours of the sunrise' (no purging fires here); to take sannyasin names and to wear *malas* bearing his image. The uniform dress, the malas, the trappings of disciple-hood, were all marks of initiation into what Rajneesh called his 'Buddhafield', a sign that devotees were serious in their commitment. They also had the effect, of course, of separating the initiates from their past, driving a wedge between the world they had embraced and the world they had left behind that would become more pronounced as time passed. Intoxicated by Rajneesh's promise that 'I teach rejoicing', the 'neo-sannyasin' was required to give up nothing except their discernment.

'The old concept of Sannyas,' he said, 'was to give you a rigid discipline, to give you a character, to give you a certain form, a pattern, a lifestyle. My Sannyas is not like that at all—it is a radical change.'[9] Rajneesh did not believe in 'character'—an artificial, inauthentic social construct—and he abhorred the idea of 'cultivating' character: 'To me the man of character is a dead man.'[10] Real morality, he argued, is not to be cultivated but comes as a result of being aware, or realised.

He happily called himself 'the rich man's guru'. He had no use for pieties about the virtuous poor. True religion, he argued, is a luxury that can come only after one's survival needs are met. Rich people are seekers; the poor are 'merely survivors', too preoccupied with the cares of the world to truly understand religion. Only when a person has everything and comes to the realisation that it actually amounts to nothing, can the search for illumination begin: 'Yes, sometimes a poor man can also be religious, but for that, very great intelligence is needed. A rich man, if he is not religious, is stupid ... I am a rich man's guru. Absolutely it is so.'[11]

In a sense, Rajneesh was the first authentic 'me generation' guru, preaching a philosophy perfectly attuned to the sensibilities of a generation that took material comforts for granted, that advocated the supremacy of personal 'experience' over authority, tradition and conventional morality. 'The more dangerously you live,' he told his followers, 'the more risks you take, the more you grow, the more you become integrated, crystallised ...

Live life totally, love life totally, get involved with your life! Don't hold back.'

The pursuit of pleasure and of enlightenment were not, after all, mutually incompatible. Disciples were urged to follow their desires without guilt. Nothing was to be suppressed. 'Be selfish,' he urged his followers, 'Only then can you be altruistic. Just look for the beautiful; forget the ugly.' Not surprisingly, this philosophy would prove enormously attractive to the children of the 'free love' generation.[12]

The centrepiece of Rajneesh's methods was what he called 'dynamic meditation', a form of intense catharsis designed, as Rajneesh put it, to 'release your insanity'. There were five stages of dynamic meditation. The first ten minutes of a session, known as 'the Chaotic', consisted of deep, rapid, vigorous breathing—according to Rajneesh, 'to create a chaos within your repressed system. If you can destroy the settled patterns of breathing then all the patterns in all your bodies (e.g. physical, psychic, spiritual) will be loosened.' At the sound of a gong, participants were then encouraged to let themselves go in a frenzy of shouting, screaming, rage and laughter. This was followed by a third, ten-minute stage of jumping up and down vigorously, with arms raised, while repeatedly shouting 'Hoo, hoo!' 'Hoo', Rajneesh claimed, was a sound 'invented by the Sufis' which supposedly meant 'Who am I?' and which went 'directly to the sex centre', to raise sexual energy. This stage ended in a sudden 'stop', with participants freezing in a position of 'perfect stillness' for fifteen minutes before the session ended in a further fifteen minutes of wild dancing and singing.

A film from 1972 that was taken at one of his meditation camps shows disciples engaging in dynamic meditation—jumping, shouting and weeping in a frenzy of hyper-activity, before finally collapsing in a state of spent exhaustion while Rajneesh watches impassively from his chair. He looks every inch the stereotypical Indian swami, with his long, flowing black beard and tufts of black hair fringing a bald pate, dressed in a simple cotton lungi and shawl, accepting the obeisance of his disciples with a clasped hand *namaste*. Rajneesh did not join in with the 'dynamic meditation' himself. He suffered from asthma and a raft of allergies; for all his intellectual sharpness and acuity he moved sluggishly.

Peter Brent, one of the first Western writers to encounter Rajneesh, described meeting him in the home of a wealthy disciple (Rajneesh was evidently already displaying his facility to magnetise people with money), taking note of his 'plump and hairy stomach', his black oiled ringlets and his 'rolling, slightly goatish light brown eye'.[13]

He already had all the trappings of a guru: a following, a holy name, a sense of mission, a promise of redemption. A banner at the gate of the meditation camps he held at Mount Abu, a hill station in Rajasthan popular with tourists, urged visitors to 'Surrender to me and I will transform you. That is my promise—Rajneesh.'[14] Yet the very concept of the guru, he told Brent, was 'basically irreligious and unspiritual ... There should be disciples, there must be disciples—but no gurus.' A guru 'means a person who says "I have known" and to me this very assertion is absurd'.[15] His object, he said, was not to create believers, 'but to create individuals, lovers, meditators, who can stand on their own, and each one become a light':

> The seeker may go from method to method, teacher to teacher, but it is only when the seeker finds that this pursuit has ended in total failure that the 'I' is dissolved. Only when the Buddha had exhausted every avenue, every method—abandoned even the spiritual dream—did realisation come to him. 'I have not brought it, it has come to me.'[16]

His followers, he promised, would be the embodiment of a 'New Man'—one who combined the spirituality of the Buddha with the lust for life embodied in the character of Zorba the Greek, the hero of Nikos Kazantzakis' novel of the same name (a favourite book of Rajneesh's): 'He should be as accurate and objective as a scientist ... as sensitive, as full of heart, as a poet ... [and as] rooted deep down in his being as the mystic.'[17] Disciples compared him to Buddha, Pythagoras and Jesus—comparisons that he did little in his discourses to discourage.

In 1974 Rajneesh left Bombay for Poona (now Pune). The pollution in Bombay was bad for his asthma, and it was becoming harder for him to move around the city without being bothered. Furthermore, Rajneesh needed an ashram to match his grandiose dreams of building the 'New Man', and property was expensive in Bombay. Poona, 100 miles to the south, was a smaller city without the chaos and suffocating pollution of Bombay, but with good transport links for Rajneesh's growing body of followers from the West.

With money provided in part by Catherine Venizelos, the newly established Rajneesh Foundation purchased a villa in 6 acres of land in the residential suburb of Koregaon Park, and established the first Rajneesh ashram. At first, Rajneesh was available to all who had made the pilgrimage to see him. He would receive visitors in his garden, seated on a lounge chair, while they sat on the grass in front of him. He would often greet newcomers with the words, 'I have been waiting for you' or 'Here you are at last.' A familiar trope of the guru, it intimated both that he had some gift of prescience, and that he and they had been connected since birth, and possibly over many lifetimes. It flattered them to believe they were special, the elect.

As the number of visitors increased, an auditorium was erected to the side of his house, where Rajneesh gave discourses in the morning and *darshan* in the evening. The private meetings became fewer, and then, unless you were important or a donor, stopped altogether.

\* \* \*

What would Edwin Arnold—or Vivekananda, or Annie Besant, or Ramana Maharshi—have made of Rajneesh? Could they have possibly foreseen that the West's earnest pursuit of spiritual enlightenment would have led to a guru who ridiculed holy cows and espoused sexual freedom? But then Rajneesh was unlike any other guru before, or indeed since.

A philosopher before he was a holy man, he had read extensively in the literature of twentieth-century psychology and psychiatry. He was particularly disdainful of the fathers of modern psychoanalysis. Sigmund Freud, Carl Jung, Alfred Adler and others (Rajneesh didn't make much distinction between them) were all 'just children playing on the sand of time. They have gathered beautiful pebbles, beautiful coloured stones, but when you look at the ultimate, they are just children playing with the pebbles and stones. These stones are not real diamonds. And whatsoever they have gained is very, very primitive.'[18] 'Mind,' Rajneesh taught, 'is the disease':

> This is the basic truth the East has discovered. The West says that mind can become ill, can be healthy. Western psychology depends on this. But the East says that mind as such is the disease, it cannot be healthy. No psychiatry can help. At the most, you can make it normally ill.[19]

True self-realisation, he argued, came not from intellectual enquiry or analysis but from 'dropping' the mind and the whole notion of self-enquiry entirely.

Rajneesh's ideas about the neurosis of modern life, sexual repression, the suffocating authoritarianism of social convention and the dangers of being separated from 'real' feelings—in a phrase, the corrosive effects of the 'inauthentic' life—all struck a distinct chord with the nostrums of a movement that was blossoming 15,000 miles away, on the other side of the world.

The Human Potential Movement had first come to prominence in California in the early 1960s, finding its spiritual home at the Esalen Institute at Big Sur. The Institute was founded in 1962 by Michael Murphy (a devotee of Sri Aurobindo) and Richard Price—a former psychiatric patient who had suffered the most damaging treatments that conventional Western psychiatric treatment had to offer. Esalen was a mixture of residential community, teaching institute and mystical hothouse, offering a portmanteau of experimentation and instruction on matters ranging from radical psychology to Eastern philosophy and mind-expanding drugs.

At the core of the Human Potential Movement was a fundamental break with the two cardinal orthodoxies that had successively dominated psychology for a hundred years—Freudianism and behaviourism. Freud saw the human animal as, at its core, a raging, neurotic, irrational inferno of unconscious emotions that needed to be repressed and controlled if the person was to function in society. But in the 1950s and 1960s, a new generation of psychologists and psychoanalysts began to challenge this view, arguing that it was not the self that was the problem; it was society that was to blame for people's neuroses and unhappiness. The self did not need to be repressed or 'adjusted' to social norms, but set free, like a butterfly, from the confining net of conditioning and societal expectation.

Underlying this new school of 'humanistic psychology' was the belief that these new approaches were not simply a way of curing the troubled mind, but offered a blueprint for rebirth into a better, saner life. The buzzword was 'liberation', the goal to reconnect the individual to their 'essential' self. As its prospectus put it, Esalen was concerned 'with those who are too well adjusted, too tight and too controlled. It attempts to release them for growth and greater integration.'

Esalen's inspiring spirit was the philosopher Frederic Spiegelberg, a refugee from Nazi Germany who taught comparative religion at Stanford University in California in the 1950s. Born in 1897 in Hamburg, as a young theology student, Spiegelberg had experienced a moment of spontaneous realisation while walking in the countryside and musing on the poet Rilke, when he was suddenly filled with a consciousness of 'something deep, something holy' that he would describe as his 'Higher self'. Coming upon a church, he was seized with the certainty that no single building, ideology or belief system could contain the feeling of holiness he was experiencing.

295

Spiegelberg's experience was to be the catalyst for his studies of mystical experience in myriad religious traditions.

He went on to study with Carl Jung, and acquired an extensive knowledge of Sanskrit and Tibetan iconography. In 1937, Speigelberg was forced to give up his post as lecturer in religious history at the University of Dresden and flee from Germany. In London, he met the youthful Alan Watts, who would go on to become one of the foremost popularisers of Zen Buddhism in the West. 'He wore a hat with an exceedingly wide brim,' Watts later wrote of Speigelberg, 'spoke English with a delicate German accent which always suggests a sense of authority and high culture, and was propagating the theory that the highest form of religion was to transcend religion. He called it "the religion of non-religion"' (a phrase echoed in Rajneesh's 'religionless religiousness').[20]

Born in 1915, Watts had developed an interest in Buddhism while a student at the King's School in Canterbury (Somerset Maugham's alma mater), striking up a correspondence with Christmas Humphreys, who was head of what was then the London Buddhist Lodge and would later become the Buddhist Society. 'We assumed from the tone and content of his letters that he was at least a senior master,' Humphreys would remember. 'In due course he turned up at a meeting, aged seventeen, and talked to us on Zen with the voice of authority.'[21]

Two years later, Watts published his first book, *The Spirit of Zen* (1936). By the age of twenty, he was secretary of the London Buddhist Lodge, publishing Spiegelberg's first essay on the subject of 'The Religion of No Religion' in the Buddhist Lodge journal, *Buddhism in England*, in 1938.

In late 1937, Spiegelberg left Britain for America (Watts would follow a year later), taking up a position as professor of comparative religion at Stanford University in Palo Alto. He quickly earned a reputation as an inspiring and highly popular teacher; a favourite device was to use popular comic strips and newspaper advertisements to illustrate metaphysical points. In 1949 he was awarded a Rockefeller Grant, and spent six months travelling in Tibet and India, where he visited the ashrams of both Ramana Maharshi and Sri Aurobindo, taking *darshan* on one of the rare occasions when Aurobindo emerged from seclusion in his room to be seen by his disciples.

Spiegelberg calculated that there were 2,200 people waiting in line to see the guru that afternoon. Aurobindo would be sitting in *darshan* for just four hours. That would leave each devotee just six and a half seconds standing (or kneeling) in front of the guru. Spiegelberg tried in vain to negotiate with an attendant for more time. The attendant pointed out that if he were paying for an X-ray exam, five seconds would be more than sufficient and any longer would burn him severely. Nonplussed by the ingenuity of this explanation, Spiegelberg took his place in front of the guru—and was duly 'X-rayed', as he would put it, down to the very ground of his being.[22] He would later dedicate his 1951 book, *Spiritual Practices of India*, 'To Sri Aurobindo, for having X-rayed the author for five seconds lasting an eternity and for thereby calling forth the *atman* within as the only reality which he notices in any visitor.'

Spiegelberg's time in India deeply informed his course at Stanford, which moved from the Brahminical scriptures, through the Vedas and Upanishads, to Buddhism, St Paul and Plotinus, to Ramakrishna as the exemplar of the unity of world religions and Sri Aurobindo as the philosopher of the future. His teachings galvanised one student in particular—a 20-year-old named Michael Murphy. Born in 1930, the son of a lawyer, Murphy had grown up in Salinas, northern California, where his grandfather was the town's much-loved doctor—whose accomplishments included bringing the infant John Steinbeck squawking into the world and supposedly saving his life when he had pneumonia. Steinbeck acknowledged him by naming the physician in his novel *East of Eden* 'Dr Murphy'.

Murphy's family were literate and cultured—H. L. Mencken, Jonathan Swift, George Bernard Shaw and Clarence Darrow were his father's heroes—and not particularly religious; but the young Murphy was an altar boy, and for a period in his adolescence thought that he might become an Episcopalian priest. The family expectation was that he should become a doctor like his grandfather, and he enrolled at Stanford as a pre-med student. It was curiosity that led him to one of Spiegelberg's comparative religion classes. As Murphy remembers:

> To be highly technical, I was blown away. He came out on the stage—German, tall, handsome. And he stood there in utter silence in front of these 650 Stanford students, who were habitually and chronically restless, until it fell quiet. And then, in this very powerful voice—'Atman is Brahman' ... That single sentence lit me up, and by the end of that lecture I knew I was going to stay on that course and that I would never be the same.[23]

Spiegelberg's accounts of his meetings with Ramana Maharshi and Sri Aurobindo would touch a particular chord in Murphy. As a high school student he had read everything by Somerset Maugham, and the book and film of *The Razor's Edge* had left a deep impression on him. It was a thrilling experience to listen to someone who had actually met the figure that inspired the guru of Maugham's book. 'Spiegelberg said that Ramana Maharshi just radiated the most unbelievable radiance', Murphy recalls,

> He said he would sit there and kind of glow in the dark. Spiegelberg described vividly asking him, but what about evolution? What about the world? And Ramana Maharshi waved his hand in front of his face, as if a windscreen wiper was clearing the water off a car, and said 'You, you Westerners, are in love with the shadows. Universe is all shadows ...' Maya, you know ...
>
> Then Ramana Maharshi would always say, 'Who is doing the asking?' He would always go back to that. *Atman.*
>
> I would say Ramana Maharshi was deeply realised. I see him as a gold standard for integrity. But his world view was incomplete and when he says the world is all shadows I think he's wrong.

More enthralling still to Murphy was Sri Aurobindo. At Spiegelberg's suggestion, he read Aurobindo's book *The Life Divine* (1939), in which the philosopher argued that the next step in evolution would be the development of a higher state of consciousness that Aurobindo called the 'Supermind'. Aurobindo's teaching about the evolution of consciousness and what Murphy described as 'its power to transform flesh', struck a deep chord: 'For me, it's a fact. And, as it were, I took vows that this is what I was going to spend the rest of my life furthering.'

Leaving university, Murphy served his obligatory spell in the army, where he passed most of his tour of duty in Puerto Rico, reading, meditating and playing baseball and—his other great life passion—golf. On his discharge in 1955, he returned to Stanford and enrolled in a doctoral programme in the philosophy department. But he quickly grew unhappy with the course, and in 1956 he dropped out and, following in Spiegelberg's footsteps, set off for India—stopping off in Scotland on the way to play a round of golf at the famous Old Course at St Andrews.

Murphy made his way to Pondicherry and to what Sri Aurobindo had called his 'laboratory of evolution'. Aurobindo had died six years earlier, and the ashram was now under the sole guidance and control of the Mother. For Murphy, the ashram provided the perfect environment in which to 'anchor my practice', as he put it. Granted the privilege of meditating in Aurobindo's room, he lost consciousness of the outside world almost immediately, immersed in the lingering radiance of Aurobindo's presence.

Murphy also threw himself into the ashram's sporting and physical fitness regime, coaching swimming and basketball and setting up a softball team—'Somebody had to do it. And it was a really good gig.' But he grew to dislike the 'cult-like' features of the ashram, and the personality worship of Aurobindo and the Mother: 'The Mother was a phenomenal human being. I would say she did not like some of this cult-like behaviour that grew up around the ashram—but it's not just a matter of not encouraging it; you have to actively work against it. And that she did not do.'[24]

After sixteen months in Pondicherry, Murphy returned to California. He took a part-time job as a bellhop in a hotel in Palo Alto, and spent every free hour meditating and working on a metaphysical adventure novel about a golfer-guru named Shivas Irons, set on a course based on the Old Course at St Andrews. Published in 1971, *Golf in the Kingdom* would go on to sell over a million copies and be translated into some twenty languages.

In 1960, Murphy moved to San Francisco and took a room in a meditation centre called the Cultural Integration Fellowship, that had been set up by a follower of Sri Aurobindo named Haridas Chaudhuri. It was there he met Richard Price.

The son of Jewish immigrants from Lithuania, Price had been a student at Stanford at the same time as Murphy, although the two had never met. After graduating in 1952 with a BA in psychology, Price studied briefly at Harvard and spent time in the military before returning to Stanford, where he enrolled in a course taught by Spiegelberg on the Bhagavad Gita. Just as it had with Murphy, Spiegelberg's passion lit a spark in Price. For the first time, he would later recall, he began to see religion as something more than 'a system of deceit and the enforcement of social rules'.

At Spiegelberg's suggestion, he began to take classes at the American Academy of Asian Studies, which Spiegelberg had founded, and where Alan Watts was now Dean and principal teacher. At the same time he immersed himself in the bohemian milieu of the North Beach, mixing with the Beat poets and writers including Lawrence Ferlinghetti, Allen Ginsberg and Gary Snyder.

Price contemplated becoming a Buddhist monk, then married, and in short order suffered a mental breakdown, which resulted in lengthy hospitalisation, during which he was diagnosed as paranoid schizophrenic and subjected to an intensive regime of insulin-shock and electro-shock treatments. He left hospital a broken man, his marriage over (his

299

parents had arranged for an annulment while he was committed), but with a bruising personal understanding of how psychiatric illness was conventionally perceived and treated. As he would later put it:

> Rather than seeing someone through a particular type of experience, it was an effort to suppress and negate in every possible way what I was going through ... The disease, if any, was the state previous to the 'psychosis'. The so-called 'psychosis' was an attempt toward spontaneous healing, and it was a movement toward health, not a movement toward disease.[25]

Price moved back in with his parents and took a job working as a clerk in an uncle's sign-making business. For three years he dutifully went through the motions of leading a conventional life, until he learnt that a group of his old friends in San Francisco had founded a cooperative called East-West House. Price quit his job and flew west. It was not long afterwards, on the advice of a friend, that he went looking for Michael Murphy.

Murphy was now working for two days a week as a proof-reader on a trade journal called *Pacific Shipper*. But he was thinking of moving down to Big Sur, 120 miles south of San Francisco down Highway 1, where his grandparents owned a property perched on land that was high on a cliff above the Pacific coast, adjacent to a natural hot spring known as Slates Springs. Murphy hoped it would be the perfect place to meditate, study and write. He invited Price to join him.

Big Sur was infused with a distinctly rackety flavour. Henry Miller, fresh from his interlude in Paris and his tempestuous affair with Anaïs Nin, had settled there in 1946 and was a frequent visitor to the Springs. In the wake of Miller came a small community of artists and free spirits inhabiting cabins in the surrounding woods. At weekends, the Springs were also a popular, if surreptitious, attraction for gay men who had made their way there from San Francisco.

The Murphy property, which comprised a large house and a number of small cabins, was being run in a haphazard fashion as a guest house, managed by a Mrs Webb, a member of a fundamentalist Christian church called the First Church of God of Prophecy. On Saturday nights, members would gather for their services, lustily singing hymns and speaking in tongues.

Murphy and Price arrived at Big Sur one April night in 1961. The guest house was deserted. Price took one of the guest rooms, and Murphy took the master bedroom. In the middle of the night he awoke to find a figure standing at the foot of his bed holding a flashlight and a billy club, demanding to know who the hell he was and what the hell he was doing in the house. The man was the caretaker, employed by Murphy's grandmother; nobody had told him that Murphy and Price were coming. The caretaker was a 23-year-old who had taken the job to earn money while he was writing his first novel. One day, he would tell people, to indulgent laughter, he would be as famous as Henry Miller. His name was Hunter Thompson.

Murphy had the idea of taking over the running of the motel, at the same time conducting seminars on meditation and the new thinking in spirituality and psychology that was fermenting around people such as Spiegelberg and Alan Watts, who—catching the mood of the times— was arguing that in Buddhism, Taoism, Vedanta and Yoga one did not find religion and philosophy as understood in the West, but 'something more resembling psychotherapy'.

Both men would lend their encouragement to the project, as did Aldous Huxley, whose book *The Doors of Perception* and lectures on what he called 'human potentialities' had made him the paterfamilias of what was becoming a gathering movement. Less enthused by Murphy's grand scheme was his grandmother, Bunny, who was initially reluctant to hand over the running of the property, concerned that her grandson would 'give it away to the Hindoos'. But by the autumn of 1962, Murphy and Price had established a programme of events, and a new name for the enterprise—Esalen—after one of the Native American tribes that had inhabited the coastline for thousands of years. For Murphy, the core of Esalen's inspiration remained the teachings of Aurobindo; for Price it was Zen Buddhism and the new thinking in psychology. Esalen would be a place where East would meet West. 'Arnold Toynbee lectured in Esalen in 1962,' Murphy remembers,

> and he told us that one of the great events of the twentieth century would
> be the coming of Buddhism to the West; what he really meant was Eastern
> thought—this whole migration of thought and culture was underway.
> And Esalen in those days was the central location. People in those days
> would say, we're all Vietcong but you're Hanoi.[26]

But Murphy and Price were adamant on one point; that no one teacher or method would ever, as Murphy, put it, 'capture the flag'; Esalen would never be allowed to take on the trappings of a cult.

The first Esalen brochure featured on its cover an infinitesimal calculus from Bertrand Russell and the iconic lotus from Buddhist and Hindu symbolism. Inside was a statement of the organisation's mission:

> A new conception of human nature is emerging in the field of psychology, a conception that is gradually superseding the views of classical psychoanalysis and strict behaviorism, a conception oriented toward health, growth and the exploration of our psychic potentialities. Creativity research, work with the 'mind-opening' drugs and the discoveries of parapsychology (psychical research) complement this development, pointing as they do toward a profounder human possibility.

Murphy had quietly dreamed that Esalen might one day evolve into a small 'college of consciousness', similar to the Aurobindo ashram, but without the paralysing fixation on a single teacher. But in a platform that brought together religion, science, psychology and psychedelic exploration—its synthesis of East and West—Esalen quickly established itself at the forefront of what Murphy would describe as a 'consciousness revolution', and which would come to be known as the Human Potential Movement.

Esalen offered seminars and courses under the tutelage of a wide range of speakers and residential psychologists. Foremost among these were Abraham Maslow, who devised the theory of 'self-actualisation' and the 'peak experience', and a cantankerous German psychologist named Fritz Perls, the father of Gestalt therapy. An enthusiastic apostle of sexual freedom—he happily characterised himself as a 'dirty old man'—who was described variously as looking like Father Christmas, Martin Buber and 'the oldest carny man in the world', Perls quickly established himself as the Institute's eminence grise. Chain-smoking furiously and speaking in a guttural *mittel*-European accent, Perls presided over group sessions in which participants were invited to take their turn in the 'hot seat' while Perls ruthlessly and systematically took them apart, dismantling their defence mechanisms and zeroing in on their every tic, verbal interaction and mannerism.

Perls' sessions were to prove remarkably transformative. The author Jeffrey Kripal writes of how Perls had a wall in his room decorated with eyeglasses from group participants who had supposedly recovered normal eyesight following Gestalt sessions.[27]

Group therapy at Esalen took an even more volatile turn in 1967, with the arrival of a psychologist named Will Schutz. A balding, muscular man with an overbearing manner, Schutz practised what he called 'open encounter' sessions, where participants were encouraged to confess their own neuroses and to criticise others in the group.

His approach often employed a pedantically literal interpretation of a person's particular hang-up or problem. A man complaining of being 'held down' by life, for example, might find the entire group piling on top of him until he had to fight his way out. Another exercise, Pandora's Box, involved women exposing their vaginas, which the group would scrutinise intently —as Kripal describes it, 'processing the feelings, fears and desires together, acting out of the myth, as it were, in order to transcend its fundamental misogyny'.[28] To consolidate the upbeat theme of 'joy', Schutz would finish his sessions by playing a recording of the schmaltz anthem, 'To Dream the Impossible Dream'.

'Encounter sessions, particularly of the Schutz variety, were often wild events', wrote the novelist Tom Wolfe in his essay 'The "Me" Decade and the Third Great Awakening' for New York Magazine in August 1976:

Such aggression! such sobs! tears! moans, hysteria, vile recriminations, shocking revelations, such explosions of hostility between husbands and wives, such mud balls of profanity from previously mousy mommies and workadaddies, such red-mad attacks! Only physical assault was prohibited.

... Outsiders, hearing of these sessions, wondered what on earth their appeal was. Yet the appeal was simple enough. It is summed up in the notion: 'Let's talk about Me.' No matter whether you managed to renovate your personality through encounter sessions or not, you had finally focused your attention and your energies on the most fascinating subject on earth: Me.[29]

Graffiti painted on the entry sign of Esalen put it more bluntly: 'Jive shit for rich white folk'. But by the late 1960s, the encounter group and the new creed of 'personal growth', with its vocabulary of discovering 'the authentic self' and 'living in the now', had spread far beyond the confines of Big Sur into the bourgeois purlieus of middle America, the subject of a popular Hollywood movie, Bob & Carol & Ted & Alice (1969), that was synonymous with hot-tubs, sexual swinging, Nehru collars and marijuana as a dinner-party aperitif.

\* \* \*

In a curious case of circularity, just as the philosophy of the Indian guru Aurobindo had planted the seeds of Esalen, so the nostrums of the new humanistic psychology cultivated in California now began to take root in the ashram of another India guru.

Rajneesh's ideas about the need to liberate the individual from the stultifying effects of social conditioning, his 'dynamic meditation' to release the negative energies blocked in the body and 'bring your insanity out'; his combination of the contemplative aspects of the Buddha with the joyful and uninhibited life-affirming force of Zorba the Greek; his claim that he was 'less a guru and more like a psychiatrist (*plus* something)'— all of this appeared to chime perfectly with the work being done at Esalen.[30] At Rajneeshpuram, the vocabulary of humanistic psychology and the spiritual path would become interchangeable: 'healing' became synonymous with 'enlightenment'.

One of the first of the Human Potential psychotherapists to make his way to Rajneesh was an Englishman named Paul Lowe. Born in Birmingham in 1933, Lowe had spent much of the 1960s hitch-hiking around the world, working in a variety of jobs, including in an advertising agency in Hong Kong, before eventually arriving at Esalen, where he lived for a year and participated in the encounter groups runs by Will Schutz. Lowe had no formal training as a psychologist, but in 1970 he returned to Britain and established Quaesitor, which claimed to be the first 'growth centre' in Europe.

Hearing of Rajneesh, in 1972 Lowe made his way to Bombay, where he quickly became a disciple. He was given the sannyasin name Swami Teertha. He returned to London and turned Quaesitor into a Rajneesh meditation centre, but after a year moved back to India permanently. When Rajneesh established his ashram at Poona, Teertha assumed the role of chief therapist, or as some sannyasins saw it, 'head monk'. Teertha was one of the few people whom Rajneesh authorised to 'give sannyas'.

He was followed by other therapists from the Human Potential Movement, who were invited to set up their own groups within the ashram. Bernie Gunther, who had been a leading figure at Esalen, arrived at Poona, taking the name Swami Amrit Prem. Leonard Zunin, a Californian psychologist who sat on the American Board of Psychiatry and Neurology, became Swami Prem Siddha; Michael Barnett, the author of a book called *People, Not Psychiatry* (1973), became Swami Anand Somendra; and Robert Birnbaum, a clinical psychologist from Walnut Creek, California, became Swami Prem Amitabh.

As 'chief therapist', Teertha led most of the encounter groups. Teertha had the bony, ascetic face of a medieval penitent, if not the thirst for renunciation. He applied himself to the principles of sexual freedom with particular zeal. 'He was ready to go to bed with every woman who showed interest in him,' Ma Anand Sheela, who would become Rajneesh's secretary and closest confidante, would recall, 'And surprisingly there were many of them.'[31]

Teertha had none of the gravitas or authority of a Fritz Perls; none of the macho bravura of Will Schutz; but he was devoted to Rajneesh, and he demonstrated a singular fluency in vapid psycho-babble. 'It's not that the way you are now is bad,' Teertha told new arrivals at Poona, 'it's just that it's not working. You're not living in bliss—and bliss is possible.'

In his role as a group leader, Teertha styled himself as merely the lightning rod for powerful and inexplicable processes: 'Most of the things that go on in the group, I don't understand with my mind at all. They feel absolutely right, absolutely harmonious but I'm not in touch with them on an intellectual level. They just happen through me.' The function of a group leader was 'not to be there' but to be 'out of the way ... to just say or do whatever comes through'. This principle of saying or doing 'whatever came through' was to prove distinctly hazardous. Stripped naked—often literally—in encounter groups, participants were encouraged to unleash their inhibitions and give physical expression to their most repressed feelings, in order to release the 'energy blocks' in the body. Unlike at Esalen, physical assault was not discouraged—rather, the opposite.

Sessions in which people were encouraged to act out their aggression often resulted in hurt bodies as much as hurt feelings, and sometimes in broken bones. Hugh Milne, a devotee who would subsequently turn against Rajneesh, wrote that injuries during these encounter sessions became so commonplace that they prompted a new diagnosis at the local hospital—'falling off a ladder at Shree Rajneesh Ashram'.

Rajneesh was quick to welcome the therapists and the therapies, and to appropriate the jargon of the new psychology into his own teachings, which he now took to describing as a 'unitive psychology'. The Eastern methods, he said, were 'more individualistic, more inward going', concerned with 'the person and his integrity'. The Western methods were more concerned with the group and with 'community and relationships'. Bringing them together was uniting 'the two polarities' of human consciousness: 'love and meditation'.

The public confession of inhibitions, problems and hang-ups was a 'base normal' in group encounters. Sexual freedom was actively encouraged. Possessiveness and jealousy were bad. Marital fidelity was worthless. 'The very word "fidelity" is ugly, dirty ...'[32] 'Rajneesh tells his followers that they are perfect, beautiful exactly as they are, and does not recommend any discipline of the mind and body', noted the psychologists Susan J. Palmer and Frederick Bird in one study,

On the contrary, he tells them to 'loosen up', 'let it all hang out', and accept themselves in the 'herenow'. He is a warrant for distancing themselves from the authoritative claims of parents, teachers, priests and for dismissing the judgements of others. In the place of these external authorities from the past, the inner authority of feelings and impulses is evoked in the therapy groups.[33]

Rajneesh was held to be the living example of his teachings—the playful child, unburdened by care or responsibility, irreverent, scornful of authority and convention, free of the petty morals, bourgeois inhibitions and hang-ups of society.

Therapists were described as 'channels for Bhagwan', and 'Bhagwan's energy' was frequently invoked as a catalyst in therapeutic exercises. Rajneesh insisted that his teachings and methods went further than Esalen or other growth groups in the West, offering more self-awareness because 'it goes beyond all boundaries—boundaries of sex, boundaries of violence, anger, rage'.

Of course, there was another essential difference. The therapists and group leaders of Esalen and other growth centres did not command personal devotion; did not insist their participants observe a strict dress code of orange robes, or wear their picture on malas around their necks. As Philip Roth observed in *American Pastoral* (1997), 'one price you pay for being a god is the unabated dreaminess of your acolytes'.

By 1979, Poona was styling itself as 'the greatest human growth centre in the world', and offering more than sixty different therapies and techniques for unleashing inhibition and connecting to the 'authentic self', including Rolfing, postural integration, Gestalt, bioenergetics, neo-Reichian rebirthing—the full smorgasbord of every radical and newly fashionable psychotherapeutic method and diversion known to man—along with 'Eastern oriented' groups teaching a range of yoga and meditation techniques from vipassana to zazen.

Visitors to the ashram were urged to participate in the different groups as fully as possible; they were a lucrative source of income, after all. Ma Anand Sheela would recount how the guru would consult a chart showing which therapies were selling well and which badly, tailoring his recommendations accordingly.

A statement filed with the Maharashtra State charity officials in 1980 stated that therapy accounted for $188,253 of the movement's savings (about $591,287 in 2020 money). It would also prove a valuable source of revenue from abroad, as the techniques spread to Rajneesh groups in

America, Europe and Australia through visiting therapists, who would arrive like semi-divine emissaries, brimming with 'Bhagwan's energy'.

Underpinning it all was one of the many paradoxes that characterised Rajneesh's teachings—in this case, that no amount of method or technique would get you 'there'; that you were, in fact, 'there' already if you would but realise it. As Swami Prem Amitabh (Robert Birnbaum) would put it, what Raneesh was doing was giving his disciples ample opportunity to discover that no techniques actually worked.

\* \* \*

Christine Ryder arrived in Poona in 1976. Born in the north of England, she had grown up in a working-class family, trained as a graphic designer and, in her early twenties, moved to London to find work. There, she had been drawn into the alternative culture of underground newspapers, the Arts Lab and people's cooperatives: 'I didn't know what a guru was; I didn't know what a spiritual journey was. I didn't even know I was looking.'[34]

Forty years later, she met me at the railway station of the small town in the north of England where she lived, a handsome woman in her sixties, and we walked in the rain back to her small flat, immaculately tidy, with books on psychology, religion and philosophy stacked on shelves and a single Buddha statue on a sideboard.

In London, she said, she had been introduced to a personal growth centre called 'Community' run by Michael Barnett, who would later become Swami Anand Somendra. It was 'an intense encounter group that had people shouting at me and sent me running down a rabbit hole for two years,' Christine said, continuing:

> I was curious and interested without really understanding what the interest was. For some people there was a real rejection of either the family situation, or some other personal issue. For me it was a rejection of the materialism of our society. There was an idealism there from the beginning. But did I understand that in spiritual terms? No I did not.

In 1976, a friend invited her to join her on a trip to India to visit the Rajneesh ashram:

> She lent me one of Bhagwan's books, of which I read one chapter. I saw a photograph of him, and I rang her the next morning and said, I don't know why, but I'm going to come with you. It was not a thinking decision for me. But when I arrived in Poona—and I can't rationalise this—I just knew I was in the right place.

There definitely was the feeling that I was less of an oddball there than I had felt in most of my life—without realising that I had felt like an oddball. It was—ah, ok, these are people like me.

She took a room in a nearby hotel, visiting the ashram each day:

I loved getting up every morning and doing dynamic meditation—it was really like coming alive. Then somebody said to me, would you like to go to *darshan*, so I said yes.

And there was a real quality of peace about it. Bhagwan was talking in Hindi, which of course I didn't understand, so it wasn't to do with the contact of the words. But just sitting there listening, there was something that was communicated to some part of my soul that was very impactful.

I never thought of Bhagwan as a God, but I did recognise something— or I would say my soul recognised something. It was like being bathed in something that was beneficent.

Here I was having my first contact with somebody with a level of realisation that was impacting myself and others, within a community where things were being done together and where there was a lot of benign feeling and more capacity to be more emotionally open.

But after only a week, Christine fell ill and had to return to England. 'In retrospect,' she says, 'that was the real moment, the turning from looking out to looking in.'

Before leaving, she was asked if she would like to take *sannyas* with Rajneesh and said yes. She returned to London and to her work, following the instructions of Rajneesh to continue wearing her new orange robe and the mala bearing his image. 'Turning up for meetings in ad agencies in a long orange robe, felt like a statement of me saying "this is really who I am",' she said, 'That was one of the things about being a sannyasin; you were both making a statement about who you were, but you were also making yourself different, separating yourself.' That, she continued, would eventually prove to be one of the biggest downfalls of Rajneeshpuram— 'setting ourselves against the world'. After nine months in London, Christine returned to Poona. For the next ten years her life would be spent with Rajneesh:

In many ways, my move was away from the [Western] culture rather than my family situation or any other reason. The whole question of freedom of self-expression, the openness about sexuality—that it was no longer regarded as a bad thing, to be kept in the cupboard—these were things that drew so many people to Bhagwan.

There was that feeling that you just knew you'd landed in the right place at the right time. I couldn't necessarily explain to somebody why I was feeling that way. But it was enough that it was worth giving my energy to. I felt like my life and work was meaningful.

By the late 1970s, the Poona ashram was entertaining up to 5,000 people at any given time—some living permanently in the ashram itself, or in other accommodation nearby, others visiting for anything between a fortnight and three months for the various courses and treatments on offer. The Rajneesh teachings were also being 'exported' around the world, as visitors to Poona returned to establish groups in their own countries. There were centres throughout Europe, America and Australia. By 1980, there were an estimated 50,000 sannyasins worldwide.

The ashram was a flourishing financial concern. It had its own bank— an institution originally established to borrow money from sannyasins— and its own medical facility, with free treatment for ashram residents. A disproportionate number of those seeking treatment were suffering from sexually transmitted diseases. Sexual freedom had its price.

In effect, Rajneesh had created a hermetically sealed universe. Like Big Brother, his pictures were everywhere. But while Poona might have displayed many of the trappings of a cult, its residents evinced little of the drained and dead-eyed appearance of the brainwashed. The mood was more generally one of joy and laughter; people appeared to be genuinely happy, as if energised by Rajneesh's teaching that they were participants in 'a great experiment upon which the whole future of humanity depends'.

It required commitment to be there at all. Ashram workers were supported by the community, but most had to find some way to support themselves when the savings ran out. There were stories of drug dealing and prostitution.

Children were discouraged. Rajneesh had deeply ambivalent ideas about the family, no doubt stemming from his own family experiences. He did not oppose marriage per se, but believed that for the most part marriage was a breeding ground of resentments, possessiveness and neurosis. He proposed the idea of the 'liquid family', whereby couples would have no obligation to stay with each other and where children would be raised communally. Nobody could give birth in the ashram, nor were pregnant women allowed to live inside, although Rajneesh was persuaded to set up a kindergarten and school.

Sannyasins holding important positions or doing useful work in the ashram were encouraged to be sterilised. When his girlfriend Vivek became pregnant by Rajneesh, Laxmi organised for her to be given an abortion and then sterilised.[35] There were many, Christine recounted, who followed Rajneesh's suggestion of sterilisation and came to regret it. But the most important relationship in the disciple's life was with the guru. Christine's own mother died suddenly, shortly after Christine had taken up permanent residence at Poona. News of her illness came too late for Christine to return to England to be with her:

> I've always considered that as a major life mistake—not being there for her. I came home for the funeral, and then almost immediately turned around and went back to India. And I can still remember feeling that was right. My brother was quite angry with me for not staying to support my father.
>
> But at the time the words in my head were Jesus's—leave your mother and father and come follow me. There was a real delusion in me about what my spiritual life was and what its significance in the world was—a misunderstanding about everything about it in many ways.

In his discourses, Rajneesh could talk for hours without pause or recourse to notes, drawing on a myriad of references, from Mahayana and Zen Buddhism to the Upanishads and the writings of the fifteenth-century mystic and poet Kabir, larded with rambling allegorical stories, jokes of varying degrees of awfulness, and attacks on sacred cows like the Pope and Mother Teresa. (When, in 1979, Mother Teresa of Calcutta won the Nobel Prize, Rajneesh attacked her as a fraud and a 'hypocrite' for accepting the award.) These discourses would be collected into over 600 volumes and translated into 50 languages.

'It became clear that God was an intellectual snob,' wrote Gita Mehta, in her sardonic attack on Rajneesh (although he is never actually named) in her book *Karma Cola* (1979): 'He dropped only the heaviest names, Jesus. Marx. Mahavira. And Fritz Perls. His two thousand-odd devotees inhaled, writhed or listened in an ecstasy of being.'[36] In the evening *darshan*, he would invite questions from his followers about personal matters, such as relationships, jealousy or spiritual practice. Occasionally he might pick someone out of the audience and lavish them with special praise—or ruthlessly cut them down.

Sometimes sannyasins would seek confirmation about special effects they had experienced during meditation which they hoped pointed to a growing enlightenment. According to Sheela's account:

If they were rich Bhagwan sometimes confirmed it. Sometimes He declared such people enlightened on the spot. Once the purpose was achieved—meaning their pockets were emptied—He would become angry at them. And when He had had enough of a person, He would speak about it openly in the same discourses.[37]

Devotees took all the contradictions and insults as a teaching. 'You ask him about love and he'll give a long talk about ecstasy. You ask him about relationships and he would ... tell you a joke or something that he just read in a newspaper,' Michael Barnett (Swami Anand Somendra) once remarked. 'It would make you feel as if you were participating. In fact, nobody ever participated in Poona. There was only one person, really, in Poona.'[38]

Among those who took a close interest in the burgeoning growth of human potential techniques at Poona was Richard Price. He had read Rajneesh's books and listened to recordings of his discourses with growing interest, and in 1976, to the consternation of some of his Esalen colleagues, Price took sannyas by mail order (a service that Rajneesh offered, whereby applicants would get their mala and new name by return of post). Price was given the name Swami Geet Govind.

In 1977, he arrived at Poona in person. *Time* magazine noted his presence in a lengthy article on Rajneesh published in January 1978, in which it described Poona as 'Esalen East' and commented: 'Now the guru is instructing his best-connected disciple yet: Richard Price, co-founder and director of the Esalen Institute, the very fount of the encounter craze.'[39] Price, the article noted, would be returning to Big Sur in due course, 'to apply the teachings of his new master'. But any expectations that Price would be forging a partnership between Rajneesh and Esalen, or that Rajneesh was about to become Price's 'new master', were quickly disabused. Price spent two weeks happily meditating at the ashram, but was then deeply shocked when, participating in a group session on 'aggression' with Swami Teertha, an Irish woman—who happened to be former nun—had her leg broken. Shortly after the incident the woman stood up in a public session with Rajneesh and directly questioned him on whether violence was really necessary in the encounter groups. Rather than offering sympathy or an apology, Rajneesh rounded on her and tried to intimidate her into silence. Price left Poona appalled.

On his return to America, Price wrote a letter to *Time*—that was never published—anxious to put a distance between Esalen and 'Esalen East'.

Rajneesh, he wrote was 'well worth reading' and could speak 'brilliantly' of the transformative possibility of human life:

> However, the ashram 'encounter' group is an abomination—authoritarian, intimidating, violent—used to enforce conformity to an emerging orange new order rather than to facilitate growth. Broken bones are common, bruises and abrasions beyond counting. As such it owes more to the S.S. than Esalen. Until the compassion Rajneesh speaks about with such eloquence is reflected in his groups, I am content to be known as 'Richard Price' rather than 'Geet Govind'.[40]

He later wrote to Rajneesh:

> My experience in the first two weeks at the ashram in the 'meditation camp' was excellent. I felt a deepening, an enrichment, an attunement. During the last two weeks my experience was quite the opposite. I had softened up only to be confronted with Teertha's autocratic, coercive, life-negating style of 'leadership'; a style reinforcing violence and sexual acting-out of the most unfeeling kind; a style negating soft emotion and emerging sensitivity, and manipulating group pressure to force conformity. Is *this* what Bhagwan is about ... It is as if the worst mistakes of some inexperienced Esalen group leaders of many years ago had been systematized and given the stamp of 'God'.[41]

Rajneesh wrote a reply to Price explaining that it was 'objective compassion', allowing participants to vent their frustrations. But the bad publicity threatened to be damaging, and by 1979 the encounter groups had been quietly dropped. A press release from the ashram explained that Rajneesh believed that violence had 'fulfilled its function within the overall context of the ashram as an evolving spiritual commune'. Michael Murphy recalls:

> Dick was a very fiery guy and he was so horrified by what he saw going on there ... particularly in the formats that had been largely developed at Esalen, in these Gestalt therapy and encounter group things—in Dick's mind they were so deformed. So, yes, Ranjeesh's influence had reached into Esalen but it was violently rejected, starting with the co-founder. It was like throwing off an antigen—our immune system just threw it off.

Price's dismissal of Rajneesh, his concerns about the excesses of the therapy groups and what was going on in the ashram, were thrown into sharper relief the following year, when, 8,000 miles away, another charismatic religious figure lurched dramatically into the newspaper headlines.

In November 1978, the world was given a salutary glimpse into the worst possibilities of charismatic guru figures, when in Guyana, over 900 followers of the cult leader Jim Jones committed suicide or were murdered, at his behest, by drinking Kool Aid laced with poison. The events in Guyana were the grim apotheosis of the rise of cult groups that characterised the 1960s and 1970s, from Charles Manson's 'family' onwards. In India, the American Embassy despatched a representative to Poona to check on the well-being of American sannyasins, and the media took a keener interest in the ashram's activities.

An Associated Press reporter visiting the ashram paid particular attention to Rajneesh's comments, discovered on a tape for sale in the bookshop: 'This isn't going to be a democracy. You are never going to be asked what should be done and what should not be done ... Your vote will never be taken.' Asked about the encounter groups, Teertha admitted that eyes were blackened and the occasional limb broken as sexual fantasies were acted out.

Teertha was also quoted as saying he would happily commit suicide for the guru: 'I'd do anything he says. Why? Because what he has done with me so far is beyond my comprehension. Suicide is easy, cleaning toilets at 12 o'clock at night when you don't really want to, that's the real test. Suicide is nothing.' It would be charitable to assume that Teertha was attempting levity.

Rajneesh himself addressed the subject of the Jonestown massacre in a discourse, given in Hindi, in which he was quoted as saying that such an incident would be 'unthinkable' at Poona: 'Occasionally such people come to me also. They come and plead, Bhagwan we are ready to die for you. I tell them, "If you obey me, then first you should be willing to live for me as I ask you to live".' Those who drew parallels between himself and Jim Jones, he said, 'have never been here ... and never looked into my eyes, neither sat near me nor held my hands. Their words carry no values.'[42]

It had long been Rajneesh's policy to court public figures, and it was not long before people who were more accustomed to appearing in gossip columns than ashrams began to arrive at Poona. The Prince and Princess of Hanover, the Marquis of Bath ... Jaded by a life of fast cars, nightclubs and beautiful women, the actor Terence Stamp arrived in 1976, taking the name Swami Deva Veeten. 'The first weekend I was there I was invited to live in the ashram and frankly, the thing that struck me was that he was one of the greatest performers I had ever come across,' Stamp recalled:

He was like a mixture of sort of a Charles Laughton and Orson Welles; he was probably the greatest public speaker I have ever come across. He was mesmerizing, he could hold an audience, talk for an hour, no notes, nothing. So he became the focus of my attention. I became ensconced in the ashram, I had a new name, I was wearing orange, I was studying tantric sex. It wasn't uninteresting![43]

In 1980 the ashram received an unexpected publicity coup when Bernard Levin, the respected commentator and columnist for *The Times* of London, arrived at Poona with his girlfriend Arianna Stassinopoulos.[44] An enthusiast of New Age teachings, Stassinopoulos had already introduced Levin to 'Insight', a self-awareness course started by a self-styled American guru named John-Roger Hinkins, founder of the Church of the Movement of Inner Spiritual Awareness (MISA—pronounced 'messiah').[45] Enraptured by the guru's 'low, smooth and exceptionally beautiful' voice, Rajneesh, Levin wrote in *The Times*, was regarded as 'the conduit along which the vital force of the universe flows'. His followers, he continued,

[were] in general an extremely fine crop, bearing witness to a tree of choice, rare nature ... The first quality a visitor to Rajneesh ashram notices—and he never ceases to notice—is the ease and comfort with which they wear their faith ... I cannot put it better than in saying that they constantly extend, to each other and to strangers, the hand of love, though without the ego-filled demands of love as most of the world knows it.[46]

In media and intellectual circles, Levin was roundly ridiculed for his opinions.

By the time of Levin's arrival, the ashram was increasingly coming into conflict with the local community. Much of this was to do with sexual behaviour. Local people found it particularly vexing to see Western visitors kissing and fondling each other while dressed in the garb of India's holy men. One Poona newspaper editor likened it to a group of foreigners dressing up as monks and nuns and engaging in sexual activity on American streets.

By 1981, local hostility had grown to fever-pitch; furthermore, the ashram's finances were coming under increasing scrutiny from government officials, frustrating Rajneesh's attempts to secure a larger site on which to build a new ashram to accommodate his expanding following. The feud with the government resulted in the tax authorities cancelling the tax-exempt status of the ashram as a charitable, religious or educational establishment, which resulted in a demand for current and back taxes amounting to around $5 million.

To make matters worse, Rajneesh's health, never good, was now in steady decline. While he was only fifty, he looked twenty years older. The oily ringlets and wispy beard had turned grey. He was suffering from diabetes, asthma, a prolapsed disc and a multitude of allergies. Disciples were terrified of sneezing in his presence and were forbidden from wearing any perfume or scents; sniffers were deployed at the entrance to the *darshan* hall to ensure that this stricture was observed. (Happily, approved shampoo was available to buy in the ashram shop.)

Increasingly, his talks consisted of insults and jokes, often scatological—a five-minute disquisition on the various meanings and uses of the word 'fuck', for example, that would have barely raised a laugh if told by a nightclub comedian, would have his disciples obligingly laughing uproariously. The anomaly of a spiritual teacher and lavatory humour was a rich seam, it seemed, in 'waking people up' or at least keeping them amused.

Then, on 24 March 1981, something extraordinary happened. Rajneesh stopped speaking altogether. Sannyasins were told that he had entered 'a new and ultimate stage of his work ... silence'.[47] The truth was that burdened with health worries and concerns about the ashram, Rajneesh was sliding into a state of depression and indifference to everything around him.

The daily discourses were replaced by a ritual where he would sit silently with his disciples for an hour, listening to music. Declaring himself 'a medium for Bhagwan', Swami Teertha began to perform the initiation ritual of taking sannyas and presiding over 'energy darsana'. With life in Poona becoming impossible, Rajneesh instructed his secretary Laxmi to come up with a solution to the tax problem, and to find land elsewhere in India, fit for the development of his 'new society'. But Rajneesh's name was poison. No regional government could be found to grant the necessary permissions for land use. When Laxmi was unable to deliver what Rajneesh demanded, he fired her.

Her place was taken by a woman named Ma Anand Sheela, who would come to play an important, and ultimately catastrophic, role in Rajneesh's life. Sheela was the daughter of a farmer and businessman, who had been a close disciple of Mahatma Gandhi and had at one time served as his appointment secretary. At the age of eighteen, she went to America to study art at a small college in Montclair, New Jersey, where she met and married fellow student Marc Silverman. In 1972, on a visit back to India, her father, who had become an admirer of Rajneesh, took her to meet the guru. For Sheela, it was love at first sight. 'I just sat there, drowned in Him, lost in Him,' she wrote in her autobiography, 'I heard everything that was spoken, and yet I heard nothing. I was there and yet I was not there.'[48]

Abandoning her plans to become an artist, she and Silverman soon became sannyasins. She took the name Ma Anand Sheela while her husband became Chinmaya. Sheela made regular visits back to America, and in 1975 she established a Rajneesh centre in Montclair. In 1980, Silverman died of Hodgkin's disease. Sheela married another sannyasin, a former New York banker named John Shelfer, who became known as Swami Jay.

But there was truly only one man in her life. More than a mere secretary to Rajneesh, she quickly assumed the role of confidante, *consigliera*, trusted adviser and gatekeeper. Reading her autobiography, it is hard to know who was controlling whom. She writes that

> Rajneesh was King of my heart … But He was not too unlike other men. In fact He had many weaknesses of the ordinary man. This understanding of Him helped me a lot in dealing with Him objectively … Bhagwan suffered from the same domestic problems as every married man. Toothache made Him grumpy. Bad weather made Him depressed. He nagged when things did not run as He wanted them to run. There were days when He behaved as if nobody could do anything right for Him. On such days He needed me. He loved me. He trusted me. I was able to reassure Him by just being present. He felt safe with me just as I felt safe in His presence.[49]

In May 1981, matters became critical for Rajneesh when the Indian government instructed its embassies overseas to stop issuing visas to foreigners wishing to visit the Poona ashram. Together, Rajneesh and Sheela began making plans to relocate to America, and on 1 June, Rajneesh and a small group of devotees left Poona, en route for New York. Residents of the ashram were told that Bhagwan was in 'grave danger' medically if he remained in India, and that he needed to go to America for treatment.

It was the first time Rajneesh had ever been on a plane. While he, Vivek and Sheela sat in first class drinking champagne, the handful of other sannyasins travelling with him flew economy. On his arrival, he announced to the waiting media: 'I am the Messiah America has been waiting for.' He was admitted to the country on a three-month medical visa, and installed in a property in Montclair called Kip's Castle, which had been bought by a devotee for use as a meditation centre. While Sheela travelled around America, scouting for a site for a new ashram, Rajneesh, apparently inspired by the splendours of Mammon around him, embarked on a spending spree, buying his first cars—a Mercedes for Sheela and a two-tone convertible Rolls-Royce for himself.

On 13 June 1981, the Chidvilas Rajneesh Meditation Center, a New Jersey Corporation headed by Ma Anand Sheela, paid $5.75 million for one of the biggest ranches in Oregon, a 64,229-acre property called the Big Muddy Ranch. With the arrival of the Indian guru, it was given a new name: Rancho Rajneesh.

# 14

# DOWN ON THE RANCH

Rancho Rajneesh was set in the arid, sparsely populated countryside of hills and canyons in Wasco County. The nearest town of Antelope, little more than a hamlet with a population of fewer than fifty, was 18 miles away. Madras, the largest town in the area, 50 miles away, had a population of just 2,300.

An immense fund-raising and development programme was launched, in which devotees coming to Oregon were encouraged to donate all their money or income from investments in the form of either donations or low-interest loans. The first new residents began to arrive in July. Concerns among the local populace about the sudden influx of strangers were mollified with reassurances from Sheela that the project was an agricultural commune, with no more than forty residents.

By October the population had grown to around 180. By 1985, when the ashram dissolved, the population would number around 4,000, and Rancho Rajneesh—or Rashneeshpuram, as it became known—was a self-contained town including a hotel, an airstrip, a sewage reclamation plant and a shopping centre.

From the moment of her arrival in Oregon, Sheela had launched a charm offensive, meeting local ranchers and politicians, buying fifty head of cattle from a Wasco County commissioner and hosting a dance in Madras, where cowboys drank and danced until dawn. But relations quickly deteriorated after the ashram was given permission by the local county court to incorporate the ranch as 'a city', and then applied to build an office complex and printing plant in the nearest town of Antelope, where they had already acquired a handful of properties for extra housing. Local residents objected, but in November 1982 the issue was finally settled in the Rajneeshees' favour when, in a town council election, Rajneeshees out-voted the town's residents, allowing them to take control over the town council. Main Street was renamed Mevlana Bhagwan Street and the town's general store became the Zorba the Buddha Restaurant. Nudity in the public park was legalised. Angry and disgusted, local people began to pack up and leave town.

Within the space of a year, an experiment ostensibly born of an aspiration to unify and save mankind had mainly succeeded in unifying a bewilderingly diverse range of antagonists—including ranchers, conservatives, liberals, fundamentalist Christians, public officials and large elements of the media—who denounced the Rajneeshees as cultists and freaks. Rajneeshees might have protested that the objections to them were rooted in 'bigotry' and prejudice. But the local people had legitimate complaints about broken promises over land use, and quite understandable fears of being taken over by the newcomers.

Rajneeshpuram had grown at a phenomenal pace. It had its own sewage plant, a cement plant, a recycling centre, a landing strip for aircraft, water storage tanks and electrical generators. There were restaurants and boutiques offering a kaleidoscopic variety of clothes, in any colour—echoing Henry Ford's maxim—as long as it was orange. There was an ashram newspaper, *The Rajneesh Times*, and a printing press churning out copies of Rajneesh's discourses and teachings for sale in the ashram bookshop—dozens of volumes of them, his every utterance preserved as holy writ. (Apart from Rajneesh, the journalist Frances FitzGerald noted, the most popular author on the ranch was the writer of formulaic westerns, Louis L'Amour.)

The 'agricultural commune' the Rajneeshees had assured the local people they were establishing now more closely resembled a medium-sized town, or—given the presence of its own 'Peace Force', a cadre of weapons-trained sannyasins armed with rifles—a small nation state. Hundreds of acres were being farmed with modern equipment, providing 90 per cent of all the vegetables consumed in the ashram; there was a poultry farm, a dairy farm and a bus service. The ashram also purchased a hotel in Portland, which was used primarily by sannyasins on their way to and from the ashram, but which also accommodated other tourists, many coming for the therapies and encounter groups which now came under the aegis of the newly inaugurated Rajneesh Institute for Therapy and the Rajneesh Institution for Meditation and Inner Growth.

The rapid growth of Rajneesh's 'intentional community' provided an unparalleled opportunity for social scientists to explore a utopian community in action—a hermetic society, populated by educated and for the most part highly intelligent participants, rejecting social norms and guided by its own set of beliefs, principles and ideas about community, work and religion. A survey conducted by the University of Oregon in 1983, revealed that 54 per cent of the ashram residents were female, with an average age of 33.9 years. The average age among males was 34.7 years. Of the respondents, 95 per cent had graduated from high school and 64 per cent from university, while 11 per cent had graduate degrees in psychiatry or psychology. Some 74 per cent of respondents reported that they were married, 14 per cent were single, 10 per cent divorced and 2 per cent widowed or separated (the high incidence of marriage could most likely be attributed to sham 'marriages of convenience' for immigration purposes; a major cause of trouble in the future). Of the respondents, 25 per cent reported having children, but fewer than half of these had children living at Rajneeshpuram (there were no children living in the ashram itself; the few who were part of the ashram lived in Antelope).

About half of the respondents had been sannyasins for five years or more; 40 per cent characterised themselves as having been 'religious' prior to becoming a sannyasin; and 61 per cent characterised themselves as being either 'radical', 'very liberal' or 'somewhat liberal'. None characterised themselves as 'conservative'; 36 per cent characterised themselves as 'neither liberal nor conservative'.

On a graph of 'life satisfaction', 93 per cent reported being in the top two categories of 'extremely satisfied' and 'best ever'. The ratings for 'perceived stress' and depression were far below the mean norm; ratings for self-esteem were far above.[1]

The ashram president, Ma Yoga Vidya, was a former systems analyst for IBM. The mayor, Krishna Deva, was a clinical psychologist. The city planner, Swami Deva Wadud, was a practising psychic who had been a city planner in San Mateo, California. His wife, another psychic, was the ranch's air-traffic controller.

\* \* \*

In 1988, John Updike published a satirical novel, S., about a religious commune in Arizona run by a guru named Shri Arhat Mindadali. S. tells the story of a middle-aged woman, Sarah, disillusioned with haute-bourgeois life, who leaves her husband to join the guru's ashram. Sarah's experiences are told through a series of letters to her husband, her daughter, her mother and Midge, her friend from the suburban yoga class where she first learned of the mysteries of 'the Arhat'.

On her arrival in Arizona, she tells Midge, she was asked the pro forma questions: 'Did I have any venereal disease and how much money was I bringing to the Treasury of Enlightenment ... credit cards ... access to jointly held securities?' Taking the name Ma Prem Kundalini, she throws herself into the free-love ethos of the commune, at the same time abiding by the ashram dictat of work/worship for twelve to fourteen hours a day. Like Rajneesh, the Arhat enjoys parading before his adoring followers in expensive cars. 'You wouldn't believe the *peace* he generates,' Sarah writes, 'even at thirty miles an hour.'[2]

Updike, who described himself as 'a card-carrying Episcopalian', wickedly mocks the affectations of mystical jargon—'Deep down in my atman, beneath all these sniffles and this hysterical physical pace,' Sarah tells Midge, 'I am absolutely at peace.' Sarah is hypnotised by the Arhat's liquid eyes, the hypnotic, hissing sibilance of his voice. When he speaks, 'it's like a fist inside me relaxing, like a lens that keeps opening and opening to let in more light'. The ashram activities are not

> [the] usual repulsive little anatomical stunts like sucking things back up through your anus and cleaning out your sinuses with a silk string, but a lot of group encounter and hydrotherapy, and some primal scream, and strange things like food fights and blue movies—anything to wake people up, was the Arhat's approach.[3]

Just as at Poona and Rajneeshpuram, the ashram is run largely by women: 'The Arhat has this theory that women are stronger in selflessness than men, which may be a nice way of saying they're subservient.' Sarah is soon employed using her talents as a secretary, ghost-writing letters from the Arhat to prospective new sannyasins:

> I ask merely that for the duration of your life here under my protection and guidance—may it be eternal!—your financial savings be placed in the care of the vigilant and efficient custodians of our Treasury of Enlightenment ... Demand for places amid our limited facilities is such that we must ask a minimum deposit of ten thousand dollars (U.S.) ...
> I return your love a million-fold and with tranquil exultation await your reply.[4]

Such is her dedication that she rises to the position of ashram administrator, while at the same time practising energetic tantric sex with the Arhat.

Updike's ultimate joke is that the guru turns out to be not an Indian mystic at all, but Art Steinmetz, from Massachusetts, 'just one more bright good Jewish boy, who even put in a few terms at Northeastern studying sales engineering and business administration before the peace movement got to him and he took off'. 'The human hunger for a god,' Sarah notes, as she slips away from the ashram, bound for a Caribbean island to enjoy the money she has been siphoning off from the ashram accounts, 'will always reward those with the temerity—the inner density and vacuity—to call themselves gods.'[5]

Rajneesh too, if not a nice Jewish boy from Massachusetts, remained largely a mystery; his mantra of complete transparency for his followers did not extend to himself. They were encouraged to dig deep in self-interrogation, to bare their minds and souls—and their bodies—to the community; yet any questions about Rajneesh were discouraged. He remained totally opaque, the Wizard of Oz behind the curtain.

In 1988, a year after the dissolution of Rajneeshpuram, Ronald O. Clarke, a professor of religious studies at Oregon State University, offered a study of Rajneesh's character and behaviour through the American Psychiatric Association's *Diagnostic and Statistical Manual of Mental Disorders* (*DSM*). Clarke concluded that Rajneesh was suffering from classic narcissistic personality disorder: a lack of empathy with others; grandiose feelings of entitlement; interpersonal exploitiveness; a complete absence of social reciprocity; excessive vanity (Rajneesh was always meticulously groomed and would spend an inordinate time in front of a mirror); an insatiable need for adulation; and a sense of self-importance or uniqueness that 'seems to possess no limits'.

In short, wrote Clarke, rather than ego-lessness, his condition was one of ego-inflation, manifest in his claims to be greater than Jesus, to be the 'midwife' assisting in the birth of a 'New Man' on the planet, and that he had personally progressed beyond enlightenment and transcended the 'untranscendable'.[6] Implicit in Rajneesh's self-concept, Clarke noted, his constant reiteration of his uniqueness, and his entitlement to the adoration and largesse of his followers, was his assumption that his very presence on earth—the result of his decision to accept a final earthly embodiment—constituted a great gift of existence to the human species.

Martyrdom was a recurring theme of Rajneesh's pronouncements. He constantly talked about the threats he posed to organised religion and society and warned against the reprisals that would surely follow; his prediction of acts of violence against himself and the ashram became almost a self-fulfilling prophecy in light of his constant provocations. The more he baited the authorities and the world at large, the more he was distrusted, and the more he was able to play the card of persecution and martyrdom.

He took an enormous delight in provoking anger, shock and controversy. His extravagance was a calculated rebuttal to those who believed a holy man should be self-denying. As a popular bumper-sticker at Rajneeshpuram had it, 'Jesus Saves, Moses Invests, Bhagwan spends'. The Rolls-Royces and diamond watches were indeed a joke about the false gods of materialism—but a joke at the expense of the devotees who paid for them. Rajneesh did not hold his baubles in contempt or even the serene indifference of non-attachment—he craved them and loved them; the more he had, the more he wanted.

Neither of the ashrams at Poona and Oregon had pretended to be democracies. Rajneesh scorned democracy, on the grounds that 'it only gives power to those who stand at the lowest'. Nor would any of the sannyasins have described them as dictatorships—although that is effectively what they were.

Since arriving in Rajneeshpuram, Rajneesh had only communicated with a small group of close disciples; but that circle now narrowed to just one, after Sheela announced that Bhagwan would henceforth speak only with her. Theoretically, Sheela made the major policy decisions in consultation with Rajneesh; she in turn would then meet with a group of ashram 'co-ordinators', who would pass edicts down through a series of department heads. The majority of these co-ordinators were women, a loyal inner circle who were known among other sannyasins as 'moms'. Christine Ryder says:

> I think he understood the patriarchy of the world, and that was a genuine attempt to say 'Let's see what happens if we put women in charge.' One of the things that is often said in therapy work is 'if it's not one thing, it's your mother ...', because our relationship to our mother is how we relate to the world. And in a sense Rajneeshpuram was a therapy community.
>
> In some situations Bhagwan would put a strong, difficult woman in charge and all sorts of authority numbers would come up. I don't think it was because he believed women were less of a challenge to his authority, or easier to manipulate than men. If he did think that, it was a mistake.[7]

Since few people had direct access to Rajneesh, it was difficult for ordinary sannyasins to know exactly how much control he had over Sheela (or how much control she had over him) and which of the policy decisions were truly his. It was a system in which the word of the guru was absolute—

without anybody ever being completely sure what the word of the guru actually was.

Sheela was becoming an increasingly provocative presence. At a school board meeting in Antelope, in front of television cameras from a Portland television station, she described the children of local ranchers as looking 'retarded'. In an interview on Australian television, she accused the interviewer of using prostitutes. On another occasion, she mocked the cardinals in the Vatican as being 'lousy businessmen' who 'only know the missionary position'. She reached the nadir of bad taste in an interview for NBC in which she described the Holocaust as 'five hundred Jews in an ashtray'.

Rajneesh encouraged her outbursts—and on occasion scripted them. Outrage, he believed, kept the ashram in the public eye, and attracted more devotees. A document, *Osho: The Last Testament, Volume 1*, published in 1985, reproduces a conversation between Rajneesh and a woman sannyasin, in which she asks whether he was 'offended' by Sheela's pronouncements. He replies:

> Whenever she came back, I hit her hard, because she was not the way I would like her to be—really outrageous! She was falling below the standard. And I was continuously telling her, 'Don't be worried, we don't have anything to lose. We have the whole world to gain and nothing to lose. Be outrageous!' ... It has to be sensational. I have been sharpening her like a sword. 'Go, and cut as many heads as you can!'

As one sannyasin, Dyhan John (aka John Wally), put it, Sheela was 'just a funnel for everything that happened, right down to where plants went in hallways and the colour of carpet in the bathroom of the mall'.[8]

She consolidated her power by 'blacklisting' sannyasins who displeased her and encouraging other sannyasins to spy on them for 'negativity'. At her behest, a system of wiretapping and electronic eavesdropping was secretly installed on payphones and in the guest rooms where visitors to Rajneeshpuram, including journalists, stayed. Later, there would be allegations that troublesome sannyasins had been drugged and poisoned to keep them quiet. 'A lot of people will pin the downfall of Rajneeshpuram on Sheela—and there are good reasons for that,' Christine Ryder remembered,

> But the truth is Rajneeshpuram wouldn't have existed without her. She was a highly charismatic person who didn't understand the word 'impossible', and who had the capacity in the earlier years to inspire people to go with that, and to do extraordinary things.

Rajneeshpuram did become authoritarian, and I think that has more to do with what happens when one commits to an ideal and the commitment is so deep you start getting blinders about the choices you make in that commitment. People talk about fascism in relation to what happened at Rajneeshpuram, but I think communism is a much better analogy. It started as idealism; it was not about seeking power. We had that belief that we were doing something that was important and right for the world, and we were right to defend it. And out of that you get all sorts of lunacy.

\* \* \*

Within two years of Rajneesh arriving in Oregon, the ashram had started buckling under a multitude of problems. It was fighting legal cases with the state over zoning and land use, and also coming under increasing government scrutiny over its tax affairs, and the number of sham marriages arranged among sannyasins to circumvent American immigration laws.

The main target of the Immigration and Naturalization Service (INS) was Rajneesh himself, who had been admitted to America on a tourist visa, issued in light of his plea that he needed urgent medical treatment. But in two years he had not been admitted to any hospital, nor sought any medical treatment whatsoever. In 1983, when he applied for permanent residency, the INS began to assemble a case to deny his application on the grounds that he had made false statements on his original visa application, and at the same time to deny him classification as a religious worker.

In a strategy designed to thwart the authorities' case, the ashram administrators, in the guise of a body called the Academy of Rajneeshism, attempted to establish 'Rajneeshism' as a formal religion. According to a founding document, *Rajneeshism: An Introduction to Bhagwan Shree Rajneesh and His Religion* (1983), the organisation of the church comprised three categories of 'ministers': Acharyas, Arihantas and Siddhas, and 'The category into which a candidate is placed depends on the particular type of energy he or she possesses: introverted, extroverted or a synthesis of the two.'[9]

Sheela, apparently, was an acharya, and so too was Teertha. Quite how much of this was the design of Rajneesh was unclear. He had consistently decried any form of religious institution, and often insisted that it would be impossible to make a fixed doctrine out of his teachings. Fluidity, paradox, contradiction—all were essential parts of Rajneesh's 'game mind'. If, as many sannyasins believed, Rajneesh was divine, an enlightened Buddha, then whatever he did, no matter how paradoxical or irrational it might seem, must have some deeper meaning and purpose, even if that was not immediately apparent.

What was apparent was that the threat to Rajneesh and the ashram from the outside world was growing. Rajneesh had always emphasised that his disciples were the chosen ones, in the vanguard of a new world order—and as the threats appeared to grow, so it seemed self-protection became more necessary. The fear, paranoia and delusions that—according to Rajneesh—characterised the world outside, now flourished within the ashram itself. The list of enemies, both real and imagined, grew.

Following an incident in which a man brought a bomb into the ashram's Hotel Rajneesh in Portland, accidentally blowing himself up (the incident was never explained), a rigorous security regime was introduced at the ranch. Everyone entering and leaving was body-searched by guards and cars were checked by sniffer dogs. Fearing plots to assassinate him, the guard detail on Rajneesh's compound was increased, and he ordered Sheela to build him an underground bunker, equipped with survival rations and emergency health care.

Paradise was becoming a prison camp, and as the paranoia increased so the regime became more authoritarian, the rhetoric of conflict more heated. Readying for a violent stand-off with the authorities, the ashram had been stockpiling weapons. According to a report in *The Oregonian*, by the autumn of 1984, sannyasins had amassed an arsenal of at least twenty-eight semi-automatic rifles, along with silhouette targets for target practice and $25,000 worth of ammunition (more than half of what the city of Portland spent in that year). An air of impending apocalypse now enshrouded Rajneeshpuram.

Rajneesh had long propounded a vision of the world being destroyed by nuclear war or some other man-made catastrophe by the 1990s—a view he shared with Paul Brunton, Meher Baba and sundry lesser apocalyptic prophets. That had not (yet) come to pass. In the face of mankind's imminent demise there was but one route to salvation, according to Rajneesh: 'Rajneeshism is creating a Noah's Ark of consciousness ... I say to you that except this there is no other way.'[10]

If not nuclear annihilation, then Aids—the scourge predicted by Nostradamus, according to Rajneesh—would be the instrument of death: he talked of the possibility of the disease killing 'two-thirds of the world's population' before the end of the twentieth century.[11] Sannyasins were instructed to wear condoms and rubber gloves and to refrain from kissing during intercourse. But for most, the new precautions had little personal relevance. The fervour of free love had diminished considerably since the years of Poona. Most sannyasins were too exhausted by the long, laborious hours of work as 'worship' and the increasing air of foreboding and uncertainty about the ranch to have either the time or energy to give vent to their sexual feelings.

By the summer of 1984, the ashram was beginning to fall apart. Rajneesh had been refused permanent residence status. The number of incomers had dropped, and so too had revenue. The network of centres and ashrams in Europe was also in decline, not least because of growing resentments over Sheela's authoritarian leadership. Factions began to open up within the movement. Swami Anand (Michael Barnett), who had established a Rajneesh centre in Brussels, was expelled after showing disturbing signs of an independent mind and cultivating his own following.

Legal problems were also mounting. When the ashram came into conflict with Wasco County for annexing land without the county's consent, a plan was hatched to have a Rajneeshnee run for county officer, and to influence the turn-out in elections by debilitating voters. A suggestion to poison the water supply was abandoned as impractical. Instead, salad bars at ten local restaurants were contaminated with salmonella bacteria, resulting in 751 people falling ill and 45 being hospitalised.

Even more bizarre was a plan inaugurated in August 1984, known as the 'Share A Home' programme, to move homeless people into the ashram. The scheme was announced as a demonstration of Rajneesh's largesse— an opportunity for the most dispossessed in society to join the ranks of the 'New Man' and 'inspire a life of dignity with love and respect'. In fact, it was a cynical attempt to boost the electoral register in the ashram's favour.

Rajneeshees were despatched to Portland, Seattle and San Francisco to round up homeless people, offer them a place to stay with three meals a day, and then bus them to the ashram. More than 4,000 indigents were recruited, with as many as 2,500 living at the ashram at any single time, outnumbering the permanent residents. Local people reeled at the influx of drunks, drug users, the desperate and the mentally ill.

The new arrivals at Rajneeshpuram were given instructions on voting, and the more volatile and troublesome were sedated with 'pacification-tea'. When wholesale voter registration was blocked by the State, the 'Share A Home' programme was abandoned. Most of the new residents barely stayed for a week. The failed bid to fix the elections cost the ashram $1 million.

On 30 October 1984, Rajneesh, recognising that the ashram was now tearing apart at the seams, broke his three-year silence, recording videos of speeches that were played in the main hall. Rajneeshpuram was coming increasingly to resemble the last days of Rome. Sheela was now styling herself as 'Bodhisattva Ma Anand Sheela' and disporting herself in long red 'ceremonial' robes and a mala studded with diamonds or pearl beads.

Rajneesh too, his moods now moderated by a daily regimen of Valium, the tranquilliser meprobamate and regular hits of laughing gas, had adopted a berserk flamboyance, with glittering robes and diamond watches. He was now driven the few hundred yards from his house to the lecture hall in a chauffeur-driven stretch Rolls-Royce, accompanied by security vehicles and sometimes two helicopters, as disciples threw rose petals in his path—a performance Frances FitzGerald noted was 'a cross between Oscar night and the evening out of a Latin American dictator'.[12]

By Sheela's account, his appetite for Rolls-Royces and expensive watches had become insatiable: 'It had gone beyond being a funny off-beat way of Bhagwan to make people see that there was no inherent value in such material possessions. His appetite for these luxuries was in fact, growing, worsening.' His demands no longer seemed merely idiosyncratic; 'they appeared to be the product of a deteriorating being'.[13] Sheela would later maintain that the ashram had expended more than $11 million on Rolls-Royces and $8 million on watches and jewellery.

Sheela's authority in the ashram was now being challenged by the arrival of a new group of sannyasins—Hollywood high rollers, bringing with them a much-needed injection of funds. Among them were Françoise Ruddy, a former soldier in the Israeli Defense Forces (IDF) and the ex-wife of Albert Ruddy (who had produced *The Godfather* in 1972), and John Wally, a Los Angeles physician who had made a fortune in emergency room medicine. Françoise became Ma Prem Hasya; Wally was Swami Dhyan John.

Known as 'the Hollywood mafia', the newcomers installed themselves in their own housing, with expensive furnishings and artwork, and declined to eat in the ashram restaurant, instead making frequent trips to Madras in their Jaguar for their own provisions. The promise of new funds quickly endeared them to Rajneesh, and provided a threat to Sheela's exclusive proximity to the guru. Before long, cementing her connection to the inner circle, Ma Prem Hasya had married the guru's British doctor, Devaraj—previously George Meredith.

Sheela, in a bid to consolidate her position and demonstrate her continuing usefulness to Rajneesh, allegedly now drew up a 'hit-list' of enemies including Devaraj, Rajneesh's close companion Vivek, an investigative reporter for *The Oregonian* newspaper and the United States Attorney for the District of Oregon, Charles Turner, who had been appointed to head the investigation into immigration fraud at the ranch.

Vivek would later give evidence to a Grand Jury about how she had been invited to Sheela's home for a meeting for the first time in June 1985, and became violently ill immediately after drinking a cup of tea that Sheela had given her, experiencing hot sweats, retching and a rise in her pulse rate to between 160 and 170 bpm—twice the normal rate. Devaraj seems to have become a target after an outside doctor questioned his competence, and suggested that Devaraj might be responsible after Rajeesh had been diagnosed with blood poisoning.

When Sheela asked for a volunteer from among her inner circle to 'get rid of' Devaraj by shooting him full of adrenalin, a woman named Ma Shanti Bhadra (Jane Stork in an earlier life) had stepped forward. On 6 July 1985, the ashram was filled with sannyasins from all over the world who were visiting for a festival. Devaraj was sitting cross-legged on the floor of the lecture hall, where sannyasins were dancing to pounding music, when Stork approached, leaned over him and whispered in his ear, at the same time jabbing him in the buttock with a syringe concealed in a handkerchief. Devaraj was able to stagger out of the hall and was rushed to hospital, where he almost died.

At the same time, in an action that would be nicknamed by ashramites as 'God versus the Universe', the ashram filed a suit against the US Attorney General Edwin Meese, Secretary of State George Shultz, the State Department, and the Immigration and Naturalization Service, accusing them of a programme of 'unlawful and intrusive monitoring' and surveillance which violated the ashram residents' constitutional rights. In a statement in *The Rajneesh Times*, Rajneesh lashed out at the government, threatening reprisals if 'any harm' came to the ashram:

> No American embassy all over the world will be left intact. I know also how to deal with these idiots. Our people can also hijack American planes if worst comes to worst. Then no American agency in any country can function. I have enough sannyasins everywhere. So don't be worried about power. No need to be worried.[14]

In the next issue, he declared that his remarks had been 'just a joke'.[15] But the battle lines were drawn.

* * *

On 13 September, in the face of looming legal proceedings against her for immigration fraud, Sheela wrote a letter resigning as Rajneesh's secretary. The final straw was an argument over a particularly expensive wristwatch that Rajneesh insisted he wanted.

The following day, along with three other senior ashram figures and her personal assistant and hairdresser, and leaving behind the diamond wristwatch and expensive Montblanc pen Rajneesh had given her as gifts, Sheela left the ashram for Switzerland, with the parting shot, 'To hell with Bhagwan.' Ten other senior ashram figures followed a few days later. Ma Prem Hasya took over as Rajneesh's secretary.

Two days after Sheela's departure, Rajneesh called a press conference to denounce her and her 'gang of fascists' for a series of crimes, including the attempted poisoning of Devaraj, his dentist and Vivek. He further accused Sheela of financial mismanagement and embezzlement that had left the ashram $55 million in debt. Over the following days he would add to this catalogue of crimes, alleging that Sheela had poisoned the county commissioner Judge William Hulse; plotted to crash a plane loaded with explosives into The Dalles courthouse; created a 'Stalinist' regime in Rajneeshpuram, bugging rooms and telephones—including in Rajneesh's own house; and plotted to kill or incapacitate Rajneesh with poisons prepared in 'a secret tunnel' behind Sheela's house (investigators who searched the 'secret tunnel' later found only a hot tub).

The departure of Sheela prompted a fit of revisionism worthy of Stalinist Russia. Whatever had gone wrong at Rajneeshpuram was all Sheela's fault. The 'religion' of 'Rajneeshism'—devised as a ploy to keep him in the country—was entirely Sheela's invention, and the 'religion's bible', *Rajneeshism: An Introduction to Bhagwan Shree Rajneesh and His Religion*, was, according to Rajneesh, 'not my book. I've never read it. I am not a saviour. I am not a prophet. Nobody has ever been a saviour.'[16] Following Rajneesh's instructions, copies of the 'bible' were ceremonially burned, along with Sheela's robes and belongings, as sannyasins danced around the pyre.

On 26 September, in a bid to purge the last vestiges of 'Rajneeshism', sannyasins were instructed to stop wearing their robes and malas. When they followed his orders, Rajneesh berated them for disloyalty:

You have been clapping because I have dropped red clothes, mala. And when you clap, you don't know how it hurts me. That means you have been a hypocrite! Why have you been wearing red clothes if dropping them brings you so much joy? Why have you been wearing the mala? ...

Now, I have to say one thing more and I would like to see whether you have guts to clap or not: that is, now there is no Buddhafield. So if you want enlightenment, you have to work for it individually, the Buddhafield exists no more. You cannot depend on the energy of the Buddhafield to become enlightened. Now clap as loudly as you can. Clap![17]

The following day he reassured his sannyasins that he could not withdraw the Buddhafield, because he 'loved [them] unconditionally ... It was just to give [them] a shock.'[18]

As the ashram collapsed around him, and in an attempt to curry favour with the authorities and the local community, Rajneesh now encouraged the restoration of Antelope's original name, and offered to sell commune properties back to the original residents. But the net was closing in. In October, an interagency task force of county, state and federal officers moved into the ranch, searching buildings and files and questioning sannyasins, and on 23 October a federal grand jury issued a 35-count indictment charging Rajneesh, Sheela and six others with a conspiracy to evade immigration laws.

Four days later, amid growing fears that he was about to be arrested, Rajneesh fled the ranch with a few senior disciples in two chartered Learjets. He flew to Charlotte, North Carolina, where another jet was waiting to fly him to Bermuda. As the plane waited on the landing strip for permission to take off, police boarded and arrested Rajneesh for attempting to flee prosecution. A search of his belongings revealed $58,522 in cash, thirty-eight watches, and jewellery worth over $1 million.

After a brief sojourn in a county jail and then a federal prison, on 14 November he pleaded guilty to charges dating back to his arrival in America of making false statements to federal officials and concealing his intent to reside in the United States. He received a ten-year suspended sentence, paid a fine of $400,000 and agreed not to return to America for five years without the written permission of the attorney general. The same day, he boarded a plane bound for Delhi.

Meanwhile, in West Germany, police arrested Sheela and two of her group on immigration charges. She was extradited to America, where she subsequently faced charges of wiretapping, attempted murder and conspiracy to commit murder. In 1986, Sheela and two other sannyasins, Ma Anand Puja (who oversaw the commune's medical operations) and Jane Stork (Ma Shanti Bhadra), pleaded guilty to having attempted to murder Devaraj with an injection of adrenalin. Sheela and one other person pleaded guilty to wiretapping, poisoning two state officials and causing the outbreak of salmonella poisoning in The Dalles. Sheela also pleaded guilty to immigration fraud and to setting fire to the Wasco County planning offices. She and Ma Anand Puja were given maximum twenty-year sentences, and Sheela was fined nearly $500,000. Stork was sentenced to ten years for the attempted murder of Devaraj, but was released after serving two years.

A week after Rajneesh's departure, the disciples left in charge of the ranch announced that it would be closing down. The experiment in building a new world was over. Within a few weeks, all but 200 or so sannyasins had left. The ranch and buildings were liquidated. It was reported in *The Oregonian* that an inventory of the items put up for sale included two baby-grand pianos, a $15,000 Weertman cello, a flight simulator and twenty-one Israeli-made Galil assault rifles. The Rolls-Royces were sold to a dealer in Texas.

Sheela later wrote her own account of the Rajneeshpuram debacle, and her relationship with the man she continued to call 'Bhagwan, my eternal lover, king of my heart'. This depicted her as misunderstood; the one devotee who had always remained faithful to his teachings when all others had betrayed them. Her departure from Rajneeshpuram was not a matter of self-interest, she explained. Rather, she had left because she did not wish to be 'pulled into His madness and forsake the values important for me ... I was the heart of the commune and He was the soul, the inspiration. We were a team.' But Rajneesh, she wrote, 'had lost interest in us as a community. I was not prepared to take responsibility for His people and the commune all by myself, alone. I did not have any such ambition. Moreover, I no more wanted to deal with His constant, crazy demands.'[19] She claimed that the allegations concerning the poisoning of 751 people in The Dalles with salmonella bacteria were false—'Such a pointless and heartless action would not have served any purpose'—while the allegation that she had attempted to murder the US Attorney for the District of Oregon, Charles Turner, 'was sickening and went beyond any logical evidence'.[20]

If Rajneesh believed she was guilty of all he had accused her of, why had he not called her to account earlier? 'If He had the impression that we were so evil, why did He let us go in the first place? Why did He not oppose or stop us when we were still there? Why did He not hand us over to the authorities?' she continued.[21]

The autobiography was a work of baffling contradictions. Bhagwan was her love, her dream, her master; yet at the same time he was a ruthless exploiter who had descended into madness:

> In the commune ego was a word to be avoided and detested. Nobody wanted to have anything to do with it, and yet everybody had it. We all tried to hide it. In my opinion all these big words—ego, meditation, enlightenment—were used to camouflage serious emotions and mask exploitation. Everyone was so crazy for enlightenment and so zealously anxious to be without ego and to be meditative that they could do anything for it. The Sannyasins participated in sexual activities, emptied their pockets, and proved their devotion by expensive gifts and the like. The exploitation was dirty, ugly, and repulsive, especially coming from Bhagwan. He totally exploited his people. But with Bhagwan, it was also possible to learn if one was willing and ready. This exploitation was a price that I gladly paid and paid to the fullest extent.[22]

\* \* \*

After a brief stay in India, Rajneesh left once more, spending the next seven months travelling the world in a fruitless attempt to find a country that would allow him to stay and establish a new ashram. In Crete, he was arrested and thrown out after protests from Greek Orthodox bishops. He was declared persona non grata in Switzerland. In England, he did not get past immigration. En route to Antigua, Ireland refused permission for his plane to land for refuelling. He subsequently returned once more to India.

Devotees seized on the enthusiasm of authorities around the world to have nothing to do with Rajneesh as evidence of 'persecution': the dangerous prophet being silenced. It was a sentiment reiterated by Rajneesh himself:

> It has never happened in history that the whole world should be against a single man ... So this is something to rejoice about, that I may be the first man in the whole of history who is being persecuted around the world ...
>
> But this is not bad news, it is good news. It means I have threatened all the powers of the world—religious, political, social. A single man singlehandedly has been able to prove the impotency and poverty of all the great powers, of great theologians, of great organised religions. What more reward can I receive?[23]

It was a statement that may have offered scant consolation to those disciples traumatised by the events of the past few years. But others were there to pick up the pieces. In the spring of 1986, Swami Teertha and other head therapists from Rajneeshpuram established the International Academy of Meditation in Sicily. Teertha embarked on a tour of the disintegrating ashrams around Europe and America, drumming up business for his new project and pressing his own claims to be an enlightened master. Michael Barnett founded an enterprise called the MB Energy University in Zurich, advertising Zen courses specifically designed for disillusioned sannyasins.

In 1986, *The Rajneesh Times* ran an article entitled 'The Therapists Controversy', reporting Teertha as saying

> he'd played the master-disciple game long enough; that Bhagwan was exploiting sannyasins and that he left them in financial misery; that he appreciated Bhagwan's silence, but did not want to be involved with His actions; that he was on the same level as Bhagwan and was happy doing his own thing.

Rajneesh responded in a statement issued by Ma Prem Hasya, instructing sannyasins not to participate in any of the therapy groups conducted by 'anybody who has betrayed Bhagwan'. Teertha, he went on,

> has never been a disciple, but only a politician hoping to succeed Bhagwan. As far as his therapy is concerned, it is nothing but a mind game. Bhagwan has allowed these phony people as therapists to clean the minds of those who have never known the art of meditation. But now that the therapists will not be doing their therapies in the context of a master and meditation, they can prove immensely dangerous.

The therapists, he warned, were 'full of mental problems. The rate of suicide and madness in therapists has risen; it was twice as much as other professions, now it is thrice.'[24]

Teertha would subsequently drop his sannyasin name and his Indian robes and return to being plain Paul Lowe. He set up as a life coach, conducting seminars and retreats preaching the therapeutic benefits of sexual freedom. In 2008, the London *Sunday Times* reported on a ten-day residential retreat conducted by Lowe, which he described as 'the most radical self-help workshop in the world' and which advocated sexual freedom as a path to self-realisation. Among the various techniques employed at the workshop, participants were encouraged to voice compliments to each other, such as, 'you make my vagina tingle'.[25]

After his enforced travels around the world, Rajneesh eventually returned to his original ashram in Poona. In January 1989 he dropped the title 'Bhagwan', and a few months later the name 'Rajneesh', instead calling himself 'Osho'—a Japanese term meaning a high-ranking or highly virtuous Buddhist monk. He died on 19 January 1990, his body weakened, disciples claimed, by radiation poisoning administered while he was in prison in America.

Thirty-three years after his death, the Rajneesh ashram in Poona now describes itself as 'a meditation resort', offering visitors 'Zen style air-conditioned rooms', gym, sauna, Jacuzzi and other diversions and comforts. A variety of different meditation techniques are offered under the branding of 'OSHO Active Meditations™'. Nowhere in any of the organisation's literature is there any mention of Bhagwan, Rajneesh, Rajneeshpuram, diamond watches, Rolls-Royces ... It is as if the past had never happened.

In a sense Rajneesh was the last great guru—the collapse of his dream of creating heaven on earth marked the final pangs of the Western dream of India as the repository of esoteric wisdom and the promise of enlightenment. There would be other gurus, other followers, other seekers, other saints—and other charlatans. And there will be others to come. But fewer perhaps.

In Oregon, the ranch where Rajneesh planned his new world for 'the New Man' was sold to a wealthy Montana rancher. He later turned it into a camp for Young Life, a Christian youth organisation. In Antelope, at the base of the flagpole outside the Post Office, flying the Stars and Stripes, there is now a commemorative plaque memorialising the tumultuous period when the small community became Rajneeshpuram. It reads: 'Dedicated to those of this community who throughout the Rajneesh invasion and occupation of 1981–1985 remained, resisted, and remembered ...' At the bottom is a quotation from Edmund Burke: 'The only thing necessary for the triumph of evil is for good men to do nothing.'

'We made a mess of it, but we did our best,' Christine Ryder told me, sitting in her flat under the implacable gaze of the Buddha statue. She went on:

> I hold huge remorse for anybody that was harmed by this experiment, within the community and outside of it. It certainly was nobody's intention. But I also think we're pretty lucky if we manage to go through life without causing harm at any time in our lives. And we tried to do

something extraordinary that impacted many, many people in many ways, that was crazy and wonderful.

She paused for a moment, lost in thought. 'Most of the people I know,' she said at last, 'wouldn't have missed the experience for anything.'[26]

# NOTES

## 1. THE LIGHT OF ASIA

1. Emerson Arnold, 'Author of "The Light of Asia", Edwin Arnold', *Buddhism in England* (July/August 1932).
2. From the late 1870s, women were able to attend lectures and take examinations and gain honours in those examinations at Oxford colleges. They were, however, unable to receive the degree to which their examinations would have entitled them had they been men. The new University statute of 1920 admitted women to full membership of the University, and enabled women who had previously taken and gained honours in University examinations to return to matriculate (i.e. go through the formal ceremony of admission to the University) and have the degree to which they were now entitled conferred on them, again at a formal ceremony. Consequently, at the very first ceremony at which women were able to graduate, more than forty women did so.
3. Edwin Arnold, trans., Preface to *The Book of Good Counsels: From the Sanskrit of the Hitopadésa* (London: Smith, Elder, 1861).
4. Emerson Arnold, 'Edwin Arnold'.
5. Quoted in Francis Wheen, *Karl Marx* (London: HarperCollins, 1999).
6. George Augustus Sala, *The Life and Adventures of George Augustus Sala* (London: Cassell & Co., 1896).
7. Lord Burnham, *Peterborough Court: The Story of The Daily Telegraph* (London: Cassell & Co., 1955).
8. Emerson Arnold, 'Edwin Arnold'.
9. Sir Edwin Arnold, *The Light of Asia* (London: Kegan Paul, Trübner & Co., 1902).
10. The film *Prem Sanyas* (*The Light of Asia*) was made in 1925 and directed by Himanshu Rai and Franz Osten.
11. Cited in Philip Almond, *The British Discovery of Buddhism* (Cambridge University Press, 1988).
12. Quoted in Kim Knott, *Hinduism: A Very Short Introduction* (Oxford University Press, 2000).
13. Quoted in P. J. Marshall, ed., *The British Discovery of Hinduism in the Eighteenth Century* (Cambridge University Press, 2009).
14. Ibid.
15. Ibid.

16. Ibid.

17. Ibid.

18. *Monthly Review* (1785), quoted in Mishka Sinha, 'Corrigibility, Allegory, Universality: A History of the Gita's Transnational Reception, 1785–1945', *Modern Intellectual History* 7.2 (2010).

19. Emerson did more than anybody in America to embrace and promulgate Hindu philosophy, informing his readers about a school of philosophy that held that 'what we call Nature, the external world, has no real existence—is only phenomenal. Youth, age, property, conditions, events, persons—self, even—are successive *maias* (deceptions) through which Vishnu mocks and instructs the soul.'

20. Mr Roy, Asiatic Society secretary, interview with the author, 27 November 2018.

21. Sir William Jones, 'The Third Anniversary Discourse, on the Hindus', Asiatick Society, 2 February 1786, in *Sir William Jones: Selected Poetical and Prose Works*, ed. M. J. Franklin (Cardiff: University of Wales Press, 1996).

22. Marshall, *The British Discovery of Hinduism*.

23. 'Minute by the Hon'ble T. B. Macaulay', 2 February 1835, http://www.columbia.edu/itc/mealac/pritchett/00generallinks/macaulay/txt_minute_education_1835.html.

24. Thomas R. Trautmann, *Aryans and British India* (Oakland: University of California Press, 1977).

25. G. R. Welbon, *The Buddhist Nirvana and its Western Interpreters* (University of Chicago Press, 1968).

26. Ieuan P. Ellis, 'The Intellectual Challenge to "Official Religion"', in *The British: Their Religious Beliefs and Practices, 1800–1986*, ed. Terence Thomas (London and New York: Routledge, 1988, 2017).

27. Quoted in Michael J. Dodds, *Unlocking Divine Action: Contemporary Science and Thomas Aquinas* (Washington, DC: University of America Press, 2012).

28. Quoted in Donald S. Lopez, *From Stone to Flesh: A Short History of the Buddha* (University of Chicago Press, 2013).

29. Quoted in Elizabeth Puttock, '"Why has Boddhidharma Left for the West?" The Growth and Appeal of Buddhism in Britain', *Religion Today* 8.2 (1983).

30. F. Max Müller, *India: What Can It Teach Us?* (New York: Funk & Wagnalls, 1882), https://www.gutenberg.org/files/20847/20847-h/20847-h.htm.

31. *Funny Folks*, 3 June 1882.

32. Quoted in Brooks Wright, *Interpreter of Buddhism to the West: Sir Edwin Arnold* (New York: Bookman Associates, 1957).

33. Sir Edwin Arnold, *The Light of Asia*.

34. Sir Edwin Arnold, *Seas and Lands* (London: Longmans, Green, & Co., 1891).

35. Quoted in Sinha, 'Corrigibility, Allegory, Universality'.

36. *Birmingham Daily Post*, 13 November 1885, quoted in Sinha, 'Corrigibility, Allegory, Universality'.

37. Emerson Arnold, 'Edwin Arnold'.

38. Ibid.

39. Quoted in Charles Allen, *The Buddha and the Sahibs* (London: John Murray, 2003).

40. Sir Edwin Arnold, *Seas and Lands*.

41. Four years before Arnold's arrival in Ceylon, Panadura had been the site of a famous debate between the Buddhist scholar and orator Migettuwatte Gunananda Thera, described as 'the boldest, most brilliant and most powerful champion of Sinhalese Buddhism', and a Christian missionary, Father David de Silva, which had proved an important foundation stone in the revival of Buddhism in Ceylon.

42. Sir Edwin Arnold, *Seas and Lands*.

43. *San Francisco Call*, 25 March 1904.

44. Sir Edwin Arnold, *Seas and Lands*.

## 2.　THE SWAMI COMES WEST

1. Swami Vivekananda, 'At the World's Parliament of Religions, Chicago, 11 September 1893', https://www.swamivivekananda.guru/1893/09/11/response-to-welcome/.

2. See https://www.swamivivekananda.guru/2017/05/07/annie-besant/.

3. Quoted in Gopal Stavig, *Western Admirers of Ramakrishna and his Disciples* (Kolkata: Vedanta Press/Advaita Ashrama, 2011).

4. *The Civil and Military Gazette*, Lahore, May 1895.

5. *The Civil and Military Gazette*, Lahore, 23 April 1895.

6. 'A March through the Cow-Rioting Districts', *Pioneer*, Allahabad, 7 February 1894.

7. Swami Nikhilananda, *Vivekananda: A Biography* (New York: Ramakrishna-Vivekananda Center, 1953).

8. Hastie was undoubtedly one of the first Westerners to take note of Ramakrishna, but the first writing about Ramakrishna to appear in the West was a sketch by the Orientalist scholar Max Müller in the magazine *The Nineteenth Century* in 1896, based on Müller's conversations with Vivekananda, who visited Müller's Oxford home that year. 'The visit was really a revelation to me,' Vivekananda wrote, 'That nice little house in its setting of a beautiful garden, the silver headed sage, with a face calm and benign, and forehead smooth as a child's in spite of seventy winters, and every line in that face speaking of a deep-seated mine of spirituality somewhere behind.' Müller's book *Ramakrishna: His Life and Sayings*, to which Vivekananda supplied biographical material, was published in 1899. http://www.ramakrishnavivekananda.info/vivekananda/volume_4/writings_prose/on_professor_max_muller.htm.

9. Quoted in 'The Parliament of Religions', http://www.ramakrishnavivekananda.info/vivekananda_biography/07_the_parliament.htm.

10. From 'The Influence of Indian Spiritual Thought in India', a speech given at the Star Theatre, Calcutta, 11 March 1898.

11. Quoted in Narasingha Prosid Sil, *Swami Vivekananda: A Reassessment* (Selinsgrove, PA: Susquehanna University Press, 1997).

12. Quoted in Parama Roy, *Indian Traffic: Identities in Question in Colonial and Postcolonial India* (Oakland: University of California Press, 1998).

13. Letter to Josephine MacLeod, 2 September 1902, http://www.ramakrishnavivekananda.info/reminiscences/358_skb.htm.

14. The original 1832 pamphlet was published under the title *Fruits of Philosophy, or the Private Companion of Young Married People*.

15. Michael Holroyd, *Bernard Shaw* (London: Chatto & Windus, 1997).

16. Objects as set out in 1905 at Chennai. See https://www.ts-adyar.org/content/mission-objects-and-freedom.

17. Quoted in Harry Oldmeadow, *Journeys East: 20th Century Western Encounters with Eastern Religious Traditions* (Bloomington, IN: World Wisdom Books, 2004).

18. Edward Carpenter, *My Days and Dreams: Being Autobiographical Notes* (London: G. Allen & Unwin, 1916).

19. Mohandas K. Gandhi, *An Autobiography* (Boston: Beacon Press, 1957).

20. Max Müller, 'Esoteric Buddhism', *The Nineteenth Century* (May 1893).

21. Quoted in Theodore Besterman, *Mrs Annie Besant: A Modern Prophet* (London: Kegan Paul, Trench, Trübner & Co., 1934).

22. The wayward curate was initiated into the Theosophical Society at the same time as the physicist and chemist William Crookes, the discoverer of the element thallium and the inventor of the radiometer. Crookes was also a believer in spiritualism, a noted investigator of psychical phenomena and a member of the occult group, the Hermetic Order of the Golden Dawn.

23. *The New Zealand Craftsman and Masonic Review* 1.11 (March 1885), http://nzetc.victoria.ac.nz/tm/scholarly/tei-Stout14-t9-body-d15.html.

24. Quoted in Gregory Tillett, *The Elder Brother: A Biography of Charles Webster Leadbeater* (London: Routledge, 2015).

25. The Akashic records were an invention of Theosophy, deriving from *akasha* or *ākāśa*, the Sanskrit word for 'sky', 'space', 'luminous' or 'aether'. Madame Blavatsky described the *akasha* as a sort of life force, and referred to 'indestructible tablets of the astral light' that recorded both the past and future of human thought and action, but she did not use the term 'akashic'. The term 'akashic record' is attributed to the Theosophist Alfred Sinnett, who, in his book *Esoteric Buddhism* (1884), wrote of a Buddhist belief in 'a permanency of records in the Akasa' and 'the potential capacity of man to read the same'.

26. Charles Leadbeater, *How Theosophy Came to Me* (Adyar, India: Theosophical Publishing House, 1930).

27. Holroyd, *Bernard Shaw*.

28. Quoted in Tillett, *The Elder Brother*.

29. Mary Lutyens, *Krishnamurti: The Years of Awakening* (London: John Murray, 1975).

30. P. G. Wodehouse did not much share his brother's enthusiasm for the mystic East or esoteric philosophy. In his comic short story, 'Leave it to Jeeves', published in the collection *My Man Jeeves* (1919), the bumbling Bertie Wooster likens his butler Jeeves' ability to materialise in a room when needed to 'one of those weird chappies in India who dissolve themselves into thin air and nip through space in a sort of disembodied way and assemble the parts again just where they want them. I've got a cousin who's what they call a Theosophist, and he says he's often nearly worked

the thing himself but couldn't quite bring it off, probably owing to having fed in his boyhood on the flesh of animals slain in anger and pie.'

31.  Emily Lutyens, *Candles in the Sun* (London: Rupert Hart-Davis, 1957).

3.   LADY EMILY'S DILEMMA

1.   Jane Ridley, *Edwin Lutyens: His Life, His Wife, His Work* (London: Pimlico, 2003).
2.   E. Lutyens, *Candles in the Sun*.
3.   Ridley, *Edwin Lutyens*.
4.   E. Lutyens, *Candles in the Sun*.
5.   Ibid.
6.   Ridley, *Edwin Lutyens*.
7.   Annie Besant, *London Lectures of 1907* (CreateSpace Independent Publishing Platform, 2015).
8.   E. Lutyens, *Candles in the Sun*.
9.   Ibid.
10.  The promotion of Krishnamurti as the putative World Teacher caused deep divisions within Theosophy, leading the German branch under Rudolf Steiner to break away altogether.
11.  M. Lutyens, *Krishnamurti*.
12.  E. Lutyens, *Candles in the Sun*.
13.  Ibid.
14.  Ridley, *Edwin Lutyens*.
15.  E. Lutyens, *Candles in the Sun*.
16.  Ibid.
17.  Quoted in ibid.
18.  Ridley, *Edwin Lutyens*.
19.  Clayre Percy and Jane Ridley, eds., *The Letters of Edwin Lutyens to his Wife, Lady Emily* (London: Hamish Hamilton, 1988).
20.  Ibid.
21.  E. Lutyens, *Candles in the Sun*.
22.  Quoted in Peter Washington, *Madame Blavatsky's Baboon* (New York: Schocken Books, 1996).
23.  Quoted in M. Lutyens, *Krishnamurti*.
24.  In the 1960s, Baron Philip's descendant Frederik van Pallandt, performing as one half of the popular folk singing duo Nina & Frederik, would enjoy hits with the Christmas songs 'Mary's Boy Child' and 'Little Donkey'. He was subsequently arrested on drugs charges and later shot dead. The last Theosophical Camp was held at Ommen in 1938. Following the German invasion of Holland, the site became a concentration camp.
25.  Rom Landau, *God is My Adventure* (London: Faber & Faber, 1943), https://archive. org/details/godismyadventure032951mbp/page/n114/mode/1up.
26.  E. F. Benson, *Queen Lucia* (London: Hutchinson, 1920). Benson was one of the four sons of Edward White Benson, the Archbishop of Canterbury from 1883. Like his

brothers, Benson was homosexual; his friend, the novelist Somerset Maugham, described him as 'not an obtrusively masculine sort of person'. Benson was a prolific and highly popular author of the day. His other accomplishments included composing the words to the song 'Land of Hope and Glory'. Benson had himself visited India in 1912 to join his friend Francis Yeats-Brown, an officer in the British Indian Army and an avid practitioner of yoga, who would later write an acclaimed memoir, *The Lives of a Bengal Lancer* (1930). Benson's stay was brief; he was taken ill shortly after his arrival and returned to England.

27. M. Lutyens, *Krishnamurti*.
28. Quoted in Roland Vernon, *Star in the East: Krishnamurti the Invention of a Messiah* (London: Constable, 2000).
29. M. Lutyens, *Krishnamurti*.
30. E. Lutyens, *Candles in the Sun*.
31. Ibid.
32. M. Lutyens, *Krishnamurti*.
33. E. Lutyens, *Candles in the Sun*.
34. Ibid.
35. Ibid.
36. Ibid.
37. Ibid.
38. M. Lutyens, *Krishnamurti*.
39. Ibid.
40. Ibid.

4. THE BHIKKU AND THE BEAST

1. Paul Brunton, 'Bhikku Ananda Metteyya: A Pioneer Western Buddhist', *Ceylon Daily News*, May 1941.
2. Aleister Crowley, *The Confessions of Aleister Crowley* (London: Arkana, 1989).
3. Ibid.
4. Elizabeth J. Harris, *Ananda Metteyya: The First British Emissary of Buddhism* (Kandy, Sri Lanka: Buddhist Publication Society, 1998).
5. John L. Crow, *The White Knight in the Yellow Robe: Allan Bennett's Search for Truth*, MA Thesis, University of Amsterdam, 2009.
6. It is highly likely the Order was founded on the basis of a fraud. According to William Wynn Westcott, in decoding the manuscripts he discovered the address of an elderly lady named Fraulein Anna Sprengel, or Sapiens Dominabitur Astins, as Westcott called her—an adept within a German Rosicrucian group and a member of the mystical hierarchy of so-called Secret Chiefs. In fact, Sprengel seems to have been a figment of Westcott's imagination. Giving the mythical Fraulein an accommodation address in Germany, Westcott arranged for the forgery of five letters ostensibly sent from Sprengel, among them one conferring the honorary grades of Adeptus Exemptus on Westcott and his two fellow members of the Societas Rosicruciana, Samuel Mathers and William Woodman, along with a

charter to found a Golden Dawn temple in which to practise the rituals outlined in the cipher manuscripts.

Westcott was a member of the Quatuor Coronati Masonic lodge, which also numbered among its members Adolphus Woodward and Sir Walter Besant, whose brother Frank was the husband of Annie Besant. Another lodge member was Sir Charles Warren, the Commissioner of the Metropolitan Police, who conspicuously failed to apprehend the serial killer known as Jack the Ripper, who mounted a reign of terror in the East End of London in 1888, murdering at least five women. The filmmaker and author Bruce Robinson speculates in his book, *They All Love Jack* (2015), that Warren knew the killer was a Freemason (named Michael Maybrick) and that as a Freemason himself, Warren deliberately obstructed the enquiry.

7.  In Paris, Mathers cemented his own links with 'the Secret Chiefs', while remaining distinctly coy about their identities. 'I can tell you nothing,' he wrote, 'I know not even their earthly names. I know them only by certain mottoes. I have but very rarely seen them in the physical body; and on such rare occasions the rendezvous was made astrally by them at the time and place which had been astrally appointed beforehand.' He was, however, able to describe the experience of encountering one of them: 'The sensation was one of being in contact with so terrible a force that I can only compare it to the *continued* effect of that usually experienced momentarily by a person *close* to whom a flash of lightning passes during a violent storm; coupled with the difficulty in respiration similar to the half-strangling effect produced by ether.' See S. L. MacGregor Mathers, *Mathers Manifesto* (1896), https://www.scribd.com/doc/160787911/Mathers-manifesto.

8.  Crowley, *The Confessions*.

9.  W. B. Yeats, in his book *Autobiographies* (1955), describes visiting Mathers and his wife and playing Enochian chess, ostensibly based on an Indian board game called chaturanga. Enochian chess required four players, so while Yeats partnered with Moina, Mathers would take as his partner an invisible spirit: 'Mathers would shade his eyes with his hands and gaze at the empty chair at the opposite corner of the board before moving his partner's piece.' Alas, Yeats did not record who won these contests.

10. Brunton, 'Bhikku Ananda Metteyya'.

11. Crow, *The White Knight in the Yellow Robe*. 'MacGregor' was a name adopted or bestowed on several members of the Golden Dawn. Mathers' wife took to signing her illustrations as 'M. Bergson MacGregor', and Aleister Crowley claimed that Mathers had bestowed the name on him to establish 'an astral link'. Mathers died in Paris in 1919. An obituary published in *The Occult Review* noted that 'Amidst many weaknesses he possessed of course his good points, a certain sincerity in his occultism—amidst several queer devices—and a considerable fund of undigested learning.'

12. Initiation into the Order included a ceremony involving the candidate being led from darkness into light, and undertaking 'to prosecute with zeal the study of the occult sciences, seeing that this Order is not established for the benefit of those who desire only superficial knowledge thereof'. In time, the initiate would progress to

the Inner Order of the Rose of Ruby and the Cross of Gold, vowing to 'purify and exalt my Spiritual nature, that with the Divine aid, I may at length attain to be more than human, and thus gradually raise and unite myself to my Higher and Divine Genius and that in this event I will not abuse the Great Power Entrusted to me'. As the writer Gerald Yorke pointed out, the hazard in these vows was that unless specific precautions were taken, the initiate might well begin to imagine that being 'more than human' was tantamount to declaring that rather than being a servant of God, the initiate was God himself.

13. Aleister Crowley, 'My Wanderings in Search of the Absolute', *The Sunday Referee*, 10 March 1935.

14. Crowley, *The Confessions*.

15. Among the practices that would have occupied Bennett was Enochian magic, as devised by the Elizabethan astrologer John Dee and his assistant Edward Kelly to contact angels. These include 'The Magical Invocation of the Higher Genius' and 'The Ritual for the Evocation unto Visible Appearance of the Great Spirit Taphthartharath', a ritual that Bennett wrote at the request of another Golden Dawn member, Florence Farr. Among Bennett's correspondence one finds a fascinating shopping list for some of the ingredients necessary for the ritual: 'Ammoniacum, two ozs; Coriander seed. About 1/2lb of spermaceti [a wax present in the head cavities of the sperm whale] … as I find I shall have to make a great Magic Candle to give light to read by. Also we shall need about a pint of olive oil.' Letter in Gerald Yorke Collection, Warburg Institute, University of London (Yorke Collection hereafter cited as GYC).

16. Crowley, *The Confessions*.

17. Ibid.

18. Kenneth Grant, *The Magical Revival* (London: Starfire Publishing Ltd, 2015).

19. Godfrey is described as twenty-three, a bachelor and professional agent, of 39 Cedars Terrace, Queen's Road, Battersea. At the same time Allan Bennett was living at 42 Dorothy Road, Clapham, SW11, in a row of modest terraced houses—a short walk from Cedars Terrace. Was Bennett living with his sister, perhaps?

20. Undated letter (GYC). There is no evidence that Bennett ever found work teaching.

21. Letter from Charlotte Bennett (GYC).

22. Crowley, *The Confessions*. According to John Crow in *The White Knight in the Yellow Robe*, Goetia means 'howling', but is also the technical word employed to cover all the operations of Magic that deal with gross, malignant or unenlightened forces, purportedly used by the biblical King Solomon to build the first temple in Jerusalem.

23. Aleister Crowley, 'At the Fork of the Roads', *The Equinox* 1.1 (1909).

24. Crowley, *The Confessions*. Spelling 'Magick', with a 'k' was Crowley's affectation.

25. http://www.hermetics.org/pdf/magick_revival.pdf.

26. C. R. Cammell, *Aleister Crowley: The Black Magician* (London: Richards Press, 1951).

27. Crowley, *The Confessions*.

28. Ibid.

29. Ibid.

30.  Cammell, *Aleister Crowley*.

31.  Letter from Aleister Crowley (GYC).

32.  Letter from Edward Bryant to John Symons (GYC).

33.  Letter from Aleister Crowley to Gerald Festus Kelly (GYC).

34.  Crowley, *The Confessions*.

35.  Ibid.

36.  Aleister Crowley, 'Duty: A Note on the Chief Rules of Practical Conduct to be Observed by Those who Accept the Law of Thelma', https://lib.oto-usa.org/crowley/essays/duty.html.

37.  Clifford Bax, *Inland Far* (London: Lovat Dickson, 1933). Crowley continued to correspond with Bax. A year later he wrote to him from Hong Kong, advising that 'by rights you should get ordeals and initiations and things', but that a really good student could 'make it all up himself', and that if he had the 'wit to interpret alright' he had no need of a teacher: 'One should work as if one had omnipotence at one's command and eternity at one's disposal', he urged, adding that one should resolve 'to interpret everything in life as a spiritual fact, a step on the Path, a guide to the Light' (ibid.).

38.  Roger Hutchinson, *Aleister Crowley: The Beast Demystified* (Edinburgh: Mainstream Publishing, 2016).

39.  [Allan Bennett], 'The Miraculous Element in Buddhism', *Buddhist Review* 11 (Buddhist Society of Great Britain and Ireland, July 1920).

40.  Ibid.

41.  Ibid.

42.  Ibid.

43.  Crowley, *The Confessions*.

44.  Crow, *The White Knight in the Yellow Robe*.

45.  [Allan Bennett], 'On Devotion in Buddhism', *Buddhist Review* 2 (n.d.), pp. 11–30.

46.  Crow, *The White Knight in the Yellow Robe*.

47.  Ibid.

48.  Ibid.

49.  'English Buddhist: A MacGregor Who is Not a Scot: A Strange Incident', *The Dundee Evening Telegraph & Post*, 23 April 1908, https://www.100thmonkeypress.com/biblio/acrowley/articles/1908_04_23_dundee_evening_telegraph.pdf.

50.  'Scotchman as Buddhist Monk', *The Taranaki Herald*, 12 June 1908, p. 8. The Scottish accent seems to have been imagined by the reporter, no doubt suggested by Bennett apparently being introduced as 'Allan Bennett MacGregor'—his homage to his old mentor Mathers. There are no accounts elsewhere of Bennett speaking with a Scottish accent, and as an Englishman it would have been surprising if he had done so. Confusingly, one report also described Bennett as 'a graduate of Cambridge University', although there is no record of him having ever attended Cambridge, or any other university.

51.  *Ashburton Guardian*, 29 June 1908.

52.  'Scotchman as Buddhist Monk', *The Taranaki Herald*, 12 June 1908, p. 8.

53.  Letter from Edward Bryant to John Symons (GYC).

54. [Allan Bennett], 'Followers of the Buddha', *Buddhist Review* 1 (c.1908).

55. Quoted in Christmas Humphreys, ed., *A Buddhist Students' Manual* (London: The Buddhist Society, 1956).

56. Reid's non-conformist spirit lived on in his great-nephew, the artist Jamie Reid, who provided the graphic images for the Sex Pistols.

57. The latter was a reference to the Fellowship of the New Life, whose members included Havelock Ellis and Edward Carpenter, which was dedicated to the cultivation of 'a perfect character in each and all' through a regimen of simple living, vegetarianism and pacifism. The Fellowship of the New Life would subsequently give rise to the socialist Fabian movement.

58. Crow, *The White Knight in the Yellow Robe*.

59. Letter to MacGregor Reid (GYC).

60. Ibid.

61. Letter from Ethel Powell-Brown to Gerald Yorke (GYC); also adapted and published under the name Rhona Galley in *The Westminster Gazette*, 1952.

62. Crowley, typically perverse, later maintained he was working on behalf of British intelligence.

63. Bax, *Inland Far*.

64. Ibid.

65. Ibid.

66. Ibid.

67. Brunton, 'Bhikku Ananda Metteyya'.

68. Ibid.

69. Bax, *Inland Far*.

70. Gerald Yorke, *Aleister Crowley, the Golden Dawn and Buddhism: Reminiscences and Writings of Gerald Yorke* (New York: Teitan Press, 2001).

71. Letter from Edward Bryant to John Symonds (GYC).

72. Quoted in Humphreys, *A Buddhist Students' Manual*.

73. Letter from Edward Bryant to John Symonds (GYC).

74. Crowley, *The Confessions*.

5.   HYMAN, THE BOOTMAKER'S SON

1. Paul Brunton, *The Hidden Teaching Beyond Yoga* (London: Rider & Co., 1969).

2. Paul Brunton, *The Notebooks of Paul Brunton*, 16 vols. (Burdett, NY: Paul Brunton Philosophic Foundation/Larson Publications, 1987).

3. Ibid.

4. Kenneth Thurston Hurst, *Paul Brunton: A Personal View* (Burdett, NY: Paul Brunton Philosophic Foundation/Larson Publications, 1989).

5. Ibid.

6. Ibid.

7. Michael Juste [Michael Houghton], *The White Brother: An Occult Autobiography* (London: Rider & Co., 1927).

8. Ibid.

9.   G. E. O. Knight, *Intimate Glimpses of Mysterious Tibet and Neighbouring Countries* (Delhi: Pilgrims Book, Pvt Ltd, 1930).

10.  Ibid.

11.  F. M. Bailey, Report to Foreign and Political Department, Simla, 22 September 1922.

12.  Knight, *Intimate Glimpses of Mysterious Tibet*.

13.  Ibid.

14.  Ibid.

15.  Ibid. Knight's book is one of the most diverting and entertaining travel accounts of the period and region, not least for its laconic tone of voice.

16.  F. M. Bailey, Report to Foreign and Political Dept., Simla, March 1923.

17.  J. E. Ellam, in *The Darjeeling Advertiser*, 21 March 1923.

18.  William McGovern, *To Lhasa in Disguise: A Secret Expedition through Mysterious Tibet* (New York and London: Century Co., 1924).

19.  Ibid.

20.  Major F. M. Bailey, letter to India Office, Gangtok, Sikkim, 28 October 1924.

21.  Bhikku Prajnananda, *Buddhism in England* 5.3 (1930).

22.  Ibid.

23.  Bhikku Prajnananda, *Buddhism in England* 3.8 (1929).

24.  Paul Brunton, *A Search in Secret India* (London: Rider & Co., 1934).

25.  Meher means 'kindess' in Hindi, or in Persian, 'sun'.

26.  C. B. Purdom, *The God-Man: The Life, Journeys and Works of Meher Baba* (London: G. Allen & Unwin, 1964).

27.  Ibid.

28.  Ibid.

29.  Ibid.

30.  On 18 June 1927, Meher prophesied 'There will be a terrible war in the future, and it will be more destructive and horrible than the last one. America will play the most important role in it. Millions will die, and the war will be so horrendous that there will not even be time to dispose of the heaps of corpses. It will be then that I manifest myself as the Avatar.' See http://www.meherbabadnyana.net/life_eternal/Book_Two/2_America.htm. On 28 May 1930, he reiterated that

> A great war will break out and rage between the Western countries—Russia, America, England, Italy, Germany and others. There will be such chaos and confusion throughout the world that not one leader will understand what to do. And out of this confusion and chaos, the Avatar will appear, to guide misguided humanity onto the path of peace and prosperity—toward eternal bliss. But that will take time and require great upheavals throughout the world. These disorders, disturbances and unrest are necessary to make the world turn its face toward spirituality, and ensure its future salvation.

See http://www.meherbabadnyana.net/life_eternal/Book_One/Coming_Attractions_1.htm.

31.  D. H. Lawrence, 3 September 1917, in *The Letters of D. H. Lawrence*, Vol. 3: *October 1916–June 1921*, ed. J. T. Boulton and A. Robertson (Cambridge University Press,

1984). Starr had staged a concert in St Ives in aid of the Red Cross, which led local residents to complain of 'buffoonery'. Starr replied with an apology, but then followed with a second letter attempting to justify the buffoonery, in which he named Aleister Crowley as 'by far the greatest living artist in England', and cited Augustus John and D. H. Lawrence, 'the celebrated author', as believing that 'ninety-nine percent of British art is worse than buffoonery'.

32. Raphael Hurst [Paul Brunton], 'The Meher League in England', *The Meher Gazette* 1.2 (August 1930).

33. Brunton, *A Search in Secret India*.

34. Meher Baba's prophecy of the date of his death was not far off. He died in January 1969 at the age of seventy-four—not at the hand of Parsees but peacefully.

35. *The Meher Gazette*, March 1931. The same issue took note of Meredith Starr founding his retreat in Devon, dedicated to Meher, quoting a letter from Starr which claimed that 'the power of love is so strong that many visitors have broken down in tears on the second or third day'.

36. Avatar Meher Trust, digital library, https://avatarmeherbabatrust.org/online-library-2/.

37. Brunton, *A Search in Secret India*.

38. Ibid.

39. Purdom, *The God-Man*.

40. *A Search in Secret India* was published in 1934 with an introduction by Sir Francis Younghusband. The leader of the British expedition to Tibet in 1903–4, Younghusband had himself become something of a latter-day mystic, cultivating a belief in telepathy and the existence of a Messiah-like 'world leader' transmitting spiritual guidance by means of telepathy from his home on the planet 'Altair'.

Brunton would write in his *Notebooks* how Younghusband had once told him of an encounter while travelling in the Gobi Desert with 'a strange Mongolian,' who 'without uttering a single word aloud, purely by telepathic contact, had powerfully influenced his mind and given it a greatly broader outlook'. Many years later, Brunton claimed that he had met this same man, then living in exile in Cambodia, and wrote that 'Through the services of an educated Chinese disciple who was with him, we were able to converse about Buddhism and other matters.' The mysterious Mongolian gave Brunton a teaching which, he wrote, 'formed the basis of mentalism and was occasionally so subtle it went above my head, but which I understood sufficiently to revolutionize my outlook', and which he subsequently incorporated into his books *The Hidden Teaching Beyond Yoga* (1941) and *The Wisdom of the Overself* (1943). Given that Younghusband apparently made no mention of the name of his mysterious Mongolian, the mind boggles at the marvellous twist of fate that delivered him to Brunton some years later, and 1,000 miles away (Brunton, *The Notebooks*, chapter 15, 'The Orient'. © Copyright 1984–1989, The Paul Brunton Philosophic Foundation).

## 6.  MEHER BABA COMES TO THE WEST

1.  Ibid.

2.  Bhau Kalchuri, *Lord Meher: The Biography of the Avatar of the Age, Meher Baba.* 14 vols., 1998, https://www.lordmeher.org/rev/index.jsp.

3.  Delia De Leon, 'The English Scene, Early and Late', *The Awakener* 17.2 (1977).

4.  Filis Frederick, 'Heroines of the Path: Baba's Work with Women in the West', *The Awakener* 20.2 (1983).

5.  Ibid.

6.  Kalchuri, *Lord Meher.*

7.  Ibid.

8.  Christmas Humphreys, *Both Sides of the Circle: The Autobiography* (London: G. Allen & Unwin, 1978).

9.  Quoted in Kevin R. D. Shepherd, *Meher Baba: An Iranian Liberal* (Cambridge: Anthropographia Publications, 1988).

10.  Frederick, 'Heroines of the Path', pp. 43–5.

11.  Kalchuri, *Lord Meher.*

12.  Ibid.

13.  Ibid.

14.  Jean Adriel, *Avatar: The Life Story of the Perfect Master Meher Baba: A Narrative of Spiritual Experience* (Santa Barbara, CA: J. F. Rowny Press, 1947).

15.  Ibid.

16.  Quoted in Bal Natu, *Glimpses of the God-Man* (Myrtle Beach, SC: Sheriar Foundation, 1987).

17.  *The Awakener* 18.1 (1978).

18.  Adriel, *Avatar.*

19.  Kalchuri, *Lord Meher.*

20.  Ibid.

21.  Among the visitors at Harmon was a man named Max Wardell, an erstwhile Theosophist who had spent time with Krishnamurti, Annie Besant and Charles Leadbeater at Adyar. When Wardell asked Meher Baba for his opinion on Krishnamurti, Baba replied that Krishnamurti was 'not as advanced as some think. He does good and will come to me one day. I will help him advance on the path' (Kalchuri, *Lord Meher*, p. 1469). Malcolm Sloss later wrote to Krishnamurti suggesting that he should correspond with Meher Baba, with a view to the two men meeting. But Krishnamurti rebuffed the suggestion: 'I hope you understand that it is not rudeness on my part not to correspond with him, but I really have nothing to say.' Meher Baba offered a further comment, that while Krishnamurti was 'on the right path' he would not 'fulfill himself or become truly great as long as he does not come to visit me'. The two men never met (Kalchuri, *Lord Meher*).

     Meher Baba remained disparaging about Krishnamurti. Comparing him to Ramakrishna, he said that Ramakrishna was 'Rama and Krishna personified! Krishnamurti is living in all majesty and splendor, pomp and power, and moving about England in aristocratic, fashionable circles, playing tennis and golf, leading a most comfortable life. He does not have the slightest idea—not even a wisp—of the Real Truth' (ibid., p. 816). He was equally dismissive of the Theosophists, telling Paul Brunton, 'Their chief wire-pullers are supposed to be somewhere on the Himalayas in Tibet. You will find nothing but dust and stones in their supposed abodes.'

22. Kalchuri, *Lord Meher*.
23. Ibid.
24. Ibid.
25. Ibid.
26. Ibid.
27. Ibid.
28. Landau, *God is My Adventure*.
29. Ibid.
30. '"Miracle Man" Talks to The Daily Mirror', *Daily Mirror*, 9 April 1932.
31. Message to Paramount News Reel on Meher's arrival in London, 4 October 1932, in *Messages of Meher Baba Delivered in the East and West*, compiled by Adi K. Irani (Avatar Meher Baba Trust eBook, June 2011); copyright © 1943 Adi K. Irani; copyright © Avatar Meher Baba Perpetual Public Charitable Trust, Ahmednagar, India.
32. '"Miracle Man" Talks to The Daily Mirror', *Daily Mirror*, 9 April 1932.
33. 'Baba Wears a Paper Hat', *Daily Mirror*, 11 April 1932.
34. 'Baba Makes a Prophecy', *Daily Mirror*, 13 April 1932.
35. Douglas himself had fixed ideas on how to redeem mankind. A fierce moralist, he waged a campaign against *The Well of Loneliness*, a 1928 lesbian novel by the British author Radclyffe Hall. 'I would rather give a healthy boy or a healthy girl a phial of prussic acid than this novel', Douglas wrote. He described authors whom he believed guilty of moral 'degeneracy' as 'lepers', and his aim was to force society to undertake the 'task of cleansing itself from the leprosy of these lepers'. https://www.bbc.com/culture/article/20221121-the-well-of-loneliness-the-most-corrosive-book-ever.
36. Kalchuri, *Lord Meher*, p. 1525.
37. Quoted at http://stephenjcastro.blogspot.co.uk/2012/01/critics-of-meher-baba-paul-brunton-and.html.
38. Kalchuri, *Lord Meher*.
39. 'Biblical Scene: Indian Mystic Arrives at Combe Martin', *Ilfracombe Chronicle*, 22 April 1932.
40. Purdom, *The God-Man*.
41. 'Holy Man of the Hindu Yogis Who Hasn't Spoken A Word For 8 Years [*sic*] and Claims He Can Perform Miracles, Will Try To Start A Colony of Mystics in America', *The Milwaukee Sentinel*, 8 May 1932.
42. Quoted in Carey McWilliams, *Southern California: An Island on the Land* (Salt Lake City, UT: Gibbs Smith, 1946).
43. Ibid.
44. See http://layoga.com/community/spiritual-history-of-los-angeles/.

45. Leadbeater further prophesied that by then all mankind would be under the rule of a world government led by a reincarnation of Julius Caesar.

46. 'Baba to Give Up His "Uh"', *Kansas City Evening Star*, 27 May 1932.

47. Stephen Sakellarios, 'A Tapestry of Meher Baba's Connections with the West', https://www.ial.goldthread.com/Meher_Baba.html.

48. Copyright © Avatar Meher Baba Perpetual Public Charitable Trust, Ahmednagar, India—taken from *Meher Baba's Early Messages to the West: The 1932–35 Western Tours* (North Myrtle Beach, SC: Sheriar Foundation, 2009). A full version of Meher Baba's Hollywood speech, beautifully set to illustrative clips of films from the period, may be viewed at http://www.youtube.com/watch?v=mVZu9wMZkCo.

49. Kitty Davy, *Love Alone Prevails: A Story of Life with Meher Baba* (North Myrtle Beach, SC: Sheriar Foundation, 2001).

50. Kalchuri, *Lord Meher*, p. 1795.

51. An alternative telling of this story by the art historian John Richardson has it that through de Acosta 'you could get to anyone—as it were, from Pope John XIII to John Kennedy—in one move'. See Mercedes de Acosta, *Here Lies the Heart* (London: Andre Deutsch, 1960).

52. Ibid.

53. Robert A. Schanke, *'That Furious Lesbian': The Story of Mercedes de Acosta* (Carbondale, IL: Southern Illinois University Press, 2003).

54. De Acosta, *Here Lies the Heart*.

55. Ibid.

56. Ibid.

57. Ibid.

58. Schanke, *'That Furious Lesbian'*.

59. Hugo Vickers, *Loving Garbo: The Story of Greta Garbo, Cecil Beaton and Mercedes de Acosta* (London: Jonathan Cape, 1994).

60. De Acosta, *Here Lies the Heart*.

61. Ibid.

62. Kalchuri, *Lord Meher*, p. 1940.

63. Quoted in Schanke, *'That Furious Lesbian'*.

64. Ibid.

65. Ibid.

66. Ibid.

7. RAMANA MAHARSHI

1. [Major A. W. Chadwick] Sadhu Arunachala, *A Sadhu's Reminiscences of Ramana Maharshi* (Tiruvannamalai: Sri Ramanasramam, 2005).

2. Ibid.

3. Ibid. Chadwick adds that during Ramana's last days, 'He certainly appeared to suffer terribly, at night when he was unaware that anybody could hear him, he lay on his couch, groaning and calling out. At that time it was indeed difficult to realize

that he, as a *Jnani* did not feel pain in the same way as we, but that he saw it as something apart from him, as a dream which could be regarded objectively.'

4.  Ibid.

5.  Ramananda Swarnagiri, *Crumbs from His Temple* (Tiruvannamalai: Sri Ramanasramam, 1995).

6.  Chadwick, *A Sadhu's Reminiscences.*

7.  David Godman, *Living by the Words of Bhagavan* (Tiruvannamalai; Sri Annamalai Swami Ashram Trust, 1994).

8.  Quoted in David Godman's blog, http://sri-ramana-maharshi.blogspot.com/2008/06/yes-but-what-do-i-do.html.

9.  Swami B. V. Narasimha, *Self-Realization: The Life and Teachings of Sri Ramana Maharshi* (Tiruvannamalai: Sri Ramanasramam, 2002).

10. Paul Brunton was not the first Westerner to visit Ramana Maharshi, nor to write about him. Frank Humphreys was just aged twenty when in January 1911 he arrived in India to take up the position of assistant superintendent of police in Vellore, Tamil Nadu. Humphreys evidently had an interest in Theosophy, for one of his first questions to the man who had been appointed to teach him Telegu, was whether he knew of any Mahatmas in the vicinity—the 'ascended Masters' with whom Blavatsky and Besant had been in communication. Humphreys was led to a man named Ganapati Sastri, a disciple of Ramana Maharshi, who took the young policeman to the Virupaksha cave on the south-eastern slope of the hill where Ramana was then living. Humphreys saluted the sage and then sat silently in front of him. His account of the meeting has a distinctly Christian ring to it. 'For half an hour I looked him in the eyes which never changed their expression of deep contemplation,' Humphreys wrote. 'I began to realise somewhat that the body is the Temple of the Holy Ghost—I could only feel His body was not the man, it was the instrument of God, merely a sitting motionless corpse from which God was radiating terrifically. My own sensations were indescribable.'

    Humphreys became a frequent visitor to Ramana, recording his impressions in a series of articles for the English publication *The International Psychic Gazette*, edited by the Fabian and spiritualist Felicia Scatcherd. These articles were later collected into the first book on Ramana published in the English language, and would also form the basis for the first major biography of Ramana, *Self-Realization: The Life and Teachings of Sri Ramana Maharshi*, written by his disciple Swami B. V. Narasimha. After two-and-a-half years in India, Humphreys returned to England. He was ordained as a Dominican priest, taking the religious name Brother Nicholas. He spent the rest of his life in South Africa, ministering to the poor and needy, where he died in 1975.

11. Brunton, *A Search in Secret India.*

12. Ibid.

13. The article was first published in September 1931 in the monthly magazine *PEACE*, the journal of Swami Omkar's Shanti Ashrama in Andhra Pradesh. It was later reprinted in *Mountain Path* (April 1966).

14. Brunton, *A Search in Secret India.*

15. Ibid.
16. Ibid.
17. Ibid.
18. Ramana Maharshi located the centre of spiritual awareness on the right side of the chest. Some ashram publications connect this with the verse from Ecclesiastes 10:2: 'A wise man's heart is at his right hand, but the fool's heart at his left.' See Arthur Osborne, *My Life and Quest* (Tiruvannamalai: Sri Ramanasramam, 2008).
19. *Talks with Sri Ramana Maharshi* (Tiruvannamalai: Sri Ramanasramam, 2006).
20. Ibid.
21. 'The Maharshi with Swami Yogananda and Paul Brunton', 29 November 1935, http://www.youtube.com/watch?v=4_ZleDVogJI.
22. *Talks with Sri Ramana Maharshi*, 26 December 1936, Talk 304.
23. Ibid.
24. Baird Spalding was the author of the multi-volume series *Life and Teaching of the Masters of the Far East*. Chadwick, in *A Sadhu's Reminiscences*, thought that Spalding 'obviously suffered from delusions' and was 'slightly mad'.
25. Chadwick, *A Sadhu's Reminiscences*.
26. Ibid.
27. Osborne, *My Life and Quest*.
28. De Acosta, *Here Lies the Heart*.
29. Quoted in Schanke, 'That Furious Lesbian'.
30. Garbo and Meher Baba would never meet, but Garbo would continue to express some interest in the spiritual life. She became a good friend of Krishnamurti in Hollywood, and later took up Transcendental Meditation.
31. The Hindi word *mast* actually translates as something like 'numbskull'.
32. Purdom, *The God-Man*.
33. Quoted in Schanke, 'That Furious Lesbian'.
34. De Acosta, *Here Lies the Heart*.
35. Ibid.
36. Ibid.
37. Paul Brunton pointed out what he called the striking phenomenon, confirming the prediction of the West bringing spiritual tuition to the East, that the largest yoga ashram in all India, with more than 1,000 disciples, was headed by a Westerner; and the largest yoga monastery of the Jain religion, situated at Mount Abu in Rajputana, had a European—a Swiss popularly known as 'George'—as its guru.
38. And she did. Margaret Woodrow Wilson died in Pondicherry in 1944 from uraemia.
39. De Acosta, *Here Lies the Heart*.
40. Ibid.


8.    MERCEDES AND SOMERSET

1. Ibid.
2. Ibid.
3. Ibid.

4.   Schanke, *'That Furious Lesbian'*.

5.   W. Somerset Maugham, *A Writer's Notebook* (London: William Heinemann, 1949).

6.   Ibid.

7.   Ibid.

8.   Ibid.

9.   Crowley, *The Confessions*.

10.  Ibid.

11.  Robin Maugham, *Conversations with Willie: Recollections of W. Somerset Maugham* (New York: Simon & Schuster, 1978).

12.  Ibid.

13.  Ibid. Robin Maugham's account might be taken with more than a pinch of salt. In his introduction to *The Magician*, Somerset Maugham states that after leaving Paris in 1905 he never saw Crowley again: 'Once, long afterwards, I received a telegram from him that ran as follows: "Please send twenty-five pounds at once. Mother of God and I starving. Aleister Crowley." I did not do so, and he lived on for many disgraceful years.' Maugham notes that the publication of *The Magician* in 1908 coincided with the production and success of *Lady Frederick* (1907). Preoccupied with writing for the stage, he did not write another novel for five years. When he did, in 1915, the novel's title—*Of Human Bondage*—would have an ironic bearing on the story of him having sold his soul to Crowley.

14.  Quoted in Ted Morgan, *Maugham: A Biography* (London: Simon & Schuster, 1984).

15.  W. Somerset Maugham, *The Summing Up* (London: William Heinemann, 1938).

16.  Quoted in Morgan, *Maugham*.

17.  Humphreys, *Both Sides of the Circle*.

18.  Morgan, *Maugham*.

19.  Maugham, *The Summing Up*.

20.  Chadwick, *A Sadhu's Reminiscences*.

21.  Maugham, *A Writer's Notebook*.

22.  Ibid.

23.  Ibid. A slightly different account from that given by Maugham appears in the ashram publication *Talks with Sri Ramana Maharshi*, which records that

> Somerset Maugham, a well-known English author, was on a visit to Sri Bhagavan. He also went to see Maj. Chadwick in his room and there he suddenly became unconscious. Maj. Chadwick requested Sri Bhagavan to see him. Sri Bhagavan went into the room, took a seat and gazed on Mr. Maugham. He regained his senses and saluted Sri Bhagavan. They remained silent and sat facing each other for nearly an hour. The author attempted to ask questions but did not speak. Maj. Chadwick encouraged him to ask. Sri Bhagavan said, 'All finished. Heart talk is all talk. All talk must end in silence only.' They smiled and Sri Bhagavan left the room.

24.  Maugham, *A Writer's Notebook*.

25.  Chadwick, *A Sadhu's Reminiscences*.

26.  W. Somerset Maugham, 'The Saint', in *Points of View* (London: William Heinemann, 1958); see https://www.theculturium.com/w-somerset-maugham-the-saint/.

27.  Ibid.

28.  Chadwick, *A Sadhu's Reminiscences*.

29.  Maugham, *A Writer's Notebook*.

30.  Ibid.

31.  Ibid. The metaphor of the rope and snake is a familiar trope handed down from Shankara's teachings of Advaita Vedanta. In semi-darkness, a person becomes convinced that a snake is coiled in the corner of a room, and with such conviction come attendant fears that enhance the perception. To the person who thinks there really is a snake, the snake exists. Only when a light is shone on the object of perception—when the snake is revealed to be a coil of rope—can truth be established and misconception banished.

32.  Maugham, *A Writer's Notebook*.

33.  Letter to Karl Pfeiffer, 2 February 1938. Quoted in Selina Hastings, *The Secret Lives of Somerset Maugham* (London: John Murray, 2010).

34.  Maugham, *A Writer's Notebook*.

35.  W. Somerset Maugham, *The Razor's Edge* (London: Vintage, 2000).

36.  Ibid.

37.  Ibid.

38.  Ibid.

39.  Maugham, *A Writer's Notebook*.

40.  Christopher Isherwood, *The Wishing Tree: Christopher Isherwood on Mystical Religion* (Hollywood, CA: Vedanta Press, 1987).

41.  Christopher Isherwood, *My Guru and His Disciple* (Minneapolis: University of Minnesota Press, 2001).

42.  Christopher Isherwood, *Diaries, 1939–1960* (London: HarperCollins, 1966).

43.  Maugham, *The Razor's Edge*.

44.  Ibid.

45.  Isherwood, *My Guru*. Isherwood was equivocal about Maugham's book. He thought Larry Darrell 'a lively, natural normal, typical American boy', who made a plausible 'Mr Jones'—the sort of 'everyman' who could conceivably became a saint. But he opined that the trigger of Larry's calling—his experiences in the First World War—was 'rather vague'. See Isherwood, 'The Problem of the Religious Novel', in the volume of collected writings, *The Wishing Tree*.

46.  Dennis Wills, email correspondence with the author, 25 August 2013.

47.  Brunton, *The Notebooks*.

48.  V. S. Naipaul, *Half a Life* (New York: Alfred A. Knopf, 2001).

49.  Questioning Ramana on his years of silence while living in the temple before moving to Arunachala, Major Chadwick asked the sage whether he had actually taken a vow of silence. Ramana replied there was never any such vow, but that when living in the temple he had found himself seated for a time by a Sadhu who was observing such a vow, and he saw how convenient it was since the crowds did not worry the Sadhu in the same way that they worried him: 'So for convenience he pretended to copy him. "There was no vow, I just kept quiet, I spoke when it was necessary," he explained. I asked him how long this had continued. "For about two years," he replied.' Chadwick, *A Sadhu's Reminiscences*.

50.  Naipaul, *Half a Life*.

51.  Letter to Karl Pfeiffer, 12 May 1943. Quoted in Hastings, *The Secret Lives*.

52.  Isherwood, *Diaries*.

53.  R. Maugham, *Conversations with Willie*.


9.    THE LIFE AND DEATH OF PAUL BRUNTON

1.   Paul Brunton, *The Secret Path: A Technique of Spiritual Self-Discovery* (New York: E. P. Dutton & Co., 1935).

2.   Brunton, *The Notebooks*.

3.   Ibid.; Brunton, *The Secret Path*.

4.   Chadwick would join in the criticism of Brunton, describing him as 'a plagiarist of the first water' who 'undoubtedly wrote a lot of rubbish afterwards'. Nevertheless, Chadwick was obliged to admit that many (himself included) had come to Ramana as a result of *A Search in Secret India*, and had been grateful for it.

5.   Quoted in Godman, *Living by the Words of Bhagavan*.

6.   Ibid.

7.   Brunton, *The Hidden Teaching*.

8.   Ibid.

9.   Brunton, *A Search in Secret India*.

10.  Brunton, *The Hidden Teaching*.

11.  Brunton, *The Notebooks*.

12.  Ibid.

13.  Ibid.

14.  Ibid.

15.  Jeffrey Masson, *My Father's Guru: A Journey through Spirituality and Disillusion* (Reading, MA: Addison-Wesley Publishing Co., 1993).

16.  Brunton, *The Notebooks*.

17.  Jeffrey Masson, interview with the author, 22 December 2014.

18.  Paul Brunton, letter to Gordon Gillies, 21 October 1956.

19.  Masson, *My Father's Guru*.

20.  Brunton, *The Notebooks*.

21.  British Library: Departmental Papers, Political (External) Files and Collections: IOR/L/PS/12/4321.

22.  Masson, *My Father's Guru*.

23.  Hurst, *Paul Brunton*.

24.  Evangeline Glass, interview with the author, 26 October 2014.

25.  Brunton maintained that he would also answer enquiries telepathically. In *A Hermit in the Himalayas*, he wrote: 'When the exquisite pulsation of the sacred silence overwhelms me with its sublimity, I telegraph it, as by telepathy, to those faithful souls.' See Paul Brunton, *A Hermit in the Himalayas* (London: Rider & Co., 1975).

26.  Melody Talcott, interview with the author, 28 October 2014.

27.  The head of a monastic order believed to go back to 309 BCE.

28.  Letter to Gordon Grillies, n.d., 1969.

29. Letter to Gordon Grillies, 11 July 1957.
30. Ivan Torres, 'Mystery Man Behind Palace Walls', *Toronto Globe and Mail*, 1965.
31. According to Jeffrey Masson, Brunton said that he had plans for Masson to marry the Queen's daughter, Sofia: 'He claimed that [Queen Frederica] wanted him to arrange for her daughter to marry a spiritual man, and I was that person. I have no clue how real that was. We never had any proof that he knew any of these people, but he said he did, and nobody never questioned it' (Jeffrey Masson, interview with the author, 22 December 2014). Born in 1938, Princess Sofia of Greece and Denmark was the eldest child of King Paul of Greece and Frederica of Hanover. In 1962, she married Prince Juan Carlos of Spain.
32. Masson, *My Father's Guru*.
33. Hurst, *Paul Brunton*.
34. Masson, *My Father's Guru*.
35. Ibid. Masson's disappointment was compounded by what he saw as Brunton's misrepresentation of his academic qualifications. Brunton styled himself as 'Dr' on his book jackets and his letter-headed notepaper, engraved in an elegant italic script. When Masson pressed him on the subject, Brunton told him that he had received a PhD from Roosevelt University in Chicago, 'in recognition of distinguished service to the cause of Oriental research'. Masson checked this, but the university could find no record of Brunton. In fact, Brunton did have a qualification, but not from Roosevelt University: it was a mail-order doctorate, awarded to him in 1938 by an establishment called the McKinley Roosevelt Graduate College (which no longer exists) for a dissertation called *Indian Philosophy and Modern Culture*. This was published commercially the following year, and Brunton dedicated it to V. Subrahmanya Iyer. Brunton's dedication reads: 'This thesis is dedicated to you with much affection and much respect in remembrance of the jewelled time we spent among silent jungle-covered hills far from the haunts of men. There you unfolded to me the higher wisdom of your land, expounded its most ancient books and explained its most imperishable philosophy.'
36. Jeff Cox, interview with the author, 28 September 2014.
37. Brunton, *The Notebooks*. Interestingly, Sirius was also the purported destination of the fifty-three members of the Solar Temple cult who self-exterminated at two locations in Switzerland in 1994. The cult members had been told by their leader, Luc Joret, that they were on 'death voyages' that would lead to them being reborn on Sirius.
38. 'British Major, Buddhist Monk: Strange Career of Frederick Fletcher', *The Age*, 6 December 1941.
39. Ibid.

10. 'WE ARE ALL HINDUS IN OUR ESSENCE'

1. Wasson's experiments with magic mushrooms had led him to speculate that such mind-altering plants might have been 'the mighty springboard' which gave man his first glimpse of God, and thus sowed the seeds for religion. The Eden tree story

in the Book of Genesis, Wasson believed, alluded to the Amanita, or fly agaric, mushroom.

2. Timothy Leary, *High Priest* (New York: New American Library, 1968).

3. Timothy Leary, *Flashbacks* (Los Angeles, CA: Jeremy P. Tarcher, 1983).

4. Ram Dass [Richard Alpert], *Be Here Now* (New York: Crown Publications, 1971).

5. Ibid.

6. The principal psychoactive component of peyote was identified in the same year by Arthur Heffter, who named the isolate compound 'mezcalin'. See Peter Stafford, *Psychedelics Encyclopedia* (Berkeley, CA: Ronin Publishing Inc., 1992).

7. Havelock Ellis, 'Mescal: A New Artificial Paradise', *The Contemporary Review* 73 (January 1898).

8. Aldous Huxley, 'A Treatise on Drugs' (1931), in M. Horowitz and C. Palmer, eds., *Moksha* (Rochester, VT: Park Street Press, 1999).

9. It was Osmond who would later coin the word 'psychedelic', to describe the range of hallucinatory and mind-altering drugs, in a rhyme: 'To fathom hell or soar angelic / Just take a pinch of psychedelic.'

10. Aldous Huxley, *The Doors of Perception* (London: Vintage Classics, 2004).

11. Timothy Leary, *The Politics of Ecstasy* (New York: G. P. Putnam's Sons, 1968).

12. The existentialist and atheist Jean-Paul Sartre did not see God when he took mescaline under psychiatric supervision. When Simone de Beauvoir telephoned the hospital to ask how he was getting along, Sartre told her he was fighting a losing battle with a devilfish.

13. Huxley, *The Doors of Perception*.

14. Leary, *High Priest*.

15. Isherwood, *My Guru*.

16. Jay Stevens, *Storming Heaven: LSD and the American Dream* (London: William Heinemann, 1988).

17. Ibid.

18. Quoted in Robert Greenfield, *Timothy Leary: A Biography* (San Diego, CA: Harcourt Publishers, 2006).

19. Michael Hollingshead, *The Man Who Turned On the World* (London: Blond & Briggs, 1973), http://www.psychedelic-library.org/hollings.htm.

20. Leary, *High Priest*.

21. Ibid.

22. Ibid.

23. One of the ten students who had taken the placebo also reported having a mystical experience.

24. Leary, *Flashbacks*.

25. Ibid.

26. P. E. Casquet, *The 200-Year History of the War on Drugs* (London: Reaktion Books, 2022).

27. This was a phrase that Leary first coined in 1966, but which he became synonymous with after addressing the crowd at the 1967 'Human Be-In' at Golden Gate Park, San Francisco, when he urged them to 'Turn on, tune in, drop out'.

28.   Huxley, *The Doors of Perception*.

29.   Timothy Leary, *The Psychedelic Experience: A Manual Based on the Tibetan Book of the Dead* (New York: Citadel Press, 2003).

30.   William James, *The Varieties of Religious Experience: A Study in Human Nature* (New York: Longmans, Green, & Co., 1902).


11. ALLEN GINSBERG'S VISION

1.    Allen Ginsberg in conversation with Ernie Barry, *City Lights Journal* (1964). Quoted in Allen Ginsberg, *Spontaneous Mind: Selected Interviews, 1958–1996* (New York: Harper Perennial, 2002).

2.    Letter from Arthur Rimbaud to Paul Demeny, Charleville, 15 May 1871, https://my-blackout.com/2019/03/03/arthur-rimbaud-letters-1870-18719-sean-bonney-letter-on-poetics-after-rimbaud/.

3.    Ginsberg, *Spontaneous Mind*.

4.    https://www.unsoundmind.org/post/unreason-speaks.

5.    Rockland State Hospital was one of several psychiatric institutions where Ginsberg's mother, Naomi, had also been incarcerated. Carl Solomon thought 'Howl, for Carl Solomon' was 'An excellent piece of writing, and just to my taste', although he would later revise his opinion, chastising Ginsberg and complaining to the publishers, City Lights, that '"All rights reserved" is on a page of the book. Does this mean I can't use my name anymore?' Allen Ginsberg, *Howl and Other Poems* (San Francisco: City Lights, 1956).

6.    Jack Kerouac, 'Lamb, No Lion' (1958), in *Portable Jack Kerouac* (New York: Viking Penguin, 1995).

7.    Jack Kerouac, *The Letters of Jack Kerouac, 1940–1956*, ed. Ann Charters (New York: Viking, 1995).

8.    Ashvaghosa (c.80–c.150 CE) was an Indian Buddhist monk, considered the first great Buddhist poet-philosopher.

9.    Quoted in Deborah Baker, *A Blue Hand: The Beats in India* (New York: Penguin, 2008).

10.   Kerouac professed himself dissatisfied with *Some of the Dharma*: 'Some of it is now, I see, useless, because mistaken, or written on tea, or other faults.'

11.   Jack Kerouac, '15th Chorus', in *Mexico City Blues* (New York: Grove Press/Atlantic Monthly Press, 2000).

12.   Jack Kerouac, 'On the Origins of a Generation', *Playboy*, June 1959.

13.   Quoted in Carole Tonkinson, *Big Sky Mind: Buddhism and the Beat Generation* (New York: Riverhead Books, 1995).

14.   Mike Wallace, 'What is the Beat Generation?', *New York Post*, 21 January 1958.

15.   https://www.nytimes.com/2021/04/26/books/helen-weaver-dead.html.

16.   It was this attitude that led Alan Watts, writing in the essay 'Beat Zen, Square Zen, and Zen' in the *Chicago Review* in spring 1958, to criticise Kerouac's Buddhism as another word for 'anything goes'. Kerouac, he wrote,

is always a shade too self-conscious, too subjective and too strident to have the flavor of Zen ... When Kerouac gives his philosophical final statement, 'I don't know. I don't care. And it doesn't make any difference'—the cat is out of the bag, for there is a hostility in these words which clangs with self-defense. But just because Zen truly surpasses convention and its values, it has no need to say 'To hell with it,' nor to underline with violence the fact that anything goes.

When Kerouac died in 1969 at the age of forty-seven, due to an internal haemorrhage caused by cirrhosis, Allen Ginsberg wrote to Carolyn Cassady describing seeing his body in the coffin at the Archambault funeral home in Lowell: 'eyes closed, mid-aged heavy, looked like his father had become from earlier dream decades—sick first seeing him there in theatric-lit coffin room as if a Buddha in Parinirvana pose, come here left his message of illusion-wink & left the body behind'. Quoted in Carolyn Cassady, *Off the Road: My Years with Cassady, Kerouac, and Ginsberg*, new ed. (New York: Penguin 1996). Kerouac did not live to see the arrival in America of Chogyam Trungpa, the unorthodox 'crazy wisdom' teacher of Tibetan Buddhism, but he would have liked him. An important reincarnate, Trungpa had been subjected to the customary Tibetan monastic education. After fleeing to India in 1959, he travelled to England on a Spalding scholarship. With his friend Akong Rinpoche he founded Samye Ling, the first Tibetan Buddhist monastery in the West. A brilliant, if highly unorthodox, teacher, he drank like a fish, kept his audience waiting for hours for lectures and generally behaved in a totally irrational and mysterious way. In short, he was Kerouac's sort of Buddhist. Much later, Trungpa became the guru that Allen Ginsberg had been searching for all his life.

17.   Barry Miles, *Allen Ginsberg: A Biography* (London: Virgin Books, 2000).
18.   Ibid.
19.   Michael Schumacher, ed., *First Thought: Conversations with Allen Ginsberg* (Minneapolis: University of Minnesota Press, 2017).
20.   Suranjan Ganguly, 'Allen Ginsberg in India: An Interview', *Ariel* 24 (1993), https://cdm.ucalgary.ca/index.php/ariel/article/view/33620.
21.   Ibid.
22.   Allen Ginsberg letter to Jack Kerouac, 17 January 1962, in *Jack Kerouac: Selected Letters, 1940–1956* (New York: Viking, 1995).
23.   Ibid.
24.   Allen Ginsberg, *Indian Journals* (New York: Grove Press/Atlantic Monthly Press, 1996).
25.   Allen Ginsberg, 'The Vomit of a Mad Tyger', *Lion's Roar*, 2 April 2015, https://www.lionsroar.com/the-vomit-of-a-mad-tyger/.
26.   Ginsberg, *Indian Journals*.
27.   Quoted in Miles, *Allen Ginsberg*.
28.   Ibid.
29.   Leary, *Flashbacks*.
30.   Ibid.
31.   Ibid.
32.   Ibid.

33. Following the publication in 1966 of his autobiography, *The Way of the White Clouds*, Lama Angarika Govinda spent much of the last twenty years of his life travelling and lecturing in Europe and the United States. He died in San Francisco in 1985.

34. Sri Madhava Ashish, *What is Man? Selected Writings of Sri Madhava Ashish* (Delhi: Penguin Books India, 2010).

35. Leary, *Flashbacks*.

36. Ibid.

37. Krishna Prem died in 1965, shortly after Leary's visit. His last words were: 'My ship is sailing.'

38. *Esquire*, July 1968.

39. Quoted in John H. Garabedian and Orde Coombs, *Eastern Religions in the Electric Age: Why American Youth is Rejecting its Own Traditions and Seeking New Answers in the Ideas and Religions of the East* (New York: Grosset & Dunlap, 1969).

40. In 1967, American government agents seized clandestine laboratories said to have a production capacity of more than 25 million doses of LSD and LSD-like drugs per year. In 1968, the production capacity of the clandestine laboratories seized was reported to be more than 40 million doses per year. Of course, no estimate is available of the production capacity of the clandestine laboratories that remained undetected.

41. Dass, *Be Here Now*.

42. Lawrence Ferlinghetti, *A Coney Island of the Mind* (New York: New Directions, 1968).

43. Danny Goldberg, *In Search of the Lost Chord: 1967 and the Hippie Idea* (London: Icon Books, 2017).

44. Dass, *Be Here Now*.

45. Ibid.

46. Following the success of *Be Here Now*, Bhagavan Das wrote his own book, *It's Here Now (Are You?)*, its title and cover design bearing a marked similarity to those of Ram Dass' book. Bhagavan Das' book is a bizarrely entertaining account of a Zelig-like figure who seems to have encountered virtually every major living spiritual Indian teacher, with a marked susceptibility for being blissed out by all of them. The son of an Episcopalian family, Michael Riggs describes travelling to Scotland at the age of eighteen and having his first 'transcendental experience' visiting Arthur's Seat in Edinburgh—where, according to legend, King Arthur drew a sword from the rock and was named king. Hitching across Europe to Greece (lots of drugs) he finally arrives in India, where he realises his destiny is to become a saint. In Rishikesh he swims in the Ganges and gets initiated by the Maharishi Mahesh— later to become the Beatles' guru—who gives him the mantra 'Ram', the word of God. He lives as a sadhu, travelling around India encountering sundry teachers and swamis, before meeting the man who would become his and Richard Alpert's guru—Neem Karoli Baba—who gives Alpert the name Ram Dass. He becomes Karoli Baba's favourite disciple, travelling with him everywhere. At Kumbh Mela, he meets Anandamayi Ma, and touches her feet with his head: 'At that moment I realized enlightenment.'

There are momentary digressions. In Sri Lanka he becomes a nightclub singer in 'a whorehouse for sailors' under the name 'King Pleasure'—'As a bonus they let me sleep on the piano.' Back in India, he stops off at the Ramana Maharshi ashram in Tiruvannamalai, then at the Sri Aurobindo ashram in Pondicherry, where he has *darshan* with the Mother: 'I was literally blinded by the golden light. I couldn't see anything. I literally stumbled into the room.' He goes to Darjeeling and takes initiation from the great Tibetan lama Kalu Rinpoche, and runs into Zina Rachaesky, a Russian princess famous for her support of exiled Tibetan lamas, then to Sikkim to meet the Karmapa. Having tasted the nectar of divine bliss, he heads for Goa where he meets a beautiful brunette named Gay, 'falling totally in love and lust' and spending two weeks in bed while Gay 'taught me tantric sex'. On to Bodh Gaya: 'Many times I'd be walking around the temple and I'd actually see dakinis flying around the pinnacles ... these fairy beings, these miniature goddesses.'

After introducing Alpert to Neem Karoli Baba, Alpert gifts him a sitar, which Bhagavan, in defiance of centuries of musical tradition, claims to master in two weeks. He returns to Kathmandu and hooks up with a Jewish girl from Oklahama named Bhavani, who is tripping on LSD: 'She was very cool, always wanting to be there to serve me and learn from me—she became my disciple.'

It should by now be clear to the most dilatory reader that the love Bhagavan Das held for the divine was but a shadow of the love he felt for himself. With Bhavani—'I wasn't sure how I should relate to her. As my girlfriend? As my disciple? As my assistant?' He goes to Japan. While Bhagavan Das spends his days meditating, Bhavani works to support him and takes care of him, 'because I was so freaked out with all the changes'. When Bhavani becomes pregnant, they return to California. By now, Ram Dass had published *Be Here Now*. Bhagavan Das becomes a celebrity: 'People were just dying to get their hands on me. People were diving at my feet ... Everybody wanted to be in my presence ... They wanted me to name their babies.' It's a business that requires enormous self-sacrifice: there are groupies he has 'to do—it was my duty ... I was in a very crazed space and very lost. One day after having sex with three different women, I couldn't get out of bed.'

He hangs out with Allen Ginsberg—'He was a guru hunter, and I was the new guru in town'—and goes on tour with him, chanting Om Namah Shivayah. For a while he becomes a disciple of Joya, 'a middle-class Jewish housewife whose husband, Sal, was a Coca Cola truck-driver', and who is held to be a manifestation of the Divine Mother. In need of money, he becomes a car salesman. Meanwhile, his romantic attachments are becoming more complicated—a wife, and a girlfriend on the side: 'During this period I realized that my female relationships had been unsuccessful because I was first and foremost married to Kali Ma'—the Divine Mother. He suggests that his wife and girlfriend accept their position as 'wife number two' and 'wife number three'. For some reason, they reject this: 'They both wanted to be the only one. Kali wouldn't have it. She's numero uno, she destroyed the relationships.'

He goes to Hawaii and cultivates magic mushrooms, then becomes an Encyclopedia Britannica salesman—'I became the world champion three months in a row.' His wife Bhavani dies of a cocaine overdose: 'I sobbed and howled. I was mad at Bhavani for dying on me.' Now plain old Michael Riggs again, he returns to California and becomes a born-again Christian, evangelising in fast-food restaurants, 'constantly looking for souls to save'.

Now in his forties, inevitably, he has an affair with a blond, teenage choir girl 'in tight blue jeans', which results in him being branded a 'fornicator' by the church. Told he is an alcoholic, he starts attending AA meetings. Then stops. He becomes an insurance salesman, then a car salesman again, then takes up with a deeply unstable woman (who will end up in a mental institution) who counsels him that he's 'a phony' and needs to go back to being Bhagavan Das again.

After an encounter with the Indian guru Ammachi, who is making an appearance in Berkeley, he once more takes up the name given to him by Neem Karoli Baba. 'We need to break through the money, sex, and power trips we're on,' he cautions the reader in conclusion, 'and find our way back to our hearts.'

*It's Here Now (Are You?)* was published by Broadway Books in 1997. I found Bhagavan Das' website—'Teacher, performer, counter-cultural icon, lover of God: Bhagavan Das is as rich and manifold as Existence itself'—advertising his evenings of kirtan singing and drumming, and I wrote requesting an interview. A reply came from someone calling herself Kali. The correspondence is copied below.

\* \* \*

8 August 2012

Dear Mick

Thanks for writing. Bhagavan Das does not generally meet with people during events.

Also, many people requests interview for books and film, but since Bhagavan Das does not need the exposure of such things, compensation for his time would be required under the rare condition that I would 'OK' such a meeting.

If you were to come to America and attend an event, letting me know well in advance and setting up a time with me … there is the possibility of your talking to Bhagavan Das. (since I feel you are sincere and legitimate)

I would need to know how long in advance and the cost for his time is 300 dollars per hour.

Bhagavan Das's time and energy is valuable and like I said, many people want to talk to him and especially if it's free.

Thanks for your interest.

Ram Ramaya Namaha.

Kali

\* \* \*

8 August 2012

Dear Kali,

Thank you for your prompt reply. I quite understand and appreciate the terms you set out for meeting Bhagavan Das.

I am trying to work out a schedule for my trip to America, which I'll try and organise around an event. I'll certainly give you plenty of notice as to when this would be, and hope we can arrange a meeting.

I appreciate your kind and encouraging response and look forward to meeting you and Bhagavan Das.

Many thanks.

Best wishes, Mick Brown

\* \* \*

8 August 2012

Dear Mick,

Thank you.

Look forward to meeting you also.

Kali

\* \* \*

(Due to extenuating circumstances, some months passed before I was able to plan a trip to America.)

5 August 2013

Dear Kali,

You may remember that we were in contact some months ago about the possibility of my interviewing Bhagavan Das for the book I'm writing about the West's engagement with Indian religious teachings. You indicated that Bhagavan Das had kindly agreed in principle to my meeting with him.

I'm sorry to have been so long in getting back to you, but I've been trying to plan a time and place that would be good to coincide with one of his events. I see that Bhagavan Das has an event in New York on September 20th. I wonder if this would be a convenient time for him to meet, in accordance with the conditions spelled out in your previous mails.

Thank you for your time, and I hope we can pull this together.

With best wishes,

Mick Brown

\* \* \*

5 August 2013

Hi Mick,

Yes I remember ... Sept 20 will not work as we are going to be canceling the remaining east coast events to take some time off.

Thanks, Kali

\* \* \*

6 August 2013

Thanks for that Kali. Could you tell me, is Bhagavan Das still in agreement in principle to talking with me, and might you suggest a time when it would be convenient. Thank you.

Best, Mick

* * *

6 August 2013

Hi Mick,

Actually I am the one who decides these things for him. I cannot give you a time or even tell you it is still a possibility at this time because it was a year ago that you originally wrote.

* * *

6 August 2013

Hi Kali,

Thanks for that. If I may say, that's a somewhat cryptic answer. Am I to take it that while it would have been a possibility then, it is not a possibility now? If that's the case, I am very sorry to hear it. Bhagavan Das's story would have been a valuable and important chapter in a book about the history of the West's relationship to Indian religion.

All best,

Mick

* * *

6 August 2013

Hi again cryptic? funny!

Don't u live in Europe? If you want to come to Asheville NC in early October, it may be possible for an interview. $500 to meet for one hour and every 10 minutes over that is $100. no checks. If u are interested the questions/topics need to be approved beforehand.

* * *

6 August 2013

Dear Kali

I admire your chutzpah. To borrow a quote from Baba Ram Dass, from 'Be Here Now', which I'm sure you're familiar with, I have interviewed the Dalai Lama, the 17th Karmapa, numerous Tibetan lamas and spiritual teachers, and I have 'never seen hustling like this.'

I appreciate that there has been inflation since our last correspondence, but not, so far as I am aware, at the rate of 75 per cent which you seem to be proposing. I will contribute $350 to Bhagavan Das's work, for one hour, no taxi meter.

I am, of course, happy to submit questions/topics beforehand.

As ever,

Mick

* * *

6 August 2013

Hi Nick [*sic*]

You misunderstand what it is that is valuable in this situation which isn't name, fame, $ or a resume

500$ is nothing

any good hustler would agree

best of luck w your book

\* \* \*

6 August 2013

Hi Kali

It may be nothing to Bhagavan Das; it's not nothing to me.

And the name is Mick.

Thank you, and the best of luck to you both.

POSTSCRIPT: According to his website, Bhagavan Das's most recent activity, along with his partner, Amulya Maa, was running a four-day retreat 'GRAND ILLUMINATION: MOVING from Me to WE'. Price $1,008.

## 12.   LOVE IS ALL YOU NEED

1.   Timothy Leary, 'Thank God for the Beatles', *The Saturday Evening Post*, 5 August 1967.

2.   Jann Wenner, *Lennon Remembers: The Rolling Stone Interviews* (London: Penguin, 1973).

3.   Music historians will dispute whether the sitar was first played on a pop record in 'Norwegian Wood' (1965), or whether it was on the Kinks' hit of the same year, 'See My Friends'. In any event, for a short, heady period, the sitar became the necessary embellishment in pop records and film soundtracks to suggest Oriental exoticism and trippy drug experiences.

Ravi Shankar, for whom playing the sitar was as much a spiritual calling as a musical one, could be a fastidious man, and it was a cause of evident unhappiness to find the instrument he loved in lesser hands, and played in a bastardised form as a lazy musical shorthand for a wigged-out psychedelic experience. In his autobiography, he haughtily dismissed the rock audiences who came to pay homage to him as 'these strange young weirdos'; while his appearances at the Monterey and Woodstock festivals—the great quasi-religious gatherings of the counterculture— were apparently painful ordeals for Shankar, with the audiences 'shrieking, shouting, smoking, masturbating and copulating—all in a drug-crazed state … I used to tell them, you don't behave like that when you go to hear a Bach, Beethoven or Mozart concert.' See Ravi Shankar, *Raga Mala: The Autobiography of Ravi Shankar* (New York: Welcome Rain, 1999). So distressed was Shankar by the way his music was—as he saw it—misunderstood by pop audiences, that after Woodstock he decided to 'cleanse' himself by performing only in concert halls.

4. Shankar, *Raga Mala*.

5. Ibid.

6. Gary Tillery, *Working Class Mystic: A Spiritual Biography of George Harrison* (Wheaton, IL: Theosophical Publishing House, 2011).

7. I. MacDonald, *Revolution in the Head* (London: Pimlico, 1998).

8. Pattie Boyd, *Wonderful Tonight: George Harrison, Eric Clapton, and Me* (New York: Harmony Books, 2007).

9. Paul Mason, *The Maharishi* (London: Element Books, 1994).

10. Nancy Cooke de Herrera, *All You Need is Love: An Eyewitness Account of when Spirituality Spread from East to West* (San Diego, CA: Jodere Group Inc., 2003).

11. Helena Olson, *His Holiness Maharishi Mahesh Yogi* (New York: Samhita Productions, 2001).

12. Cooke de Herrera, *All You Need is Love*.

13. Maharishi Mahesh Yogi, *The Science of Being and Art of Living* (London: International SRM Publications, 1963).

14. Cooke de Herrera, *All You Need is Love*.

15. Mason, *The Maharishi*.

16. *The Daily Express*, 27 August 1967.

17. Wenner, *Lennon Remembers*.

18. *Maharishi Mahesh Yogi on the Bhagavad-Gita: A New Translation and Commentary with Sanskrit Text (Chapters 1–6)* (New York: Penguin, 1969).

19. 'Chief Guru of the Western World', *The New York Times*, 17 December 1967.

20. 'What's New in America? Maharishi and Meditation', *The Village Voice*, 9 November 1967.

21. 'Meditation: The Answer to All Your Problems?', *Time Magazine*, 13 October 1975.

22. The Maharishi was also credited as 'executive producer' on the album *Cosmic Consciousness* by one of his students, the flautist Paul Horn.

23. Peter Brown and Steven Gaines, *The Love You Make: An Insider's Story of the Beatles* (London: Macmillan, 1983).

24. Quoted in ibid.

25. Allen Ginsberg, 'The Maharishi and Me', *Los Angeles Free Press*, 19 April 1968, http://lifeofthebeatles.blogspot.co.uk/2009/10/maharishi-and-me.html.

26. Cooke de Herrera, *All You Need is Love*.

27. Eric Hedegaard, 'The Ballad of Mike Love', *Rolling Stone*, 17 February 2016.

28. Cooke de Herrera, *All You Need is Love*.

29. Wenner, *Lennon Remembers*.

30. More than thirty years later, Brian Wilson was able to recall the syllables to mind: `Ay-ni-mah. Brian Wilson, interview with the author, 22 January 1992.

31. Bruce Johnston, interview with the author, 1 June 2019.

32. 'Maharishi Links Beatles and Beach Boys', *New Musical Express*, 6 April 1968.

33. *The Chicago Tribune*, 13 May 1968.

34. Bruce Johnston, interview with the author, 1 June 2019.

35. John McLaughlin, interview by email exchange with the author, 21 January 2014.

369

36.  Chris Heath, 'The Epic Life of Carlos Santana', *Rolling Stone*, 16 March 2000.

37.  David Browne, 'The Last Word: Carlos Santana on Turning 70, Trump's Darkness', *Rolling Stone*, 13 July 2017.

38.  'Sant' in this context means someone who communes with the divine and tells others of his experiences, often through poetry.

39.  Neil McCormick, 'Nick Lowe's Quality Rock and Roll Review, Acoustic Stage, Glastonbury, Review: Played with Virtuosity and Sung with a Gorgeous, Gliding Croon', *The Daily Telegraph*, 28 June 2019.

40.  Another self-proclaimed holy man was at the same Glastonbury festival, a young man named William Jellett who called himself Jesus. Jellett had come to the belief that he was Christ one day while travelling on the London Underground, when looking at his hands he saw stigmata on his palms. 'Jesus', who was a ubiquitous figure at pop concerts, festivals and London's Speakers' Corner at the time, was once approached in Holland Park where he was playing his bongos by Brian Kitt, an acquaintance from the hippie club, Middle Earth. Kitt had recently returned from India with the Maharaj Ji. The Maharaj Ji, he told Jesus, was 'the reincarnation of Krishna, Buddha and Mohammed', and he suggested Jellett should meet him. But there is no evidence that 'Jesus' and the Maharaj Ji ever met. See https://medium.com/@JPRobinson/the-mystery-of-jesus-the-naked-hippie-dancer-9822c0da8765.

41.  There were originally eight defendants in the trial—Rennie Davis, Abbie Hoffman, Jerry Rubin, David Dellinger, Tom Hayden, John Froines, Lee Weiner and Bobby Seale. Seale's case was separated from the others during the early part of the trial. On 18 February 1970, each of the seven defendants was acquitted of conspiracy. Two (Froines and Weiner) were acquitted completely, while the remaining five, including Davis, were convicted of crossing state lines with the intent to incite a riot. On 21 November 1972, all the convictions were reversed by the US Court of Appeals for the Seventh Circuit, on the basis that the judge was biased in his refusal to permit defence attorneys to screen prospective jurors for cultural and racial bias.

42.  Rennie Davis, quoted in a letter to John Brauns, http://www.prem-rawat-talk. org/cgi-bin/anyboard.cgi/forum?cmd=get&cG=23236373&zu=32323637&v=2&gV=1&p=.

43.  Stephen A. Kent, *From Slogans to Mantras: Social Protest and Religious Conversion in the Late Vietnam Era* (Syracuse University Press, 2001).

44.  Ted Morgan, 'Middle-Class Premier Find', *The New York Times*, 9 December 1973.

45.  Ibid.

46.  Quoted in Andrea Cagan, *Peace is Possible: The Life and Message of Prem Rawat* (Delaware: Mighty River Press, 2007).

47.  The current organisation called Words of Peace Global is an independent charitable foundation set up by individuals inspired by the global ambassador of peace and author Prem Rawat's powerful and unique message.

48.  Steve Turner, *The Gospel According to the Beatles* (Louisville, KY: Westminster John Knox Press, 2006).

49. Mason, *The Maharishi*.

50. Ibid.

51. Ibid.

52. Ibid.

53. The full eight are as follows: *Anima*—Ability to be as small as one wants; *Mahima*—Ability to be as big as one may desire; *Laghima*—Ability to become light to any degree; *Gharima*—Ability to become as heavy as desired; *Prapti*—Easy grasping by hand of any object however far it may be; *Prakamya*—To have anything as soon as one desires it; *Isitva*—Power to create and control things; *Vasitva*—Subjugation of everyone and everything, even to conquering death.

54. Quoted in Mason, *The Maharishi*.

55. Gita Mehta, *Karma Cola* (New York: Simon & Schuster, 1979).

13. RAJNEESH

1. Christine Ryder, interview with the author, 22 October 2013.

2. Quoted in Harry Aveling, ed., *Osho Rajneesh and His Disciples* (Delhi: Motilal Banarsidass Publishers, Pvt Ltd, 1999).

3. Quoted in Vasant Joshi, *The Awakened One: The Life and Work of Bhagwan Shree Rajneesh* (London: HarperCollins, 1982).

4. Quoted in Aveling, *Osho Rajneesh*.

5. Osho, *The Discipline of Transcendence*, Vol. 2, chapter 1, https://www.messagefrommasters.com/Enlightenment/Osho_Enlightenment.htm.

6. Anthony Storr, *Feet of Clay: A Study of Gurus* (London: HarperCollins, 1996).

7. Osho, *Come Follow to You*, Vol. 1, chapter 1, 'The First Poor Man', https://www.osho.com/osho-online-library/osho-talks/jesus-god-concepts-2332c550-8e6?p=08c41743aa1d77e9835d3fc50bc95a16.

8. Osho, *The Book of Understanding* (New York: Harmony Books, 2006).

9. Quoted in Joshi, *The Awakened One*.

10. Ibid.

11. Osho, *Dancing in the Breeze: The Discipline of Transcendence, on Buddha's Sutra of Forty-Two Chapters* (Mumbai: Osho Media International, 1976).

12. Bhagwan Shree Rajneesh, *The Rajneesh Bible*, Vol. 1 (Montclair, NJ: Rajneesh Foundation International, 1985).

13. Peter Brent, *Godmen of India* (London: Allen Lane, 1972).

14. Quoted in Lewis F. Carter, *Charisma and Control in Rajneeshpuram: A Community Without Shared Values* (Cambridge University Press, 2010).

15. Brent, *Godmen of India*.

16. Aveling, *Osho Rajneesh*.

17. Ibid.

18. Quoted in ibid.

19. Ibid.

20. Alan Watts, *In My Own Way: An Autobiography* (London: Jonathan Cape, 1972).

21. Humphreys, *Both Sides of the Circle*.

22.  Jeffrey J. Kripal, *Esalen: America and the Religion of No Religion* (University of Chicago Press, 2007).

23.  Michael Murphy, interview with the author, 17 January 2014.

24.  Ibid.

25.  [Wade Hudson], 'Dick Price: An Interview [1985]', http://esalen.org/page/dick-price-interview.

26.  Michael Murphy, interview with the author, 17 January 2014.

27.  Kripal, *Esalen*.

28.  Ibid.

29.  Reprinted in Tom Wolfe, *Mauve Gloves & Madmen, Clutter & Vine* (New York: Farrar, Straus & Giroux, 1976).

30.  Bhagwan Shree Rajneesh, *Meditation: The Art of Ecstasy*, ed. Ma Satya Bharti (London: Sheldon Press, 1978).

31.  Ma Anand Sheela, *Don't Kill Him! The Story of My Life with Bhagwan Rajneesh* (Delhi: Fingerprint, 2012).

32.  Osho, *The Last Testament*, Vol. 1 (1985), https://oshosearch.net/Convert/Articles_Osho/The_Last_Testament_Volume_1/Osho-The-Last-Testament-Volume-1-index.html (accessed 29 October 2020).

33.  Susan J. Palmer and Frederick Bird, 'Therapy, Charisma and Social Control in the Rajneesh Movement', *Sociological Analysis* 53 (January 1992), https://www.researchgate.net/publication/261825558_Therapy_Charisma_and_Social_Control_in_the_Rajneesh_Movement.

34.  Christine Ryder, interview with the author, 22 October 2013.

35.  Sheela, *Don't Kill Him!*

36.  Mehta, *Karma Cola*. Mahavira was the twenty-fourth and last *tirthankara*, or teaching God, of Jainism.

37.  Sheela, *Don't Kill Him!*

38.  Aveling, *Osho Rajneesh*.

39.  'Religion: God Sir at Esalen East', *Time*, 16 January 1978.

40.  Quoted in Walter Truett Anderson, *The Upstart Spring: Esalen and the American Awakening* (Reading, MA: Addison-Wesley Publishing Co., 1983).

41.  Quoted in Frances FitzGerald, *Cities on a Hill: A Journey through Contemporary American Cultures* (New York: Simon & Schuster, 1987).

42.  Quoted in *The Lakeland Ledger*, 18 March 1979. The Republican congressman Leo Ryan, who had been investigating Jim Jones, was one of those killed at Jonestown. In 1981, his daughter Shannon Ryan became a sannyasin at Rajneeshpuram, Rajneesh's ashram in Oregon, and took the name Amrita Pritam. When in December 1982 she wed another sannyasin, Peter Waight (aged thirty-seven and known as Swami Anand Subhuti), in an ashram ceremony, the marriage was toasted with a bottle of champagne given to the couple that was labelled: 'With Bhagwan even Kool-Aid becomes champagne'.

43.  Brian Raven Ehrenpreis, 'Get Your Sword! Terence Stamp on Nic Roeg, Brando, And More', *Quietus*, 25 August 2018, https://thequietus.com/articles/25155-terence-stamp-interview-the-ocean-fell-into-the-drop.

44. Later Arianna Huffington.

45. Bernard Levin, who had a reputation for his acerbic turn of phrase, was greatly teased by friends for dabbling in what many regarded as a questionable fad. When Levin attended an Insight reception at the Café Royal, one reporter pointed out that Jesus Christ had not charged £150 for an introductory course in love and awareness. Levin snapped back, 'Jesus Christ did not have to hire the Café Royal.'

46. Bernard Levin, 'The Joy of Shedding their Chains', *The Times*, 10 April 1980.

47. Quoted in Aveling, *Osho Rajneesh*.

48. Sheela, *Don't Kill Him!*

49. Ibid.

14. DOWN ON THE RANCH

1. Quoted in Aveling, *Osho Rajneesh*.

2. John Updike, *S.* (New York: Alfred A. Knopf, 1988).

3. Ibid.

4. Ibid.

5. Ibid. Don DeLillo offered another parody of ashram life, undoubtedly inspired by Rajneeshpuram, in his novel *White Noise* (New York: Viking Press, 1985). He writes of the protagonist Jack Gladney's former wife, who lives in an ashram, 'She has taken the name Mother Devi and runs the business end of things. The ashram is located on the outskirts of the former copper-smelting town of Tubb, Montana, now called Dharamsalapur. The usual rumors abound of sexual freedom, sexual slavery, drugs, nudity, mind control, poor hygiene, tax evasion, monkey-worship, torture, prolonged and hideous death.'

6. Ronald O. Clarke, 'The Narcissistic Guru: A Profile of the Bhagwan Shree Rajneesh', *Free Inquiry* 82 (Spring 1988). Quoted in Aveling, *Osho Rajneesh*. See Ronald Clarke collection on Rajneesh, 1983–1991, University of Oregon Libraries, Special Collections and University Archives, https://archiveswest.orbiscascade.org/ark:80444/xv39016.

7. Christine Ryder, interview with the author, 22 October 2013.

8. Testimony of Dyhan John, aka John Wally, taken before the Wasco Grand Jury, 25 October 1985.

9. *Rajneeshism: An Introduction to Bhagwan Shree Rajneesh and His Religion* (Montclair, NJ: Rajneesh Foundation International, 1983).

10. *Rajneesh Foundation International Newsletter*, 1 October 1983, quoted in Aveling, *Osho Rajneesh*, p. 157.

11. *The Rajneesh Times*, 16, 31 October 1983.

12. FitzGerald, *Cities on a Hill*.

13. Sheela, *Don't Kill Him!*

14. *The Rajneesh Times*, 4.5, A5, 1985.

15. *The Rajneesh Times*, 4.6, B1, 1986.

16. Quoted in *The Spokesman Review*, 1985.

17. 'Clap! Now Clap!', *Sannyasnews*, 26 June 2015, http://sannyasnews.org/now/archives/5161.

18. 'Osho Cancels the Buddhafield', *Sannyasnews*, 21 March 2015, http://sannyasnews.org/now/archives/4853.

19. Sheela, *Don't Kill Him!*

20. Ibid.

21. Ibid.

22. Ibid.

23. Aveling, *Osho Rajneesh*.

24. Ibid., p. 286.

25. A flavour of Lowe's talks can be found by a clip chosen, at random, on YouTube, entitled 'You':

> Once you've found you, once you accept you, once you're with you, you find you're on a different planet. Everything's different. Your fear will go; your stress will go; your worries will go. Not that the body still won't get shaken up sometimes, and the mind and the emotions, but you … you … will be free. Once you're free everything starts to happen for you. You vibrate differently. And the world interacts differently with you. Literally. So you need to invest in you. Keep investing in yourself looking for ways for you to get free. Invest in you and then everything starts to happen all on its own. All that's needed is you decide you want it. And then it starts happening. There's many, many levels of support when you start saying yes. It gets easier and easier, now more than ever. Just say, yes. I'm going to be more awake. I'm going to be more aware. I'm going to be more real. I'm going to be more me, whatever that is in the moment. Then you'll start to feel the blessing. That's what Jesus meant when he said, seek you first the Kingdom of God and all else is added on to you. And it's not magic, it's just science. It's the law. That's what happens. The happier you become, the more happy you're going to be.

26. Christine Ryder, interview with the author, 22 October 2013.

# SELECT BIBLIOGRAPHY

Adriel, Jean. *Avatar: The Life Story of the Perfect Master Meher Baba: A Narrative of Spiritual Experience*. Santa Barbara, CA: J. F. Rowny Press, 1947. Second edition (December 1947) by Jean Adriel, *An Avatar*. Meher Baba Trust. Online Release April 2011 © 1947 by Jean Adriel, Ojai, CA.

Allen, Charles. *The Buddha and the Sahibs*. London: John Murray, 2003.

Almond, Philip. *The British Discovery of Buddhism*. Cambridge University Press, 1988.

Anderson, Walter Truett. *The Upstart Spring: Esalen and the Human Potential Movement: The First Twenty Years*. Reading, MA: Addison-Wesley Publishing Co., 1983, 2004.

Arnold, Sir Edwin. *The Light of Asia*. London: Kegan Paul, Trench, Trübner & Co., 1902.

——— *Seas and Lands*. London: Longmans, Green & Co., 1891.

Arunachala, Sadhu [Major A. W. Chadwick]. *A Sadhu's Reminiscences of Ramana Maharshi*. Tiruvannamalai: Sri Ramanasramam, 2005.

Ashish, Sri Madhava. *What is Man? Selected Writings of Sri Madhava Ashish*. Delhi: Penguin Books India, 2010.

Aveling, Harry, ed. *Osho Rajneesh and His Disciples: Some Western Perceptions*. Delhi: Motilal Banarsidass Publishers, Pvt Ltd, 1999.

Baba, Meher. *Meher Baba's Early Messages to the West: The 1932–35 Western Tours*. © Avatar Meher Baba Perpetual Public Charitable Trust, Ahmednagar, India; North Myrtle Beach, SC: Sheriar Foundation, 2009.

——— *Messages of Meher Baba Delivered in the East and West*, compiled by Adi K. Irani. Avatar Meher Baba Trust eBook, June 2011. © 1943 by Adi K. Irani; © 2009 Avatar Meher Baba Perpetual Public Charitable Trust, Ahmednagar, India.

Baker, Deborah. *A Blue Hand: The Beats in India*. New York: Penguin, 2008.

Bax, Clifford. *Inland Far*. London: Lovat Dickson, 1933.

Benson, E. F. *The Complete Mapp & Lucia*. 2 vols. Ware, Herts: Wordsworth Classics, 2011.

Blavatsky, H. P. *The Secret Doctrine*. Los Angeles, CA: Jeremy P. Tarcher, 2009.

Braden, William. *The Private Sea: LSD and the Search for God*. Chicago, IL: Quadrangle Books, 1967.

Brent, Peter. *Godmen of India*. London: Allen Lane, 1972.

Brunton, Paul. *A Search in Secret India*. London: Rider & Co., 1934.

——— *Essays on the Quest*. London: Rider & Co., 1984.

——— *The Hidden Teaching Beyond Yoga*. London: Rider & Co., 1941.

——— *The Notebooks of Paul Brunton*, Vol. 4, Part 1: *Meditation*. Burdett, NY: Paul Brunton Philosophic Foundation/Larson Publications, 1989.

# SELECT BIBLIOGRAPHY

————— *The Notebooks of Paul Brunton*, Vol. 5, Parts 1 & 2: *Emotions & Ethics, The Intellect*. Burdett, NY: Paul Brunton Philosophic Foundation/Larson Publications, 1987.

————— *The Secret Path: A Technique of Spiritual Self-Discovery*. New York: E. P. Dutton & Co., 1935.

Burnham, Lord. *Peterborough Court: The Story of The Daily Telegraph*. London: Cassell & Co., 1955.

Cagan, Andrea. *Peace is Possible: The Life and Message of Prem Rawat*. Delaware: Mighty River Press, 2007.

Cahn Fung, Annie. *Paul Brunton: A Bridge Between India and the West*. Translated from *Paul Brunton: Un pont entre l'Inde et l'Occident* (PhD thesis, Department of Religious Anthropology, Université de Paris IV Sorbonne, 1992), translation 2004.

Cammell, C. R. *Aleister Crowley: The Black Magician*. London: Richards Press, 1951.

Caquet, P. E. *Opium's Orphans: The 200-Year History of the War on Drugs*. London: Reaktion Books, 2022.

Carpenter, Edward. *From Adam's Peak to Elephanta: Sketches in Ceylon and India*. London and New York: Swan Sonnenschein/Macmillan, 1892.

————— *My Days and Dreams: Being Autobiographical Notes*. London: G. Allen & Unwin, 1916.

Carter, Lewis F. *Charisma and Control in Rajneeshpuram: A Community Without Shared Values*. Cambridge University Press, 2010.

Castro, Stephen J. 'Paul Brunton and Meher Baba: In Search of Brunton's Secret – Part Four'. 24 February 2013. http://stephenjcastro.blogspot.com/2013_02_01_archive.html

Clarke, John James. *Oriental Enlightenment: The Encounter Between Asian and Western Thought*. London and New York: Routledge, 1997.

Cooke de Herrera, Nancy. *All You Need is Love: An Eyewitness Account of when Spirituality Spread from East to West*. San Diego, CA: Jodere Group Inc., 2003.

Crow, John L. *The White Knight in the Yellow Robe: Allan Bennett's Search for Truth*. MA thesis, University of Amsterdam, 2009.

Crowley, Aleister. *The Confessions of Aleister Crowley*. London: Arkana, 1989.

Das, Bhagavan. *It's Here Now (Are You?): A Spiritual Memoir*. New York: Broadway Books, 1997.

Dass, Ram [Richard Alpert]. *Be Here Now*. New York: Crown Publications, 1971.

Davy, Kitty. *Love Alone Prevails: A Story of Life with Meher Baba*. North Myrtle Beach, SC: Sheriar Foundation, 2001.

De Acosta, Mercedes. *Here Lies the Heart*. London: Andre Deutsch, 1960.

DeLillo, Don. *White Noise*. New York: Viking Press, 1985.

Ellwood, Robert S. *Religious and Spiritual Groups in Modern America*. Englewood Cliffs, NJ: Prentice-Hall, 1973.

Feuerstein, Georg. *Holy Madness: The Shock Tactics and Radical Teachings of Crazy-Wise Adepts, Holy Fools and Rascal Gurus*. New York: Paragon House, 1991.

Franck, Harry Alverson. *A Vagabond Journey Around the World: A Narrative of Personal Experience*. New York: Century Co., 1910.

Friesen, J. Glenn. *Paul Brunton and Ramana Maharshi*. 2005. https://www.academia.edu/72272645/Paul_Brunton_and_Ramaa_Maharshi

Garabedian, John H., and Orde Coombs. *Eastern Religions in the Electric Age: Why American Youth is Rejecting its Own Traditions and Seeking New Answers in the Ideas and Religions of the East*. New York: Grosset & Dunlap, 1969.

Ginsberg, Allen. *Howl and Other Poems* (reissue edition). San Francisco: City Lights, 1956, 1986.

———— *Indian Journals*. New York: Grove Press/Atlantic Monthly Press, 1996.

———— *Spontaneous Mind: Selected Interviews, 1958–1996*. New York: Harper Perennial, 2002.

———— 'The Vomit of a Mad Tyger'. *Lion's Roar*, 2 April 2015. http://www.lionsroar.com/the-vomit-of-a-mad-tyger/

Ginsburg, Seymour B. *Masters Speak: An American Businessman Encounters Ashish and Gurdjieff*. Wheaton, IL: Quest Books, 2010.

Godman, David. *Living By the Words of Bhagavan*. Tiruvannamalai: Sri Annamalai Swami Ashram Trust, 1994.

Goldberg, Danny. *In Search of the Lost Chord: 1967 and the Hippie Idea*. London: Icon Books, 2017.

Harris, Elizabeth J. *Ananda Metteyya: The First British Emissary of Buddhism*. Kandy, Sri Lanka: Buddhist Publication Society, 1998.

Helmstadter, Richard, and Bernard Lightman, eds. *Victorian Faith in Crisis: Essays on Continuity and Change in Nineteenth-Century Religious Belief*. Stanford University Press, 1991.

Hollingshead, Michael. *The Man Who Turned On the World*. London: Blond & Briggs, 1973.

Humphreys, Christmas. *Both Sides of the Circle: The Autobiography*. London: G. Allen & Unwin, 1978.

Humphreys, Frank H. *Glimpses of the Life and Teachings of Bhagavan Sri Ramana Maharshi*. Tiruvannamalai: Sri Ramanasramam, 1999.

Hurst, Kenneth Thurston. *Paul Brunton: A Personal View*. Burdett, NY: Paul Brunton Philosophic Foundation/Larson Publications, 1989.

Huxley, Aldous. *The Doors of Perception*. London: Vintage Classics, 2004.

Isherwood, Christopher. *The Wishing Tree: Christopher Isherwood on Mystical Religion*. Hollywood, CA: Vedanta Press, 1987.

Joshi, Vasant. *The Awakened One: The Life and Work of Bhagwan Shree Rajneesh*. London: HarperCollins, 1982.

Juste, Michael [Michael Houghton]. *The White Brother: An Occult Autobiography*. London: Rider & Co., 1927.

Kalchuri, Bhau. *Lord Meher: The Biography of the Avatar of the Age, Meher Baba*. 14 vols., 1998. https://www.lordmeher.org/rev/index.jsp. Original *Lord Meher* text in Hindi © Mehernath Kalchuri and Sheela Kalchuri Fenster; English translation © Avatar Meher Baba Perpetual Public Trust. All quotes of Meher Baba © Avatar Meher Baba Perpetual Public Trust.

Kerouac, Jack. *Jack Kerouac: Selected Letters, 1940–1956*. New York: Viking, 1995.

———— *Mexico City Blues*. New York: Grove Press/Atlantic Monthly Press, 2000.

Knight, G. E. O. *Intimate Glimpses of Mysterious Tibet and Neighbouring Countries*. Delhi: Pilgrims Book, Pvt Ltd, 1930.

# SELECT BIBLIOGRAPHY

Kripal, Jeffrey J. *Esalen: America and the Religion of No Religion*. University of Chicago Press, 2007.

Laing, Adrian. *R. D. Laing: A Life*, ed. Jill Foulston. London: Laing Press, 2008.

Lawrence, D. H. *The Letters of D. H. Lawrence*, Vol. 2: *June 1913–October 1916*, ed. George J. Zytaruk and James T. Boulton. Cambridge University Press, 1982.

Leadbeater, Charles. *How Theosophy Came to Me*. Adyar, India: Theosophical Publishing House, 1930.

Leary, Timothy. *Flashbacks*. Los Angeles, CA: Jeremy P. Tarcher, 1983.

———— *High Priest*. New York: New American Library, 1968.

Lutyens, Emily. *Candles in the Sun*. London: Rupert Hart-Davis, 1957.

Lutyens, Mary. *Krishnamurti: The Years of Awakening*. London: John Murray, 1975.

———— *Krishnamurti: The Years of Fulfillment*. London: Avon Books, 1984.

Maharshi, Sri Ramana. *Talks with Sri Ramana Maharshi*. Tiruvannamalai: Sri Ramanasramam, 2006.

———— *The Teachings of Ramana Maharshi*, ed. Arthur Osborne. New York: Samuel Weiser, 1962.

Marshall, P. J., ed. *The British Discovery of Hinduism in the Eighteenth Century*. Cambridge University Press, 1970, 2009.

Mason, Paul. *The Maharishi*. London: Element Books, 1994.

Masson, Jeffrey. *My Father's Guru: A Journey through Spirituality and Disillusion*. Reading, MA: Addison-Wesley Publishing Co., 1993.

Maugham, Robin. *Conversations with Willie: Recollections of W. Somerset Maugham*. New York: Simon & Schuster, 1978.

Maugham, W. Somerset. *A Writer's Notebook*. London: William Heinemann, 1949.

———— *The Magician*. London: Vintage Classics, 2000.

———— *Points of View*. London: William Heinemann, 1958.

McGovern, William. *To Lhasa in Disguise: A Secret Expedition through Mysterious Tibet*. New York and London: Century Co., 1924.

McWilliams, Carey. *Southern California: An Island on the Land*. Salt Lake City, UT: Gibbs Smith, 1946.

Mehta, Gita. *Karma Cola*. New York: Simon & Schuster, 1979.

Miles, Barry. *Allen Ginsberg: A Biography*. New York: Simon & Schuster, 1989; revised London: Virgin Books, 2000.

Naipaul, V. S. *Half a Life*. New York: Alfred A. Knopf, 2001.

Narasimha, Swami B. V. *Self-Realization: The Life and Teachings of Sri Ramana Maharshi*. Tiruvannamalai: Sri Ramanasramam, 1993, 2002.

Oldmeadow, Harry. *Journeys East: 20th Century Western Encounters with Eastern Religious Traditions*. Bloomington, IN: World Wisdom Books, 2004.

Olson, Helena. *His Holiness Maharishi Mahesh Yogi*. New York: Samhita Productions, 2001.

Oman, John Campbell. *The Mystics, Ascetics and Saints of India*. London: T. Fisher Unwin, 1905.

Osborne, Arthur. *My Life and Quest*. Tiruvannamalai: Sri Ramanasramam, 2008.

Osho. *Osho: The Last Testament*, Vol. 1. 1985. https://oshosearch.net/Convert/Articles_Osho/The_Last_Testament_Volume_1/Osho-The-Last-Testament-Volume-1-index.html (accessed 29 October 2020).

# SELECT BIBLIOGRAPHY

Palmer, Susan J. *Moon Sisters, Krishna Mothers, Rajneesh Lovers: Women's Roles in New Religions*. Syracuse University Press, 1994.

Palmer, Susan J., and Frederick Bird. 'Therapy, Charisma and Social Control in the Rajneesh Movement'. *Sociological Analysis* 53 (January 1992). https://www.researchgate.net/publication/261825558_Therapy_Charisma_and_Social_Control_in_the_Rajneesh_Movement

Parker, Peter. *Isherwood: A Life Revealed*. New York: Random House, 2004.

Purdom, C. B. *The God-Man: The Life, Journeys and Works of Meher Baba*. London: G. Allen & Unwin, 1964.

Rajneesh, Bhagwan Shree. *The Discipline of Transcendence*, Vol. 3. Pune, India: Osho International Foundation, 1982.

———— *Meditation: The Art of Ecstasy*, ed. Ma Satya Bharti. London: Sheldon Press, 1978.

Ramesh, Jairam. *The Light of Asia: The Poem that Defined the Buddha*. Delhi: Penguin Viking, 2021.

Ridley, Jane. *Edwin Lutyens: His Life, His Wife, His Work*. London: Pimlico, 2003.

Roy, Parama. *Indian Traffic: Identities in Question in Colonial and Postcolonial India*. Oakland: University of California Press, 1998.

Schanke, Robert A. *'That Furious Lesbian': The Story of Mercedes de Acosta*. Carbondale, IL: Southern Illinois University Press, 2003.

Shankar, Ravi. *Raga Mala: The Autobiography of Ravi Shankar*. New York: Welcome Rain, 1999.

Sheela, Ma Anand. *Don't Kill Him! The Story of My Life with Bhagwan Rajneesh*. Delhi: Fingerprint, 2012.

Shepherd, Kevin R. D. *Meher Baba: An Iranian Liberal*. Cambridge: Anthropographia Publications, 1998.

Shipman, John: 'A Young American in Tibet'. *The Middle Way* 79.4 (February 2005).

Sil, Narasingha Prosid. *Swami Vivekananda: A Reassessment*. Selinsgrove, PA: Susquehanna University Press, 1997.

Sinha, Mishka. 'Corrigibility, Allegory, Universality: A History of the Gita's Transnational Reception, 1785–1945'. *Modern Intellectual History* 7.2 (2010). http://www.academia.edu/569803/A_History_of_the_Gitas_Transnational_Reception_1785-1945

Stavig, Gopal. *Western Admirers of Ramakrishna and his Disciples*. Kolkata: Vedanta Press/Advaita Ashrama, 2011.

Stevens, Jay. *Storming Heaven: LSD and the American Dream*. London: William Heinemann, 1988.

Storr, Anthony. *Feet of Clay: A Study of Gurus*. London: HarperCollins, 1996.

Stout, Adam. *Fifth Mount Haemus Lecture: Universal Majesty, Verity and Love Infinite – A Life of George Watson Macgregor Reid*. 2005. https://druidry.org/resources/the-fifth-mount-haemus-lecture-universal-majesty-verity-and-love-infinite-a-life-of-george-watson-macgregor-reid

Stump, Paul. *Go Ahead John: The Music of John McLaughlin*. London: SAF Publishing, 1999.

Swarnagiri, Ramananda. *Crumbs from His Temple*. Tiruvannamalai: Sri Ramanasramam, 1995.

379

# SELECT BIBLIOGRAPHY

Thomas, Terence, ed. *The British: Their Religious Beliefs and Practices, 1800–1986*. London and New York: Routledge, 1988, 2017.

Tillery, Gary. *Working Class Mystic: A Spiritual Biography of George Harrison*. Wheaton, IL: Theosophical Publishing House, 2011.

Tillett, Gregory John. *Charles Webster Leadbeater, 1854–1934: A Biographical Study*. PhD thesis, Department of Religious Studies, University of Sydney, 1986.

Tobler, John. *The Beach Boys*. London: Phoebus, 1977.

Tonkinson, Carole. *Big Sky Mind: Buddhism and the Beat Generation*. New York: Riverhead Books, 1995.

Updike, John. *S.* New York: Alfred A. Knopf, 1988.

Vernon, Roland. *Star in the East: Krishnamurti the Invention of a Messiah*. London: Constable, 2000.

Vickers, Hugo. *Loving Garbo: The Story of Greta Garbo, Cecil Beaton and Mercedes de Acosta*. Londo: Jonathan Cape, 1994.

Watts, Alan. *In My Own Way: An Autobiography*. London: Jonathan Cape, 1972.

———— *This Is It and Other Essays on Zen and Spiritual Experience*. New York: Collier Books, 1967.

Wenner, Jann. *Lennon Remembers: The Rolling Stone Interviews*. London: Penguin, 1973.

Wilson, Colin. *The Occult*. London: Hodder & Stoughton, 1971.

Wolfe, Tom. *Mauve Gloves & Madmen, Clutter & Vine*. New York: Farrar, Straus & Giroux, 1976.

Wright, Brooks. *Interpreter of Buddhism to the West: Sir Edwin Arnold*. New York: Bookman Associates, 1957.

Yorke, Gerald. *Aleister Crowley, the Golden Dawn and Buddhism: Reminiscences and Writings of Gerald Yorke*. New York: Teitan Press, 2001.

380

# INDEX

*Note:* Page numbers followed by "*n*" refer to notes.

16th Karmapa, 3, 239

Abbey Road studios, 253, 256
Academy of Rajneeshism, 326
Acharyas, 326
Adamic, Louis, 138–9
Adams, Robert, 156–7
Adler, Alfred, 294
Adriel, Jean, 128–9
Advaita, 156
Adyar river, 48
Adyar, 50–1
Afghanistan, 19, 249
Africa, 142
*Age, The* (newspaper), 207
Agra, 168, 185
Ahmednagar, 117
Aids, 287, 327
Ains, Douglas, 159–61
Aiwass. *See* Horus (god)
Alexander, Robert Dudley, 244–5
Alfassa, Mirra, 169–70
Alipur, 168–9
Allahabad, 164, 238
All-India Women's Congress, 289–90
Almora, 242
Alpert, George, 215
Alpert, Richard, 215–17, 246, 249–51,
    363–8n46
America, 139, 259
American Academy of Asian Studies, 299

American Civil War (1861–65), 46
*American Pastoral* (Roth), 306
American sannyasins, 313
American Tobacco Company, 261
Americans, 139, 194, 277
Ananda Maitriya Sasanajotika. *See*
    Bennett, Allan
Andover Newton Theological School,
    223
Anglo-Afghan War II (1878–80), 58
*Annual Review of Psychology, The* (journal),
    215
Antelope, 319–20, 336
anti-war demonstrations, 276
aphorisms, 286
Arabia, 164
Arabian American Oil Company
    (Aramco), 129
Arabian Sea, 123
Arangaon, 117
*Are You Upward Bound* (Delmonte and
    Fern), 103, 113
Arihantas, 326
Arizona, 322
Arnold, Edwin, 3, 5
    arrived in Colombo, 48
    death of, 75
    returned to Britain, 28–9
    returned to England, 6
    thoughts on Buddha, 16–17
Arnold, Emerson, 24–5

Arnold, Matthew, 20
Arnold, Robert Coles, 4–5
Artaud, Antonin, 231
Arunachala (holy hill), 154–5
Arunachaleswara temple, 155
Arundale, Francesca, 52
Arundale, George, 52, 64, 65
Arundale, Taormina, 64
Arya Samaj, 51
Arya Vihara. *See* Pine Cottage
Aryan race, 43
Asher, Jane, 254
Ashvaghosa, 233
Asian Music Centre (London), 256
Asiatic Society, 12
Asoka (emperor), 25
Asoka pillars, 26–7
Asquith, Cynthia, 118
*Astral Plane: Its Scenery, Inhabitants and
    Phenomena, The* (Leadbeater), 52
'Astral University', 199
atheism, 102
Atlantis, 43
Atman, 13–14
Aurobindo ashram, 162
Austin, Alfred, 4
Austin, Christina, 181, 182
Austin, Thomas, 181
Australia, 204, 259
*Autobiography of a Yogi* (Yogananda),
    176, 194
*Awakening of the Soul, The* (Tufail), 100
ayahuasca, 230, 236

Baba, Hari Dass, 250
Baba, Neem Karoli, 250–1, 363–8n46
Babajan, Hazrat, 115, 117
Bachardy, Don, 220
Bahamas, 255
Bailey, F. M., 107, 109, 110–11
Bal Bhagwan Ji, 279
Bangkok, 240, 258, 270

Bankhead, Tallulah, 140, 141–3
Baranagar, 36
Barnett, Michael, 304, 307
Barrymore, John, 146
Bartoli, Daniello, 17
*Basic Ideas of Buddhism and its Relationship
    to Ideas of God, The* (Govinda), 242
Battersea Town Hall, 90
Battle of Plassey (1757), 9
Battle of the Somme (1916), 101
Bax, Clifford, 84, 93–5, 347n37
Bay of Bengal, 169
Beach Boys, 266, 269–71
Beast in the Book of Revelation, 78
Beatles (pop group), 253–5, 262–4,
    265–6, 269–70
Beaton, Cecil, 146
Beglar, J. D. M., 26
behaviourism, 295
Behramji, 116
Benares (Varanasi), 17
Benares, 11, 168, 185, 186
Bennett, Allan, 30, 73–5, 77–8, 80–1,
    86
    *Buddhist Review* mission, 89
    death of, 96–7
    founded Buddhasasana Samagama,
        87
Bennett, Charles, 73
Benson, E. F., 67, 343–4n26
Beresford, John, 221
Bergman, Michael, 278
Bergson, Henri, 76
Bergson, Moina, 76
Berkeley, 248, 264
Besant, Annie, 32–3, 41–4, 53–4, 60–1
    death of, 72
    formally initiated into Theosophy,
        51–2
    met with Krishnamurti, 54–5
Besant, Frank, 42
'bestial blasphemy', 74

Beverly Hills, 141
Bey, Mahmoud, 114
Bhagavad Gita, 10–11, 123
Bhutanese, 106
Biddulph, Catherine, 5
*Big House, The* (film), 131
Big Muddy Ranch, 317
Big Sur, 295, 300
Bihar, 17
bioenergetics, 306
Bird, Frederick, 305–6
Birmingham, 5
Birnbaum, Robert, 304
*Black Fox* and *Doppelgangers, The* (Heard),
    189
Black Hat ceremony, 239
Black Hole, 9, 10
Blake, William, 219, 229
Blavatsky, Helena, 43–4, 45–6, 47–8,
    51, 139
Blavatsky, Nikifor, 45
*Blond Venus, The* (film), 141
Bloomsbury, 103
Blunt, Wilfred, 58
*Bob & Carol & Ted & Alice* (movie), 303
Bodh Gaya, 17, 27–8
Bodhi tree, 7, 22
Bogislav, Ruano, 163
Bogle, George, 14
Boleskine House, 81
Bombay Presidency, 5
Bond Street, 60–1
Bonney, Charles, 31
Bonny Hall (South Carolina), 186
*Book of the Law, The* (Crowley), 84
Bose, Subhash Chandra, 13
Boston, 130, 213
Boyd, Pattie, 256
Bradlaugh, Charles, 42
Brahma (god), 26
Brahmin caste, 9
Brahmins, 187

*Brave New World* (Huxley), 217
*Bremen* (ship), 136
Brent, Peter, 292–3
Brindaban, 238–9
Brinsley Schwarz, 274
Britain, 118, 134, 259
British American Tobacco Company,
    104
British Army, 101
British authorities, 82
British Buddhist Association, 104
British Buddhist Mission, 104–5
British Embassy, 57
British government, 97, 106
British India, 12, 63
British Museum Reading Room, 101
British Nature Cure Association, 89
British scholars, 9
British tax, 123
Brookes, John Ellingham, 179
Brown, Peter, 264
Brunton, Paul, 95–6, 97, 99–101, 112,
    191–2, 349n30
    arrived to Bombay, 113–14
    death of, 207
    embraced Meher as his guru,
        118–21
    marriage with Evangeline, 201–3
    met with Sri Ramana, 157–9
    relationship with Sri Ramana,
        195–8
Bryant & May factory, 43
Bryant, Edward, 89, 96
Buber, Martin, 302
Buchanan, Francis, 25
Buddhasasana Samagama. *See*
    International Buddhist Society
*Buddhism* (magazine), 90–1
*Buddhism in England* (journal), 111–12,
    296
Buddhism, 4, 17–19, 102, 109, 301
    Bennett's views on, 75, 86–7, 90–1

bond between modern science, 23
  Christianity vs, 20
  introduction in Tibet, 224
  Kerouac's engagement with, 233–5
*Buddhist Catechism* (Olcott), 48
Buddhist Defence Committee, 48
*Buddhist Review, The* (magazine), 90–1,
  95, 103
Buddhist Society, 93
Buddhist sutras, 286
Buddhist Theosophical Society, 48
Buddhist traditions, 82
Buddhist World, 109
Buddhists, 82
Buer of the Goetia, 80
Bulwer-Lytton, Edward, 58
Bulwer-Lytton, Robert, 57–8
Burdon, Arthur, 177–8
Burke, Edmund, 336
Burma, 18, 27, 86, 87, 207–8
Burmese, 26, 87
Burnouf, Eugène, 19
Burroughs, William S., 230, 232–3
Busch, Marianne, 214

Calcutta, 12, 14, 63, 164, 185
California Vedantists, 233
California, 68, 138–9, 202, 225, 303–4
Cambodia, 240
Cammell, C. R., 80
Cannes, 164
Capote, Truman, 145
Caro, Heinrich, 20
Carpenter, Edward, 47, 59–60, 348n57
Cassady, Neal, 230
Castalia Foundation, 223–4
Castle Eerde, 66, 68
Catholic Westminster Cathedral, 220
Catholicism, 145, 147, 233
Catholics, 187
Cavern Club (Liverpool), 263
Céline, Louis-Ferdinand, 231

Central Foundation School, 100
Central Hindu College, 63, 64
Ceylon, 18, 48, 82
Chadwick, A. W., 154, 156, 162,
  181–3, 185, 353–4n3
Chakravarti, Gyanendra Nath, 244
Chancery Lane apartments, 81
Chandra Mohan Jain. *See* Rajneesh,
  Bhagwan Shree
Chandran, 192–3
Chaplin, Charlie, 139
Charananand (Guru), 274
Charing Cross station, 55
charlatans, 153
Chatterji, Gadadhar. *See* Ramakrishna
Chaudhuri, Haridas, 299
Chicago Seven, 276
Chicago, 53, 139, 276
Chidvilas Rajneesh Meditation Center,
  317
China, 18, 142, 164
Chinese, 200
Chinmoy, Sri, 272–3
Chopra, Deepak, 269
Christ, 233
Christian missionaries, 48, 90, 112
Christian Science, 3, 671
Christians, 13–15, 22, 280
Church Missionary Society, 15
Church Society, 49
Churchill, Winston, 176
Circle Cinema, 135
City Temple Debating Society, 88
*Civil and Military Gazette, The*
  (newspaper), 34
Clarke, Ronald O., 323–4
Clive, Robert, 9
Cochin, 258
Cocteau, Jean, 176
Cohen, Sidney, 221
Cold War, 204
Coliseum Theatre, 126

Cologne, 204

Colombo Buddhist Theosophical
Society, 48

Colombo Engineering Company, 104

Colombo, 48, 82, 86, 167

Colorado, 275, 278

Columbia Presbyterian Psychiatric
Institute, 231

'comparative religion', 19–20

Complete Illustrated Book of Yoga
(Devananda), 255

Confucianism, 21, 31

Confucius, 46

Congress Movement, 123

Constantinople, 19

Conventional Western psychology, 289

Coombs, Orde, 254

Cooper, Gary, 140, 141

Corbyn, Mary, 73

Covent Garden, 62

Coward, Noël, 146, 164, 176

Cox, Jeff, 206–7

Craske, Margaret, 124, 126, 131–2,
144

Critical Review, The (newspaper), 10

Crockett, James, 25

Cromwell, James, 261–2

Crowley, Aleister, 73, 74, 76–7, 78–81,
96
arrived in Ceylon, 82
death of, 97
letter to Kelly, 84–5
Maugham met with, 177–8

Crowley, Edward, 78

Cuba, 145

Cuban Missile Crisis (1962), 205

Cukor, George, 180

Cultural Integration Fellowship, 299

Cunningham, Alexander, 26

Cyprus, 144


D. T. Suzuki, 31

Daggett, Charles Steward, 138

Daily Express (newspaper), 263

Daily Mirror, The (newspaper), 133–4

Daily Telegraph, The (newspaper), 4, 6,
26–7, 110

Daitoku-ji, 233

Dakshineswar, 35

Dalai Lama, 110

Dalhousie, Lord, 7

Dallas, 227

Dandi, 123

Daniélou, Alain, 47

Darjeeling, 105, 109

Darrell, Larry, 186–8, 190–1

Darrow, Clarence, 297

Darwin, Charles, 20, 23

Das Mirakel (play), 129

Das, Bhagavan, 250, 363–8n46

Dass, Bava Lachman, 34–5

Dastur, K. J., 135

Dave, Gypsy, 266

David-Néel, Alexandra, 169

Davids, T. W. Rhys, 87

Davis, Rennie, 276–8

Davy, Kitty, 124, 126, 131, 134, 164

Dawa-Samdup, Kazi, 225

de Acosta, Mercedes, 144–5, 162–4,
166–7
arrival to Maharshi's ashram, 173–6
Garbo and, 148–9
met with Gibran, 146–7

de Herrera, Luis, 260

de Herrera, Nancy Cooke, 260, 265–6

de Jonville, Joseph Eudelin, 18

de Kooning, Willem, 236

de Koros, Alexander Csoma, 18, 19

De Leon, Delia, 126, 131, 164

Deer Park, 17, 25

Dehradun, 242, 274

DeLamar, Alice, 147

Democratic National Convention, 276

Denmark, 259

Deva, Krishna, 321
Devaraj. *See* Meredith, George
Devi, Manika, 244–5
Devi, Sarada, 35
*Devil and the Deep* (drama), 140
Dharmapala, Angarika, 27, 31
*Diagnostic and Statistical Manual of Mental
    Disorders* (*DSM*), 323
Diem, Ngo Dinh, 240
Dietrich, Marlene, 141, 145
Divine Life Society, 237
Divine Light Mission, 276, 278–9
Divine Music, 275
'Divine Nectar', 275
Divine Sales, 276
Divine Will, 136
Divya Sandesh Parishad, 274
d-lysergic acid diethylamide tartrate.
    *See* LSD
Dodge, Mary, 61, 68
Dodge, William E., 61
Dolgorukov, Pavel Vasilevich, 44
*Doors of Perception, The* (Huxley), 218,
    301
Doubleday, Nelson, 186
Douglas, James, 134–5, 352n35
Dover, 133
*Downton Abbey* (television series), 105
*Dracula* (film), 150
Duce, James, 129
Duke, Doris, 261–2, 265, 267
Dulwich, 276
Duncan, Isadora, 145
Dyer, Bernard, 73
'dynamic meditation', 292

East and West: A Splendid
    Opportunity', 27–8
East Challacombe, 118, 125
East India Company, 5
East Sussex, 97
Eastern culture, 194

Eastern mysticism, 233, 242, 254
eastern Netherlands, 66
Eastern philosophy, 295
Eavis, Michael, 274
Eccleston Square, 209
Eddy, William, 45–6
Egypt, 19, 164
Egyptian Book of the Dead, 75
Eiffel Tower, 131
Elan Vital, 280
Eliot, T. S., 176
Ellam, John, 105, 106, 109
Ellis, Havelock, 216, 348n57
Ellora (caves), 168
Emerson, Ralph Waldo, 12, 340n19
English Buddhist Society, 3
Epstein, Brian, 263–4
*Equinox* (magazine), 117
Ernst Lothar Hoffmann. *See* Govinda,
    Lama Anagarika
Erskine, William, 20
Esalen Institute, 295
Esalen, 295, 301–2, 304–5, 306,
    311–12
'Esoteric Section', 52
Europe, 139, 166, 270
Europeans, 9, 194
Evangeline Glass. *See* Young, Evangeline
Evans-Wentz, Walter, 160–1, 224–5,
    242
Everest (Hil), 82
*Everyman* (magazine), 125–6

Fabian Society, 44, 60
Fairbanks, Douglas, 141
*Fairy-Faith in Celtic Countries, The* (Evans-
    Wentz), 225
Faithfull, Marianne, 262
fakirs, 34
Farmer, Sarah, 38
Farr Emery, Florence, 76
Farrow, Mia, 265–6, 269

Felt Forum, 264
Ferguson, Maynard, 222
Ferlinghetti, Lawrence, 249, 299
Fern, William G., 103–4
Fez Club, 4–5
First Church of God of Prophecy, 300
FitzGerald, Frances, 329
Fiuggi Fonte, 283
Fleet Street, 7
Fletcher, Frederick Charles, 104, 157, 208
Ford, Glenn, 260, 261, 283
Ford, Henry, 261
Foreign and Political Department (Simla), 107
Forest Hill, 76
Fort William, 9
Fort, Garrett, 150
Fortune, Dion, 102
fortune-cookie gags, 286
Four Noble Truths, 7, 17
Foyles, 101
France, 133
France, Anatole, 146
Frankenstein (film), 150
Frederica (Queen), 203–4
Freud, Sigmund, 294
Freudianism, 295
Frogmore Hall, 144
Fruits of Philosophy, A Treatise on the Population Question (Knowlton), 42

Gandhi, Mohandas, 24, 47, 123–4, 193
Ganges (river), 164, 237–8
Gangtok, 239
Garabedian, John, 254
Garbo, Greta, 142, 148–9, 151–2, 163, 175–6, 355n30
Gardner, Frank, 78
Geneva, 204
George V (King), 62

George, Lloyd, 60
Georgia, 130
Germany, 259, 296
Gestalt sessions, 302
Gestalt, 306
Ghose, Aurobindo, 168–70
Ghosh, Sri Aurobindo, 13, 296–7
Gibran, Khalil, 147
Gide, André, 231
Gillespie, Dizzy, 236
Ginsberg, Allen, 224, 229–31, 238–9, 240–1
Glass, Beaumont, 204
Glastonbury Fayre, 274
Gnosticism, 102
Gobi Desert, 46
God Realization, 150
God-Man: The Life, Journeys and Work of Meher Baba with an Interpretation of His Silence and Spiritual Teaching, The (Purdom), 126
Golden Gate Park, 247, 248, 360n27
Gonne, Maud, 76
Gopal, Ram, 146, 166
Gordon, Arthur Hamilton, 27
Govinda, Lama Anagarika, 242–4
Grace, W. G., 93
Grand Hotel (Stockholm), 152
Grant, Cary, 140
Grant, Charles, 15–16
Grant, Kenneth, 77, 80, 96
Grateful Dead, 249
Great Depression, 139
Great Exhibition (1851), 45
Great Tower Street, 73
Great War. See World War I
Great White Brotherhood, 45
Greece, 259
Greek Orthodox Church, 203
Green Acre, 38, 40
Greenly, Edward, 89
Grey, Mary, 118

# INDEX

Gunn, Battiscombe, 93–4

Gunther, Bernie, 304

Gurdjieff, George, 243

Guru Dev, 257

Guyana, 313

Gyantse, 106, 109

Hague, Guy, 174, 191

Haight Street, 247

*Half a Life* (Naipaul), 192

Halhed, Nathaniel, 11

Hamlet House, 7

Hampshire Regiment, 181

Hampstead, 209

Han dynasty, 18

Hanoi, 276

*Happy Hypocrite, The* (Beerbohm), 180

Harcourt, William, 105

Hare Krishna mantra, 281

Hare Krishna movement. *See*
    International Society for Krishna
    Consciousness (ISKCON)

Haridwar, 238, 274

Harlem God, 236–7, 240–1

Harley Street, 87

Harmon, 128, 130–1

Harrison, George, 253–6, 263, 267,
    269

Hartford Railroad, 215

Harvard Divinity School, 223

Harvard Psilocybin Project, 215, 223

Harvard, 264

Hastie, William, 36

*Hatha Yoga* (Ramacharaka), 176

Hawaii, 258

Haxton, Gerald, 178, 179–80, 181

Hayden, Tom, 277

Heard, Gerald, 194

Heathrow airport, 274

Hells Angels, 248

*Herald Express* (newspaper), 259

*Here Lies the Heart* (de Acosta), 146

Hermetic Order of the Golden Dawn,
    75

*Hermit in the Himalayas, A* (Brunton), 201

Hertfordshire, 144

Hesse, Hermann, 194

'Hierarchy of Masters', 45

Highgate Unitarian Church, 88

Hilton Hotel (London), 256, 262

Himalayas, 82, 162

Hindi Bible, 22

Hindu Tamils, 82

*Hindu, The* (newspaper), 121

*Hinduism* (Monier-Williams), 9

*Hinduism and Buddhism* (Eliot), 181

Hinkins, John-Roger, 314

*History of Indian Philosophy*
    (Radhakrishnan), 181

Hitler, Adolf, 97

Hodgson, Brian Houghton, 18–19

Hodgson-Smith, Basil, 52

Hofmann, Albert, 220–1

Hollesley Bay Colonial College, 78

Hollesley Bay, 78

Hollingshead, Michael, 221–2

Hollywood Bowl, 271

Hollywood, 138, 139, 147–8

Holmes, Oliver Wendell, Sr., 22

Holwell, John Zephaniah, 9–10

Hong Kong, 258

Horniblow, Frank, 81

Horniblow, Lilian, 81

Horniman, Annie, 76

Horniman, John, 76

Horus (god), 84

Hotel Knickerbocker, 140–1

Hotel Rajneesh (Portland), 327

Houghton, Michael, 101–3

Houston Astrodome, 276

Huddleston Gardens, 48

Hudson River, 128

Human Potential Movement, 295, 302,
    304

# INDEX

'humanistic psychology', 295

Humphreys, Christmas, 8, 125, 180, 207–8, 296

Huncke, Herbert, 230

Hungarian language, 19

Hurst, Kenneth, 104, 112–13, 191, 201, 208–9

Hussein (King of Jordan), 260

Huxley, Aldous, 189, 217–19, 222, 225, 226–7

Huxley, Maria, 225

Huxley, Thomas, 217

Hyderabad, 185

Hyperborea, 43

I Ching, 243

Immigration and Naturalization Service (INS), 326

Indian government, 109, 200, 316

Indian Home Rule, 65

Indian Mahatmas, 280

Indian nationalist movement, 41

Indian philosophy, 147

Indian Round Table Conference, 123

Indian sadhus, 8

Indian saints, 115

Indian Song of Songs, The (Arnold), 24

Indians, 8–9, 10, 16, 49, 123, 215

Indica Gallery, 267

Inspired Talks: My Master and Other Writings (Vivekananda), 176

Institute of British-American Cultural Exchange, 221

Institution of Mechanical Engineers (London), 104

International Academy of Meditation (Sicily), 259, 262, 265, 335

International Buddhist Society, 87, 88, 90

International Daisy Chain, 145

International Society for Krishna Consciousness (ISKCON), 280–1

Interpersonal Diagnosis of Personality (Leary), 215

Invisible Man, The (film), 150

Iran, 164

Irani, Rustom, 118

Irving, Ethel, 179

Isherwood, Christopher, 40, 138, 188–90, 194

Isis Unveiled: A Master-Key to the Mysteries of Ancient and Modern Science and Theology (Blavatsky), 47, 48

Islam, 21

Israeli Defense Forces (IDF), 329

Italy, 133

Iyer, Venkataraman, 153–4, 155–6, 182–3

See also Brunton, Paul

Jagger, Mick, 262

Jainism, 21, 31

Jaipur, 168

James, William, 38

Japan, 16, 17–18, 27, 240

Japanese society, 240

Al Jardine, 270, 271

Jefferson Airplane, 249

Jehanne d'Arc (play), 147, 149

John Bull, 135

John, Dyhan, 325

John, Hislop, 259

Johnson, Godfrey, 78, 92–3

Johnson, Marolyn, 279

Johnston, Bruce, 270, 271

Jones, George Cecil, 79, 80

Jones, Indiana, 105

Jones, Jim, 313, 372n42

Jones, Marc, 140

Jones, William, 12–14

Juliana (Queen), 203

Jung, Carl, 202, 294, 296

K2 (mountain), 82

# INDEX

Kabir, 310

Kagyu school, 200

Kahn, Herman, 221

Kaiser Hospital (Oakland), 214

Kaka, 164–5

Kalchuri, Bhau, 127–8

Kali (goddess), 35

Kalimpong, 239

Kali-worshippers, 255

Kandinsky, Wassily, 47

Kandy, 27

Kandyans, 82

*Kansas City Evening Star* (newspaper), 139

Kansas City, 139

Karachi, 123

Karim Baba, 164–5

*Karma Cola* (Mehta), 310

Karma Lingpa, 224

Karsavina, Tamara, 145

Kashmir, 255

Kathmandu, 249–50

Kaulback, Ronald, 200

Keightley, Bertram, 52

Kellog, Samuel, 22

Kelly, Gerald Festus, 82, 84–5

Kennedy, John, 227

Kent State University, 276

Kermit Michael Riggs. *See* Bhagavan Das

Kerouac, Jack, 230, 232–5, 361–2n16

*Key to Theosophy, The* (Blavatsky), 47

Khan, Kublai, 17

'Kinetic Light Sculptures', 267

King Edward VI School, 5

Kingdon-Ward, Frank, 200

Kip's Castle, 317

Kline, Franz, 236

Knebworth House, 59

Knight, George, 105–7, 108–9

Knothe, Helen, 68

Knowlton, Charles, 42

Koestler, Arthur, 219

Koregaon Park, 293

Krassner, Paul, 277

Kripal, Jeffrey, 302–3

Krishna (god), 11

Krishna Prem, Sri, 244–5, 246

Krishna. *See* Krishnamurti, Jiddu

Krishnamurti, Jiddu, 54–5, 57, 66–7, 343n10

    arrival in London, 60–1

    returned to Ojai, 69

kriya yoga, 262

Kuala Lumpur, 258

Kumbh Mela, 238

Kyger, Joanne, 237

Kyoto, 233, 240

*L'Introduction a l'histoire du buddhisme indien* (Burnouf), 19

Ladakh, 19

*Lady Frederick* (play), 177, 178–9

Lahiri Mahasaya, Sri, 256

Lake Dal, 255

Lake Geneva, 206

Lake Manasarovar, 201

Landau, Rom, 66–7, 132–3

Lao Tzu House, 286

laughing gas, 230

Laughton, Charles, 140, 141

Lawrence, D. H., 118

Lawrence, Frieda, 118

Laxmi Thakarsi Kuruwa, 289–90, 315

Le Chat Blanc, 177

Le Gallienne, Eva, 147

Le Mouvement Cosmique, 169

Leadbeater, Charles Webster, 49–51, 52–3, 139

Leary, Timothy, 213–15, 216–17, 220, 241–2

    returned to America, 246

    views on LSD, 222–3

Lehmann, Lotte, 204

Lemuria, 43
Lennon, John, 253–4, 263–4, 267, 268–9
Levin, Bernard, 314, 373n45
Lhasa, 104–5
Li Gotami. *See* Petit, Ratti
*Life Divine, The* (Aurobindo), 298
*Light of Asia, The* (Arnold), 4, 7–8, 21–3, 26, 29–30, 60
*Light of the World, The* (Arnold), 29
'liquid family', 309
*Lives of Alcyone*, 54
*Liza of Lambeth* (Maugham), 177
Lloyd, Harold, 139
Loch Ness, 81
London Buddhist Lodge, 296
London Clock Company, 279
Lopez, Donald, 242
Los Angeles, 68, 138, 140, 259
Louisa, Charlotte, 73, 78, 92–3
Love, Mike, 266, 270, 271
*Love's Coming of Age* (Carpenter), 59
Lowe, Nick, 275
Lowe, Paul, 304–5, 313, 335
LSD, 213, 220–1, 363n40
Lucas, Emmeline, 67
*Lucifer* (magazine), 75
Lucknow Medical College, 245
Lugano, 206
Lumbini, 17
Lutes, Charlie, 269, 283
Lutyens, Edwin, 57, 58–9, 62–5, 72
Lutyens, Emily, 55, 57–9, 64–5
  death of, 72
  loyalty to Krishnamurti, 70–1

Ma Prem Hasya. *See* Ruddy, Françoise
Ma Prem Kundalini. *See* Sarah
Macaulay, Thomas Babington, 16
MacDonald, Ian, 256
MacGregor Reid, George Watson, 89–90

Machen, Arthur, 76
MacLeod, Josephine, 40, 41
Madhava Ashish. *See* Phipps, Alexander
Madison Square Garden, 264
Madras, 48, 120, 153, 182, 287
Madurai, 153, 155, 181, 186
magic mushrooms, 213
*Magical Mystery Tour* (television film), 268
Mahabharata, 5
Maha-Bodhi Society, 27
Mahant, 25–6
Maharaj Ji (Guru), 273–5, 276–8, 279–80
Maharishi International University (Goleta), 271–2
Maharishi Mahesh Yogi, 256–7, 258–61, 264–5, 271, 281–4
  Lennon's hate for, 268–9
Mahathera, Nyanatiloka, 242
Mahavatar Babaji, Sri, 256
Mahavishnu. *See* McLaughlin, John
Mahayana Buddhism, 31, 46
Mahesh Prasad Varma. *See* Maharishi Mahesh Yogi
Maitreya, 69
Malaya, 200
Mamoulian, Rouben, 149
Manchester Regiment, 105
Mandela, Nelson, 272
Manhattan, 230
Mansfield College, 104
Manson, Charles, 267
Mao Zedong, 205
'Mapp and Lucia', 67
Mardas, Alexis, 267–8
Marine Street, 169
Marryat, Ellen, 41–2
Martin, Combe, 136
Martin, George, 253, 256
Martin, Ricardo, 163
Maslow, Abraham, 302

# INDEX

Massachusetts Institute of Technology (MIT), 219
Massachusetts, 322–3
Masson, Jacques, 198–9, 204
Masson, Jeffrey, 198–200, 205–6, 359n31, 359n35
*Master Salesman* and *How to Make Money More Easily: Being the Philosophy of the Master Money Maker, The* (Fern), 103–4
*masts*, 164, 167
Matchabelli, Georges, 130
Matchabelli, Norina, 129–30, 132–3, 142, 149, 167–8
materialism, 290
Mathers, Samuel, 75–6
Mathers, William, 75
Maugham, Robin, 179
Maugham, Somerset, 57, 176–80, 182–6, 188–9, 192–3, 356n13
MB Energy University (Zurich), 335
McCartney, Paul, 254, 256
McClure, Michael, 232
McFerrin, Bobby, 114
McGovern, William, 105–6, 109–10
McLaughlin, John, 272–3
Mechis, 106
Meenakshi temple (Madurai), 153, 181
Meerschaum pipes, 83
Meese, Edwin, 330
Meher Asramam, 120
Meher Baba, 114–15, 124–5, 136–8, 143–4, 164–6
    arrival in Hollywood, 139
    arrival in Los Angeles, 140
    de Acosta meeting with, 149–50
    returned to Europe, 163
    went into retreat at Mount Abu, 151–2
Meher League, 119
*Meher Message, The* (newspaper), 135
Meherabad, 118, 119, 167

Mehta, Gita, 310
Mehta, Jamshed, 123
Mellon, Andrew, 133
Mencken, H. L., 297
Meredith, George, 329–30
mescaline, 217–18, 236
Metro-Goldwyn-Mayer (MGM) Studios, 141
Metteyya, Ananda, 105
Metzner, Ralph, 224, 242, 246
*Mexico City Blues* (Kerouac), 233–4
Mexico, 213
Michael Hurwitz. *See* Houghton, Michael
Michael Juste. *See* Houghton, Michael
Michigan Avenue, 37
Midge, 321–2
Millbrook, 223–4, 247
Millennium '73, 276, 277, 278–9
Miller, Henry, 300–1
Milne, Hugh, 305
*Milwaukee Journal, The* (newspaper), 28–9
mind-expanding drugs, 295
'Minute on Indian Education', 16
Mirtola, 244–5
Mitchell, Weir, 216
Mix, Tom, 140
Modern Car Trust, 285
Monier-Williams, Monier, 9
Monk, Thelonious, 236
Montclair, 315–16
Montparnasse, 177
Montreux, 206
Moral Education League, 60
Morgan, Ted, 176
Morisset, Henri, 169
Morro Castle, 145
Moscow, 270
Moses, 46
Mother Teresa, 310
Mount Abu, 151, 293

# INDEX

Mount Kailash, 200, 201
Mount Meru, 154
Mouse, Stanley, 248–9
Müller, Max, 20–1, 48, 341n8
Munson, Ola, 145
Murphy, Michael, 295, 297–9, 300–2
Murray, Bill, 194
Mussolini, Benito, 96
Mylapore, 258

*Naga babas*, 238
Nagasundaram, 195–6
Naples, 204
*Narcissus: An Anatomy of Clothes* (Heard), 189
Narendra Nath Datta. *See* Vivekananda (Swami)
Narianiah, 63
NASA, 278
Nashik-Trimbak, 38
Nasik ashram, 121, 163
*National Reformer* (newspaper), 42
National Secular Society, 42
Natural Law Party, 269
*Nature Cure, The* (journal), 89
Nautchnees, 5
Nazimova, Alla, 145
Neddermeyer, Heinz, 189
Negri, Pola, 145, 147
Nelhams, Lewis Charles, 117
neo-Reichian rebirthing, 306
'neo-sannyasin', 291
Nepalese, 106
Netherlands, 203, 283
Netherwood House, 97
Neve, Felix, 20
New Delhi, 63, 185
New Haven, 215
New Jersey, 230
*New Musical Express* (magazine), 270
*New York Critique, The* (magazine), 32
*New York Herald, The* (newspaper), 33

New York Public Library, 232–3
*New York Sun* (newspaper), 46
*New York Times, The* (newspaper), 264, 277, 278
New York, 128, 136
New Zealand, 204
Nietzsche, Friedrich, 19
*nirvikalpa samadhi*, 35
Noble, Margaret, 41
North Wales, 262
'Norwegian Wood', 255
Nostradamus, 327
*Notebooks, The* (Brunton), 206, 207
Nyingma, 239

*Occult Observer, The* (magazine), 101–2, 103
Oda Sesso Roshi, 233
Ohio National Guard, 276
Ohio, 276
Ojai, 68, 69
Olcott, Henry Steel, 45–6, 48–9, 82
Oliver Haddo. *See* Crowley, Aleister
Olson, Helena, 259
Olson, Roland, 259
Olympia Press, 254
Olympian gods, 243
Oman, John Campbell, 34
Ommen, 66, 70
*On the Origin of Species* (Darwin), 20
*On the Road* (Kerouac), 232, 234–5
'Operation Shield', 204
Opher, Philo S., 199
Order of Medjidie, 6
Order of the Golden Dawn, 75–6
Order of the Silver Star, 118
Order of the Star in the East, 61, 66, 70
Order of the White Elephant, 4
Oregon State University, 323
Oregon, 319, 324, 336
*Oregonian, The* (newspaper), 327, 330, 333

Oriental religions, 243
Orlovsky, Peter, 237
Osborne, Arthur, 162
*Osho: The Last Testament, Volume 1*, 325
Osmond, Humphrey, 217–18
Ossining, 131
Ouija boards, 67
Oung, M. M. Hla, 87, 92
Ouspensky, P. D., 130

*Pacific Shipper* (journal), 300
Padmasambhava (yogi), 224
Pahnke, Walter N., 223
Pain, J. R., 87
*Pain, Sex and Time* (Heard), 189
Pakistan, 249
Palace of Peace, 276, 279
*Pall Mall Gazette, The* (newspaper), 43
Palmer, Susan J., 305–6
Palo Alto, 299
Panadura, 27, 341n41
Pandya, Amrita Nanda, 19
parables, 286
Paradise Island, 255
Paramount Company, 134
Paramount Studios, 140
Pascal, Gabriel, 142
Patanjali, 282–3
Patterson, Elizabeth, 129, 138, 163
Paul (King), 203–4
Payne, Francis, 97
'Peace Force', 320
PEAK (Peace, Education and
    Knowledge), 280
Pease, Edward, 44
*People, Not Psychiatry* (Barnett), 304
*Perennial Philosophy, The* (Huxley), 217
*Perfect Master: The Early Life of Meher Baba,
    The* (Purdom), 126
Perls, Fritz, 302, 310
Persia, 142, 187
Peru, 52

Petit, Ratti, 242
Pfeiffe, Karl, 193
Phari (Town), 107–8
Phelps Dodge Corporation, 61
Philippines, 31
Phipps, Alexander, 245
Pickford, Mary, 141, 143
*Picture of Dorian Gray, The* (Wilde), 76
Piggott, M. A., 161
Pine Cottage, 68
Plato, 46
*Playboy* (magazine), 234
Plaza Hotel, 264
Plymouth Brethren, 78
*Poems Narrative and Lyrical* (Arnold), 5
Polo, Marco, 17
Pondicherry, 162, 168–70, 245, 272,
    298–9
Poole, Abram, 147
Poona, 5, 116, 293, 309, 311
Portland, 328
Postel, Guillaume, 18
postural integration, 306
Powell-Brown, Ethel, 91–2
Power, Tyrone, 194
Prabhavananda (Swami), 40, 138, 217,
    233
Prabhupa-da, A. C. Bhaktivedanta
    Swami, 281
Prem Pal Singh Rawat. *See* Maharaj Ji
    (Guru)
Prem Rawat Foundation (TPRF), 280
Price, Richard, 295, 299–300, 311–12
psilocybin, 213, 223, 236
*Psychedelic Experience: A Manual Based
    on the Tibetan Book of the Dead, The*
    (Leary), 224, 226
Public Schools Colonial Training
    College. *See* Hollesley Bay Colonial
    College
Puerto Rico, 272
Purdom, Charles, 121, 125–6, 134, 164

# INDEX

Quaesitor, 304

Quantock, Daisy, 67–8

*Queen Christina* (play), 149

*Queen Lucia* (Benson), 67

Quicksilver Messenger Service, 249


R

Radha Krishna Temple, 281

radical psychology, 295

Raipur Sanskrit College, 289

Raja yoga, 38

Rajneesh Institute for Therapy, 320

Rajneesh Institution for Meditation and Inner Growth, 320

*Rajneesh Times, The* (newspaper), 330, 335

Rajneesh, Bhagwan Shree, 285–7, 291–3, 294–5, 305–7, 324–5, 329–30

    arrived in Oregon, 326

    death of, 336

    dynamic meditation, 303–4

    early life, 288–9

Rajneeshees, 320–1, 328

Rajneeshpuram, 285, 287, 304, 320–1

*Rajputana* (steamship), 123

Ram Dass. *See* Alpert, Richard

Ramakrishna Missions, 38

Ramakrishna, 35–7

Ramanathan, Ponnambalam, 82

Ramayana, 5, 237

Ranchi, 165

Rancho Rajneesh. *See* Big Muddy Ranch

RAND Corporation, 221

*Rangoon Times, The* (newspaper), 92

Rangoon, 111, 207, 258

Raphael Hurst. *See* Brunton, Paul

*Razor's Edge, The* (Maugham), 184, 186, 188, 190–1

Reinhardt, Max, 129

revolutionary politics, 254

*Revolver* (album), 253

Reynolds, Joshua, 12

Ricci, Matteo, 18

Richard, Paul, 169

Ridley, Jane, 64

Rig Veda, 20–1, 217

Riley, John, 253

Rinpoche, Dudjom, 239

Rishikesh, 237, 259, 265

Robbins, Tom, 285

Rodin, Auguste, 146

Rolfing, 306

Rolls-Royce, 131, 285–6, 287

Ronald Nixon. *See* Krishna Prem, Sri

Rosher, Charles, 79

Rosicrucianism, 102

Rosicrucians, 113

Ross, Margaret, 118

Rost, Ernest, 87

Roth, Philip, 306

Royal Air Corps, 244

Royal Albert Dock (London), 87

Royal Albert Hall, 269

Royal Botanic Society, 105

Rubirosa, Porfirio, 261–2

Ruddy, Albert, 329

Ruddy, Françoise, 329

Rumtek, 239

Russia, 204

Russian Empire, 44

Ryan, Mabel, 126

Ryder, Christine, 307–10, 324, 325–6, 336–7

Ryder, Japhy, 234


*S.* (Updike), 321

S.S. *Mantua* (ship), 55

Sadharan Brahmo Samaj, 36

Sadhu Arunachala. *See* Chadwick, A. W.

sadhus, 34, 238

Sahara Desert, 200

Sai Baba, 115, 259

Saidapet, 120

# INDEX

Sakori, 115

Sakya clan, 17

Sala, George Augustus, 6

'salt march', 123

Salzburg Festival, 204

*San Francisco Sunday Examiner* (newspaper), 277

San Francisco, 189, 247, 328

San Juan, 272

San Mateo, 321

Sandoz Laboratories (Basel), 220

sannyasins, 327–8, 331–2

Sanskrit, 3, 5, 9

Sarah, 321–3

Sartre, Jean-Paul, 231, 360n12

Sastri, Ganapati, 173

Savile Row, 61

Scandinavia, 259

Schanke, Robert, 152

schizophrenia, 217

Schloss, Malcolm, 128, 140

Schopenhauer, Arthur, 19

Schutz, Will, 302–3

*Science of Being and Art of Living* (Yogi), 176

Scott, Clement, 30

Scott, Margaret, 30

Scottish General Missionary Board, 36

scroungers, 153

*Search in Secret India, A* (Brunton), 99, 113, 121–2, 158–9, 197–8, 350n40

Searle, Alan, 180

Seattle, 328

*Secret Doctrine, The* (Blavatsky), 43–4, 139

Self-Realization Fellowship, 139

Sepoy Rebellion, 5

Shakyamuni. *See* Buddha

Shamballah, 46

Shankar, Ravi, 255–6, 368n3

Shankaracharya, 257–8

Shape, Tsarong, 110

'Share A Home' programme, 328

Shaw, George Bernard, 43, 51, 297

Sheela, Ma Anand, 315–17, 324–5, 326–7, 329–31, 332–3

Shelfer, John, 316

Shelley, Percy Bysshe, 161–2

Shigatse (Town), 111

Shinto temples, 241

Shintoism, 31

Shirdi, 115

Shiva (god), 154, 213

Shivadarshana, 74

Shri Ganesha, 187, 192

Shri Hans Productions, 276

Shultz, George, 330

Siam, 200

Siddhas, 326

*siddhis*, 282–3

Sikkim, 105–6, 239–40

Silverman, Marc, 316

Sinatra, Frank, 265–6

Sing-Sing prison, 131

Sinhalese Buddhists, 27

Sinhalese monks, 86

Sinhalese, 82

Sinnett, A. P., 52

Sirius (planet), 99, 199, 359n37

Skandahsram, 156

skivers, 153

Slates Springs, 300

Smith, Ray, 234

Snyder, Gary, 240, 299

Snyder, Joanne, 240

socialism, 102

Society for Psychical Research (London), 51

Solomon, Carl, 231–2

*Song Celestial, The* (Arnold), 24, 27

South America, 204

South Kensington, 7

South London, 76, 276

Southern California, 138

# INDEX

southern India, 82, 258

southern Nepal, 17

Soviet Union, 130

Spain, 187

Spalding, Baird, 162

Spiegelberg, Frederic, 295–7

*Spirit of Zen, The* (Watts), 296

*Spiritual Crisis of Man, The* (Brunton), 202

*Spiritual Practices of India* (Spiegelberg), 297

Spiritual Regeneration Movement (SRM), 258, 259

spiritualism, 31, 67, 102

Spiritualist Society, 101

Sri Aurobindo ashram, 168, 272

Sri Chinmoy Centre, 272

Sri Lanka. *See* Ceylon

Sri Parananda. *See* Ramanathan, Ponnambalam

Sri Ramana Maharshi. *See* Iyer, Venkataraman

Sri Yashoda Ma. *See* Devi, Manika

Srinagar, 255

SS *Normandie* (ship), 164

St Ignatius Loyola, 180

St Ives, 118

St Margaret, 78

Stalin, Joseph, 97

Stalinist Russia, 331

Stamp, Terence, 313–14

Stanford University, 295

Star camps, 66

Starr, Meredith, 117–18, 124, 131, 140, 143–4, 350*n*35

Stassinopoulos, Arianna, 314

Steinmetz, Art, 322–3

Sternberg, Josef von, 141

Stockholm, 152

Stokowski, Leopold, 163

Storr, Anthony, 289

*Strand, The* (magazine), 35

Stuart, Otho, 178–9

Student International Meditation Society (SIMS), 264

Students for a Democratic Society (SDS), 276

*Success* (magazine), 103

Suffolk, 78

Sufis, 187

*Sunday Express, The* (newspaper), 134

*Sunday Times* (newspaper), 335

Svareff, Vladimir, 79

Swain, Fred, 213

Swami Amrit Prem. *See* Gunther, Bernie

Swami Anand Somendra. *See* Barnett, Michael

Swami Brahmananda Saraswati. *See* Guru Dev

Swami Clang, 255

Swami Deva Veeten. *See* Stamp, Terence

Swami Jay. *See* Shelfer, John

Swami Prem Amitabh. *See* Birnbaum, Robert

Swami Prem Siddha. *See* Zunin, Leonard

Swami Teertha. *See* Lowe, Paul

Swift, Jonathan, 297

Swiss sanatorium, 129

Switzerland, 206, 283

Syria, 19

Taj Mahal, 185, 186

Talcott, Melody, 203

Tama Kurokawa, 28–9

Tamil Muslims, 82

Tamils, 82

Tank Reserve Corps, 101

Taoism, 21, 301

Tarot, 243

Teacher Training Course (TTC), 259

Tehran, 249

Tehri Garhwal, 201

# INDEX

Templeton, Elliott, 188
Texas, 276
Thant, U, 270
Thelema, 84, 97
Theosophical Society, 32, 47–9, 52–4, 60–3, 104, 342*n*22
    Jubilee Convention (Adyar), 69
    membership growth, 66
Theosophical Society's Jubilee Convention, 69
Theosophists, 47, 52–3, 57, 75, 76, 243
Theosophy, 45, 47–8, 51, 70–1, 102, 342*n*25
Theravada Buddhism, 31
Thompson, Hunter, 301
Thomsen, Martinus, 202
Thoreau, Henry David, 233
Tibet, 107, 109–10, 164, 201
    British Buddhist Mission, 105
    Buddhism introduction in, 224
    Buddhist leaders in, 27
*Tibetan Book of the Dead, The* (Evans-Wentz), 160, 224
Tibetan Buddhism, 239, 242, 253
Tibetan government, 106, 109
*Tibetan Grammar* (de Koros), 19
*Tibetan–English Dictionary* (de Koros), 19
Tibetans, 106–8, 239
*Time* (magazine), 191, 224, 264, 311
*Times, The* (newspaper), 65, 314
Tiruchuli, 153
Tiruvannamalai, 153, 182
'To Dream the Impossible Dream', 303
*To Lhasa in Disguise: A Secret Expedition through Mysterious Tibet* (McGovern), 109–10
Tod, Quentin, 139, 140
Toklas, Alice B., 145
Tolhurst, Katherine, 125
Tolhurst, Kim, 126, 127, 131

Tolkien, J. R. R., 276
Tolstoy, Ilya, 129
Tolstoy, Nadine, 129
*Tomorrow* (magazine), 175
*Top of the Pops* (show), 281
Tottrup, Karen, 103, 201
Townshend, Pete, 114
Transcendental Meditation, 256, 258–9
Treveal, 118
Turner, Charles, 330, 333

Ujjain, 238
Union Jack Field Club, 49
United States Consul, 31
'Universal Mind', 195
University of Dresden, 296
University of Jabalpur, 289
University of Oregon, 321
Upanishads, 147, 217, 310
Upasani Maharaj, 115–16
Updike, John, 321
Uruguay, 204
US Army Signals Corps, 191
Uttar Kashi, 258
Uttar Pradesh, 238–9

'Valley of the Saints', 258
Van Hook, Hubert, 54
Van Hook, Weller, 54
van Pallandt, Baron Philip, 66, 343*n*24
Vancouver, 240
Varanasi, 241
*Varieties of Religious Experience, The* (James), 38
Vedanta Hindu monk, 213
Vedanta Society (Southern California), 40, 138
Vedanta, 301
Vedantists, 14
Vedic texts, 9, 147, 220, 221
Vegetarian Society, 123

vegetarianism, 67

Venice, 133

Venizelos, Catherine, 290, 293–4

Vermont, 45–6

Vevey, 206

Victorian age, 6

Victorians, 20

Vidya, Ma Yoga, 321

Viertel, Berthold, 148

Viertel, Salka, 148

Vietnam War (1970), 276–7

Vietnam, 240, 264, 276

Villa Caldana, 164

Villa Mauresque, 176

*Village Voice* (newspaper), 264

Vinaya rules, 88

Virgin Mary, 233

Vishvakarman, 63

vitamin B3, 223

Vivekananda (Swami), 32–3, 35–6
    letter to his disciples, 40–1
    returned to United States, 39–40
    speech on amity between all
        religions, 37–8
    speech on India's spirituality, 38–9

Vlodrop, 283

von Hahn, Helena Petrovna, 44–5

Voormann, Klaus, 256


Wall Street, 129

Wallace, Alfred Russel, 47

Wallace, Mike, 235

Wally, John, 329

Warwickshire, 78

Wasco County, 319, 328

Wasson, R. Gordon, 213

Wat Dhammapadipa, 209

Watts, Alan, 8, 102, 224, 249, 296

Weaver, Helen, 235

Webb, Alexander Russell, 31

Wellcome, Syrie, 179

West Point Military Academy, 213

Westcott, William Wynn, 75, 76,
    344–5n6

Western convention, 290

Western instructors, 280

*Westminster Gazette, The* (newspaper), 91

Whalen, Philip, 235

*White Horse Inn, The* (operetta), 126

Whitman, Walt, 230

Whittaker, Glen, 276

*Who is Guru Maharaj Ji?* (Cameron), 277

Wilberforce, William, 15

Wild West (novel), 65

Wilde, Constance, 76

Wilde, Oscar, 24, 76

Wilkins, Charles, 11–12

Williams, Rowland, 22

Wills, Dennis, 191

Wilson, Brian, 270

Wilson, Margaret, 170

Wilson, Woodrow, 170

*Wisdom of the Aryas, The* (Bennett), 96–7

'Wisdom Religion', 47

Wodehouse, A. E., 55

Wodehouse, P. G., 55, 342–3n30

Wolfe, Tom, 303

Woodford, Adolphus, 75

Woodman, William, 75

Woolf, Christena, 290

Words of Peace Annual Report (2017),
    280

Words of Peace International, Inc, 280

Wordsworth, William, 36

World Columbian Exposition, 31

World Peace Corps, 276

'World Peace', 270–1

World War I, 66, 93, 102, 105

World War II, 186

World's Parliament of Religions
    (Chicago), 31, 40–1

Wyckoff, Carrie Mead, 40


Xavier, Francis, 17–18

# INDEX

Yale, 264

Yangtze River, 200

Yatung, 106

Yeats, W. B., 47, 76, 216–17, 345n9

*Yoga for the Westerner* (Krishna Prem), 245

Yoga of Synthesis, 237

*Yoga of the Kathopanishad, The* (Krishna Prem), 245

Yoga Sutras (Patanjali), 282–3

Yogananda, Paramahansa, 129, 139, 233, 256

Yorke, Gerald, 91

*Young India* (newspaper), 24

Young, Evangeline, 201–3, 204–5

Younghusband, Francis, 47, 104–5, 106

Yukteswar Giri, Sri, 256

*Zanoni* (Bulwer-Lytton), 58

Zanskar, 19

Zen Buddhism, 8, 233, 296, 301, 310

Zen koans, 286

Zetland, Lord, 200

Zodiac, 243

Zoroastrianism, 21, 31, 47

Zunin, Leonard, 304